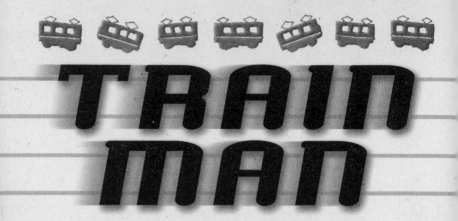

TRAIN MAN

A Shojo Manga

Manga by Machiko Ocha
Original story by Hitori Nakano

Translated and adapted by Makoto Yukon

Lettered by
North Market Street Graphics

Ballantine Books ✳ New York

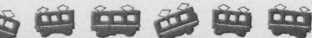

A Del Rey Trade Paperback Original

Train Man copyright © 2005 by Hitori Nakano and Machiko Ocha
English translation copyright © 2006 by Hitori Nakano and Machiko Ocha

Published in the United States by Del Rey Books, an imprint of The Random House Publishing Group, a division of Random House, Inc., New York.

DEL REY is a registered trademark and the Del Rey colophon is a trademark of Random House, Inc.

Publication rights arranged through Kodansha Ltd.

First published in Japan in 2005 by Kodansha Ltd., Tokyo, as *Densha Otoko: Bijo to Wotaku Seinen no Hatsu Love Story*.

ISBN 0-345-49619-1

Printed in the United States of America

www.delreymanga.com

9 8 7 6 5 4 3 2 1

Translator/adaptor: Makoto Yukon
Lettering: North Market Street Graphics

Contents

Honorifics Explained

Throughout the Del Rey Manga books, you will find Japanese honorifics left intact in the translations. For those not familiar with how the Japanese use honorifics and, more important, how they differ from American honorifics, we present this brief overview.

Politeness has always been a critical facet of Japanese culture. Ever since the feudal era, when Japan was a highly stratified society, use of honorifics–which can be defined as polite speech that indicates relationship or status–has played an essential role in the Japanese language. When addressing someone in Japanese, an honorific usually takes the form of a suffix attached to one's name (e.g. "Asuna-san"), is used as a title at the end of one's name, or appears in place of the name itself (e.g. "Negi-sensei" or simply "Sensei!").

Honorifics can be expressions of respect or endearment. In the context of manga and anime, honorifics give insight into the nature of the relationship between characters. Many translations into English leave out these important honorifics and therefore distort the feel of the original Japanese. Because Japanese honorifics contain nuances that English honorifics lack, it is our policy at Del Rey not to translate them. Here, instead, is a guide to some of the honorifics you may encounter in Del Rey Manga.

-san: This is the most common honorific and is equivalent to Mr., Miss, Ms., Mrs. It is the all-purpose honorific and can be used in any situation where politeness is required.

-sama: This is one level higher than -san. It is used to confer great respect.

-dono: This comes from the word "tono," which means "lord." It is an even higher level than -sama and confers utmost respect.

-kun: This suffix is used at the end of boys' names to express familiarity or endearment. It is also sometimes used by men among friends, or when addressing someone younger or of a lower station.

-chan: This is used to express endearment, mostly toward girls. It is also used for little boys, pets, and even among lovers. It gives a sense of childish cuteness.

Bozu: This is an informal way to refer to a boy, similar to the English terms "kid" and "squirt."

Sempai/ Senpai: This title suggests that the addressee is one's senior in a group or organization. It is most often used in a school setting, where underclassmen refer to their upperclassmen as sempai. It can also be used in the workplace, such as when a newer employee addresses an employee who has seniority in the company.

Kohai: This is the opposite of -sempai, and is used toward underclassmen in school or newcomers in the workplace. It connotes that the addressee is of a lower station.

Sensei: Literally meaning "one who has come before," this title is used for teachers, doctors, or masters of any profession or art.

-[blank]: This is usually forgotten in these lists, but it is perhaps the most significant difference between Japanese and English. The lack of honorific means that the speaker has permission to address the person in a very intimate way. Usually, only family, spouses, or very close friends have this kind of permission. Known as *yobisute,* it can be gratifying when someone who has earned the intimacy starts to call one by one's name without an honorific. But when that intimacy hasn't been earned, it can be very insulting.

TRAIN MAN

**A beautiful girl and an innocent fanboy.
This is their internet love story.**

Original Train Man story by Hitori Nakano

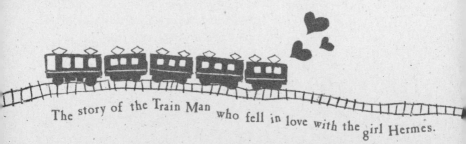

The story of the Train Man who fell in love with the girl Hermes.

```
      *   ※ ☆   ※ ※    ☆ ※   *
    *  ※ ☆   ※   ※    ※   ☆ ※   *
  *  ※ ☆   ※   ※ ※   ☆ ※   ※   ☆ ※  *
 *  ※ ☆ ※   ※ ☆   .☆ ※   ※ ☆ ※  *
 * ※ ☆ ※  ※☆      ☆※ ※ ☆ ※ *
 * ※   w00000-  (ﾟ∀ﾟ)  -00000t!  ※ *
 * ※ ☆ ※  ※※       ☆※ ※ ☆ ※ *
  * ※ ☆ ※   ※ ☆  .☆※   ※ ☆ ※ *
   *  ※ ☆ ※   ※ ※ ☆   ※   ☆ ※  *
     *  ※ ☆ ※   ※ ※   ☆ ※  *
       *   ※ ☆   ※ ※    ☆ ※   *
```

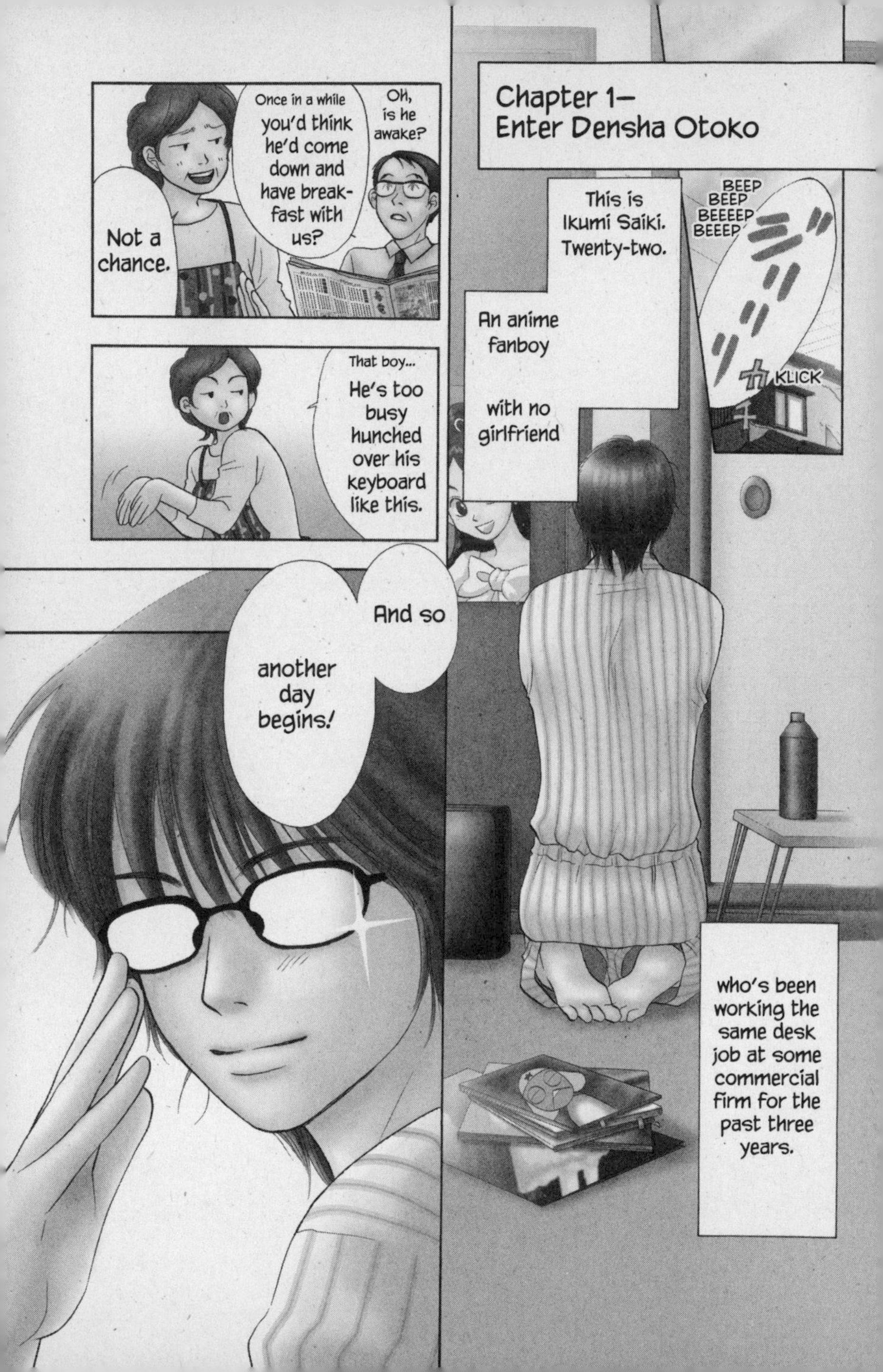
Chapter 1—
Enter Densha Otoko
BEEP BEEP BEEEEP BEEEP
KLICK
This is Ikumi Saiki. Twenty-two.
An anime fanboy
with no girlfriend
who's been working the same desk job at some commercial firm for the past three years.
Oh, is he awake?
Once in a while you'd think he'd come down and have breakfast with us?
Not a chance.
That boy...
He's too busy hunched over his keyboard like this.
And so
another day begins!

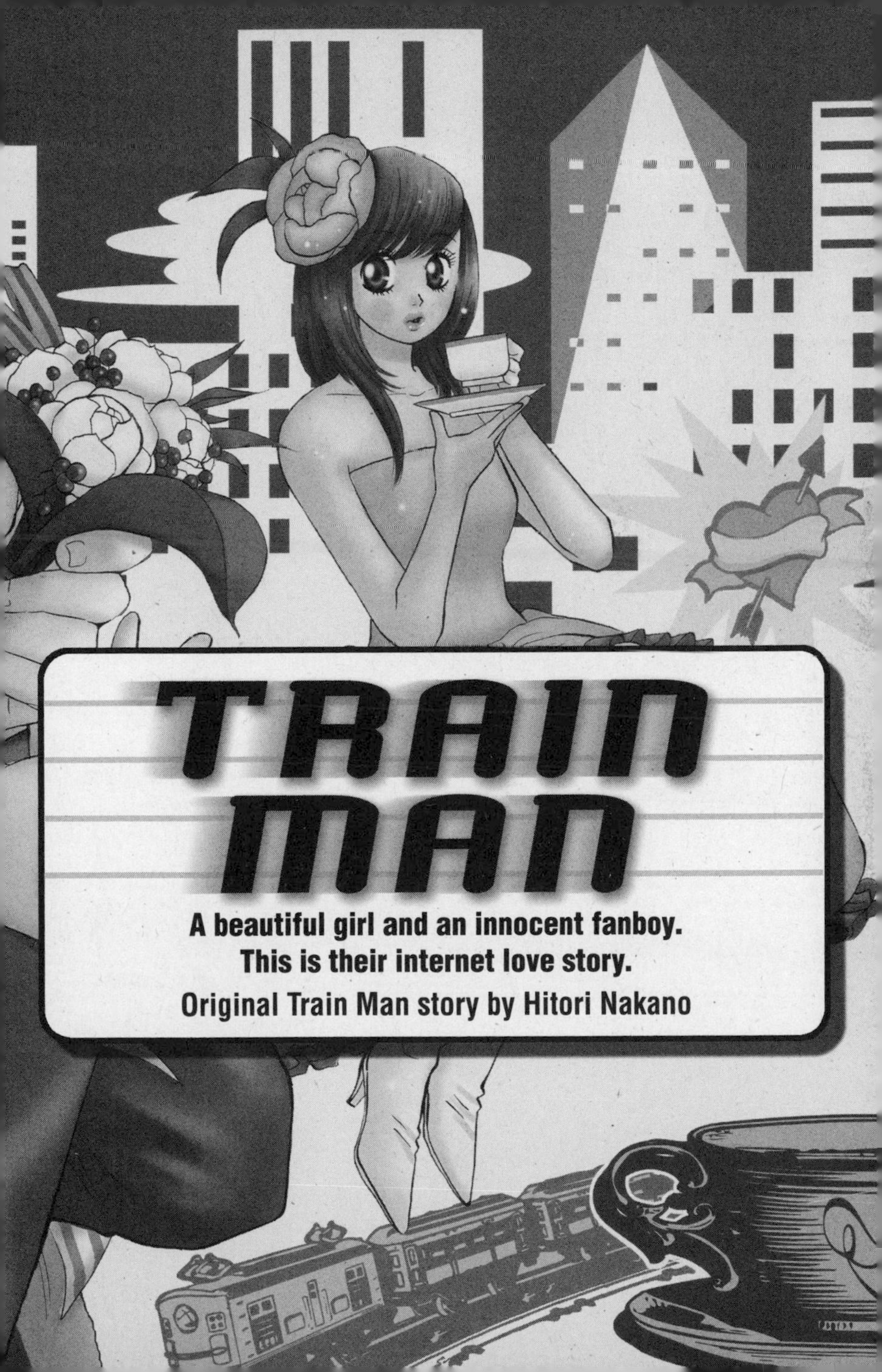
TRAIN MAN
A beautiful girl and an innocent fanboy.
This is their internet love story.
Original Train Man story by Hitori Nakano

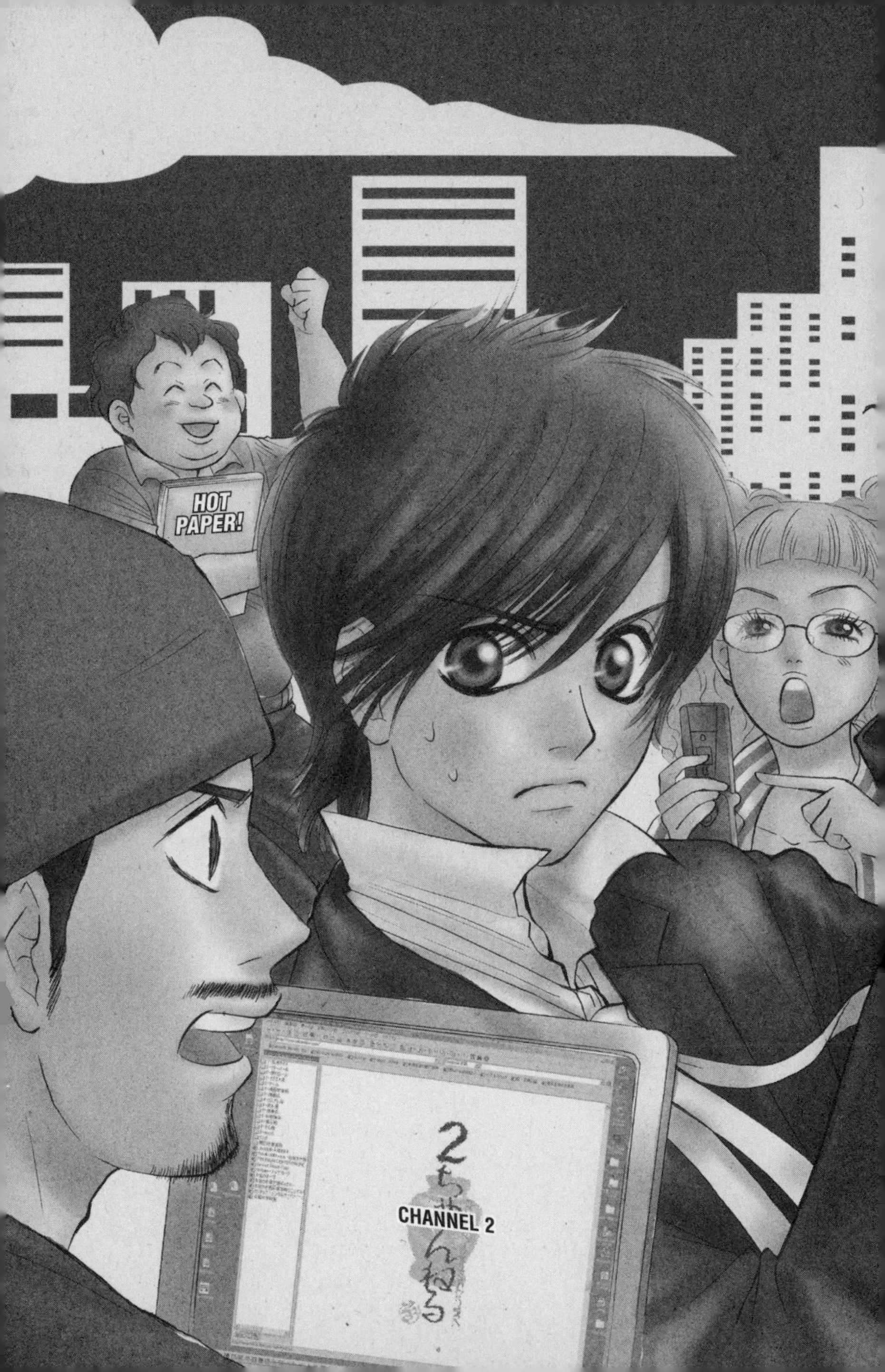
HOT PAPER!
2ちゃんねる
CHANNEL 2

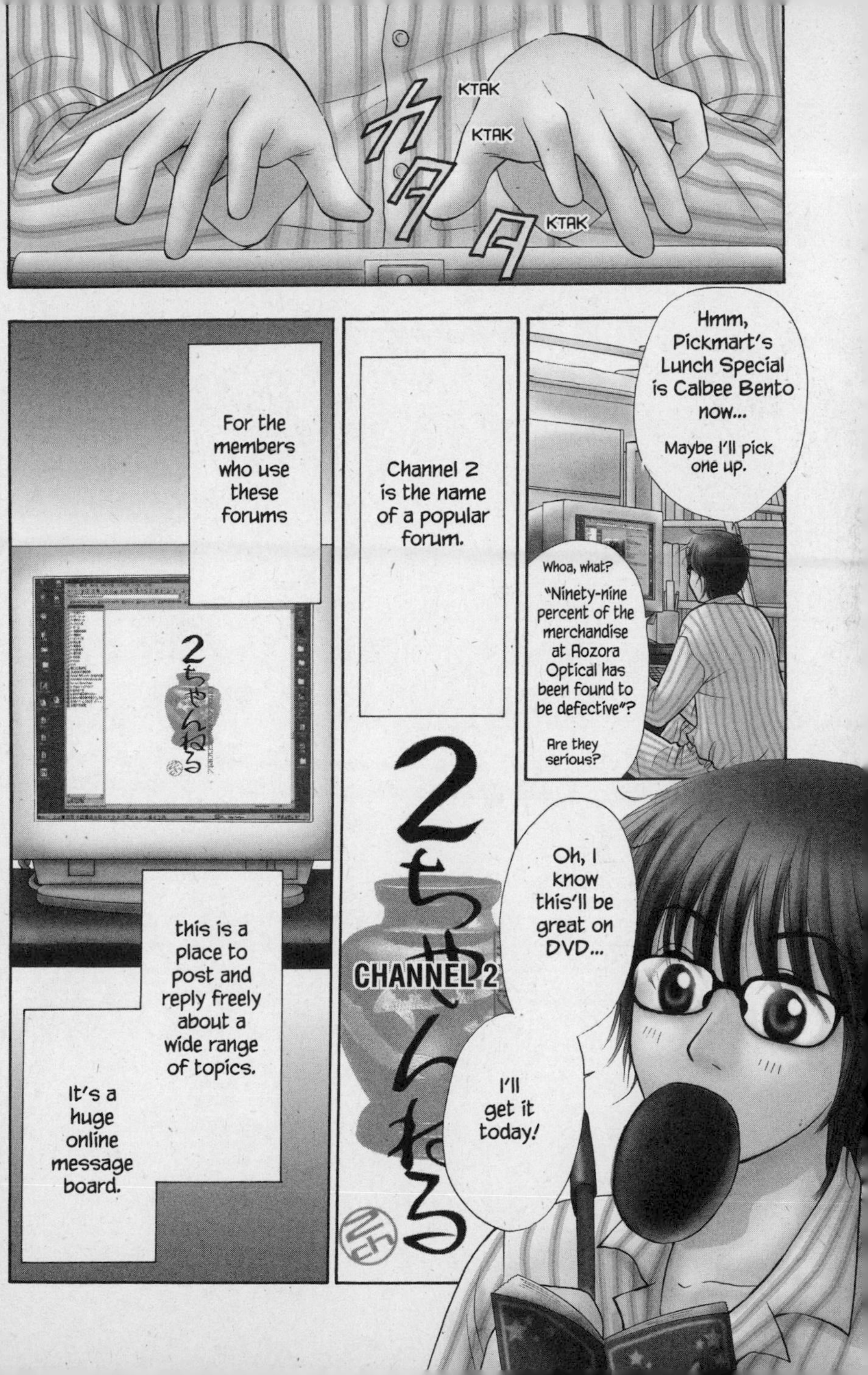
カタタ
KTAK
KTAK
KTAK
Hmm, Pickmart's Lunch Special is Calbee Bento now...
Maybe I'll pick one up.
Whoa, what?
"Ninety-nine percent of the merchandise at Aozora Optical has been found to be defective"?
Are they serious?
Oh, I know this'll be great on DVD...
I'll get it today!
Channel 2 is the name of a popular forum.
2ちゃんねる
CHANNEL 2
For the members who use these forums
2ちゃんねる
this is a place to post and reply freely about a wide range of topics.
It's a huge online message board.

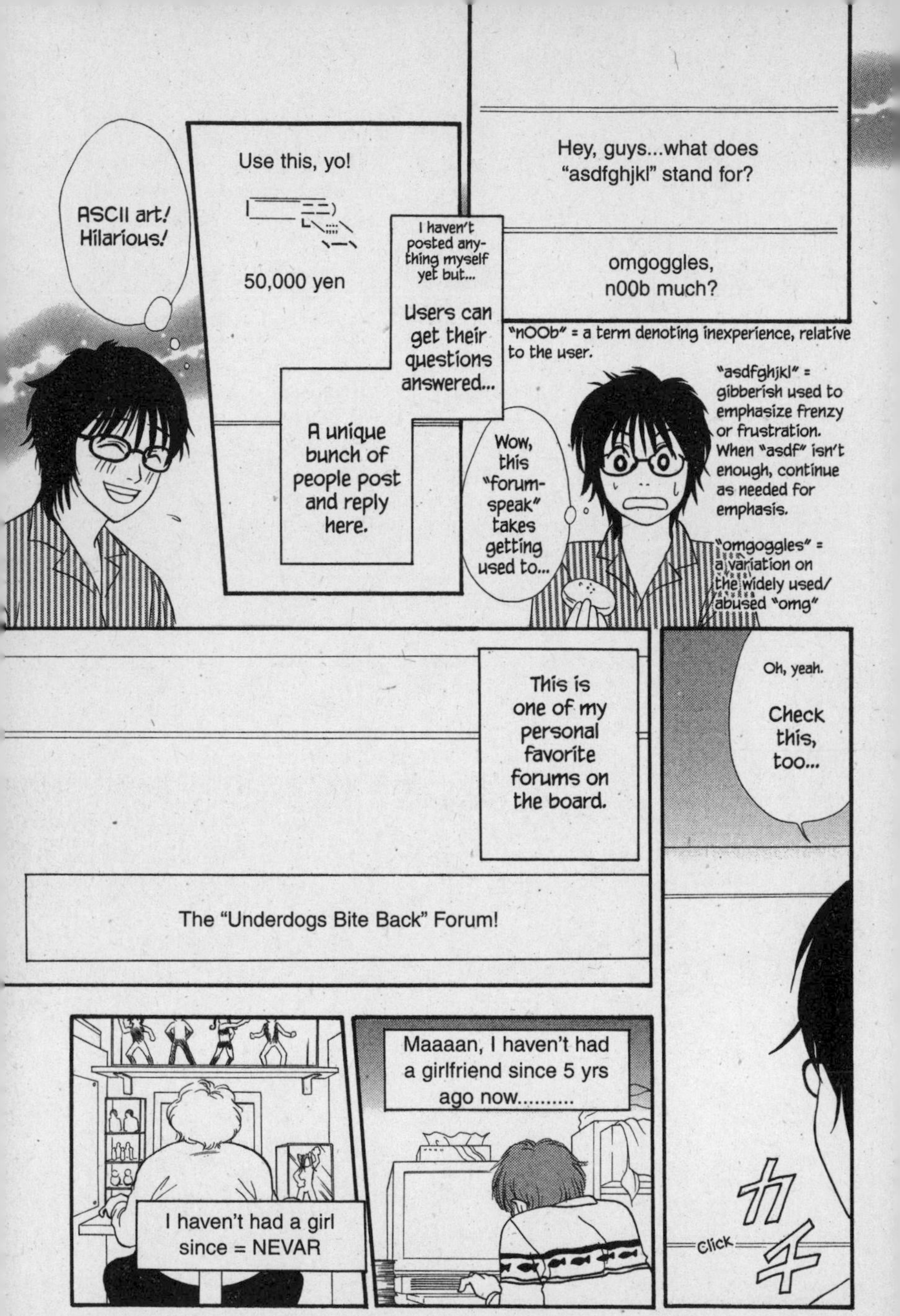
Hey, guys...what does "asdfghjkl" stand for?
omgoggles, n00b much?
"n00b" = a term denoting inexperience, relative to the user.
"asdfghjkl" = gibberish used to emphasize frenzy or frustration. When "asdf" isn't enough, continue as needed for emphasis.
"omgoggles" = a variation on the widely used/abused "omg"
Wow, this "forum-speak" takes getting used to...
I haven't posted anything myself yet but...
Users can get their questions answered...
Use this, yo!
50,000 yen
ASCII art! Hilarious!
A unique bunch of people post and reply here.
Oh, yeah.
Check this, too...
カチ
Click
This is one of my personal favorite forums on the board.
The "Underdogs Bite Back" Forum!
Maaaan, I haven't had a girlfriend since 5 yrs ago now..........
I haven't had a girl since = NEVAR

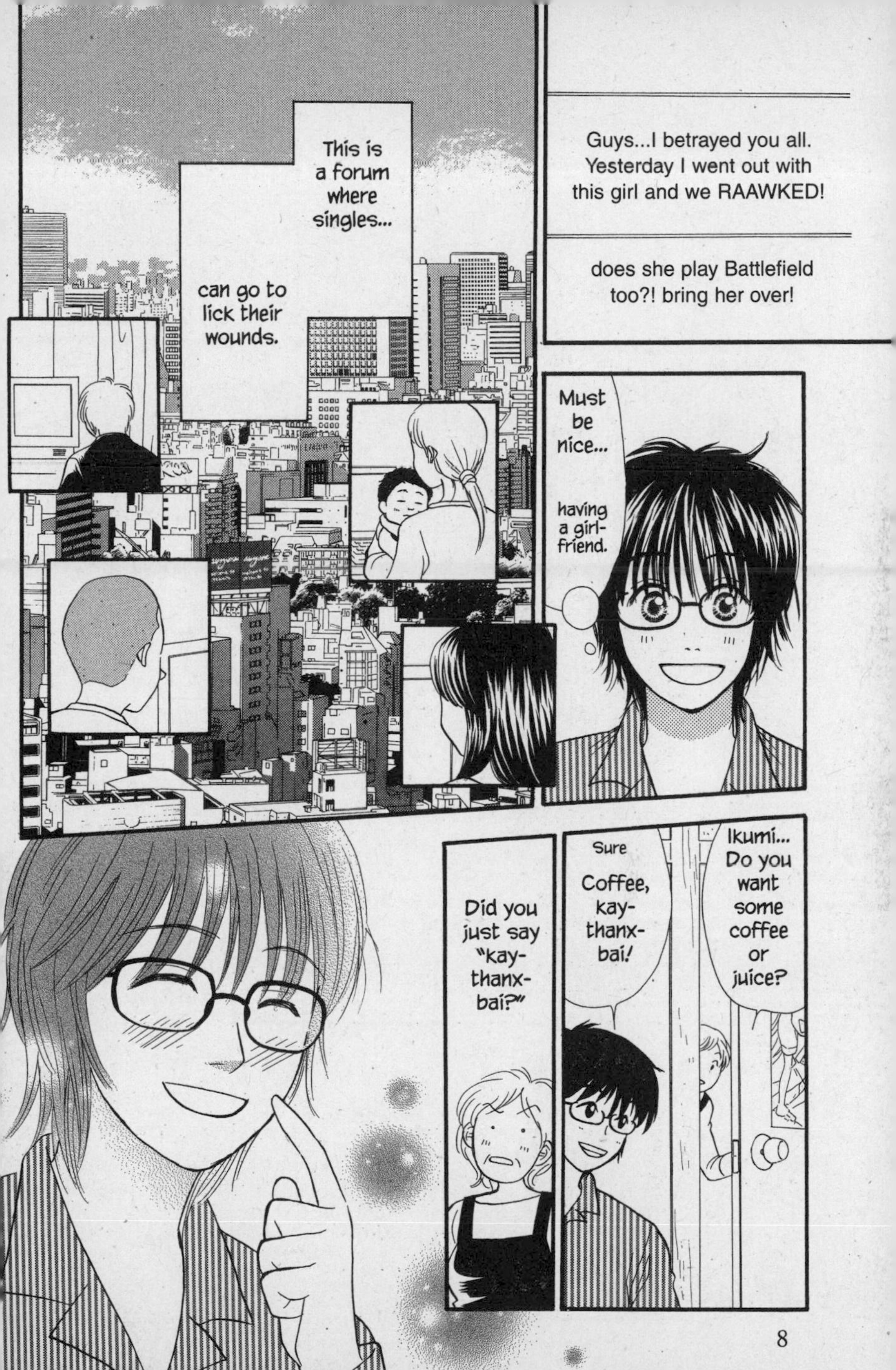
Guys...I betrayed you all. Yesterday I went out with this girl and we RAAWKED!
does she play Battlefield too?! bring her over!
Must be nice...
having a girlfriend.
This is a forum where singles...
can go to lick their wounds.
Ikumi... Do you want some coffee or juice?
Sure
Coffee, kay-thanx-bai!
Did you just say "kay-thanx-bai?"

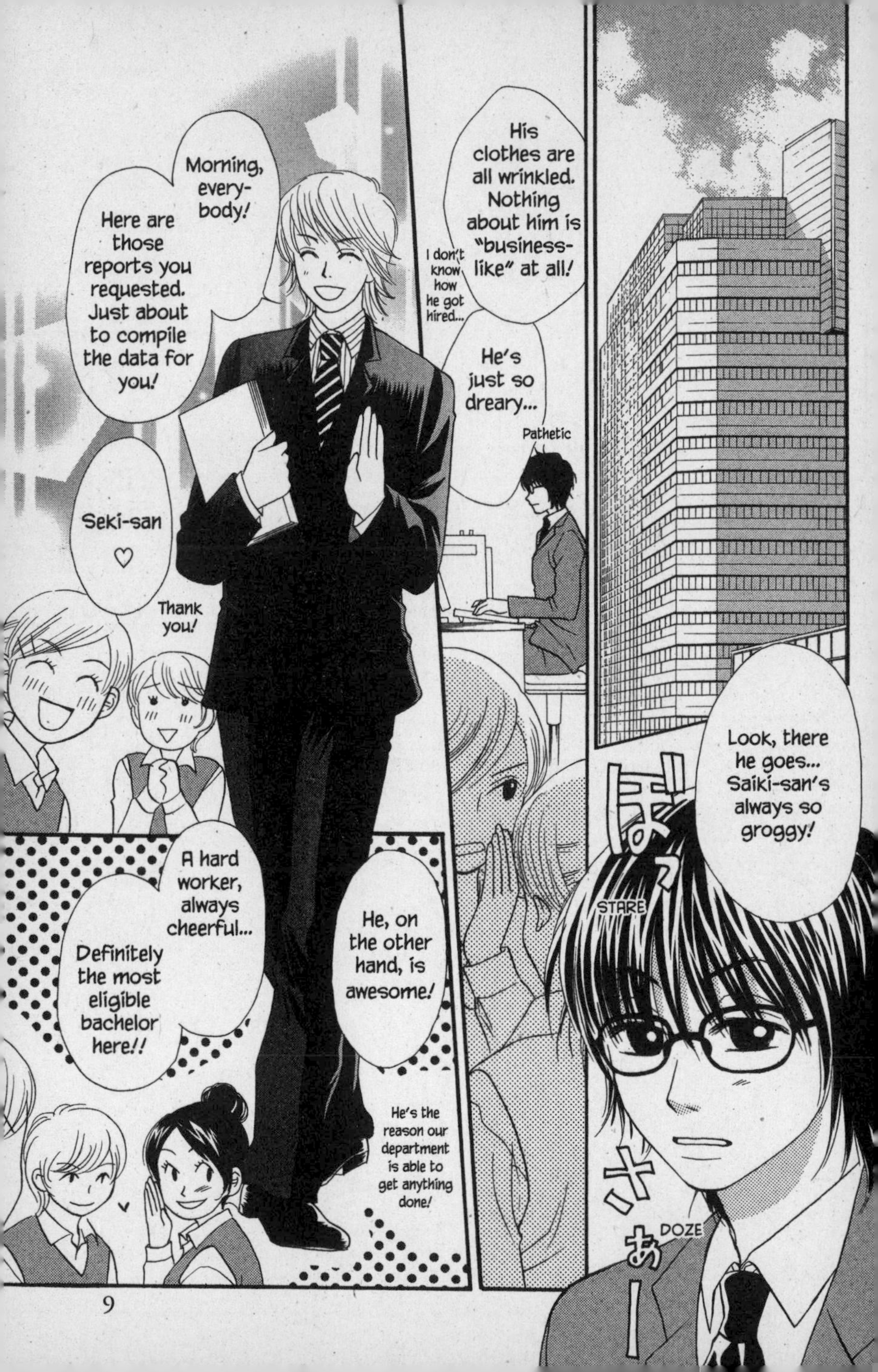
Look, there he goes... Saiki-san's always so groggy!
STARE
DOZE
His clothes are all wrinkled. Nothing about him is "business-like" at all!
I don't know how he got hired...
He's just so dreary...
Pathetic
Morning, everybody!
Here are those reports you requested. Just about to compile the data for you!
Seki-san ♡
Thank you!
He, on the other hand, is awesome!
He's the reason our department is able to get anything done!
A hard worker, always cheerful...
Definitely the most eligible bachelor here!!

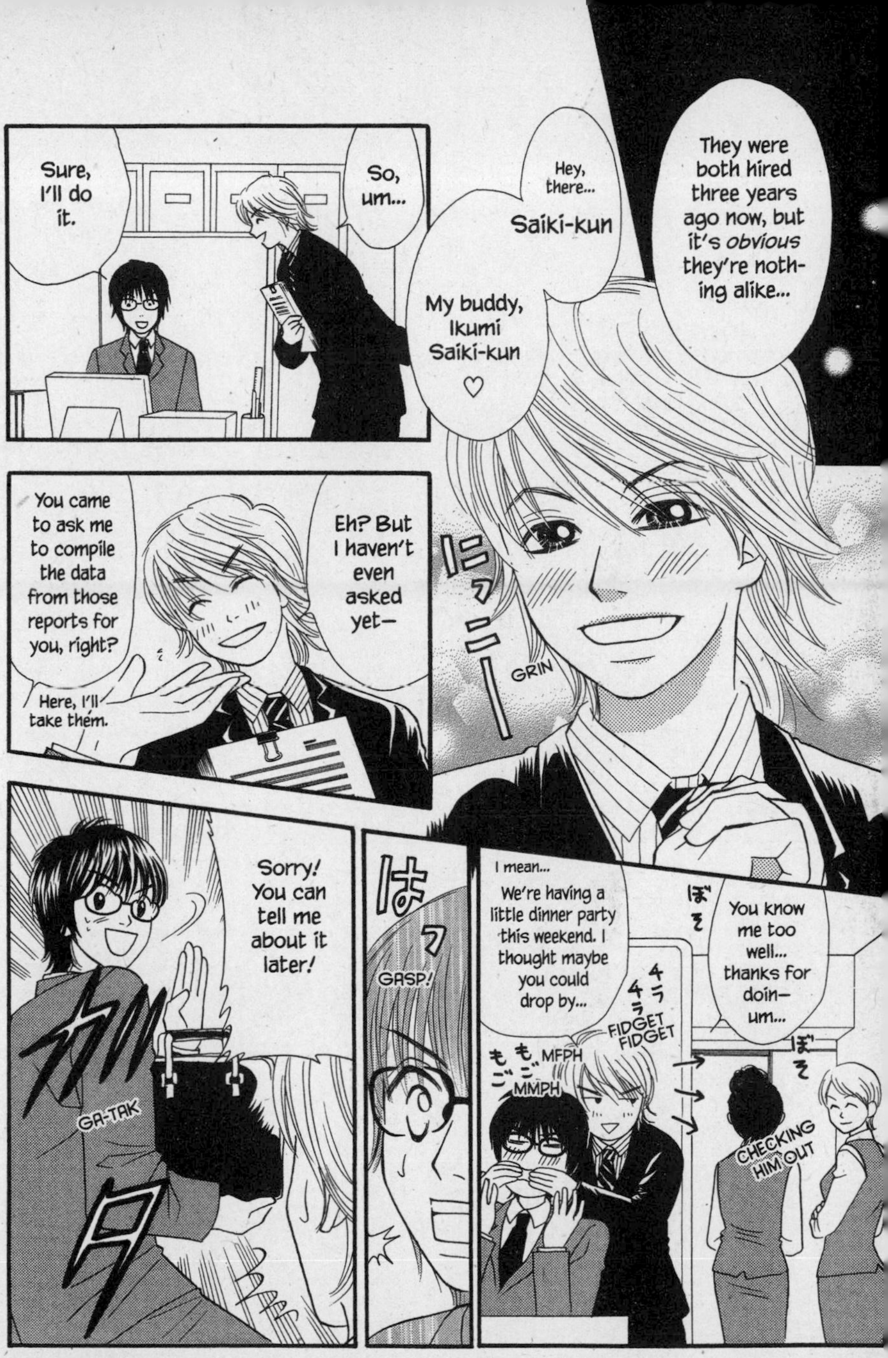
They were both hired three years ago now, but it's *obvious* they're nothing alike...
Hey, there... Saiki-kun
My buddy, Ikumi Saiki-kun ♡
GRIN
So, um...
Sure, I'll do it.
Eh? But I haven't even asked yet—
You came to ask me to compile the data from those reports for you, right?
Here, I'll take them.
You know me too well... thanks for doin— um...
I mean... We're having a little dinner party this weekend. I thought maybe you could drop by...
FIDGET FIDGET
MFPH MMPH
CHECKING HIM OUT
GASP!
Sorry! You can tell me about it later!
GA-TAK

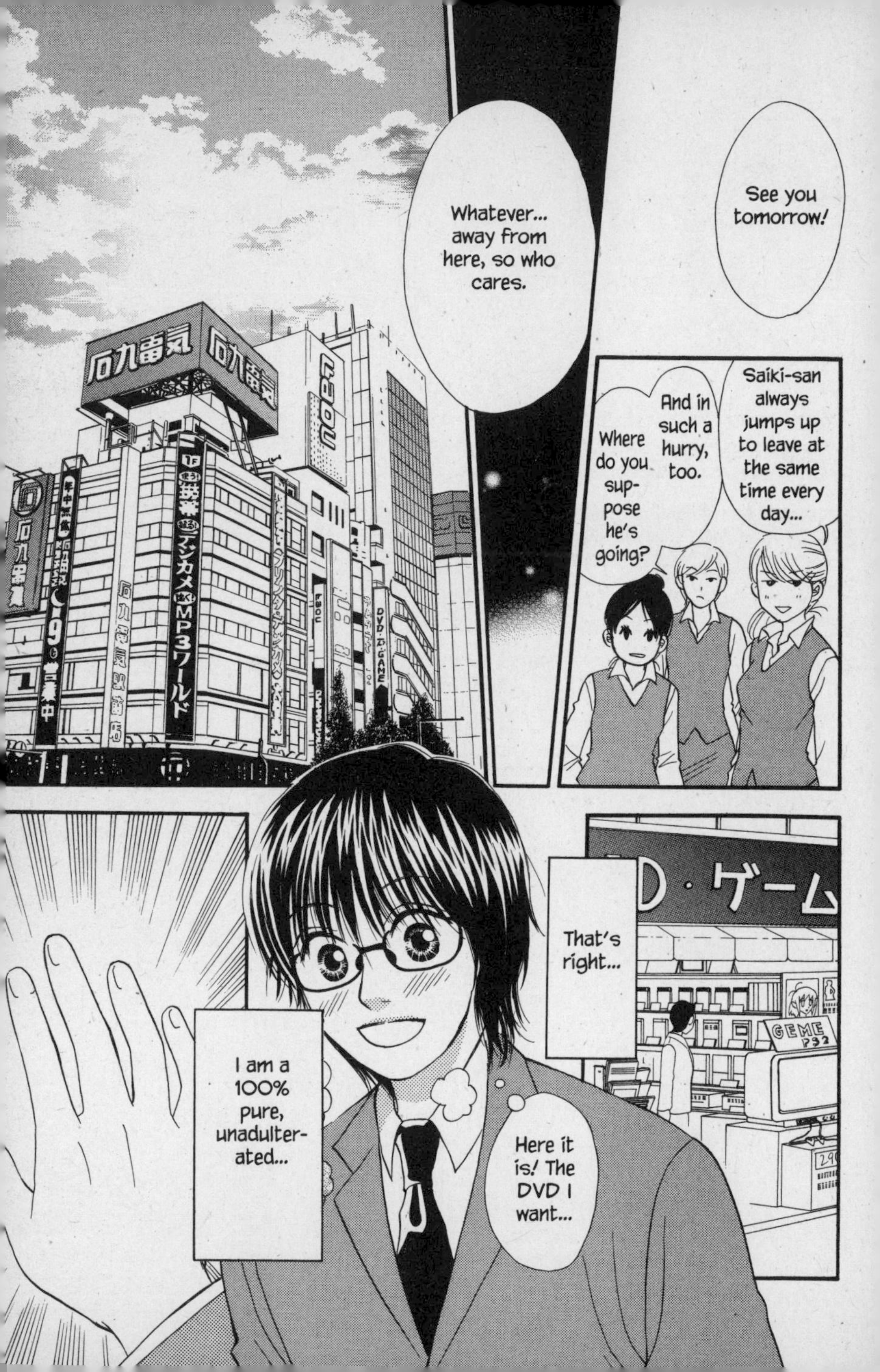
See you tomorrow!
Saiki-san always jumps up to leave at the same time every day...
And in such a hurry, too.
Where do you suppose he's going?
Whatever... away from here, so who cares.
That's right...
I am a 100% pure, unadulterated...
Here it is! The DVD I want...
D・ゲーム
GEME

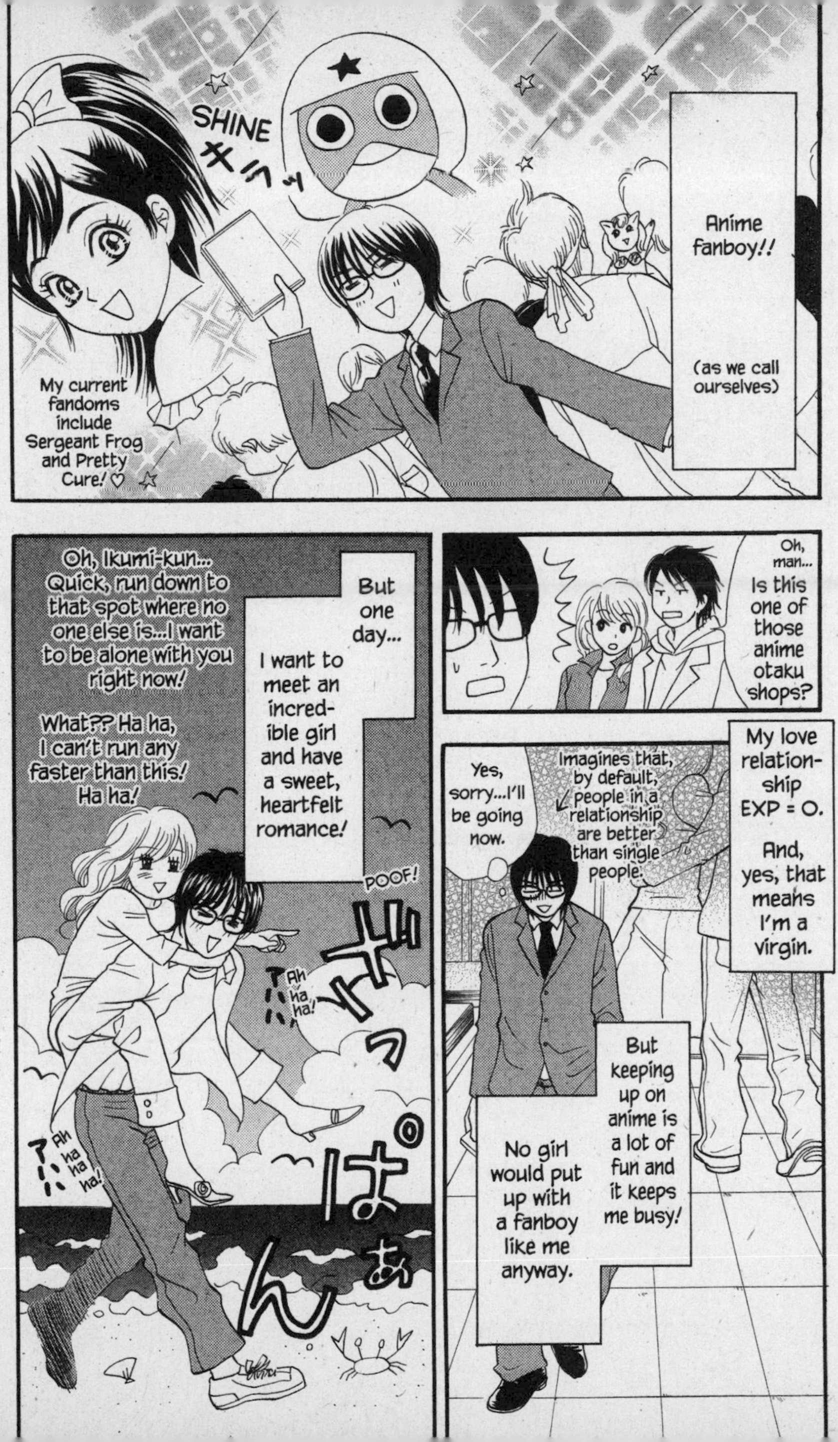
Anime fanboy!!
(as we call ourselves)
SHINE キラッ
My current fandoms include Sergeant Frog and Pretty Cure! ♡
Oh, man... Is this one of those anime otaku shops?
My love relationship EXP = 0.
And, yes, that means I'm a virgin.
Imagines that, by default, people in a relationship are better than single people.
Yes, sorry...I'll be going now.
But keeping up on anime is a lot of fun and it keeps me busy!
No girl would put up with a fanboy like me anyway.
But one day...
I want to meet an incredible girl and have a sweet, heartfelt romance!
POOF!
ぱぁん
Oh, Ikumi-kun... Quick, run down to that spot where no one else is...I want to be alone with you right now!
What?? Ha ha, I can't run any faster than this! Ha ha!
アハハ Ah ha ha!
アハハ Ah ha ha ha!

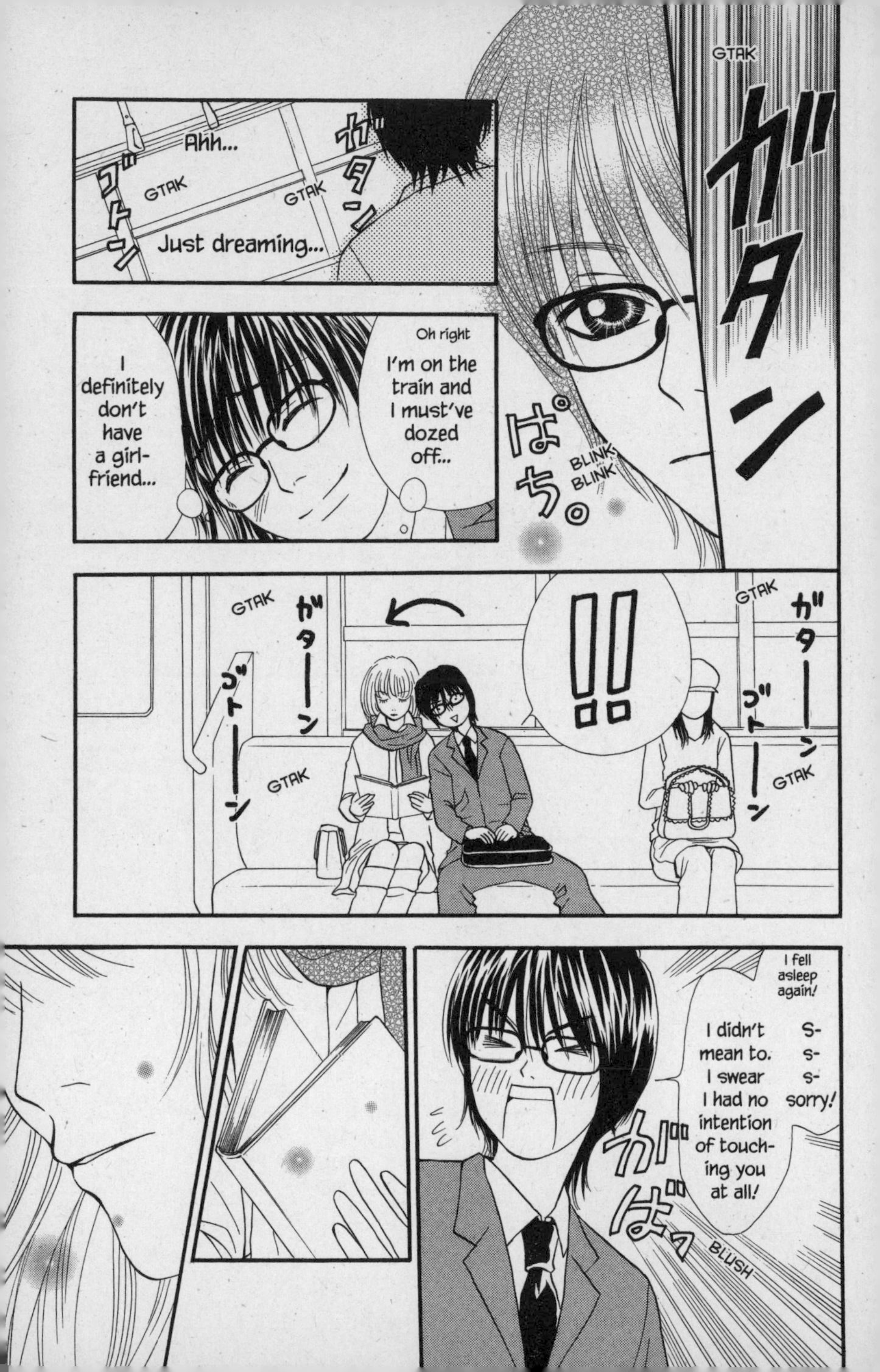
GTAK
ガタン
ぱち。
BLINK BLINK
ガタン
GTAK
Ahh...
GTAK
ゴトン
Just dreaming...
Oh right
I'm on the train and I must've dozed off...
I definitely don't have a girl-friend...
GTAK
ガターン
ゴトーン
GTAK
!!
GTAK
ガターン
ゴトーン
GTAK
I fell asleep again!
S-s-s-sorry!
I didn't mean to. I swear I had no intention of touch-ing you at all!
ガバッ
BLUSH

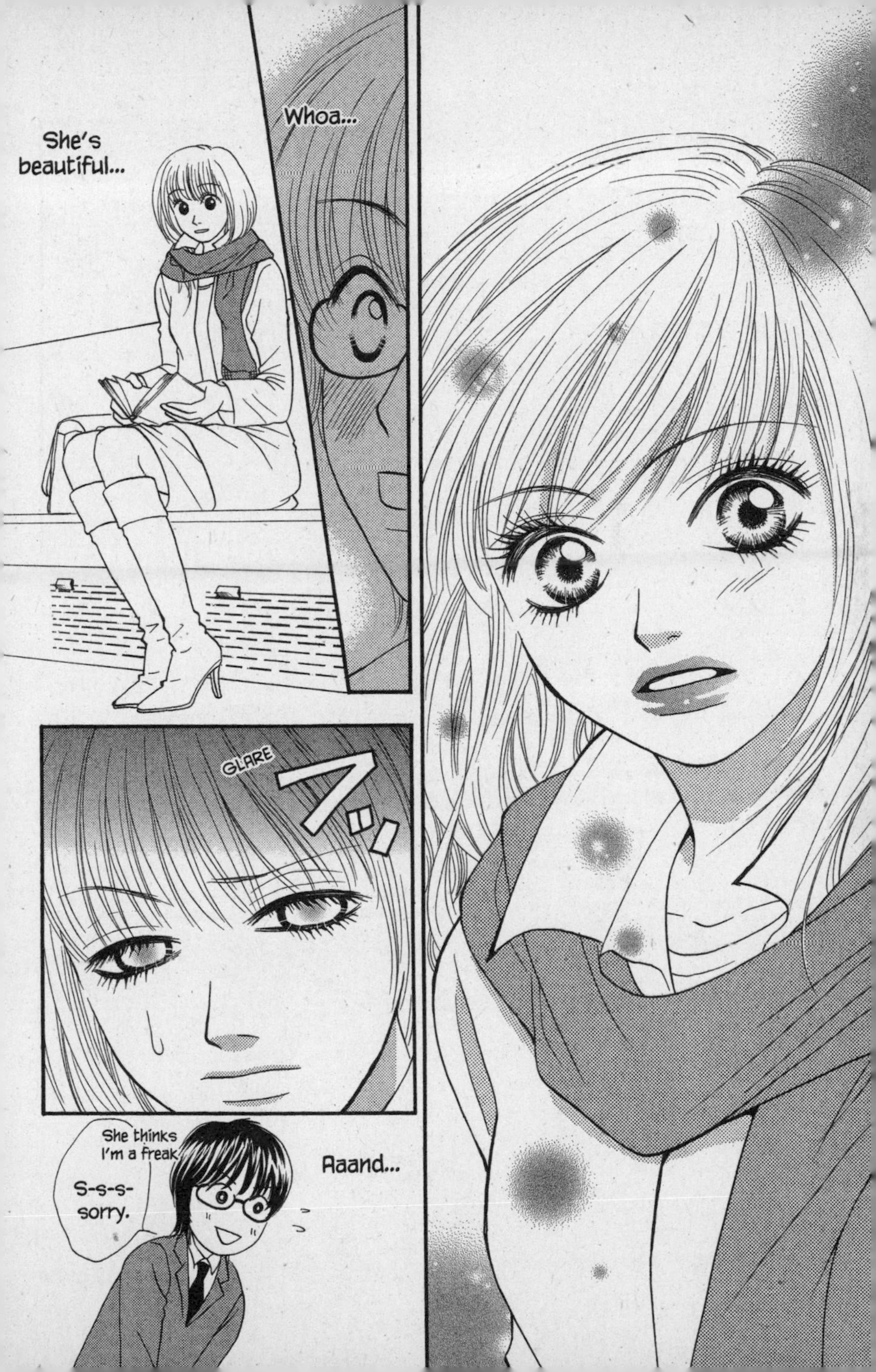
Whoa...
She's beautiful...
GLARE
Aaand...
She thinks I'm a freak
S-s-s-sorry.

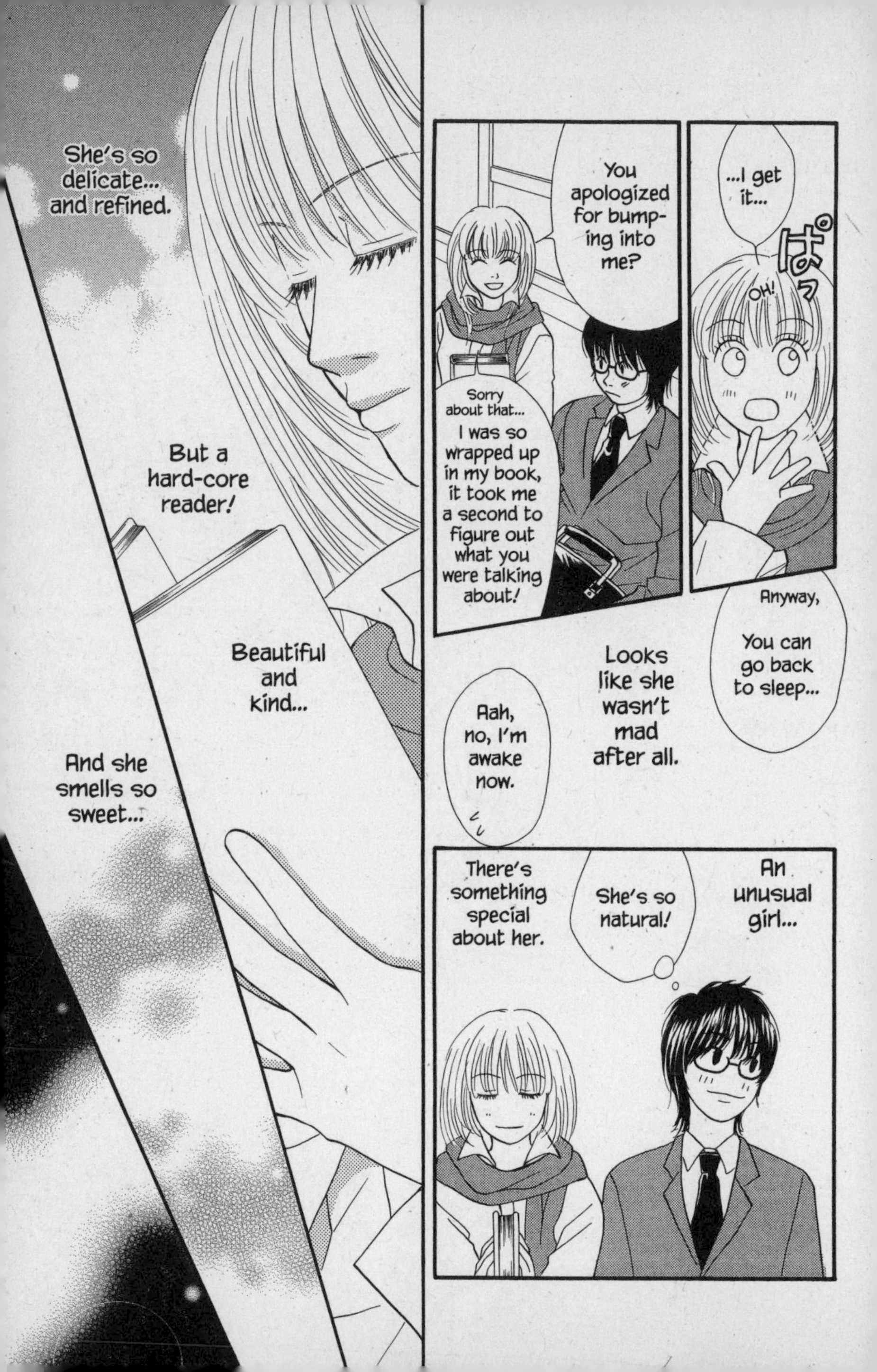
...I get it...
ぱっ
OH!
You apologized for bump-ing into me?
Sorry about that... I was so wrapped up in my book, it took me a second to figure out what you were talking about!
Anyway, You can go back to sleep...
Looks like she wasn't mad after all.
Aah, no, I'm awake now.
An unusual girl...
She's so natural!
There's something special about her.
She's so delicate... and refined.
But a hard-core reader!
Beautiful and kind...
And she smells so sweet...

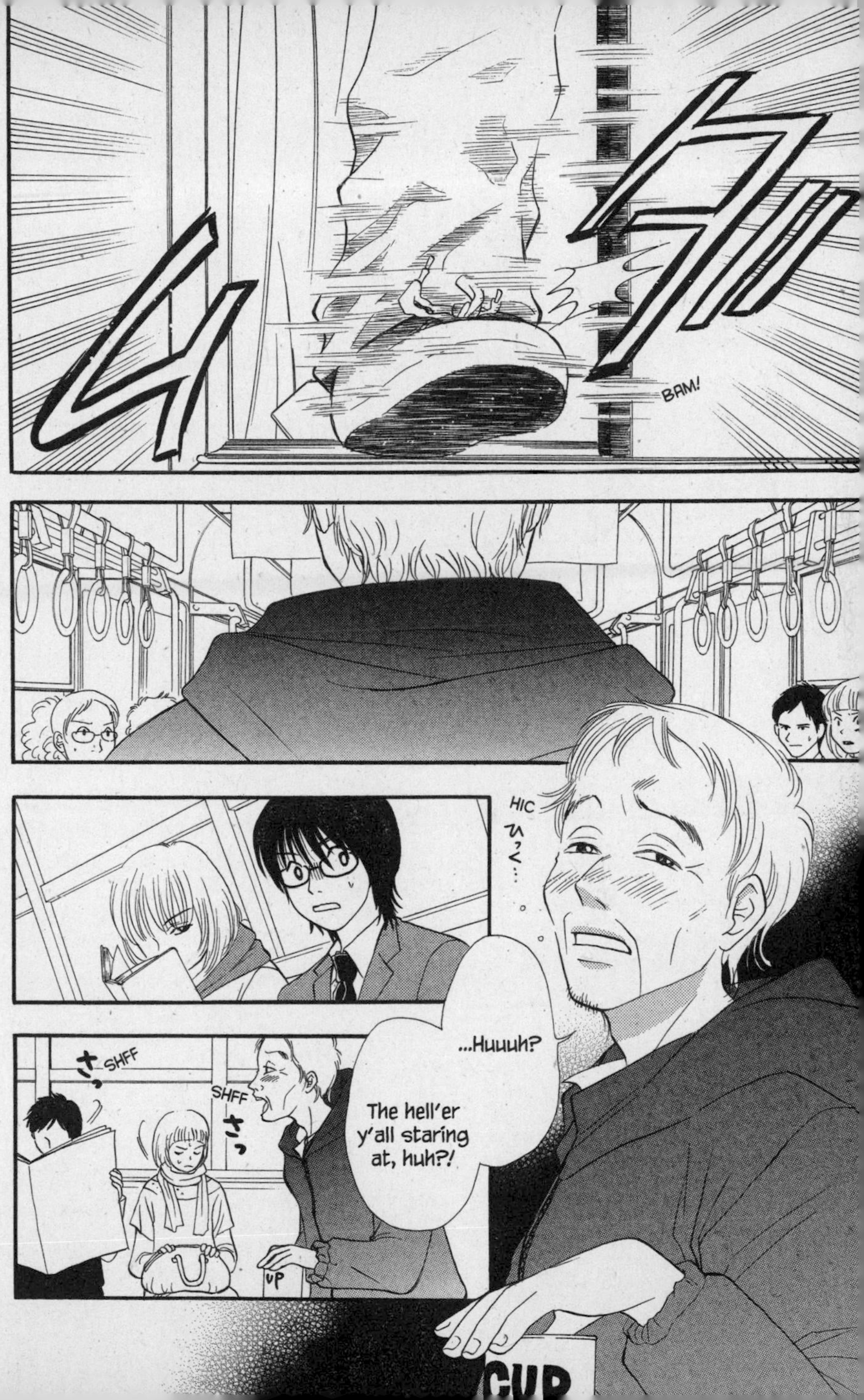
BAM!
HIC
ひっく…
...Huuuh?
The hell'er y'all staring at, huh?!
SHFF
さっ
SHFF
さっ
UP
CUP

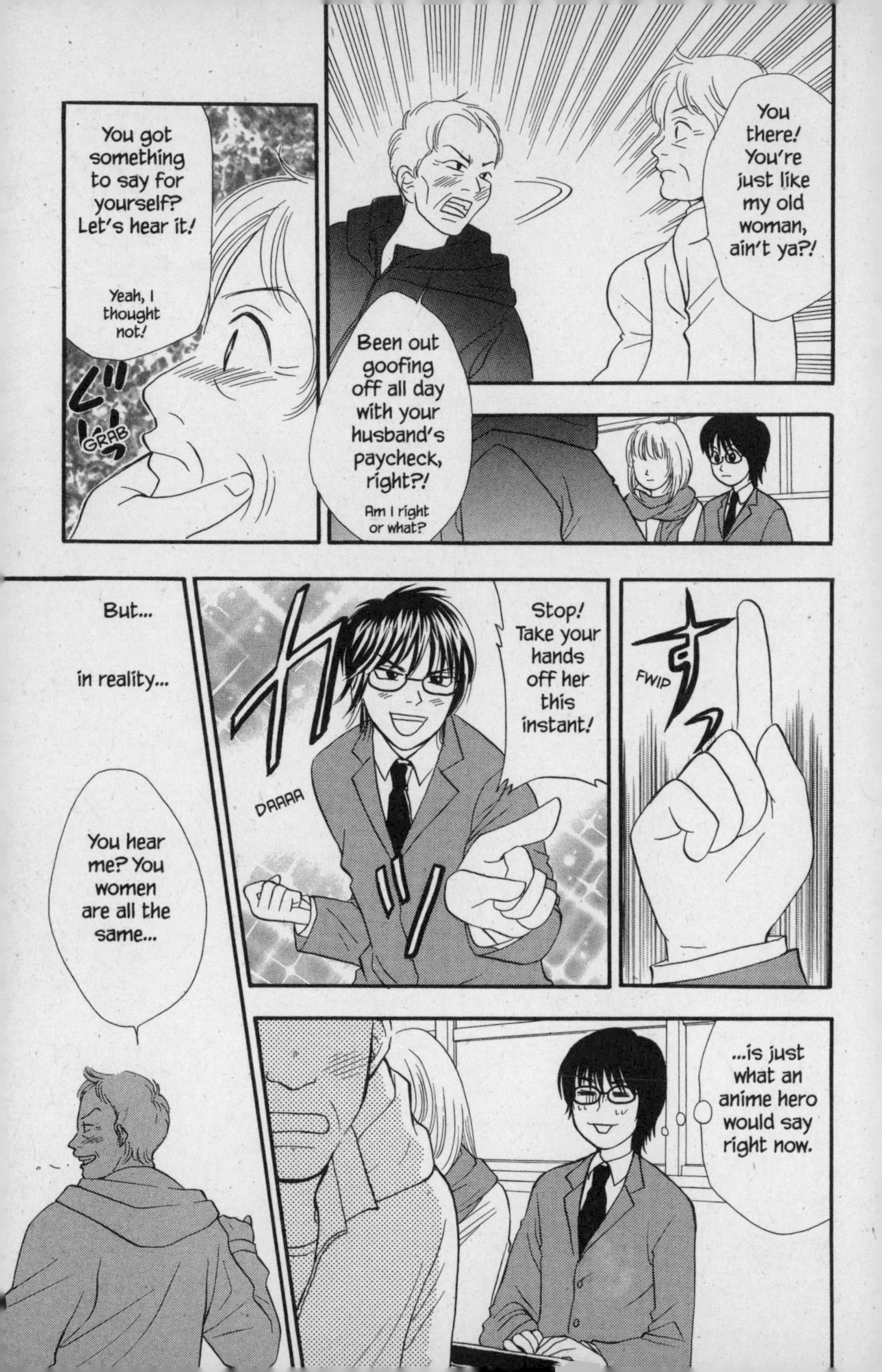
You there! You're just like my old woman, ain't ya?!
Been out goofing off all day with your husband's paycheck, right?!
Am I right or what?
You got something to say for yourself? Let's hear it!
Yeah, I thought not!
GRAB
FWIP
Stop! Take your hands off her this instant!
DAAAA
...is just what an anime hero would say right now.
But...
in reality...
You hear me? You women are all the same...

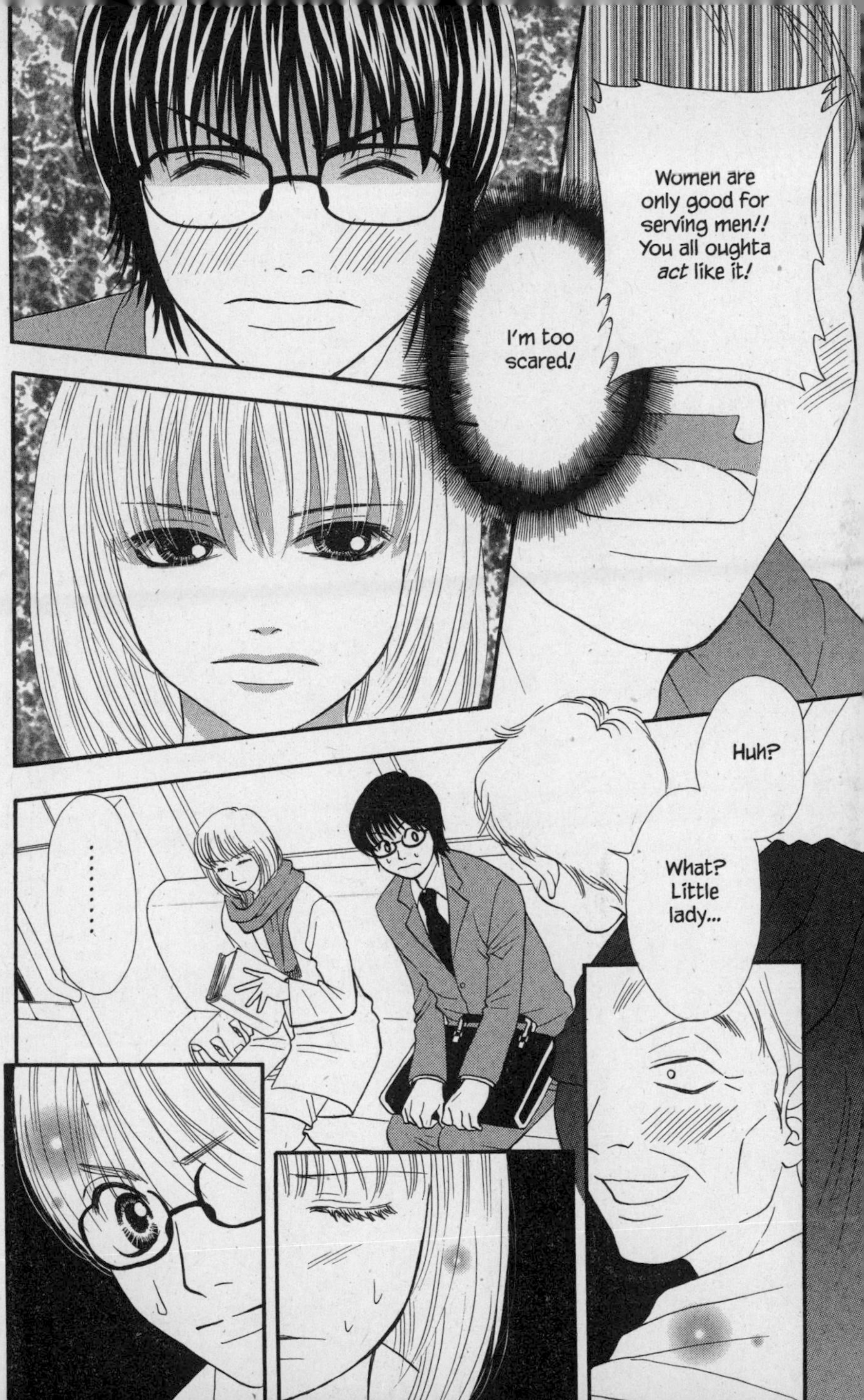
Women are only good for serving men!! You all oughta act like it!
I'm too scared!
Huh?
What? Little lady...
....

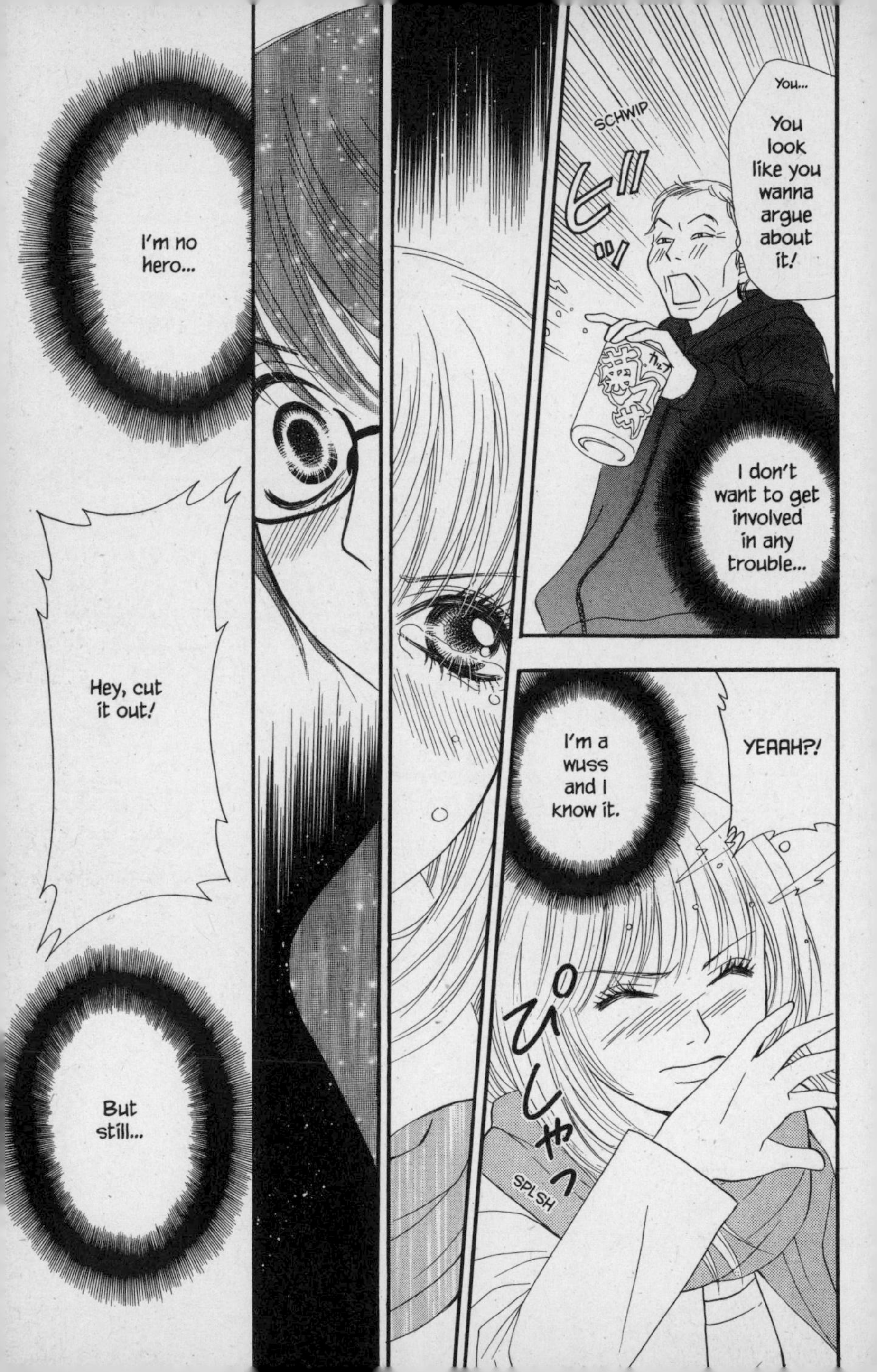
SCHWIP
You...
You look like you wanna argue about it!
I don't want to get involved in any trouble...
YEAAH?!
I'm a wuss and I know it.
SPLSH
I'm no hero...
Hey, cut it out!
But still...

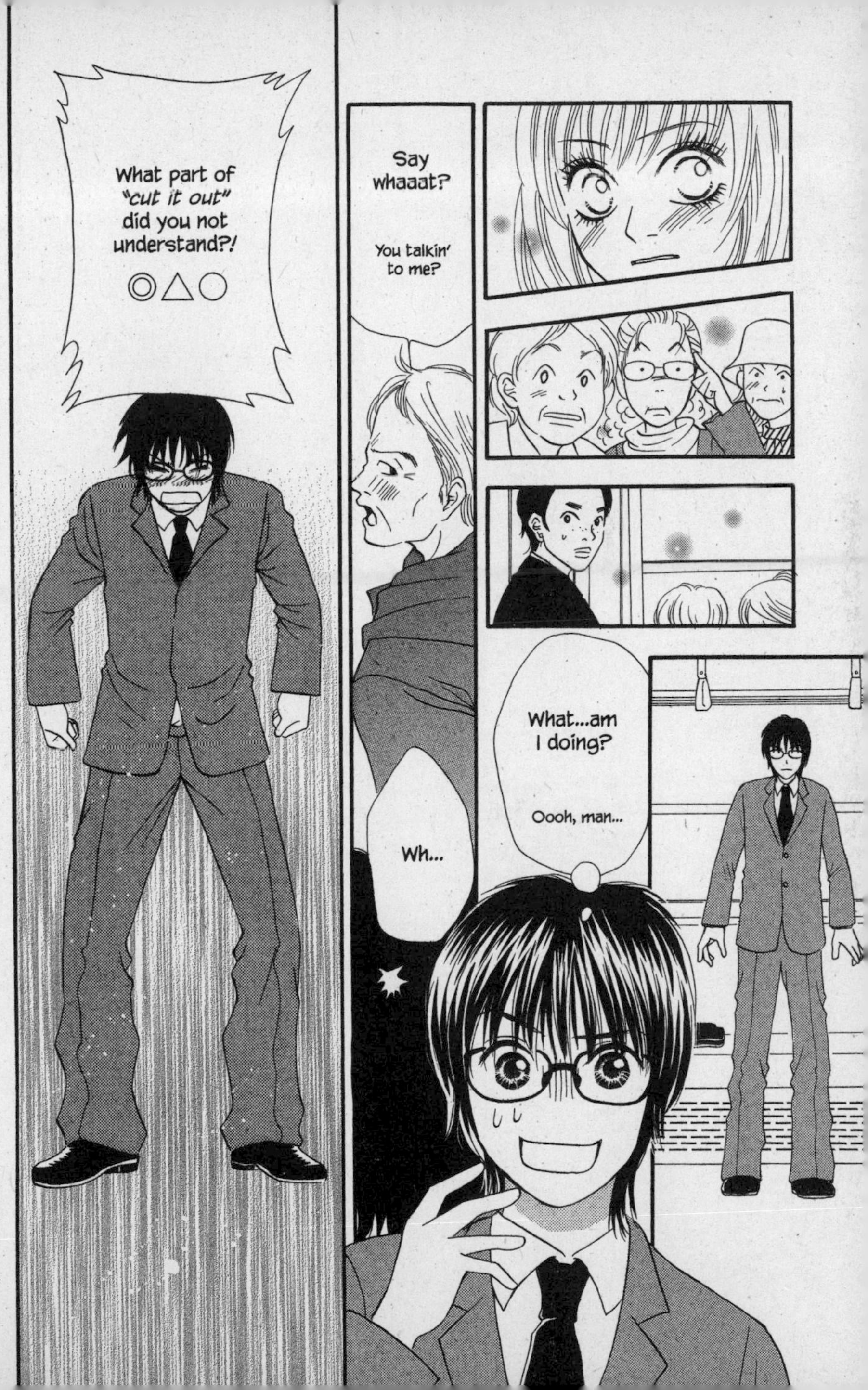
Say whaaat?
You talkin' to me?
Wh...
What...am I doing?
Oooh, man...
What part of "cut it out" did you not understand?!
◎△○

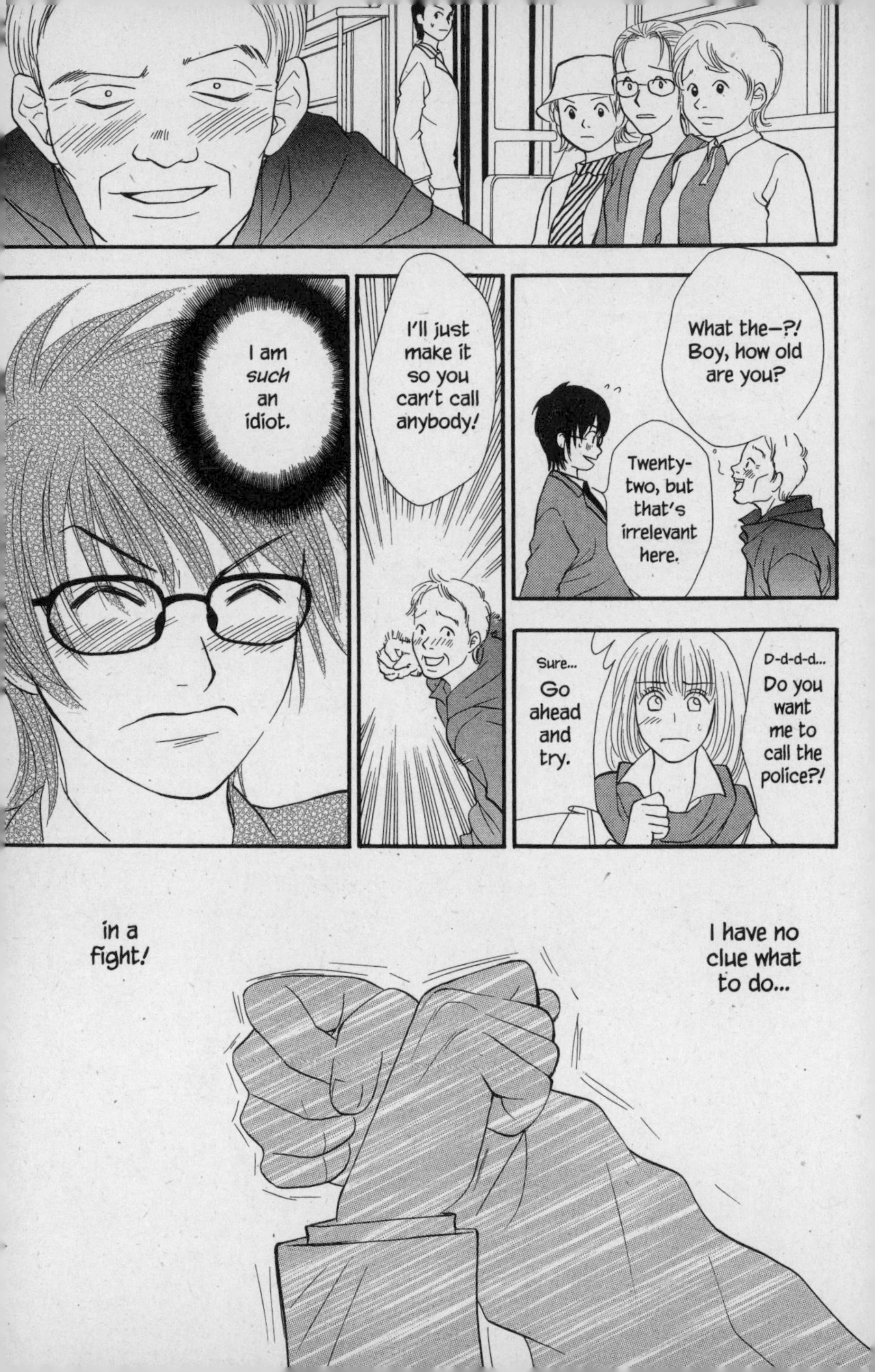
What the–?! Boy, how old are you?
Twenty-two, but that's irrelevant here.
D-d-d-d... Do you want me to call the police?!
Sure... Go ahead and try.
I'll just make it so you can't call anybody!
I am *such* an idiot.
I have no clue what to do...
in a fight!

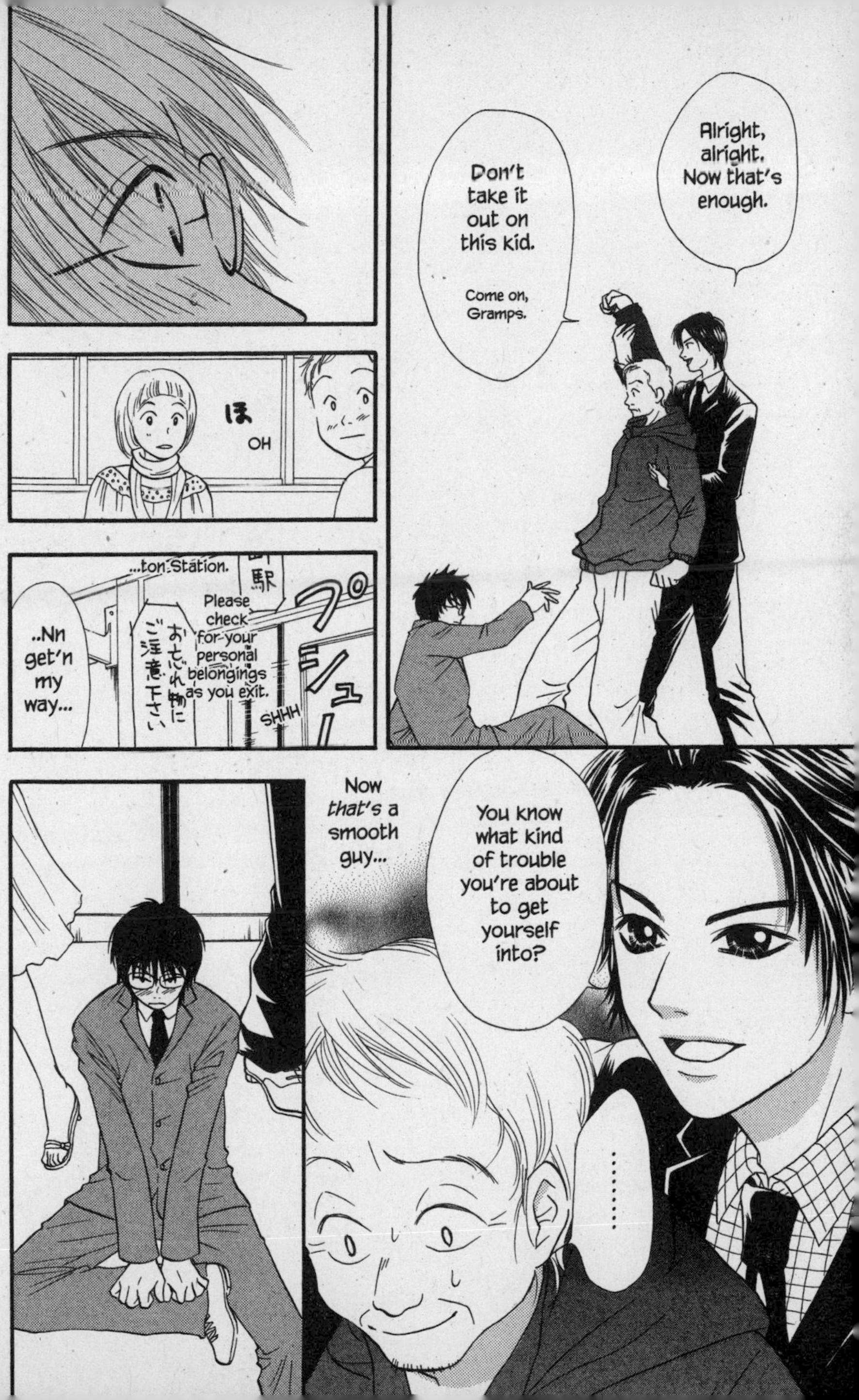
Alright, alright. Now that's enough.
Don't take it out on this kid.
Come on, Gramps.
ほ
OH
...ton Station.
駅
プシュ
SHHH
Please check for your personal belongings as you exit.
ご注意下さい
..Nn get'n my way...
You know what kind of trouble you're about to get yourself into?
Now *that's* a smooth guy...
......

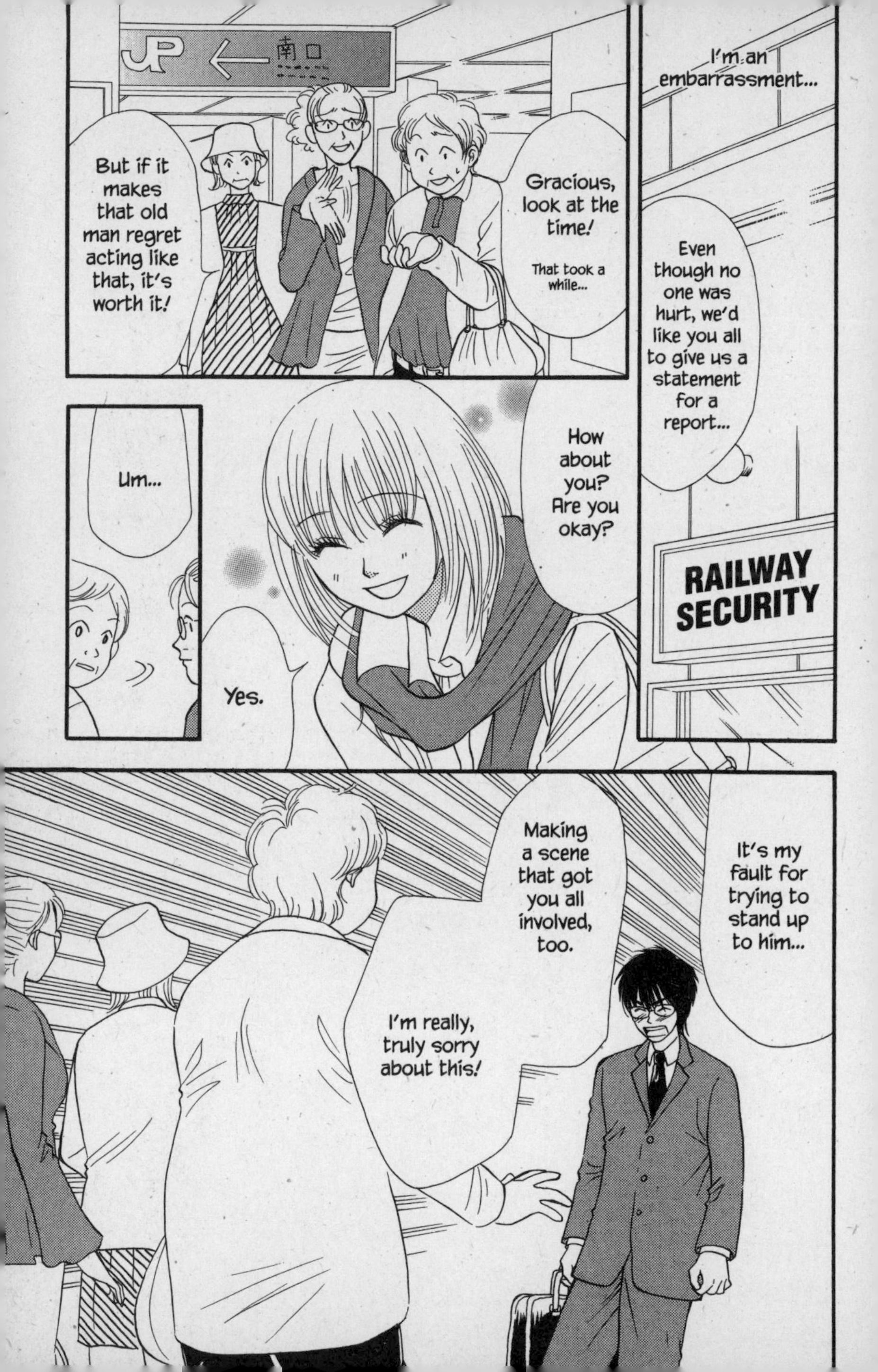
I'm an embarrassment...
Even though no one was hurt, we'd like you all to give us a statement for a report...
RAILWAY SECURITY
JP
南口
Gracious, look at the time!
That took a while...
But if it makes that old man regret acting like that, it's worth it!
How about you? Are you okay?
Yes.
Um...
It's my fault for trying to stand up to him...
Making a scene that got you all involved, too.
I'm really, truly sorry about this!

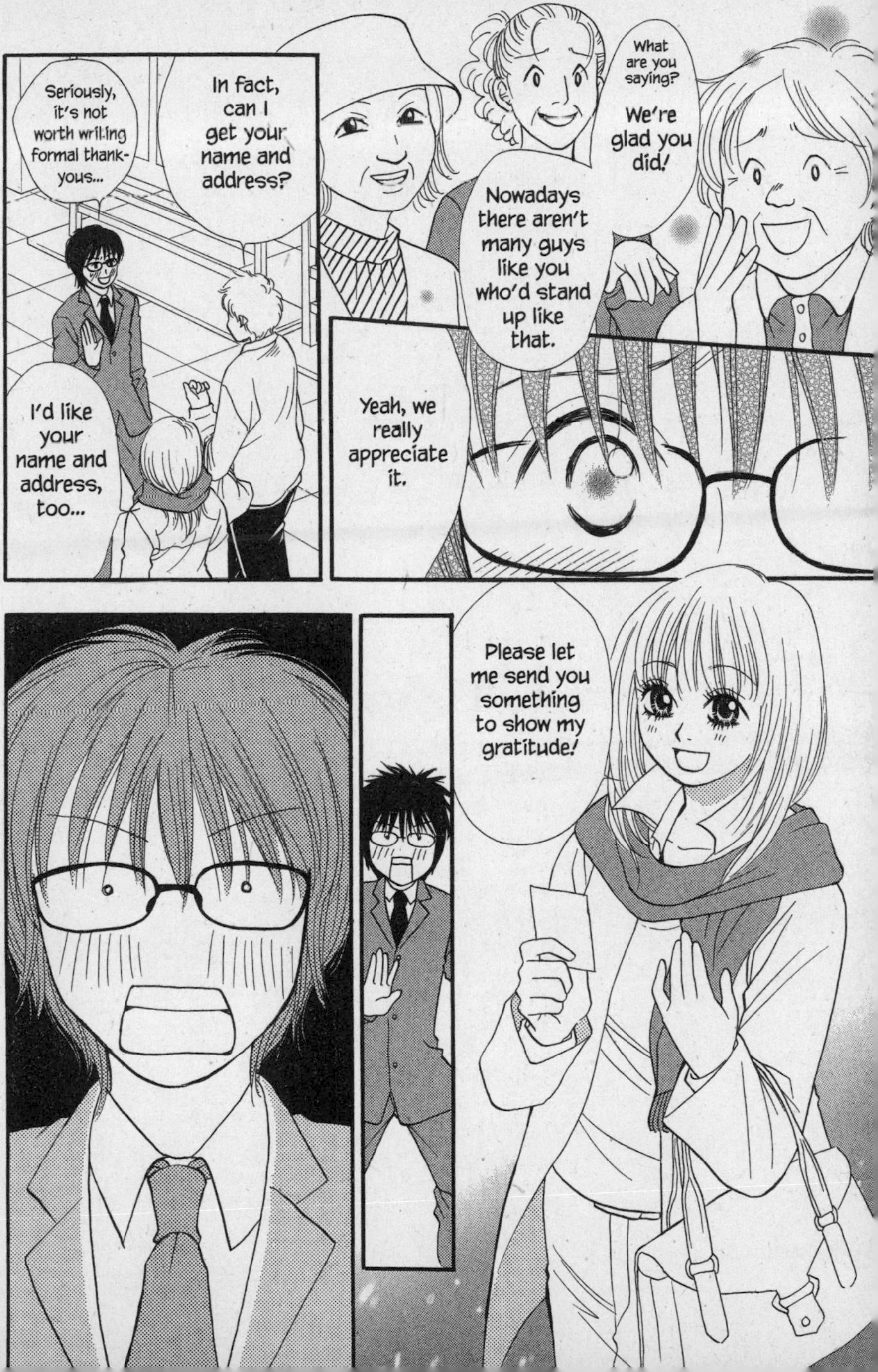
What are you saying?
We're glad you did!
Nowadays there aren't many guys like you who'd stand up like that.
Yeah, we really appreciate it.
In fact, can I get your name and address?
Seriously, it's not worth writing formal thank-yous...
I'd like your name and address, too...
Please let me send you something to show my gratitude!

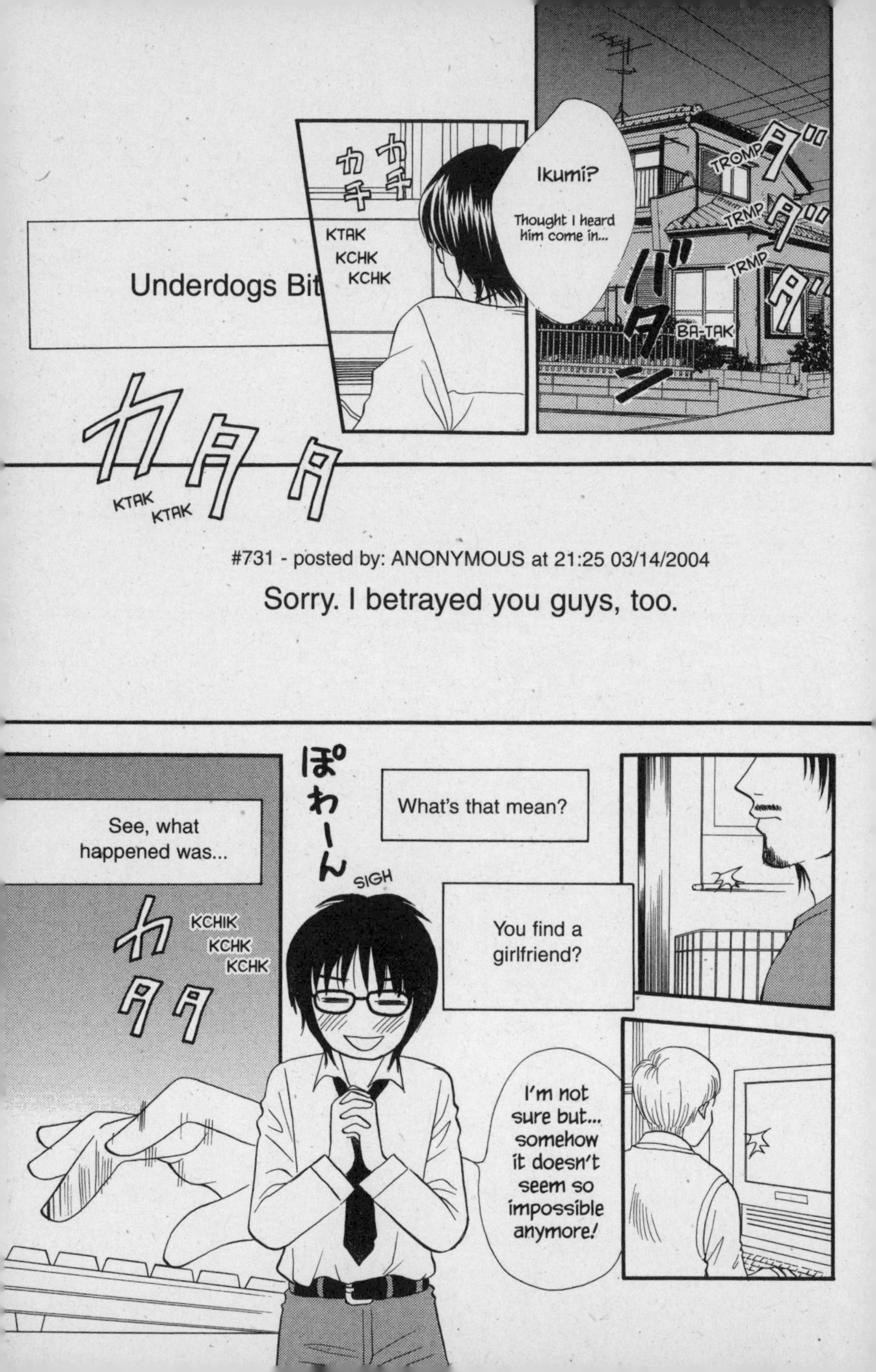

TROMP
TRMP
TRMP
BA-TAK
Ikumi?
Thought I heard him come in...
KTAK
KCHK
KCHK
Underdogs Bit
KTAK
KTAK
#731 - posted by: ANONYMOUS at 21:25 03/14/2004
Sorry. I betrayed you guys, too.
What's that mean?
You find a girlfriend?
I'm not sure but... somehow it doesn't seem so impossible anymore!
See, what happened was...
SIGH
KCHIK
KCHK
KCHK

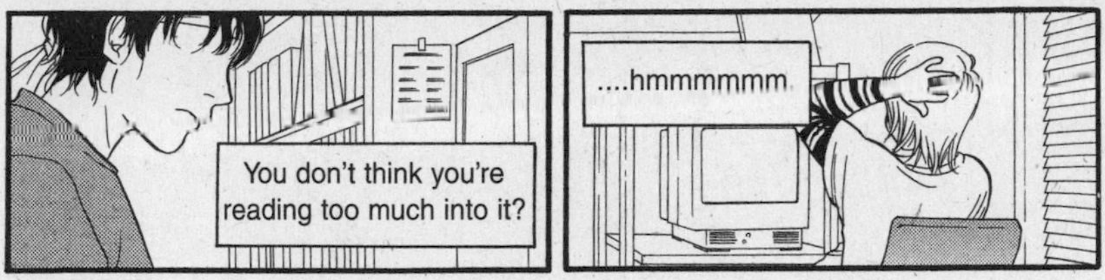
....hmmmmmm
You don't think you're reading too much into it?

#815 - posted by: ANONYMOUS

n e way, nice job. standing up like that was pretty cool of you.

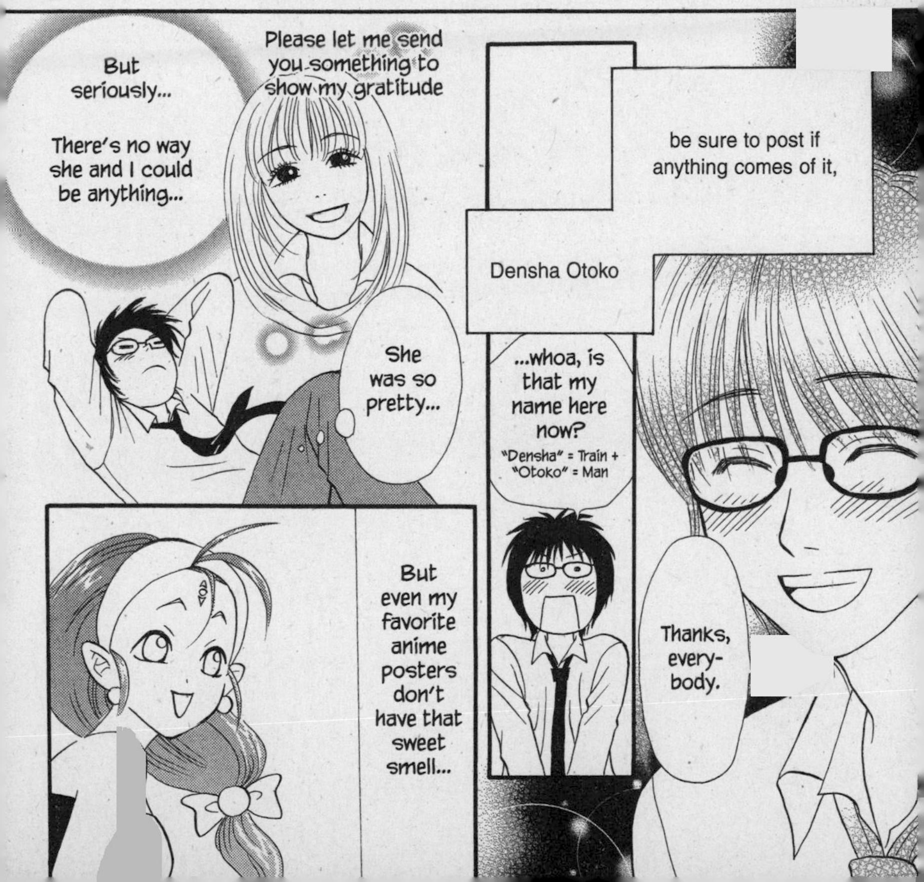
be sure to post if anything comes of it,
Densha Otoko
Thanks, every-body.
...whoa, is that my name here now?
"Densha" = Train + "Otoko" = Man
Please let me send you something to show my gratitude
But seriously...
There's no way she and I could be anything...
She was so pretty...
But even my favorite anime posters don't have that sweet smell...

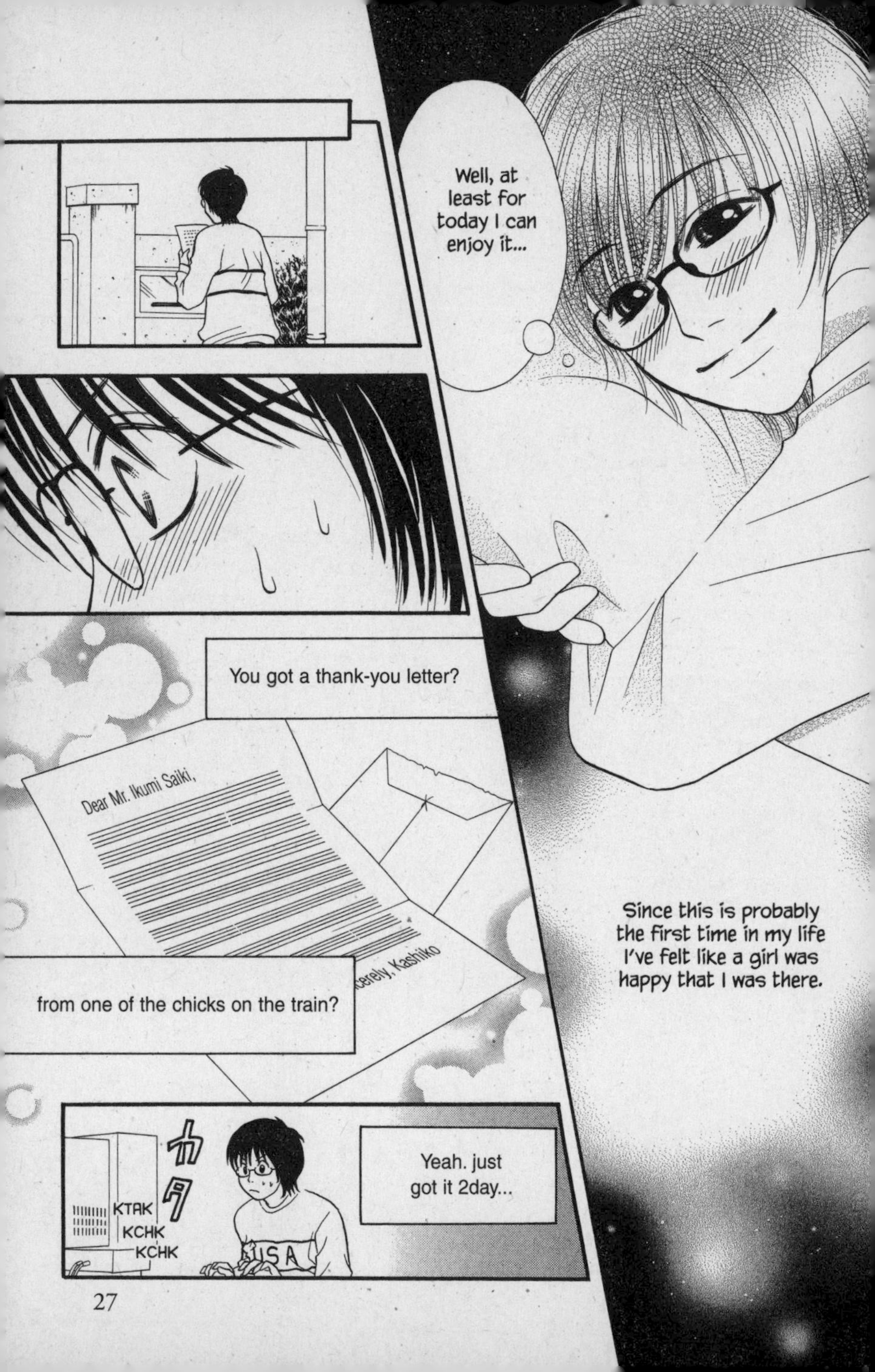
Well, at least for today I can enjoy it...
Since this is probably the first time in my life I've felt like a girl was happy that I was there.
You got a thank-you letter?
Dear Mr. Ikumi Saiki,
cerely, Kashiko
from one of the chicks on the train?
カタ
KTAK
KCHK
KCHK
Yeah. just got it 2day...

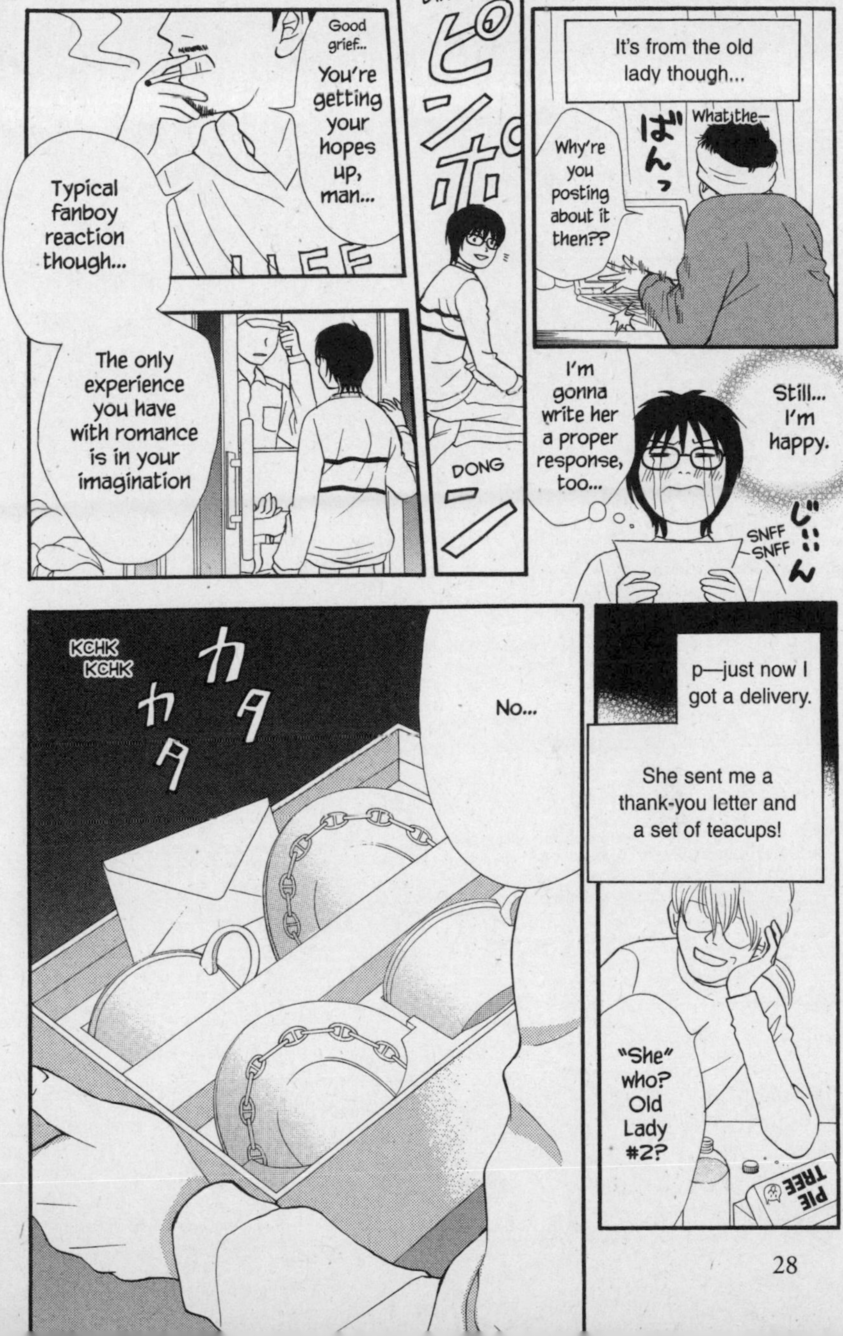
It's from the old lady though...
What the—
ばんっ
Why're you posting about it then??
I'm gonna write her a proper response, too...
Still... I'm happy.
じーん
SNFF SNFF
DING
ピンポーン
DONG
Good grief...
You're getting your hopes up, man...
Typical fanboy reaction though...
The only experience you have with romance is in your imagination
p—just now I got a delivery.
She sent me a thank-you letter and a set of teacups!
"She" who? Old Lady #2?
PIE TREE
No...
カタカタ
KCHK KCHK

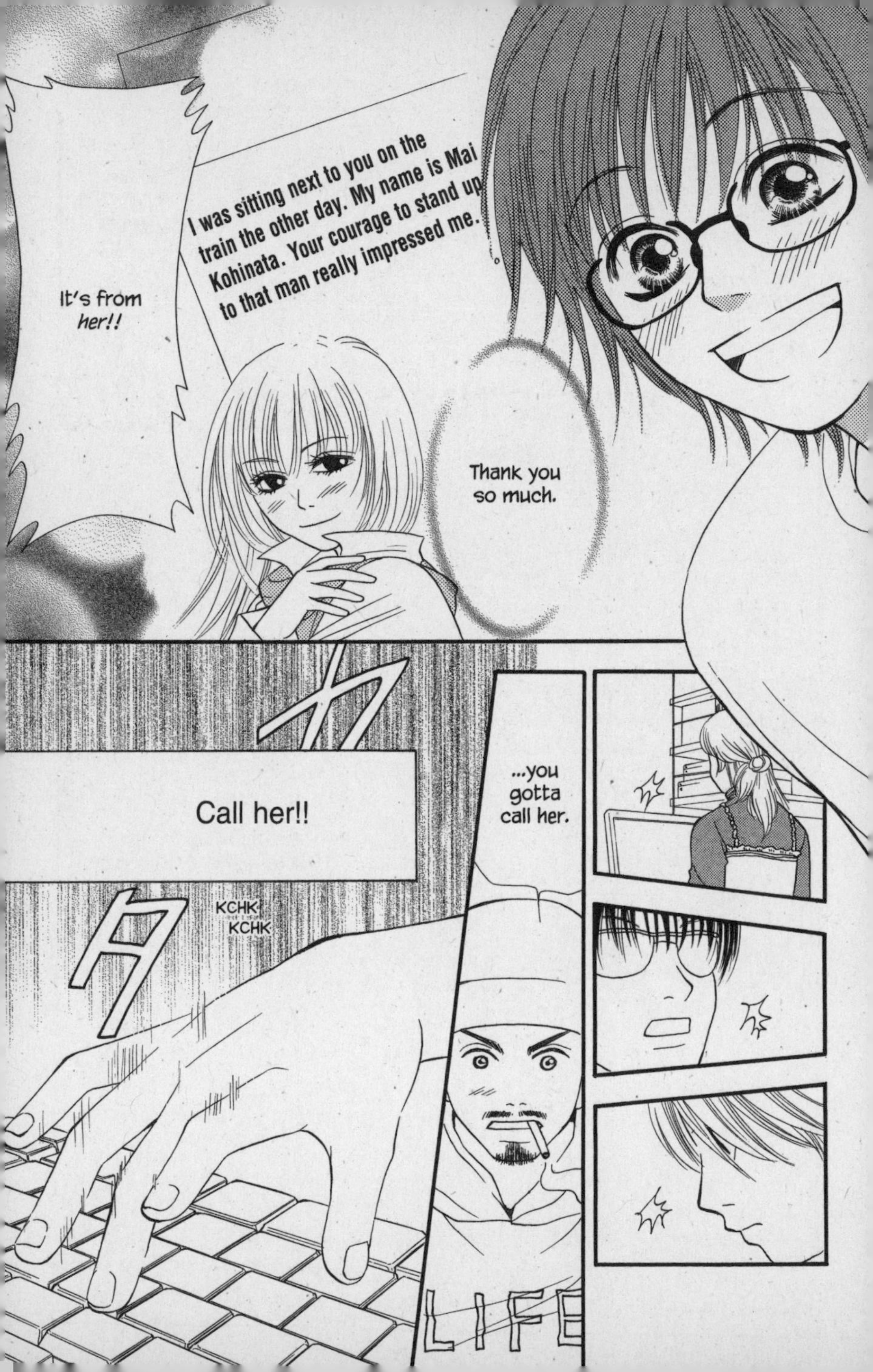
I was sitting next to you on the train the other day. My name is Mai Kohinata. Your courage to stand up to that man really impressed me.
Thank you so much.
It's from her!!
...you gotta call her.
LIFE
Call her!!
KCHK KCHK

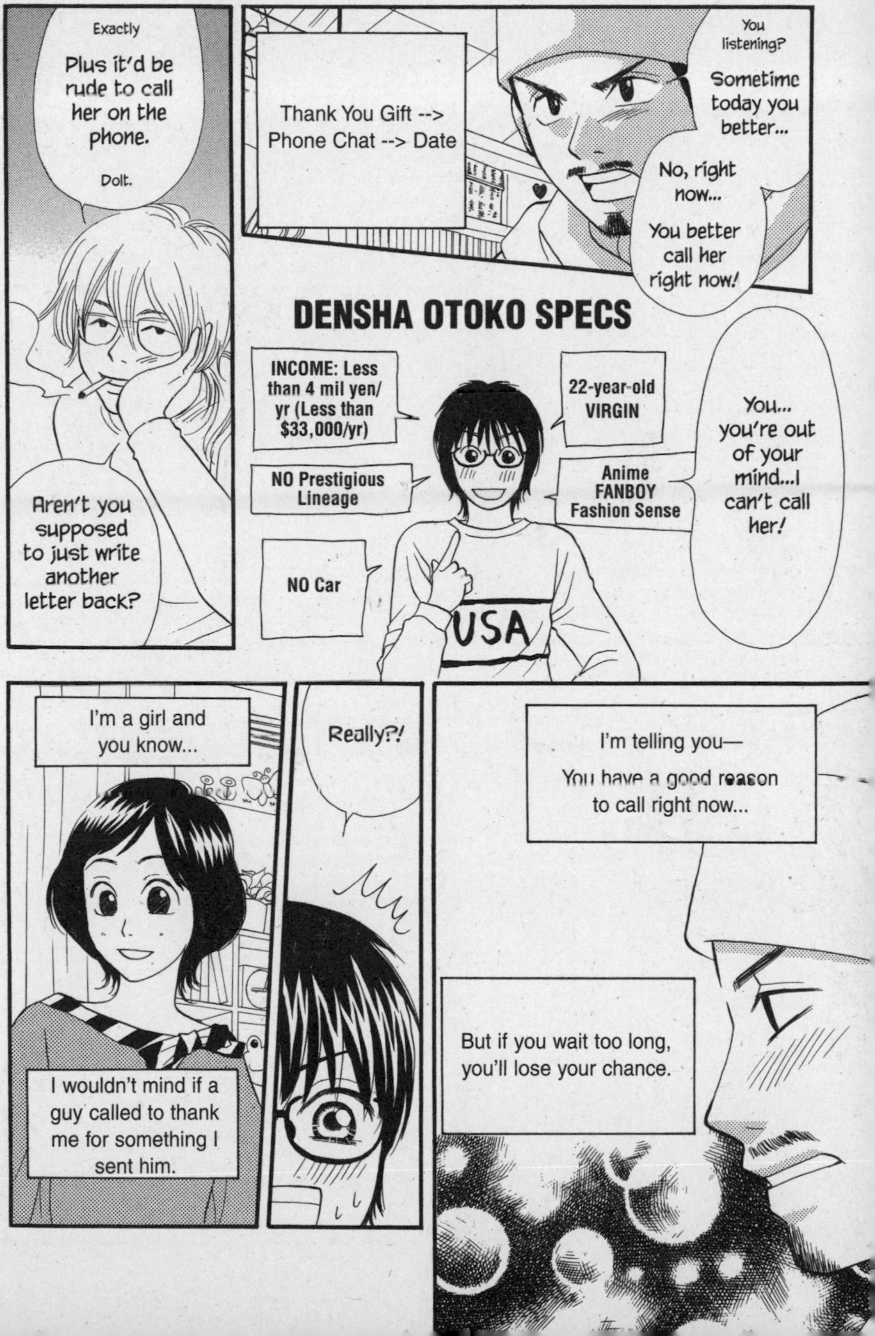
You listening?
Sometime today you better...
No, right now...
You better call her right now!
Thank You Gift --> Phone Chat --> Date
DENSHA OTOKO SPECS
You... you're out of your mind...I can't call her!
22-year-old VIRGIN
Anime FANBOY Fashion Sense
INCOME: Less than 4 mil yen/yr (Less than $33,000/yr)
NO Prestigious Lineage
NO Car
Exactly
Plus it'd be rude to call her on the phone.
Dolt.
Aren't you supposed to just write another letter back?
I'm telling you—
You have a good reason to call right now...
But if you wait too long, you'll lose your chance.
Really?!
I'm a girl and you know...
I wouldn't mind if a guy called to thank me for something I sent him.

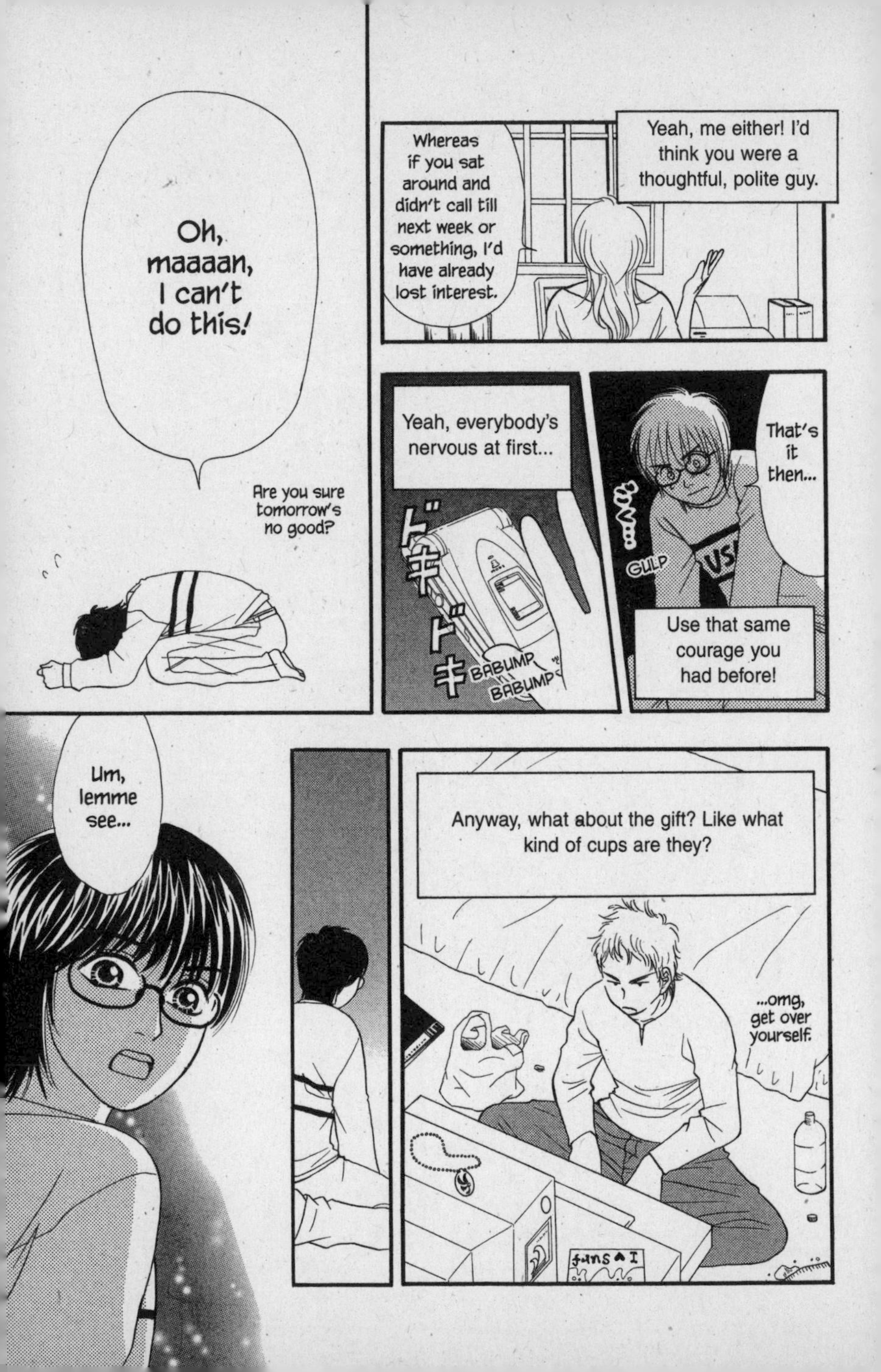
Whereas if you sat around and didn't call till next week or something, I'd have already lost interest.
Yeah, me either! I'd think you were a thoughtful, polite guy.
That's it then...
ゴクッ…
GULP
Use that same courage you had before!
Yeah, everybody's nervous at first...
ドキドキ
BABUMP BABUMP
Oh, maaaan, I can't do this!
Are you sure tomorrow's no good?
Anyway, what about the gift? Like what kind of cups are they?
...omg, get over yourself.
Um, lemme see...

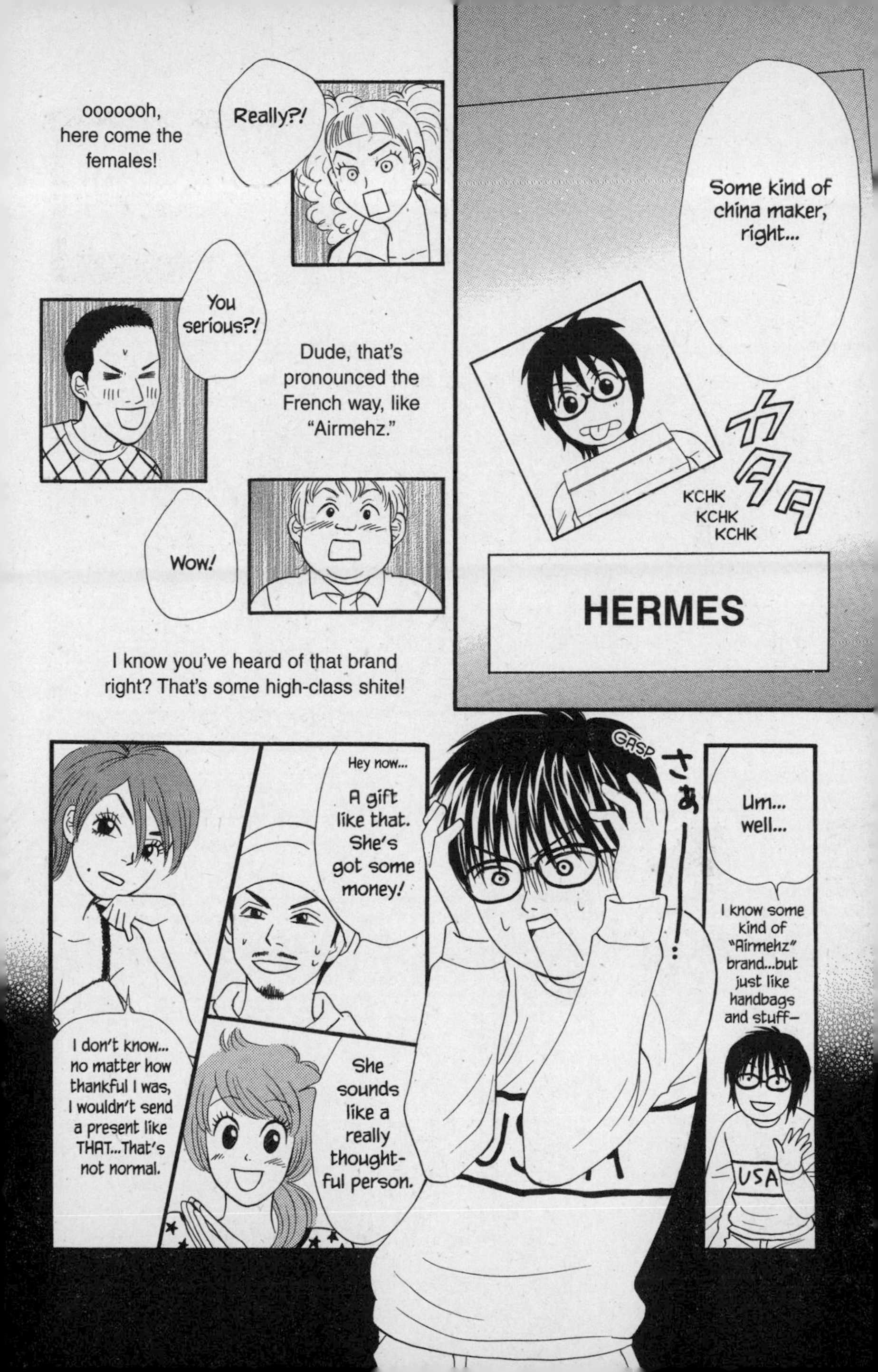
Some kind of china maker, right...
カタタ
KCHK KCHK KCHK
HERMES
Really?!
ooooooh, here come the females!
You serious?!
Dude, that's pronounced the French way, like "Airmehz."
Wow!
I know you've heard of that brand right? That's some high-class shite!
Um... well...
I know some kind of "Airmehz" brand...but just like handbags and stuff—
USA
GASP
さぁー!!
Hey now...
A gift like that. She's got some money!
She sounds like a really thought-ful person.
I don't know... no matter how thankful I was, I wouldn't send a present like THAT...That's not normal.

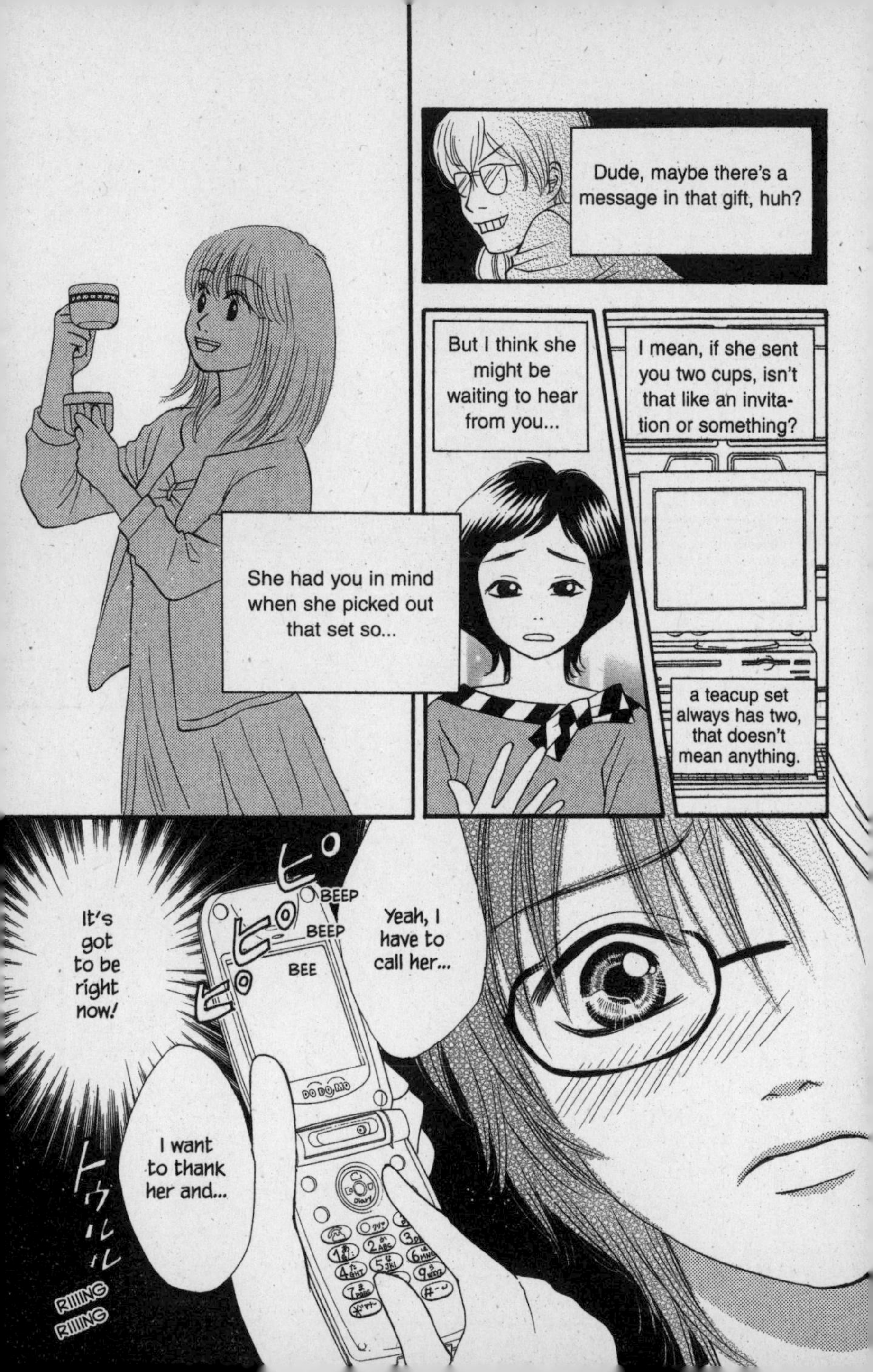
Dude, maybe there's a message in that gift, huh?
I mean, if she sent you two cups, isn't that like an invitation or something?
a teacup set always has two, that doesn't mean anything.
But I think she might be waiting to hear from you...
She had you in mind when she picked out that set so...
Yeah, I have to call her...
BEEP
BEEP
BEE
It's got to be right now!
I want to thank her and...
RIIING RIIING

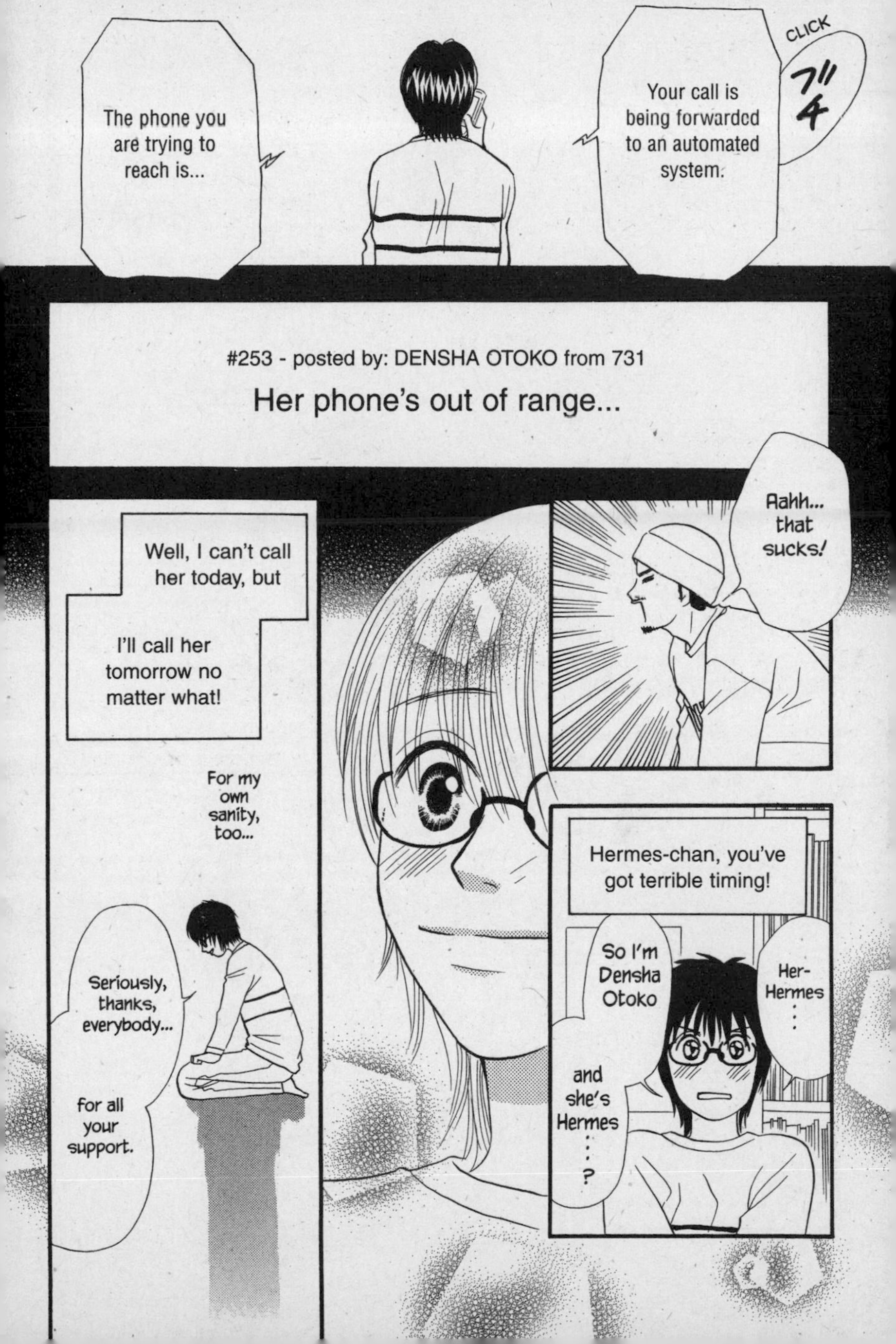
CLICK
Your call is being forwarded to an automated system.
The phone you are trying to reach is...
#253 - posted by: DENSHA OTOKO from 731
Her phone's out of range...
Aahh... that sucks!
Hermes-chan, you've got terrible timing!
Her-Hermes...
So I'm Densha Otoko and she's Hermes...?
Well, I can't call her today, but
I'll call her tomorrow no matter what!
For my own sanity, too...
Seriously, thanks, everybody...
for all your support.

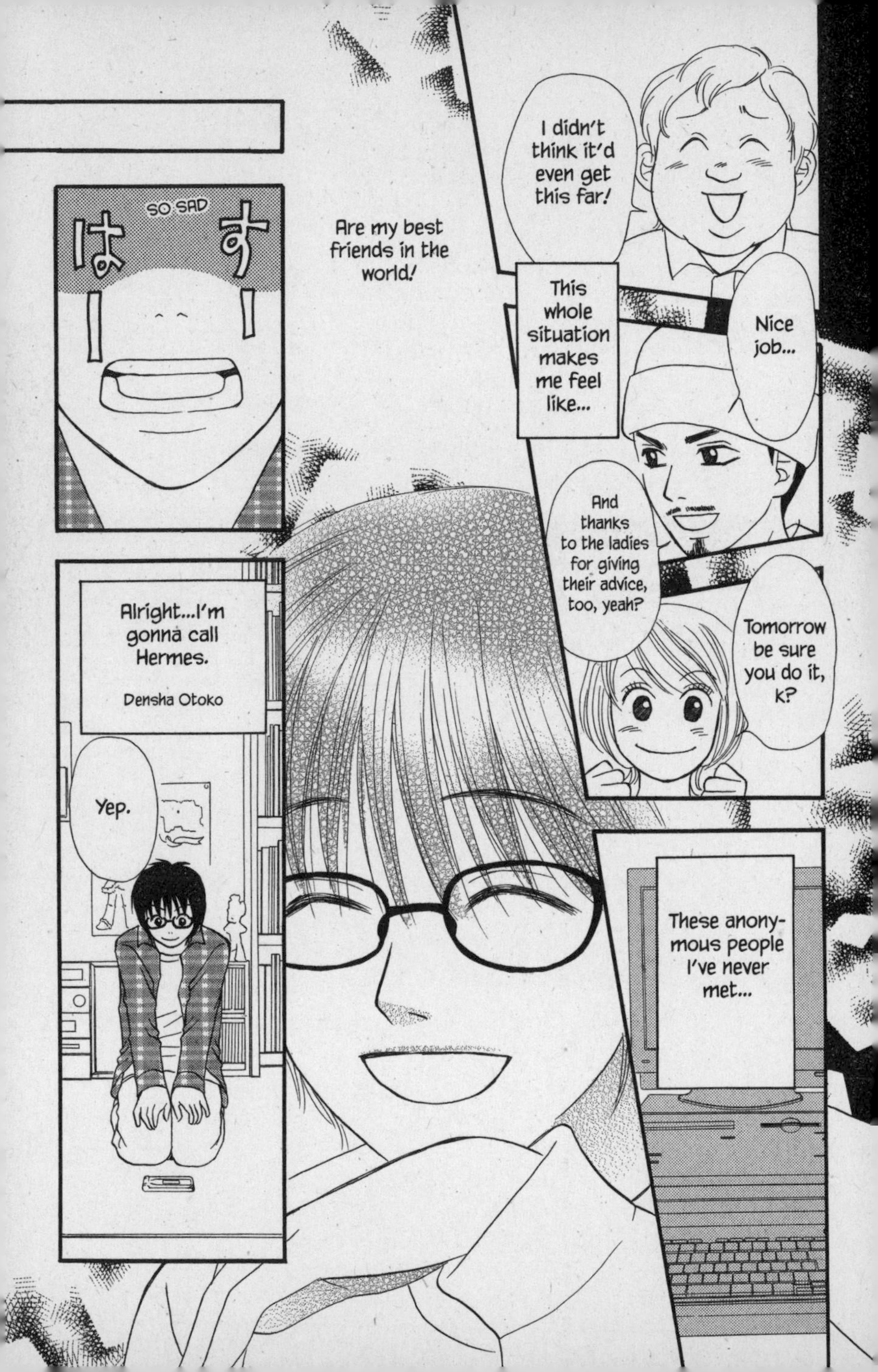

I didn't think it'd even get this far!
This whole situation makes me feel like...
Nice job...
And thanks to the ladies for giving their advice, too, yeah?
Tomorrow be sure you do it, k?
These anonymous people I've never met...
Are my best friends in the world!
すー はー
SO SAD
Alright...I'm gonna call Hermes.
Densha Otoko
Yep.

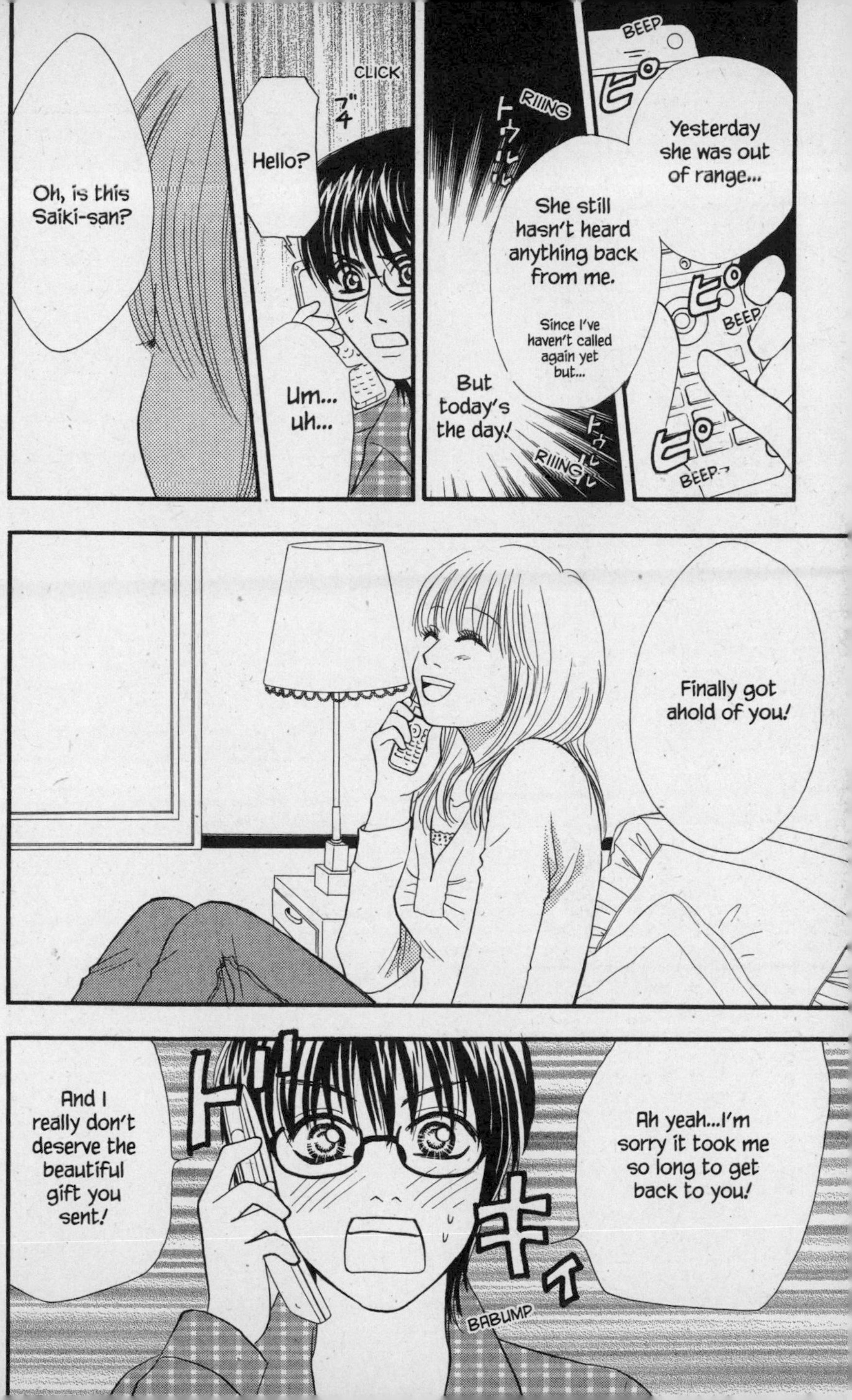
BEEP
Yesterday she was out of range...
BEEP
BEEP
RIIING
She still hasn't heard anything back from me.
Since I've haven't called again yet but...
But today's the day!
RIIING
CLICK
Hello?
Um... uh...
Oh, is this Saiki-san?
Finally got ahold of you!
Ah yeah...I'm sorry it took me so long to get back to you!
BABUMP
And I really don't deserve the beautiful gift you sent!

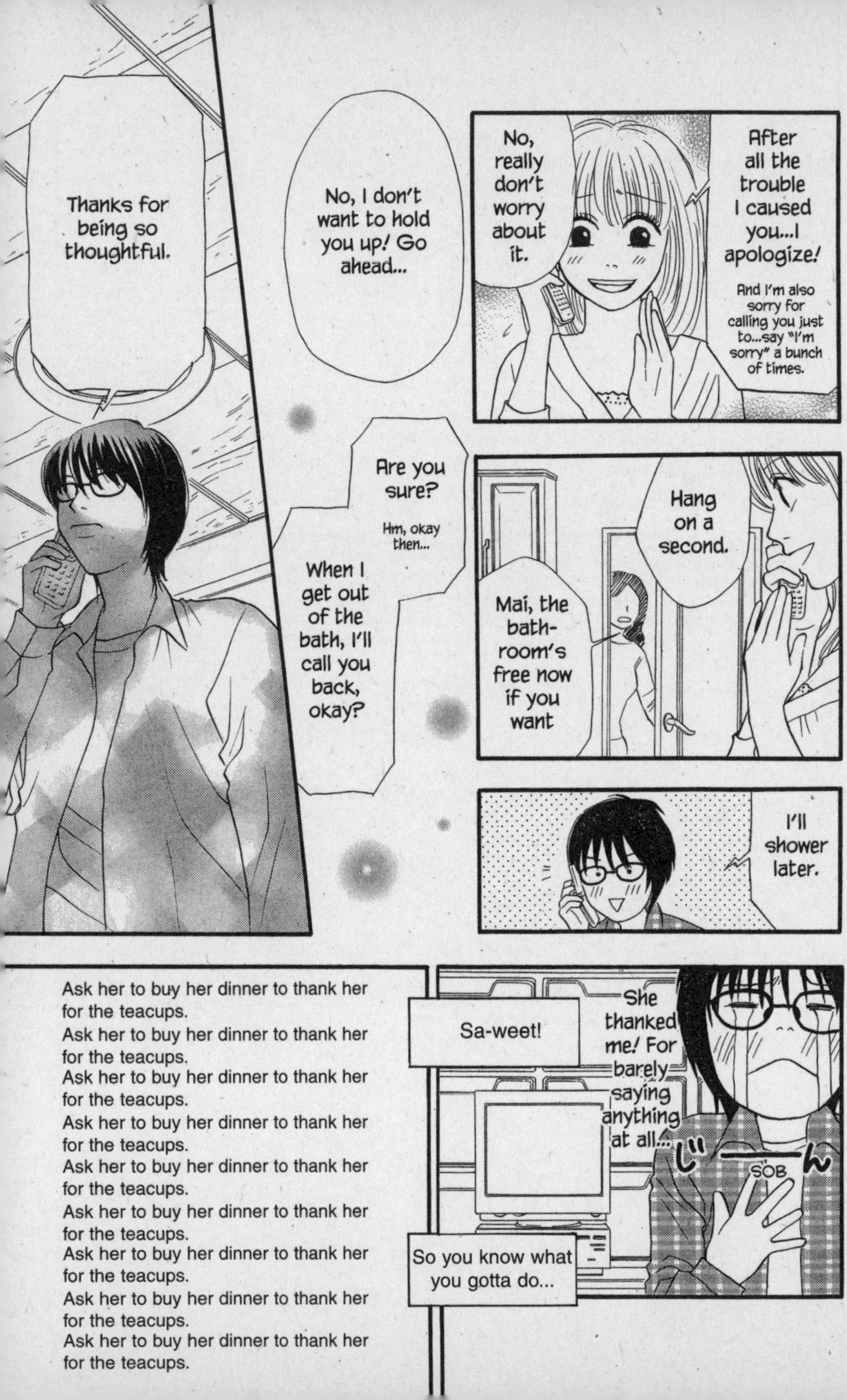
After all the trouble I caused you...I apologize!
And I'm also sorry for calling you just to...say "I'm sorry" a bunch of times.
No, really don't worry about it.
Hang on a second.
Mai, the bath-room's free now if you want
I'll shower later.
No, I don't want to hold you up! Go ahead...
Are you sure?
Hm, okay then...
When I get out of the bath, I'll call you back, okay?
Thanks for being so thoughtful.
She thanked me! For barely saying anything at all...
じ—ん
SOB
Sa-weet!
So you know what you gotta do...
Ask her to buy her dinner to thank her for the teacups.
Ask her to buy her dinner to thank her for the teacups.
Ask her to buy her dinner to thank her for the teacups.
Ask her to buy her dinner to thank her for the teacups.
Ask her to buy her dinner to thank her for the teacups.
Ask her to buy her dinner to thank her for the teacups.
Ask her to buy her dinner to thank her for the teacups.
Ask her to buy her dinner to thank her for the teacups.
Ask her to buy her dinner to thank her for the teacups.

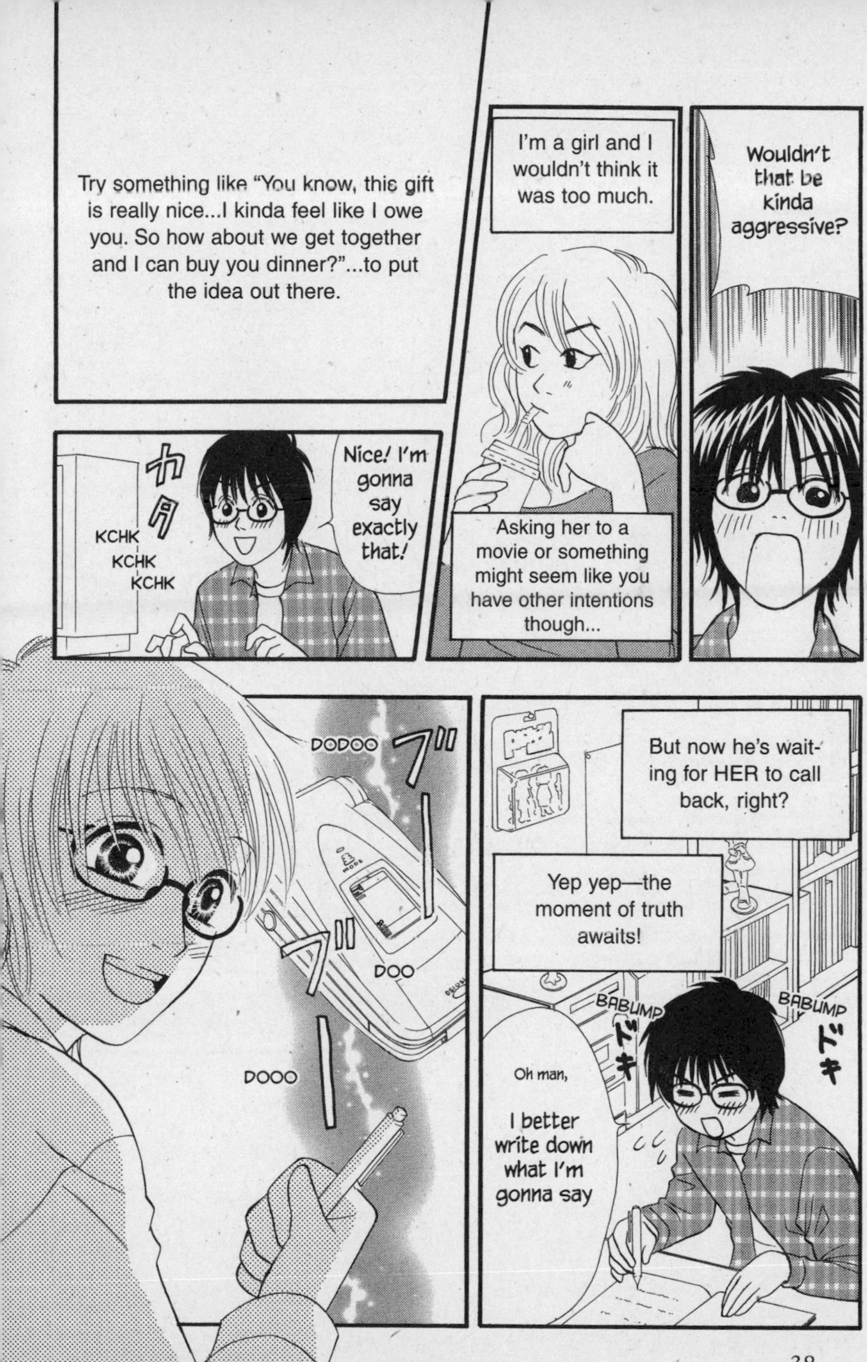
Wouldn't that be kinda aggressive?
I'm a girl and I wouldn't think it was too much.
Asking her to a movie or something might seem like you have other intentions though...
Try something like "You know, this gift is really nice...I kinda feel like I owe you. So how about we get together and I can buy you dinner?"...to put the idea out there.
Nice! I'm gonna say exactly that!
カタ
KCHK KCHK KCHK
But now he's wait-ing for HER to call back, right?
Yep yep—the moment of truth awaits!
BABUMP
ドキ
BABUMP
ドキ
Oh man,
I better write down what I'm gonna say
DODOO
ブー
DOO
ブー
DOOO

w00000t! ::phone ringing::

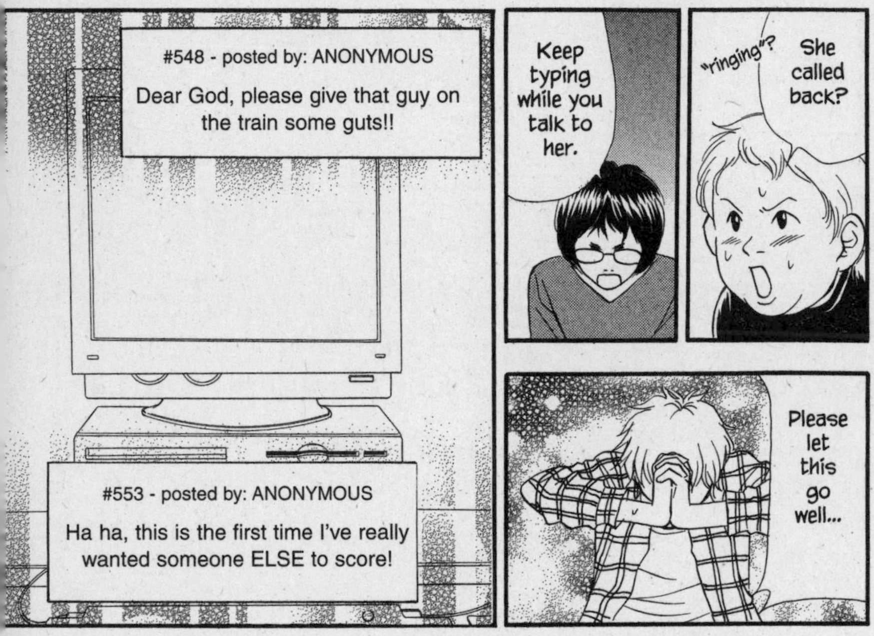

"ringing"?
She called back?
Keep typing while you talk to her.
Please let this go well...
#548 - posted by: ANONYMOUS
Dear God, please give that guy on the train some guts!!
#553 - posted by: ANONYMOUS
Ha ha, this is the first time I've really wanted someone ELSE to score!

#614 - posted by: DENSHA OTOKO from 731

good restaurants?! anybody!

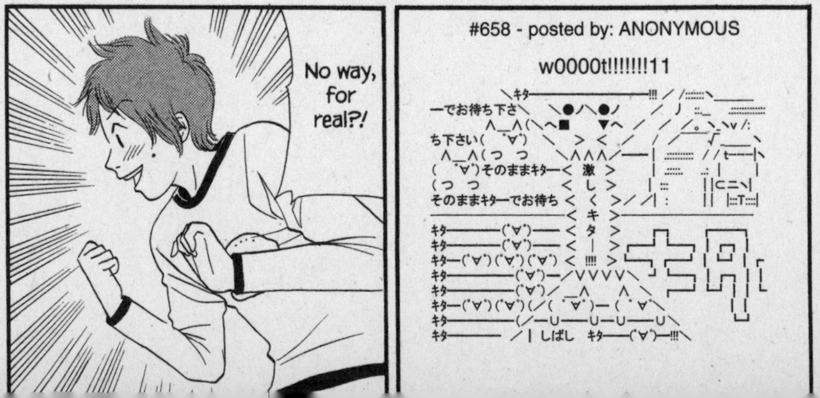

#658 - posted by: ANONYMOUS
w0000t!!!!!!!11
No way, for real?!

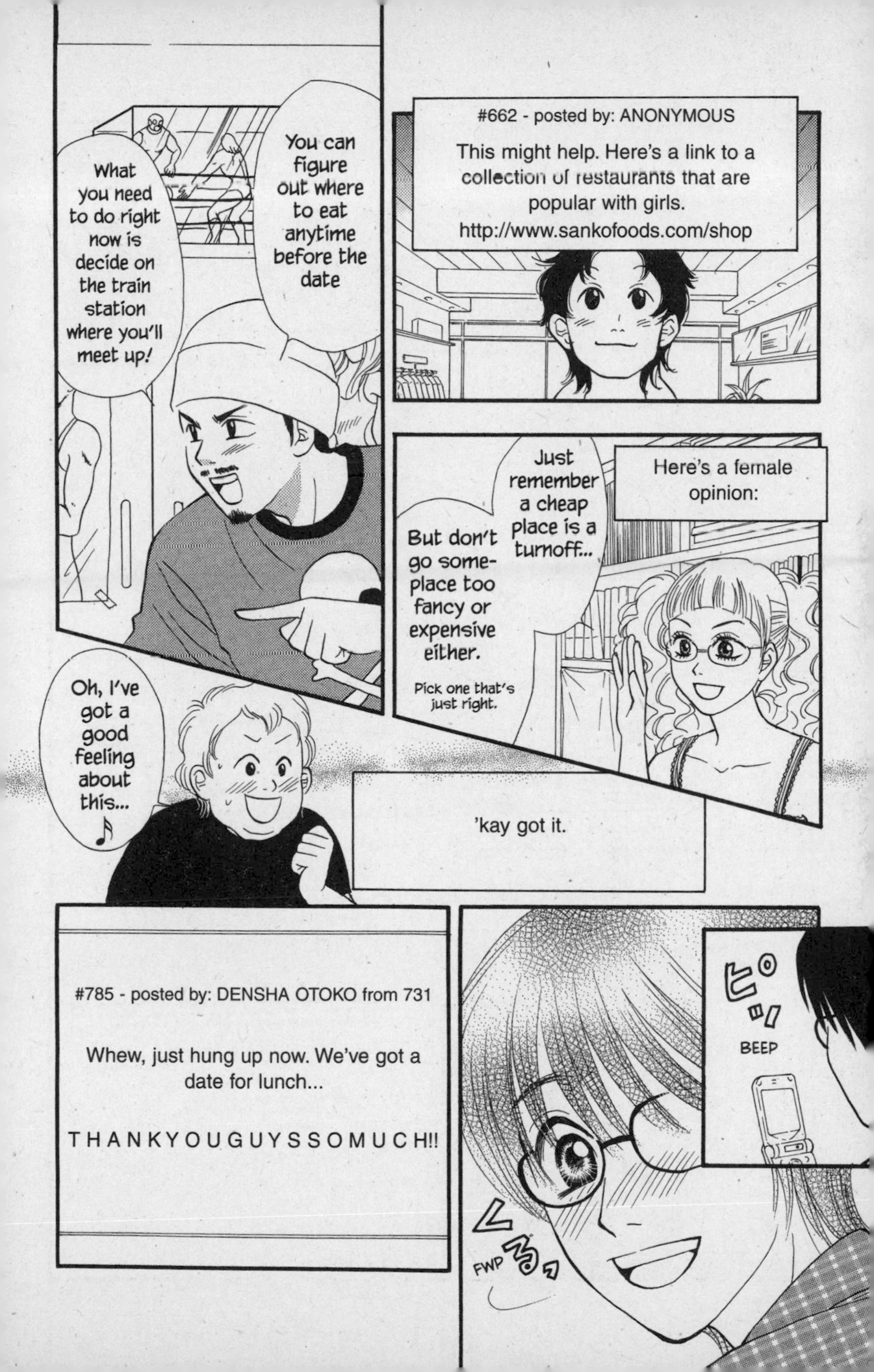
#662 - posted by: ANONYMOUS
This might help. Here's a link to a collection of restaurants that are popular with girls.
http://www.sankofoods.com/shop
Here's a female opinion:
Just remember a cheap place is a turnoff...
But don't go someplace too fancy or expensive either.
Pick one that's just right.
You can figure out where to eat anytime before the date
What you need to do right now is decide on the train station where you'll meet up!
'kay got it.
Oh, I've got a good feeling about this... ♪
BEEP
FWP
#785 - posted by: DENSHA OTOKO from 731
Whew, just hung up now. We've got a date for lunch...
THANKYOUGUYSSOMUCH!!

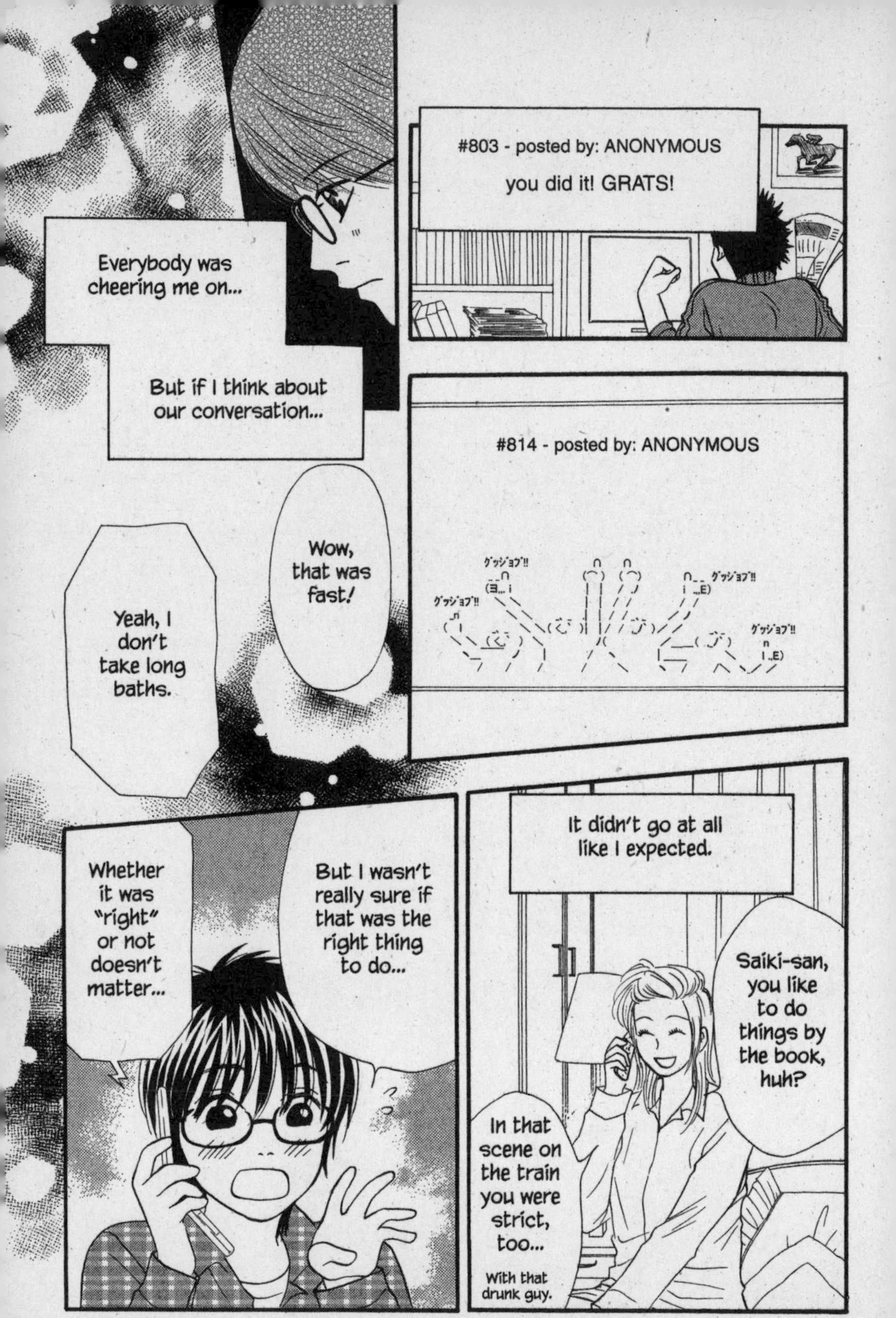
#803 - posted by: ANONYMOUS
you did it! GRATS!
#814 - posted by: ANONYMOUS
Everybody was cheering me on...
But if I think about our conversation...
Wow, that was fast!
Yeah, I don't take long baths.
It didn't go at all like I expected.
Saiki-san, you like to do things by the book, huh?
In that scene on the train you were strict, too...
With that drunk guy.
But I wasn't really sure if that was the right thing to do...
Whether it was "right" or not doesn't matter...

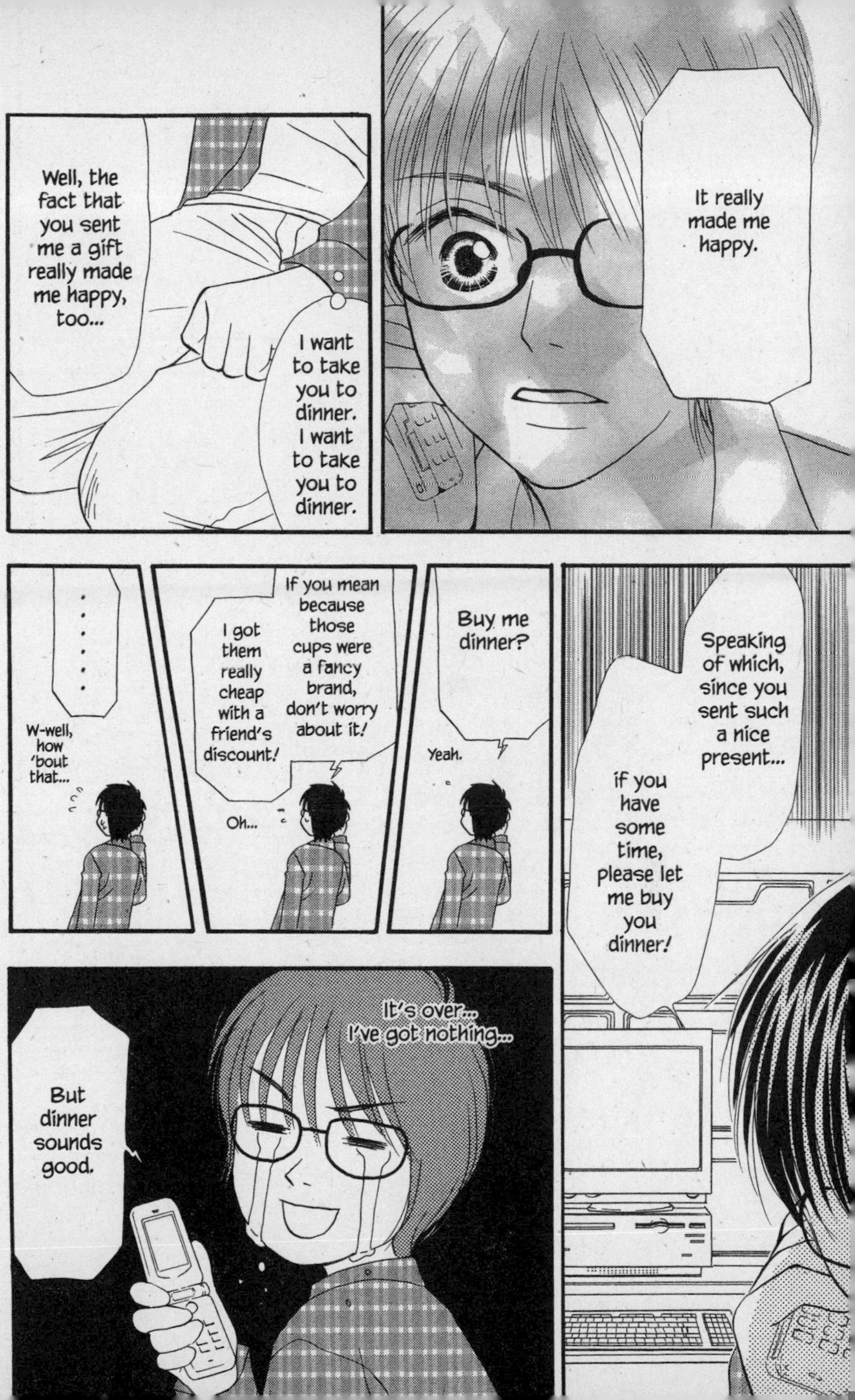
It really made me happy.
Well, the fact that you sent me a gift really made me happy, too...
I want to take you to dinner. I want to take you to dinner.
Speaking of which, since you sent such a nice present...
if you have some time, please let me buy you dinner!
Buy me dinner?
Yeah.
If you mean because those cups were a fancy brand, don't worry about it!
I got them really cheap with a friend's discount!
Oh...
......
W-well, how 'bout that...
It's over... I've got nothing...
But dinner sounds good.

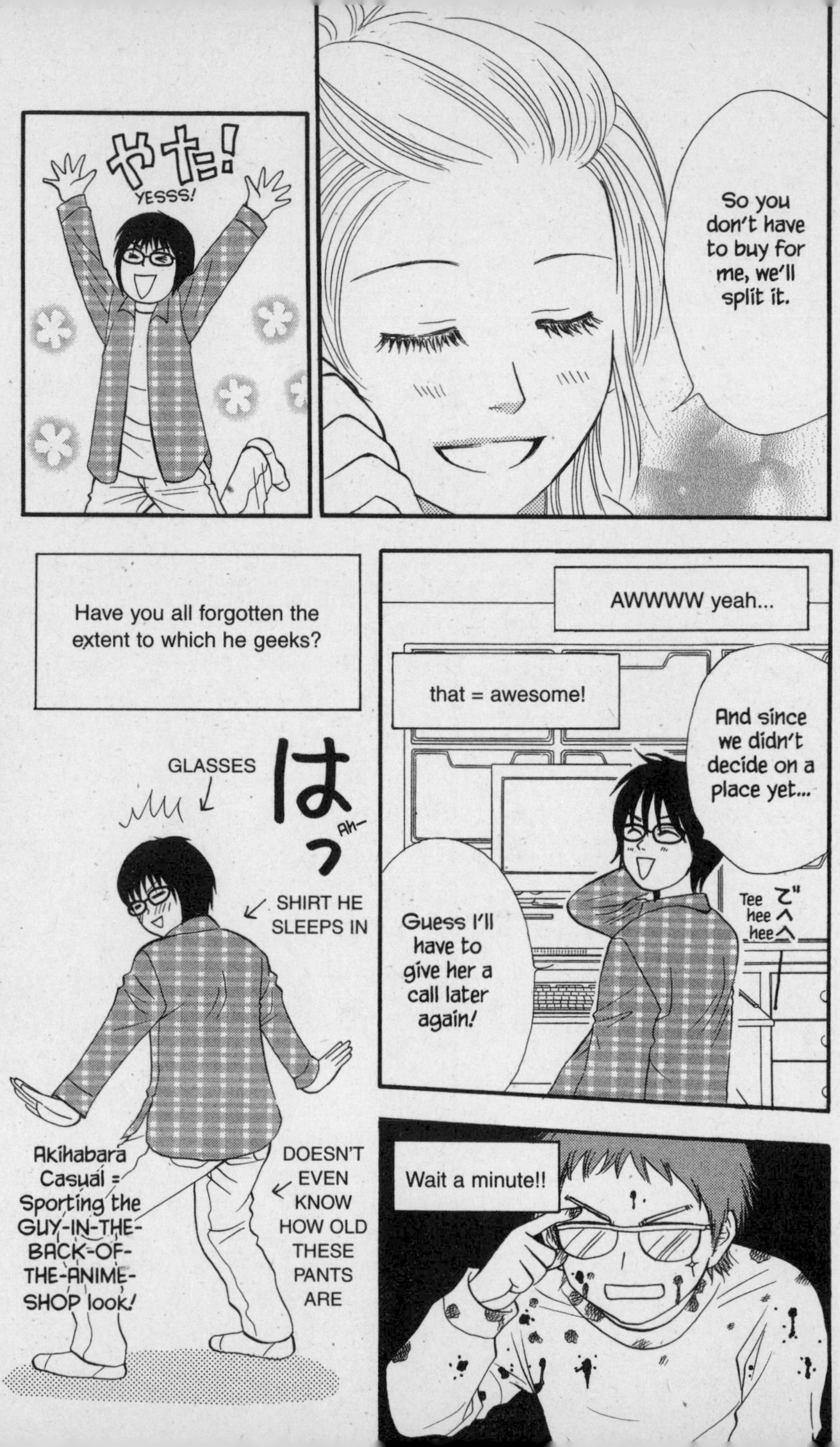
So you don't have to buy for me, we'll split it.
やた!
YESSS!
AWWWW yeah...
that = awesome!
And since we didn't decide on a place yet...
Guess I'll have to give her a call later again!
でへへ
Tee hee hee
Wait a minute!!
Have you all forgotten the extent to which he geeks?
はっ
AH-
GLASSES
SHIRT HE SLEEPS IN
Akihabara Casual = Sporting the GUY-IN-THE-BACK-OF-THE-ANIME-SHOP look!
DOESN'T EVEN KNOW HOW OLD THESE PANTS ARE

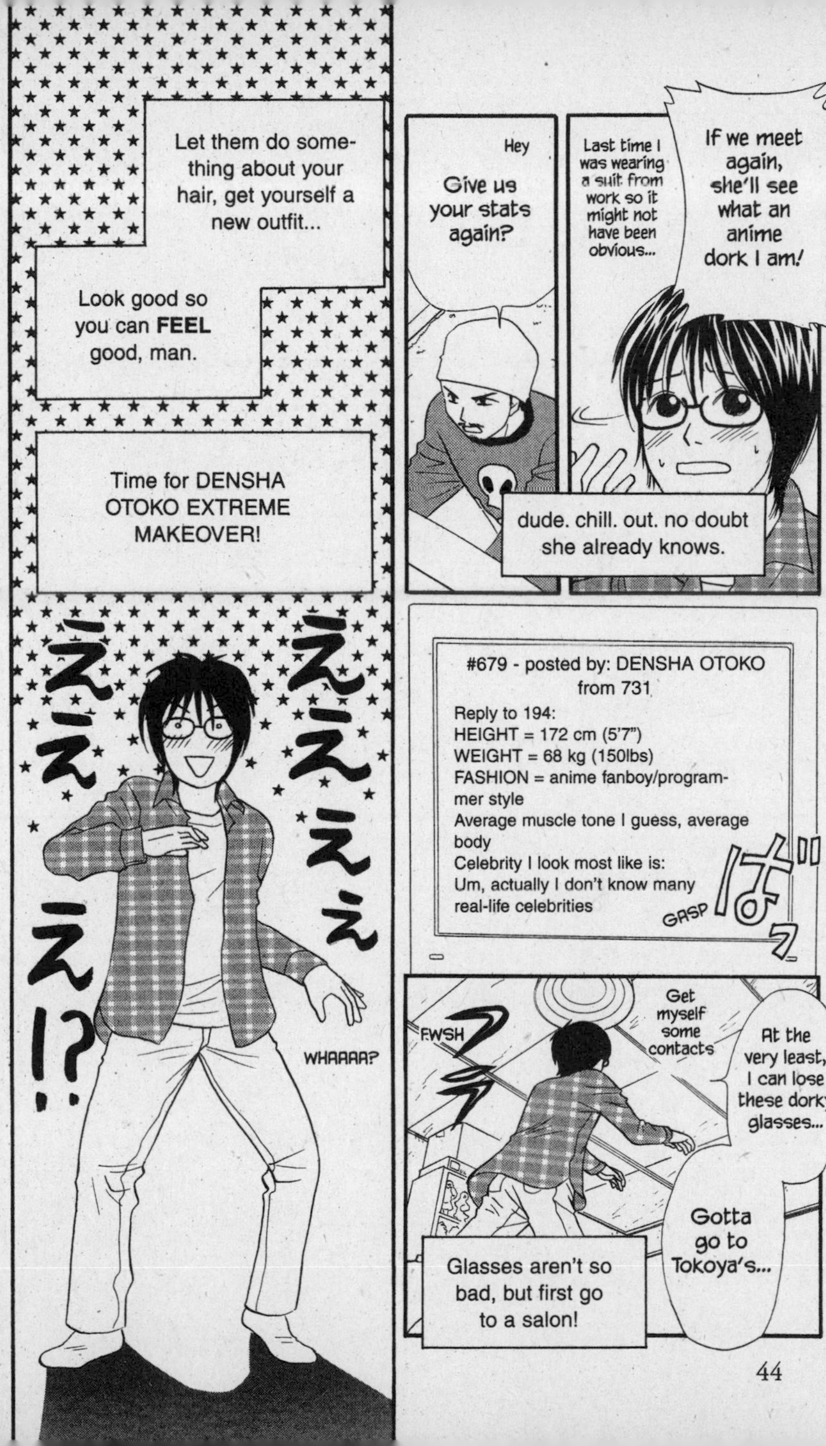

If we meet again, she'll see what an anime dork I am!
Last time I was wearing a suit from work so it might not have been obvious...
dude. chill. out. no doubt she already knows.
Hey
Give us your stats again?
#679 - posted by: DENSHA OTOKO from 731
Reply to 194:
HEIGHT = 172 cm (5'7")
WEIGHT = 68 kg (150lbs)
FASHION = anime fanboy/programmer style
Average muscle tone I guess, average body
Celebrity I look most like is:
Um, actually I don't know many real-life celebrities
ばっ
GASP
At the very least, I can lose these dorky glasses...
Get myself some contacts
FWSH
Gotta go to Tokoya's...
Glasses aren't so bad, but first go to a salon!
Let them do something about your hair, get yourself a new outfit...
Look good so you can **FEEL** good, man.
Time for DENSHA OTOKO EXTREME MAKEOVER!
えええええ
ええええ!?
WHAAAAA?

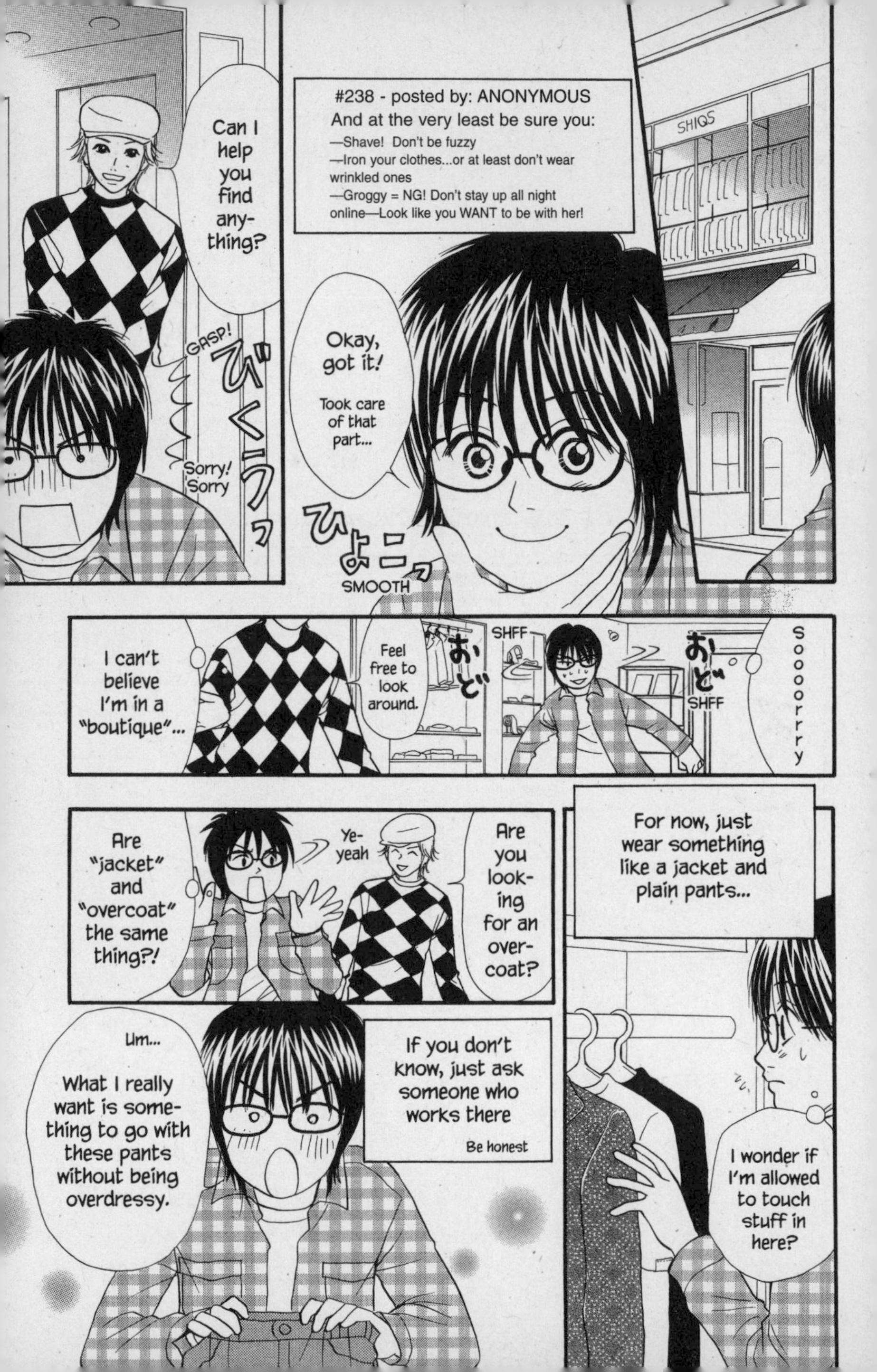
#238 - posted by: ANONYMOUS
And at the very least be sure you:
—Shave! Don't be fuzzy
—Iron your clothes...or at least don't wear wrinkled ones
—Groggy = NG! Don't stay up all night online—Look like you WANT to be with her!
Okay, got it!
Took care of that part...
SMOOTH
Can I help you find anything?
GASP!
Sorry! Sorry
Sooooorrry
SHFF
SHFF
Feel free to look around.
I can't believe I'm in a "boutique"...
For now, just wear something like a jacket and plain pants...
I wonder if I'm allowed to touch stuff in here?
Are you looking for an overcoat?
Ye-yeah
Are "jacket" and "overcoat" the same thing?!
If you don't know, just ask someone who works there
Be honest
Um...
What I really want is something to go with these pants without being overdressy.

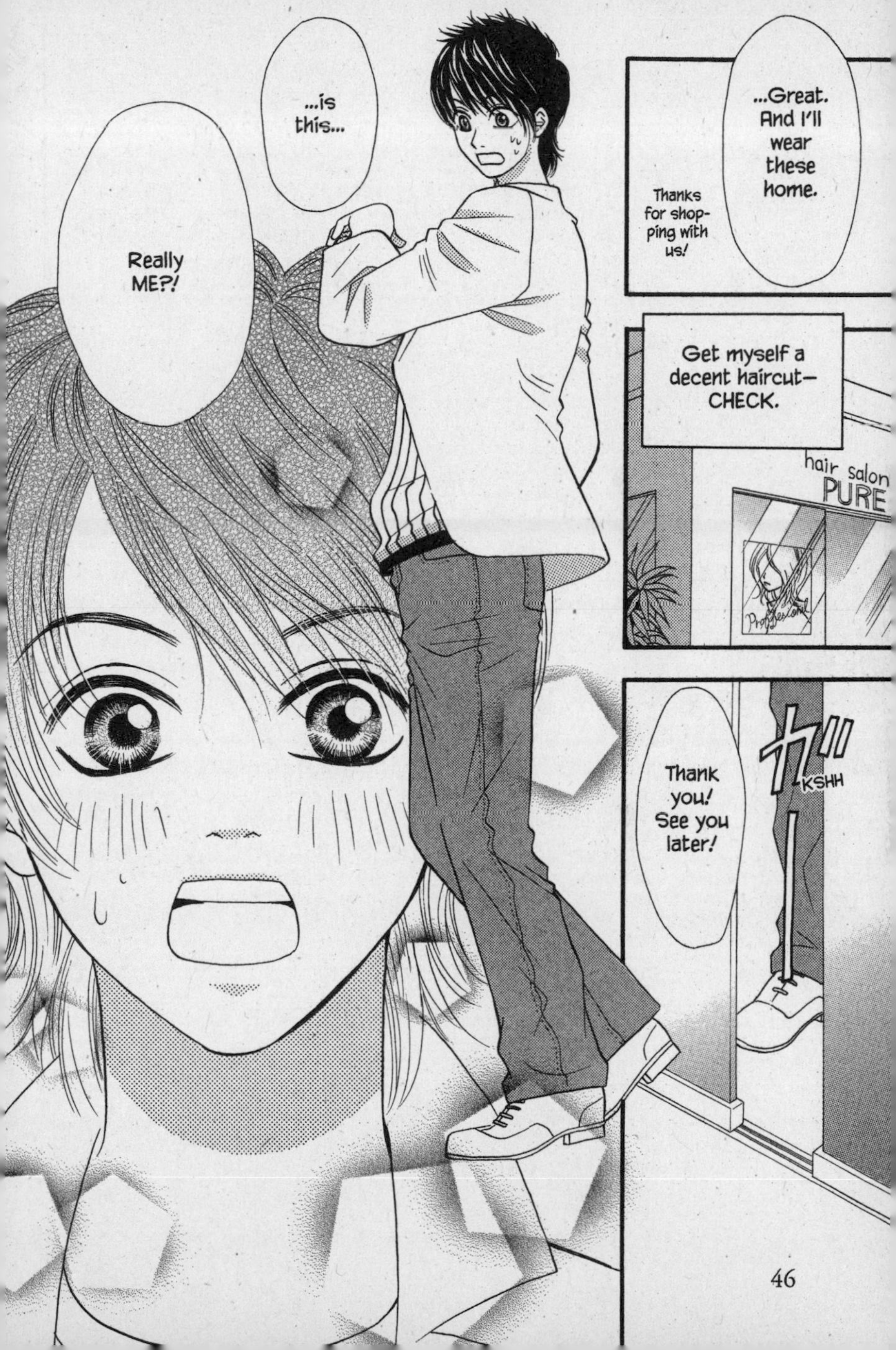
...Great. And I'll wear these home.
Thanks for shopping with us!
Get myself a decent haircut—CHECK.
hair salon PURE
Professional
Thank you! See you later!
KSHH
...is this...
Really ME?!

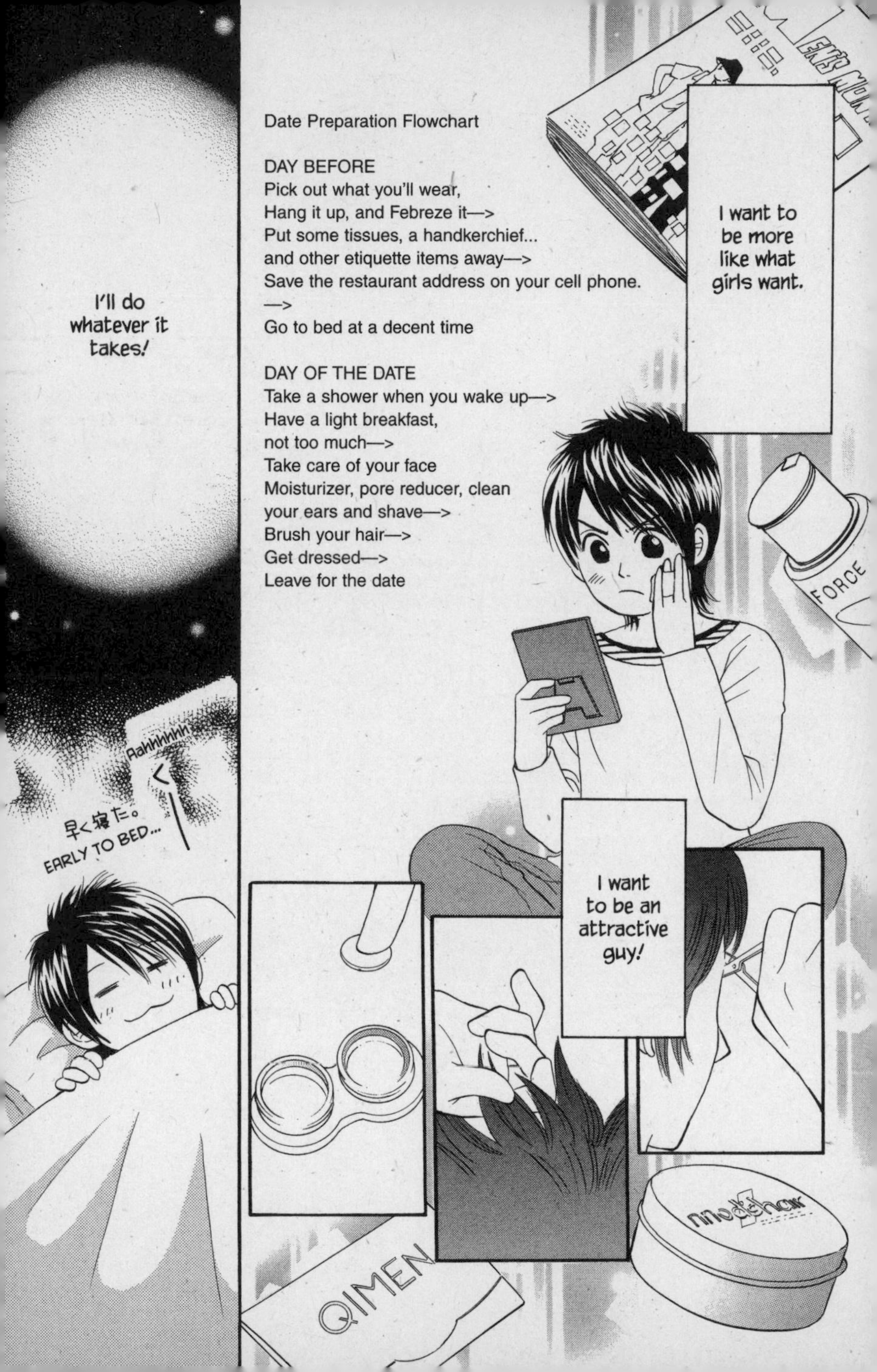

I want to be more like what girls want.
Date Preparation Flowchart
DAY BEFORE
Pick out what you'll wear,
Hang it up, and Febreze it—>
Put some tissues, a handkerchief...
and other etiquette items away—>
Save the restaurant address on your cell phone.
—>
Go to bed at a decent time
DAY OF THE DATE
Take a shower when you wake up—>
Have a light breakfast,
not too much—>
Take care of your face
Moisturizer, pore reducer, clean
your ears and shave—>
Brush your hair—>
Get dressed—>
Leave for the date
FORCE
I want to be an attractive guy!
QIMEN
I'll do whatever it takes!
Aahhhhhh
早く寝た。
EARLY TO BED...

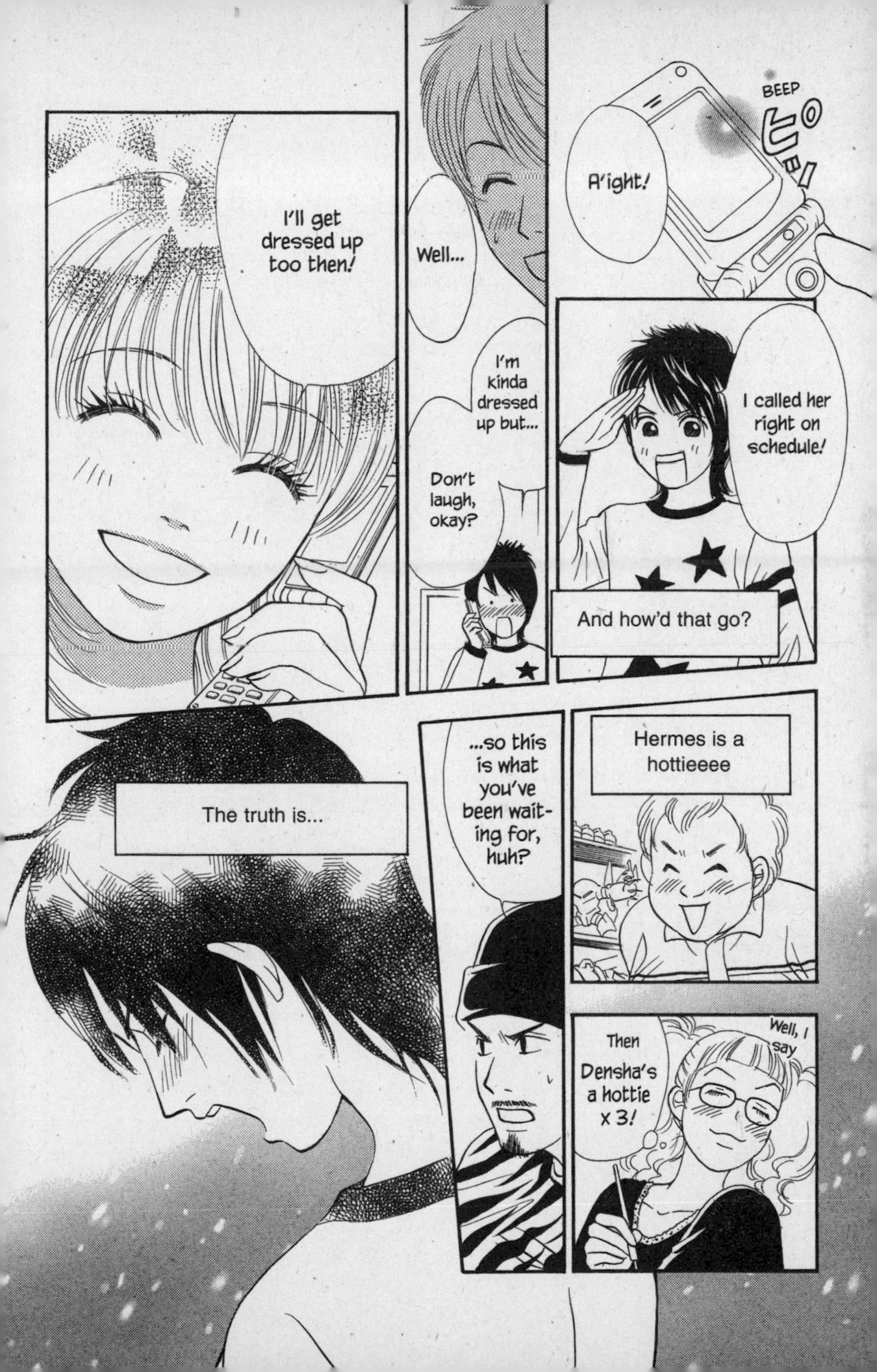
BEEP
ピ
A'ight!
I called her right on schedule!
And how'd that go?
Well...
I'm kinda dressed up but...
Don't laugh, okay?
I'll get dressed up too then!
Hermes is a hottieeee
Well, I say
Then Densha's a hottie x 3!
...so this is what you've been waiting for, huh?
The truth is...

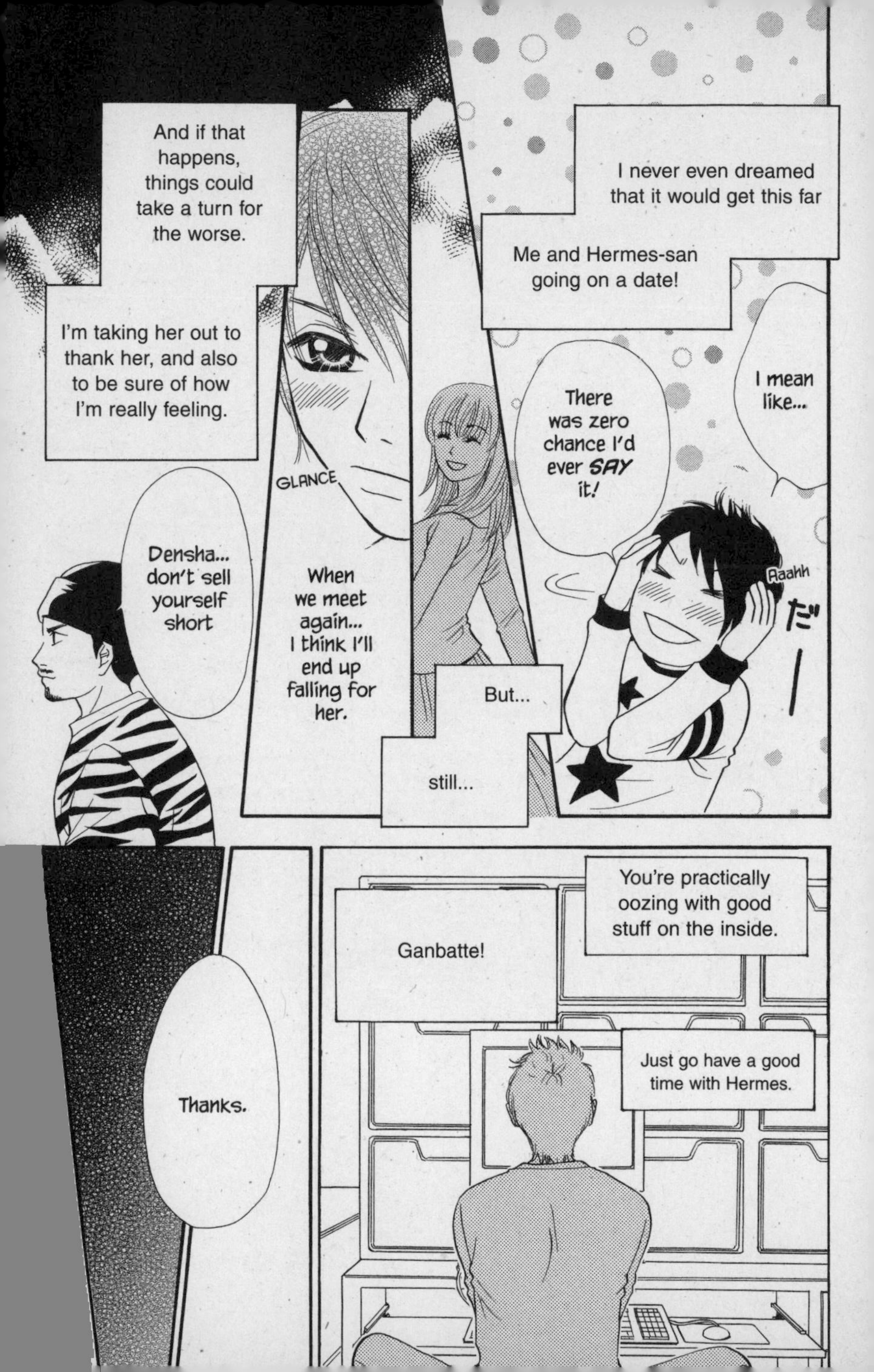
I never even dreamed that it would get this far
Me and Hermes-san going on a date!
I mean like...
There was zero chance I'd ever SAY it!
Aaahh
だ
But...
still...
When we meet again... I think I'll end up falling for her.
GLANCE
And if that happens, things could take a turn for the worse.
I'm taking her out to thank her, and also to be sure of how I'm really feeling.
Densha... don't sell yourself short
You're practically oozing with good stuff on the inside.
Ganbatte!
Just go have a good time with Hermes.
Thanks.

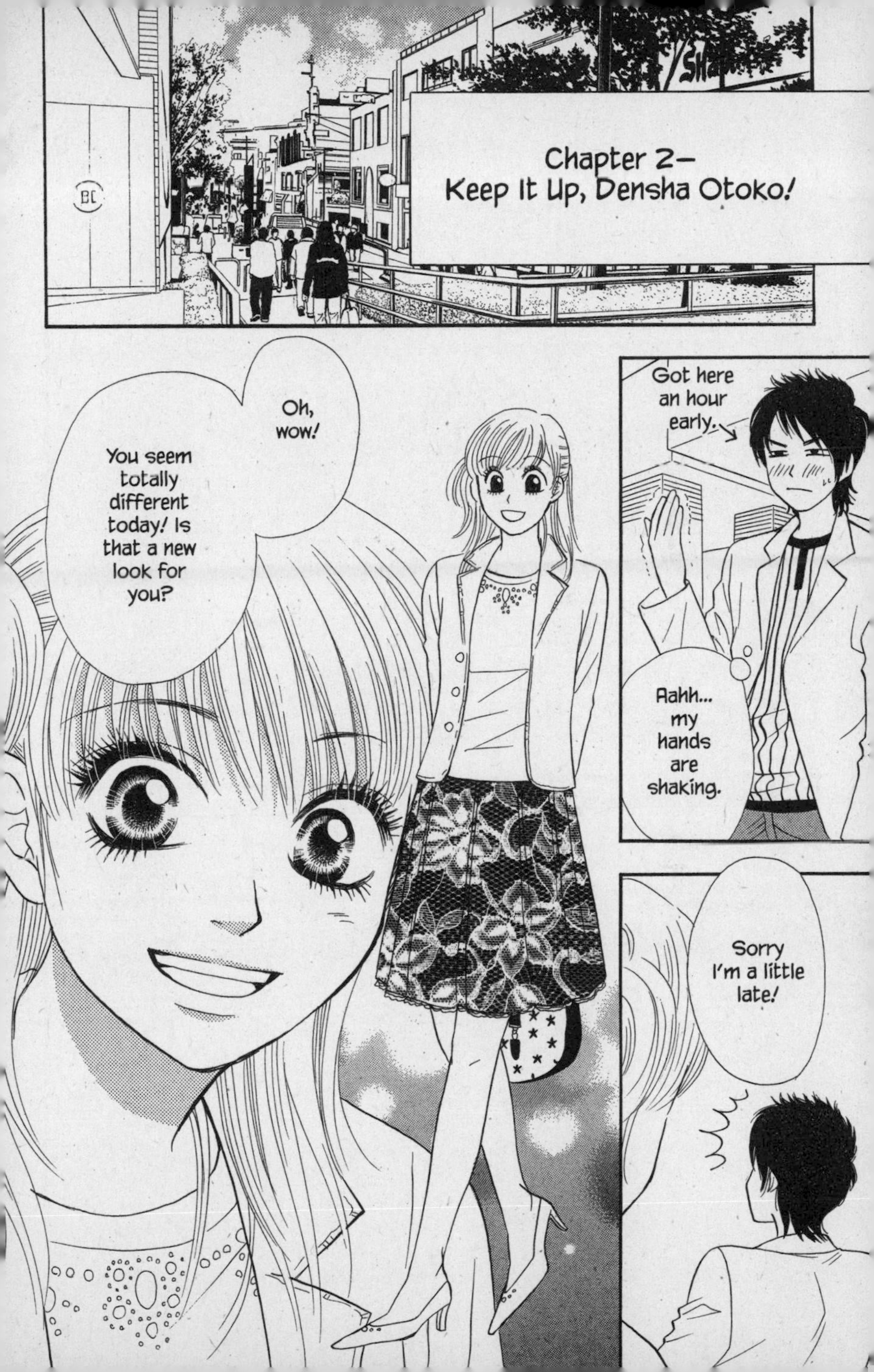
Chapter 2—
Keep It Up, Densha Otoko!
Got here an hour early.
Aahh... my hands are shaking.
Sorry I'm a little late!
Oh, wow!
You seem totally different today! Is that a new look for you?

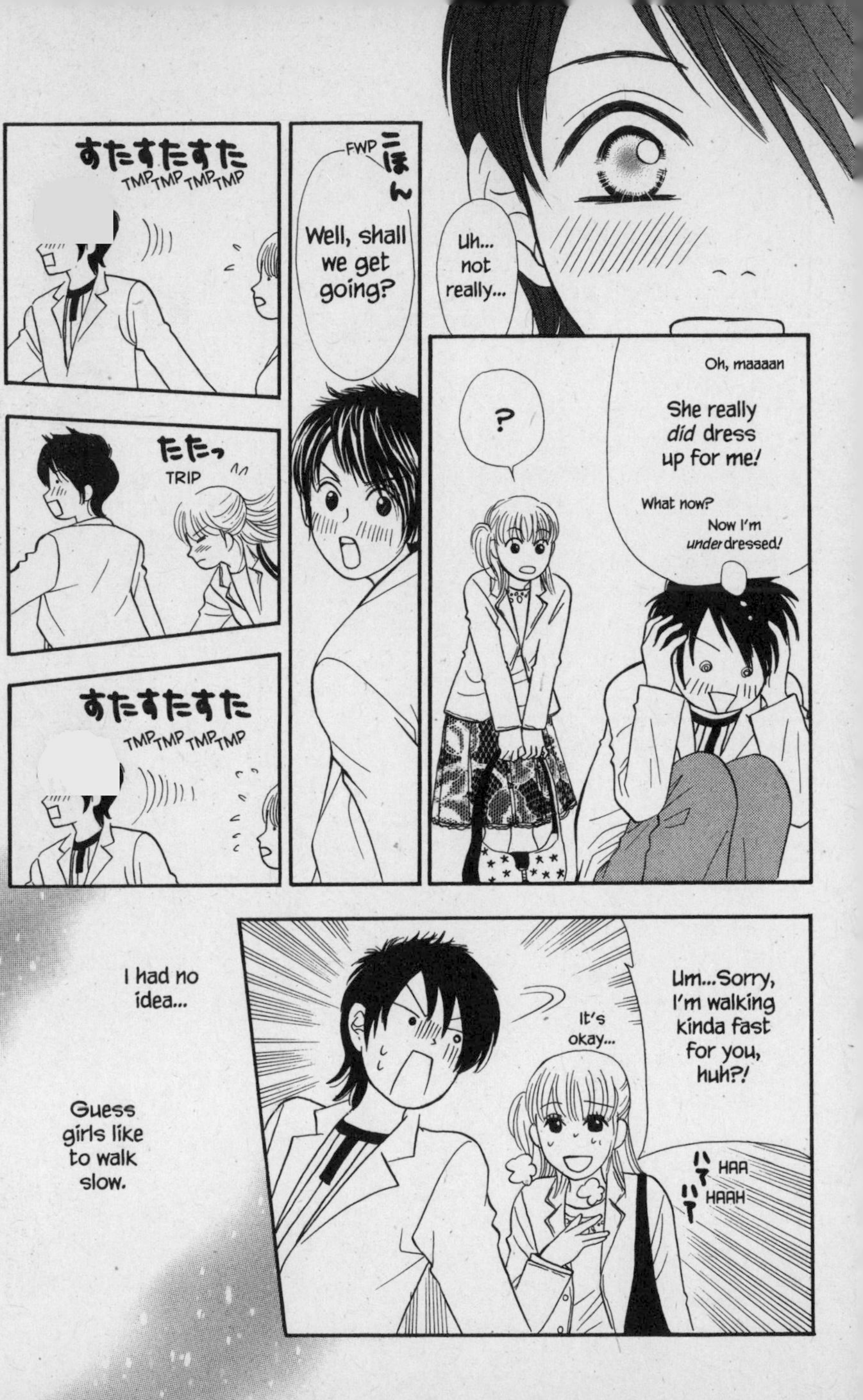
uh... not really...
Oh, maaaan
She really *did* dress up for me!
What now?
Now I'm *under*dressed!
?
FWP ごほん
Well, shall we get going?
すたすたすた
TMP TMP TMP TMP
たたっ
TRIP
すたすたすた
TMP TMP TMP TMP
Um...Sorry, I'm walking kinda fast for you, huh?!
ハァ HAA
ハァ HAAH
It's okay...
I had no idea...
Guess girls like to walk slow.

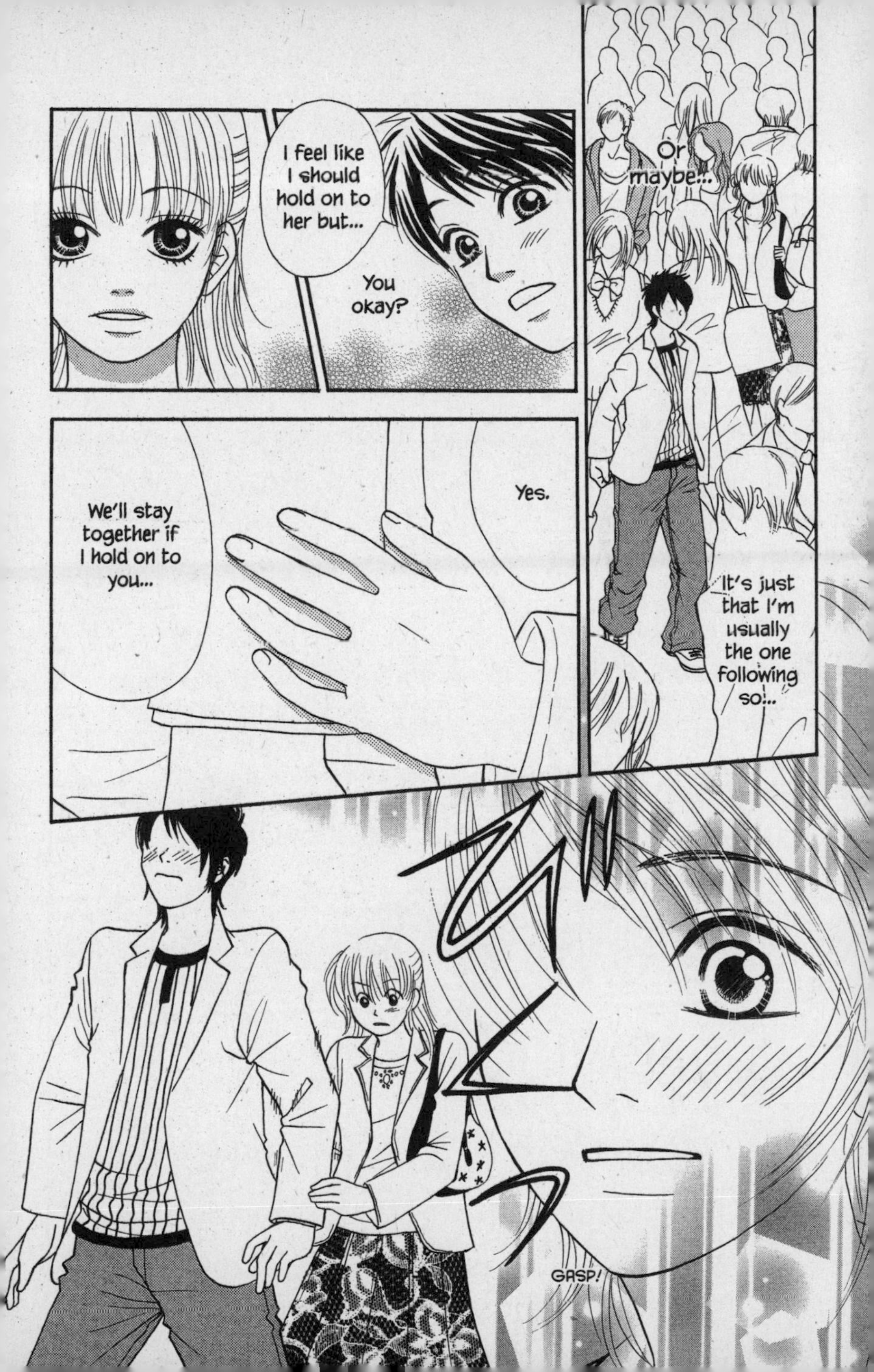
Or maybe...
It's just that I'm usually the one following so...
I feel like I should hold on to her but...
You okay?
Yes.
We'll stay together if I hold on to you...
GASP!

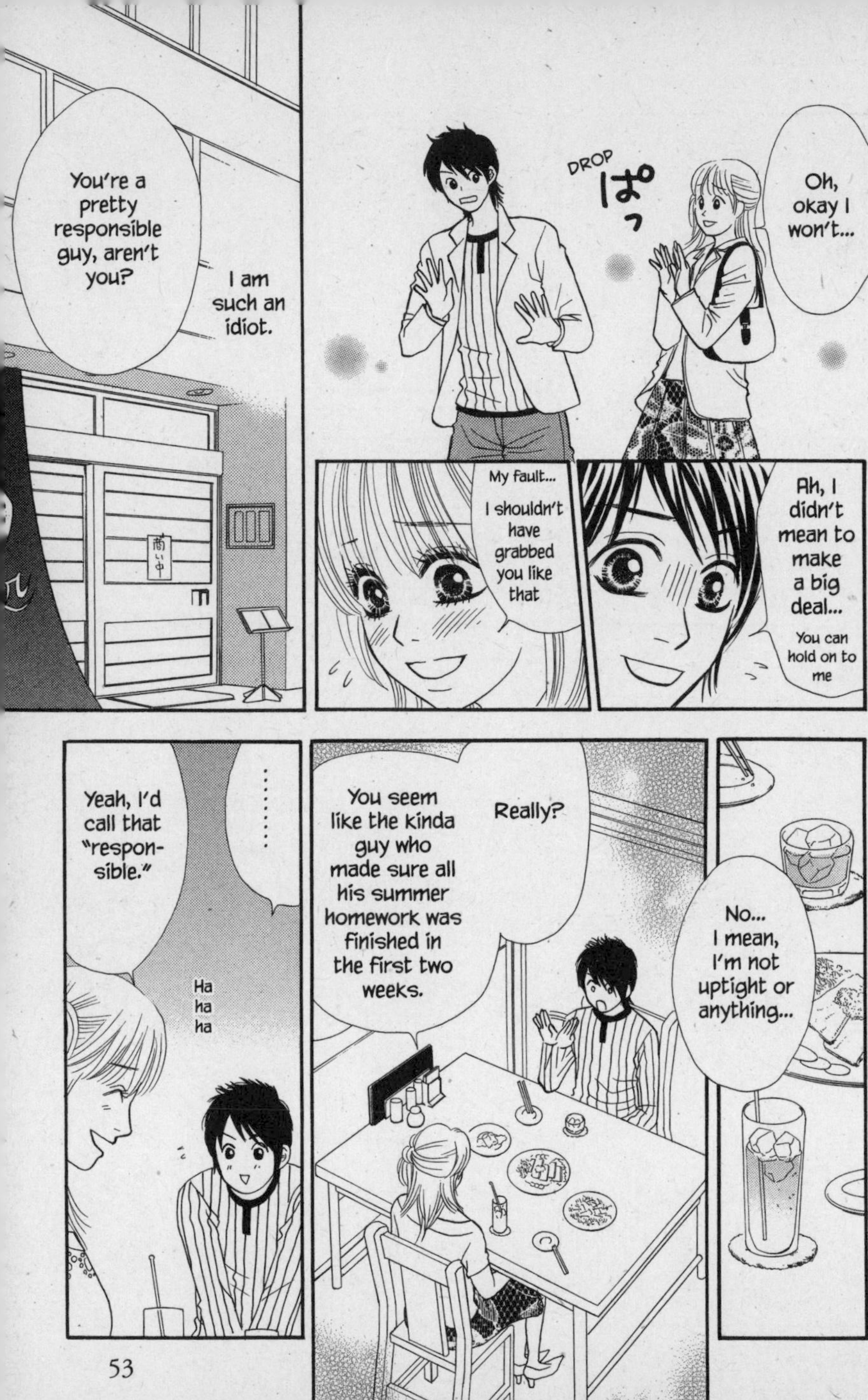
Oh, okay I won't...
DROP
ぱっ
Ah, I didn't mean to make a big deal...
You can hold on to me
My fault...
I shouldn't have grabbed you like that
I am such an idiot.
You're a pretty responsible guy, aren't you?
No... I mean, I'm not uptight or anything...
Really?
You seem like the kinda guy who made sure all his summer homework was finished in the first two weeks.
......
Yeah, I'd call that "respon-sible."
Ha ha ha

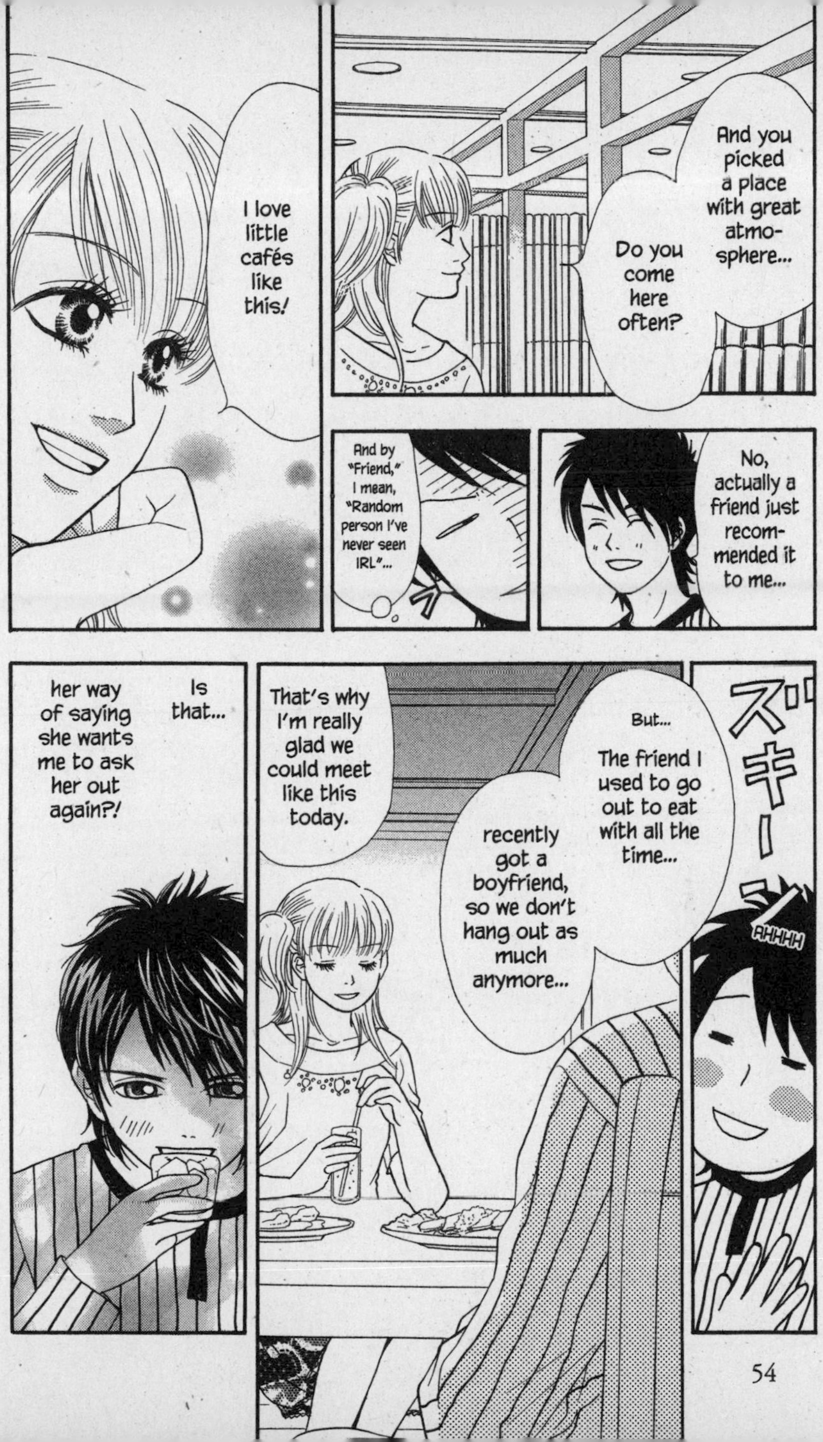

And you picked a place with great atmosphere...
Do you come here often?
No, actually a friend just recommended it to me...
And by "Friend," I mean, "Random person I've never seen IRL"...
I love little cafés like this!
ズキーン
AHHHH
But...
The friend I used to go out to eat with all the time...
recently got a boyfriend, so we don't hang out as much anymore...
That's why I'm really glad we could meet like this today.
Is that...
her way of saying she wants me to ask her out again?!

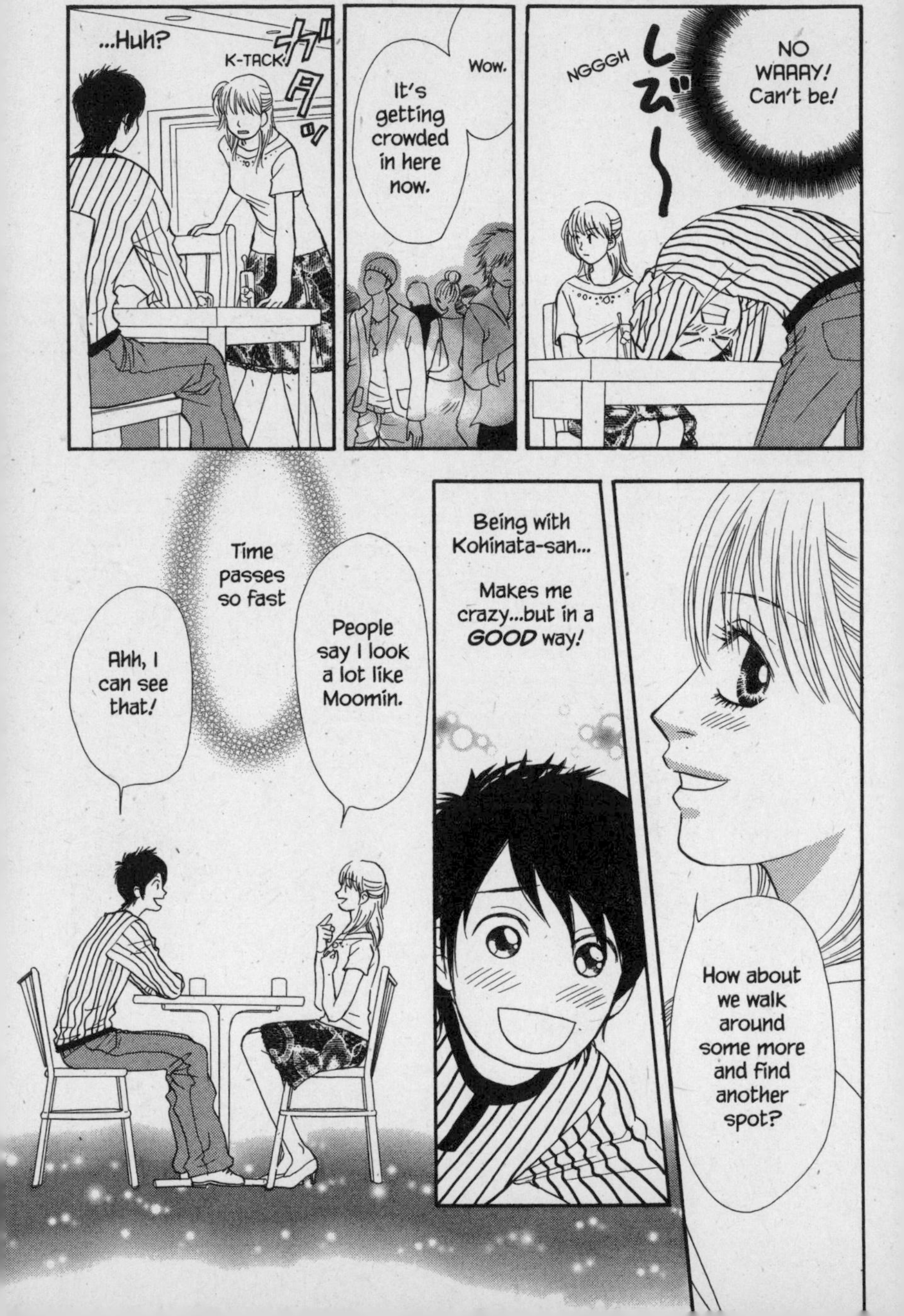
NO WAAAY! Can't be!
NGGGH
Wow.
It's getting crowded in here now.
...Huh?
K-TACK!
How about we walk around some more and find another spot?
Being with Kohinata-san...
Makes me crazy...but in a *GOOD* way!
Time passes so fast
People say I look a lot like Moomin.
Ahh, I can see that!

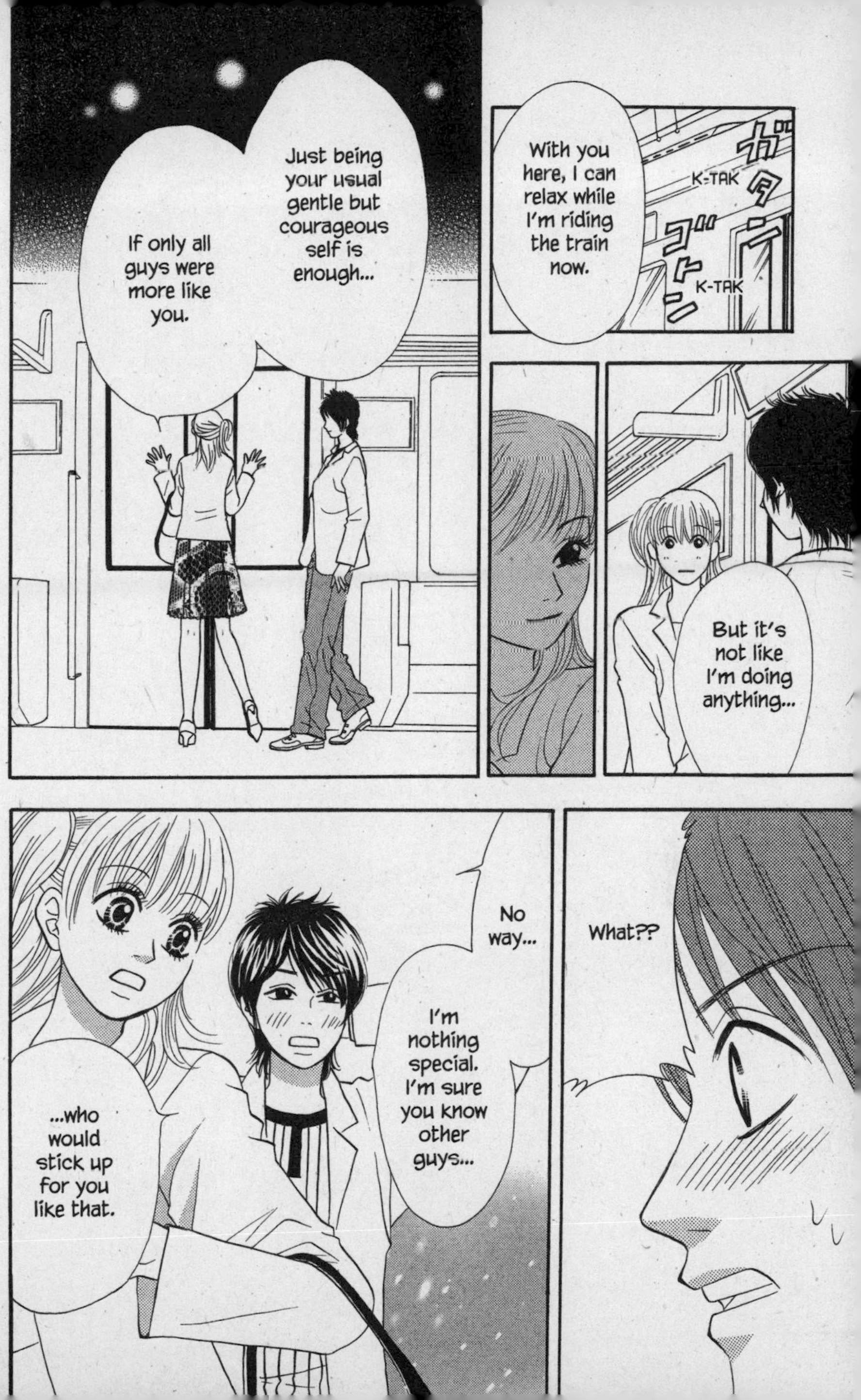
With you here, I can relax while I'm riding the train now.
ガタン
K-TAK
ゴトン
K-TAK
But it's not like I'm doing anything...
Just being your usual gentle but courageous self is enough...
If only all guys were more like you.
What??
No way...
I'm nothing special. I'm sure you know other guys...
...who would stick up for you like that.

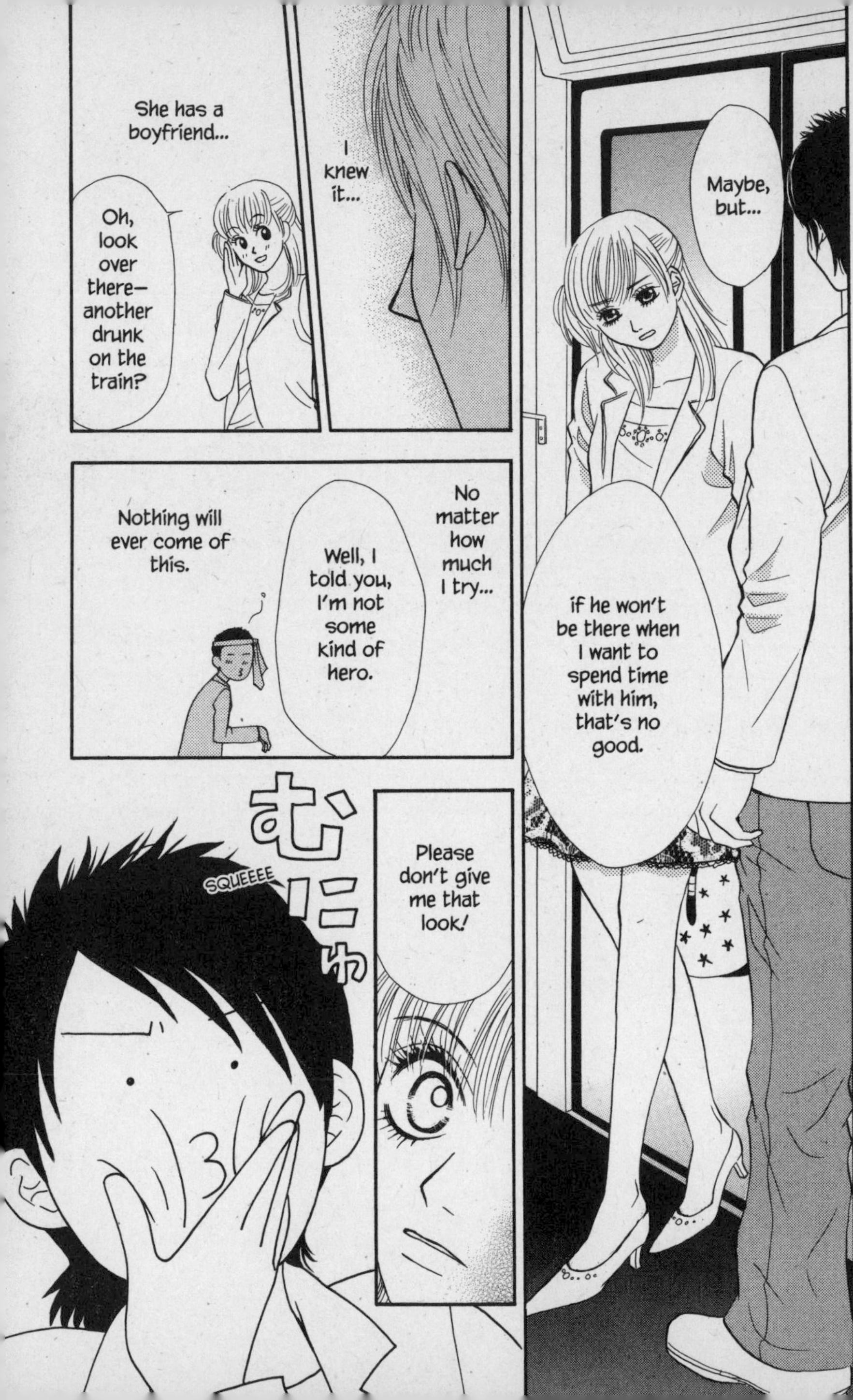
Maybe, but...
if he won't be there when I want to spend time with him, that's no good.
I knew it...
She has a boyfriend...
Oh, look over there—another drunk on the train?
No matter how much I try...
Well, I told you, I'm not some kind of hero.
Nothing will ever come of this.
Please don't give me that look!
むにゅ
SQUEEEE

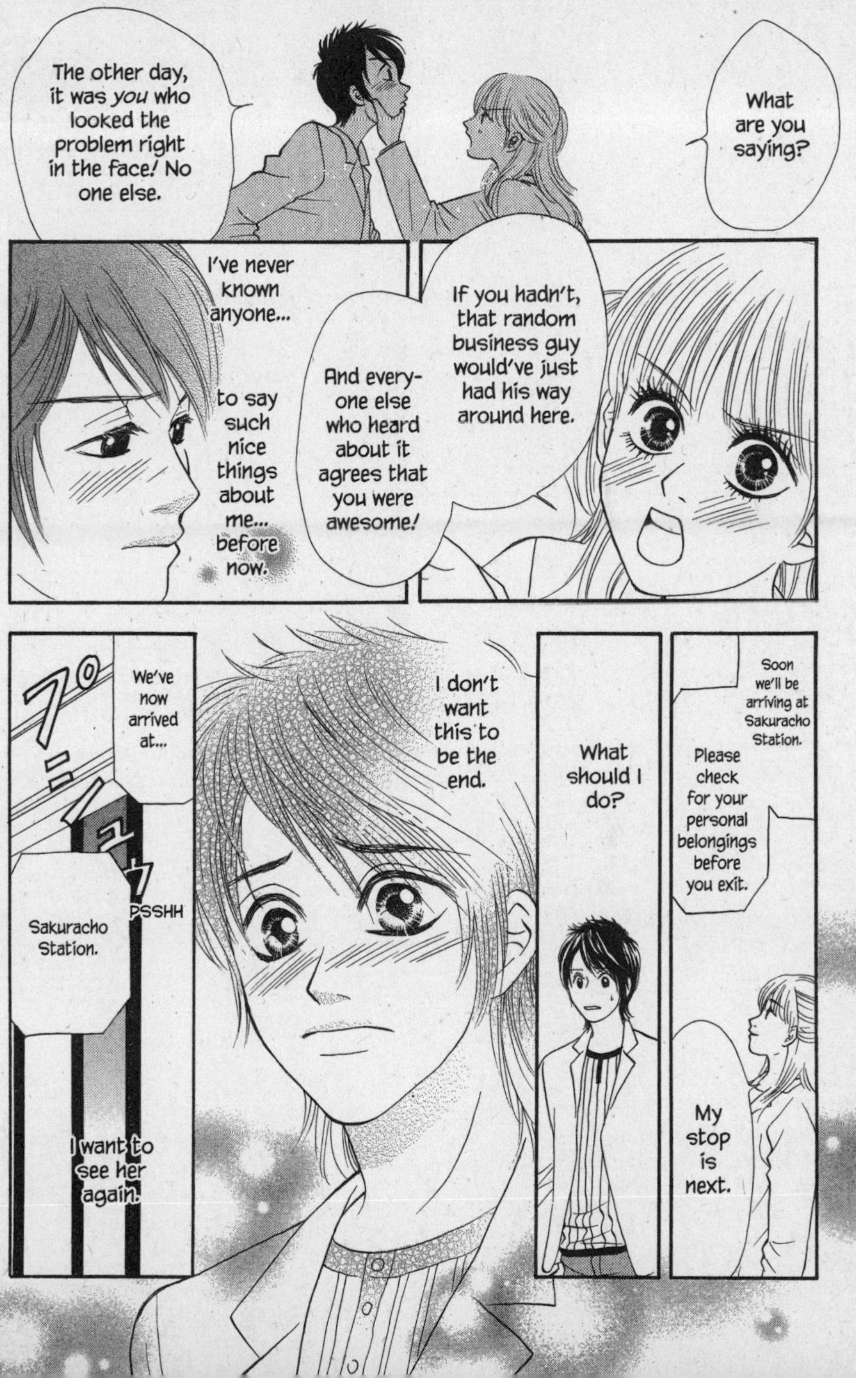
What are you saying?
The other day, it was *you* who looked the problem right in the face! No one else.
If you hadn't, that random business guy would've just had his way around here.
And every-one else who heard about it agrees that you were awesome!
I've never known anyone...
to say such nice things about me... before now.
Soon we'll be arriving at Sakuracho Station.
Please check for your personal belongings before you exit.
My stop is next.
What should I do?
I don't want this to be the end.
We've now arrived at...
PSSHH
Sakuracho Station.
I want to see her again.

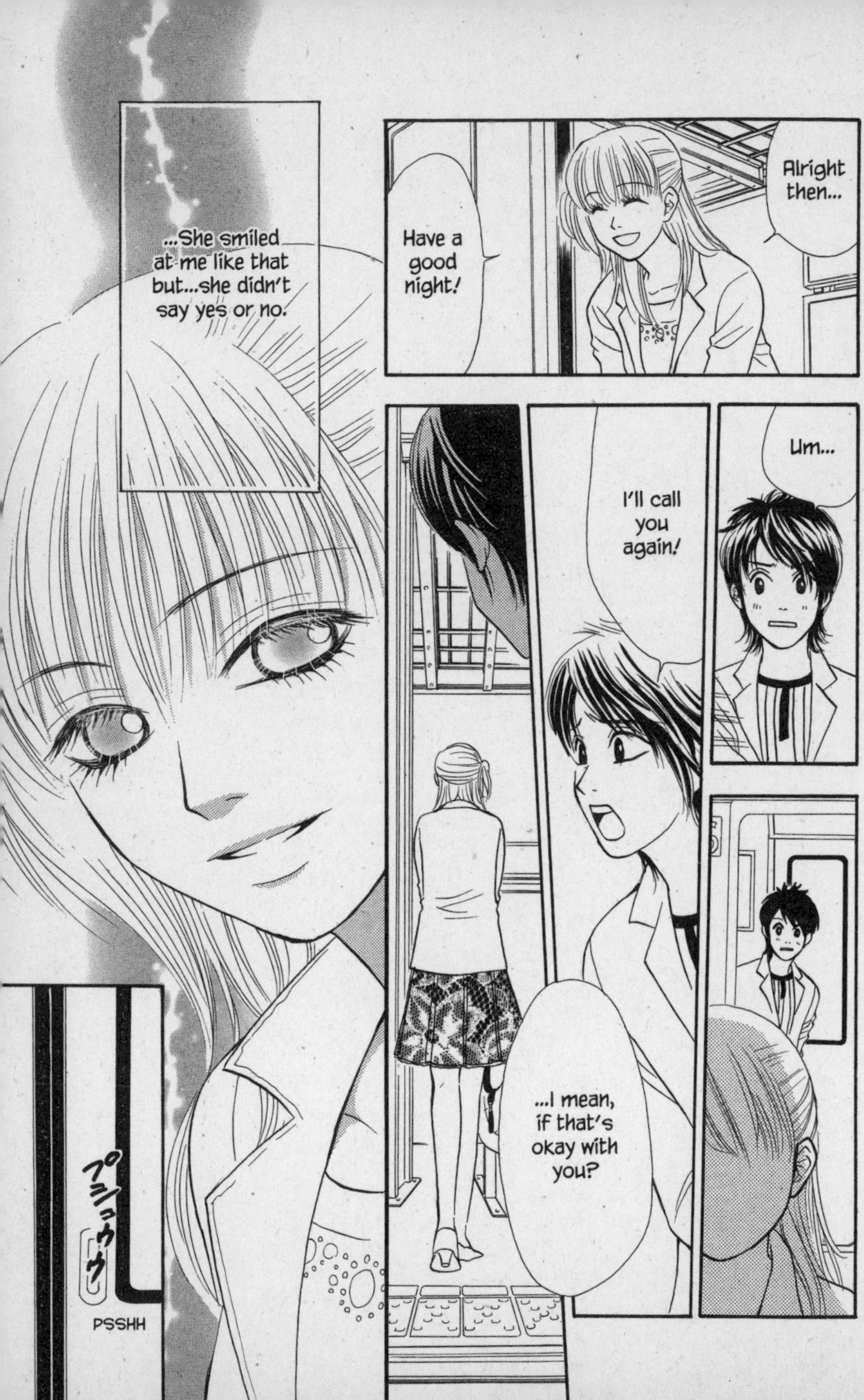
Alright then...
Have a good night!
Um...
I'll call you again!
...I mean, if that's okay with you?
...She smiled at me like that but...she didn't say yes or no.
プシュウウ
PSSHH

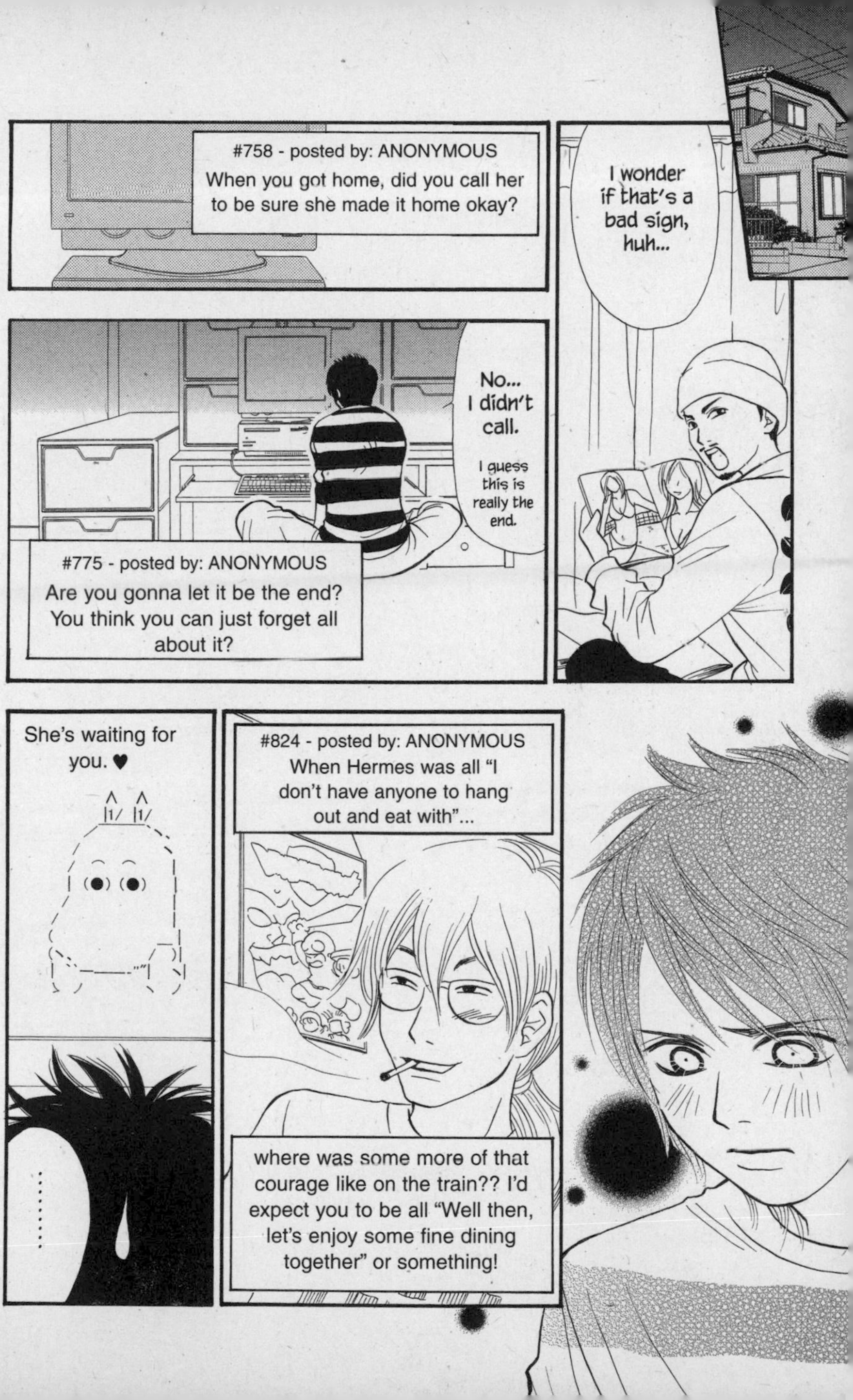
I wonder if that's a bad sign, huh...
#758 - posted by: ANONYMOUS
When you got home, did you call her to be sure she made it home okay?
No... I didn't call.
I guess this is really the end.
#775 - posted by: ANONYMOUS
Are you gonna let it be the end? You think you can just forget all about it?
#824 - posted by: ANONYMOUS
When Hermes was all "I don't have anyone to hang out and eat with"...
where was some more of that courage like on the train?? I'd expect you to be all "Well then, let's enjoy some fine dining together" or something!
She's waiting for you. ♥

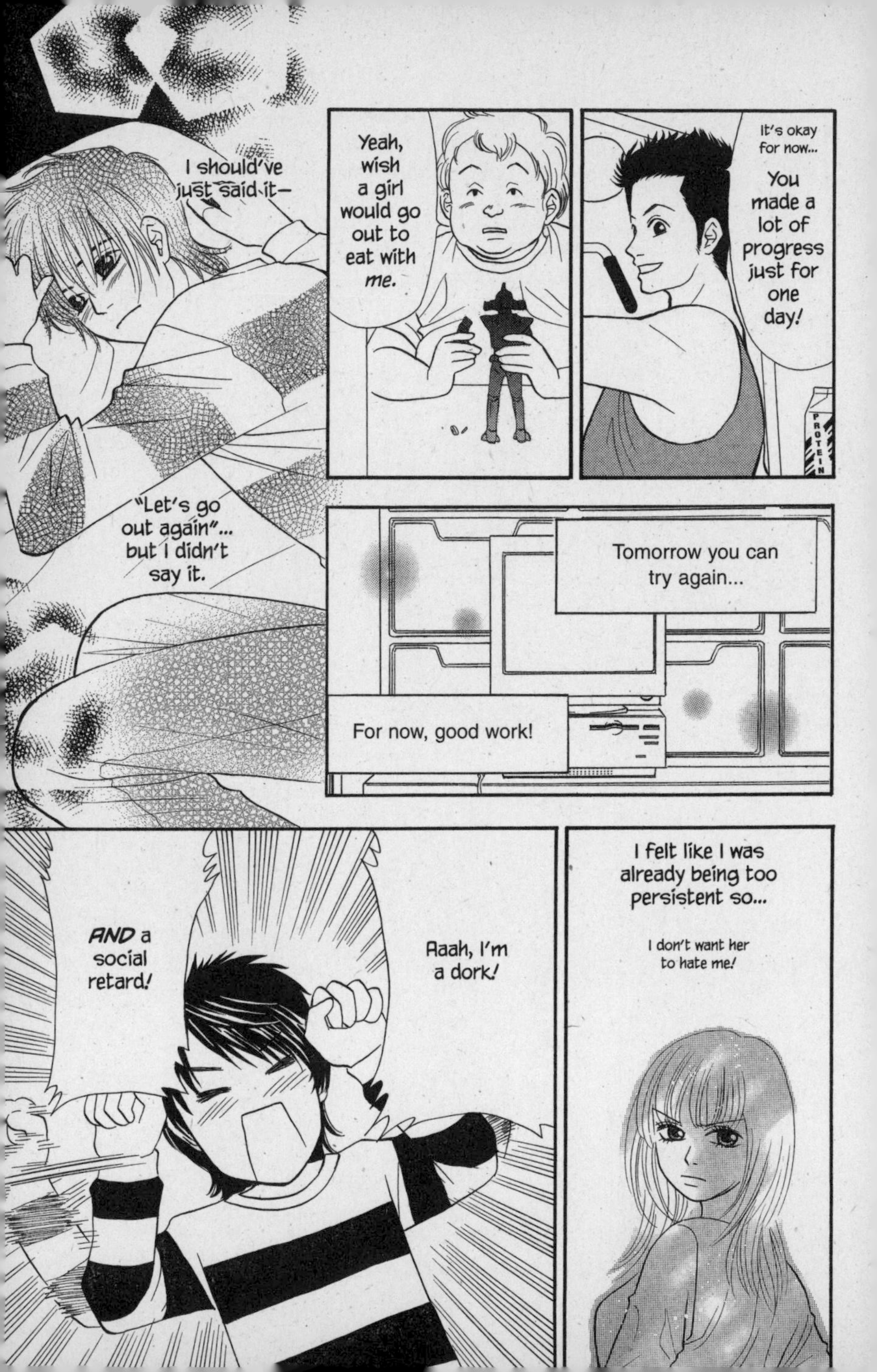

It's okay for now...
You made a lot of progress just for one day!
Yeah, wish a girl would go out to eat with *me.*
Tomorrow you can try again...
For now, good work!
I should've just said it—
"Let's go out again"... but I didn't say it.
I felt like I was already being too persistent so...
I don't want her to hate me!
Aaah, I'm a dork!
AND a social retard!

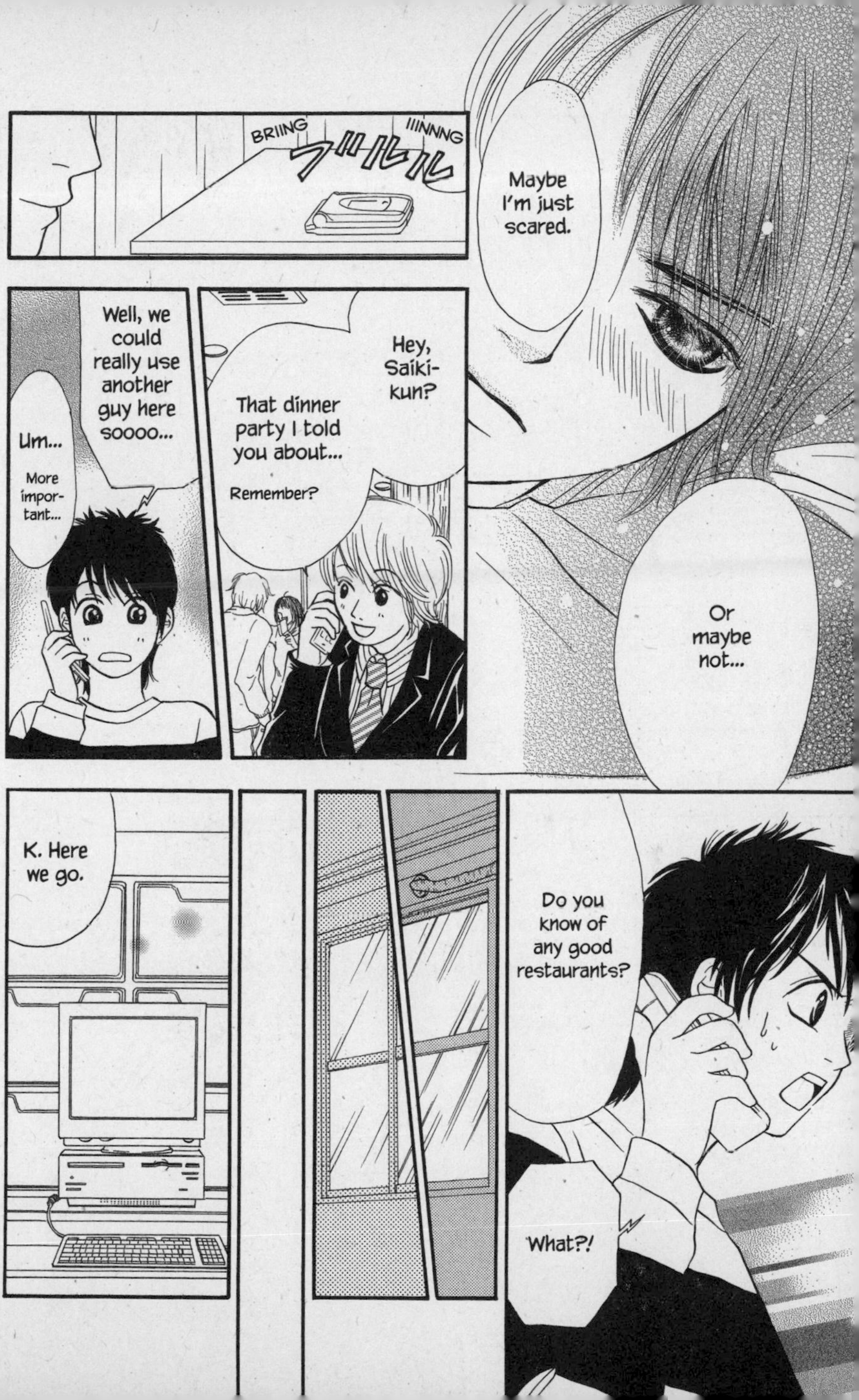
Maybe I'm just scared.
Or maybe not...
BRIING
フルルル
IIINNNG
Hey, Saiki-kun?
That dinner party I told you about...
Remember?
Well, we could really use another guy here soooo...
Um...
More impor-tant...
Do you know of any good restaurants?
What?!
K. Here we go.

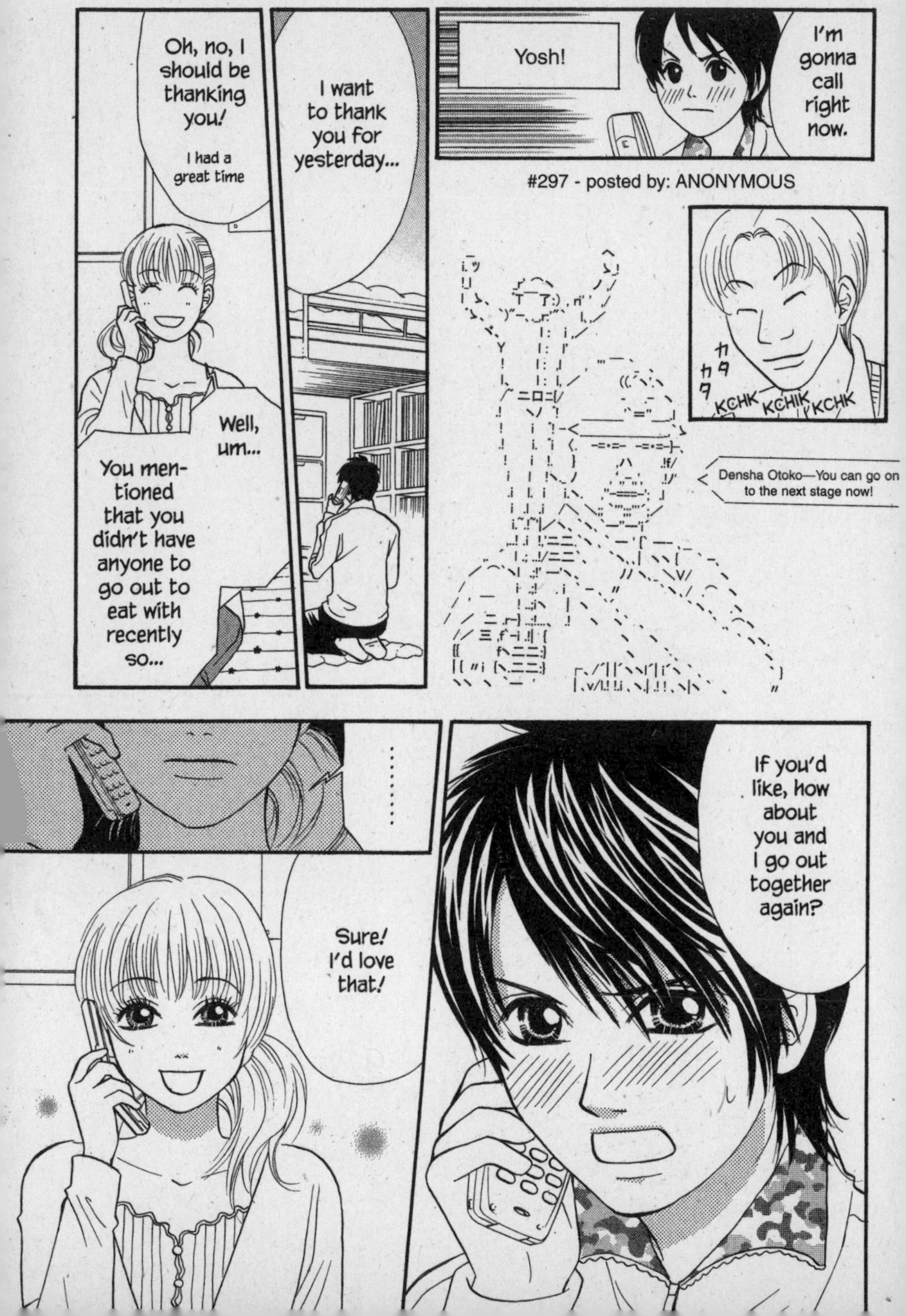
I'm gonna call right now.
Yosh!
#297 - posted by: ANONYMOUS
Densha Otoko—You can go on to the next stage now!
カタ カタ
KCHK KCHIK KCHK
I want to thank you for yesterday...
Oh, no, I should be thanking you!
I had a great time
Well, um...
You mentioned that you didn't have anyone to go out to eat with recently so...
If you'd like, how about you and I go out together again?
......
Sure! I'd love that!

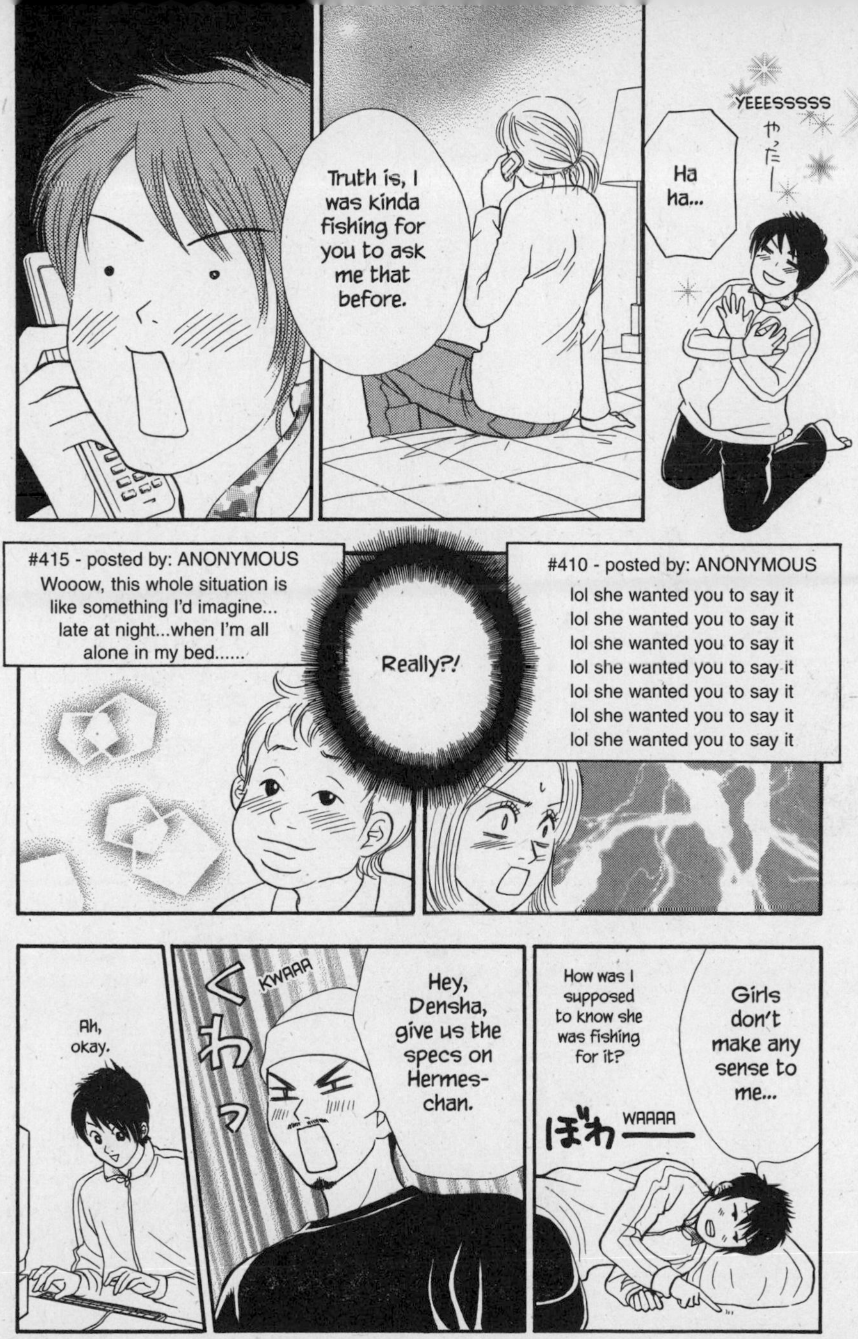
YEEESSSSS
やったー
Ha ha...
Truth is, I was kinda fishing for you to ask me that before.
#410 - posted by: ANONYMOUS
lol she wanted you to say it
lol she wanted you to say it
lol she wanted you to say it
lol she wanted you to say it
lol she wanted you to say it
lol she wanted you to say it
lol she wanted you to say it
Really?!
#415 - posted by: ANONYMOUS
Wooow, this whole situation is like something I'd imagine... late at night...when I'm all alone in my bed......
Girls don't make any sense to me...
How was I supposed to know she was fishing for it?
ぼわー
WAAAA
Hey, Densha, give us the specs on Hermes-chan.
くわっ
KWAAA
Ah, okay.

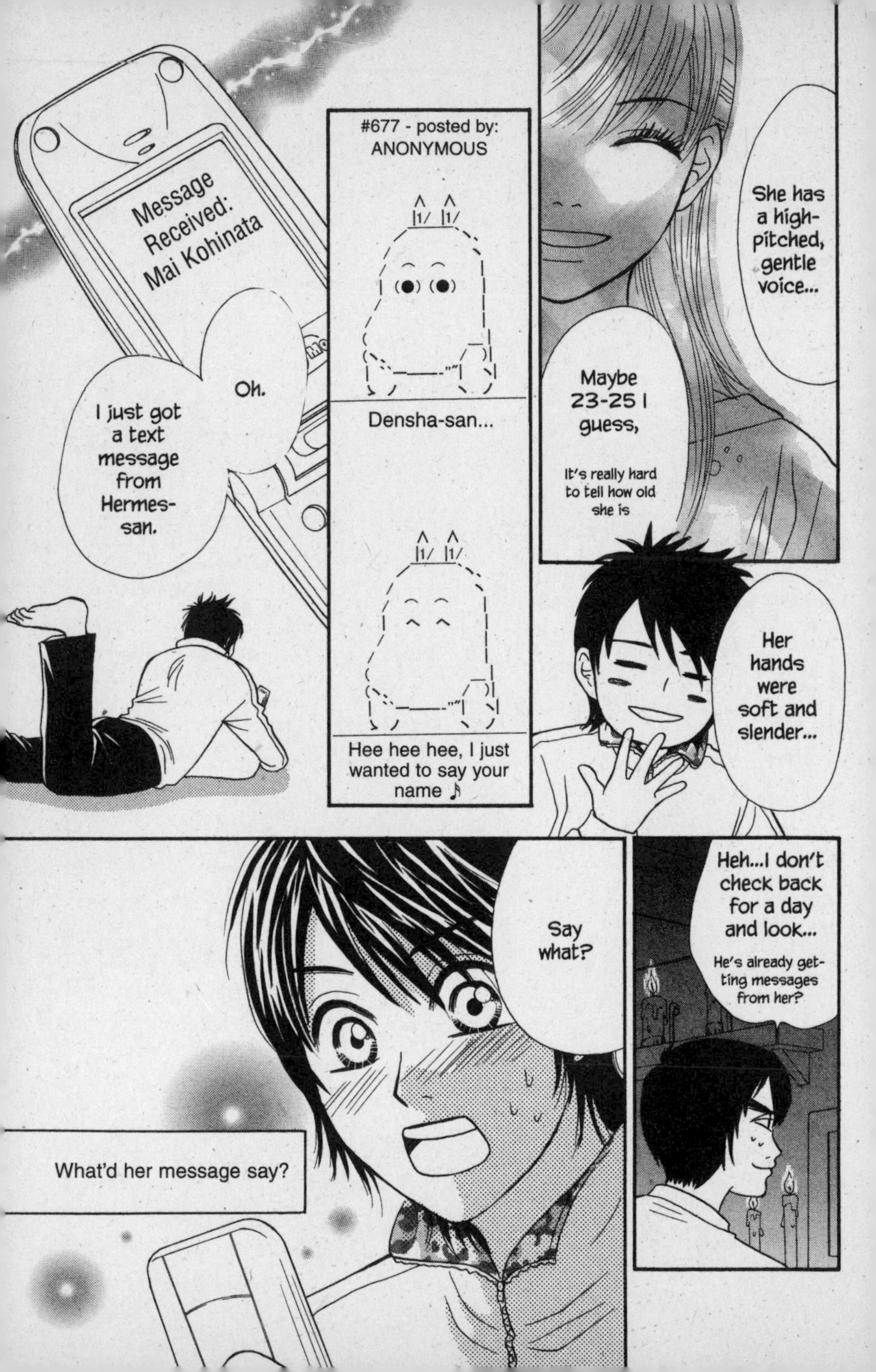
She has a high-pitched, gentle voice...
Maybe 23-25 I guess,
It's really hard to tell how old she is
Her hands were soft and slender...
#677 - posted by: ANONYMOUS
Densha-san...
Hee hee hee, I just wanted to say your name ♪
Message Received: Mai Kohinata
Oh.
I just got a text message from Hermes-san.
Heh...I don't check back for a day and look...
He's already getting messages from her?
Say what?
What'd her message say?

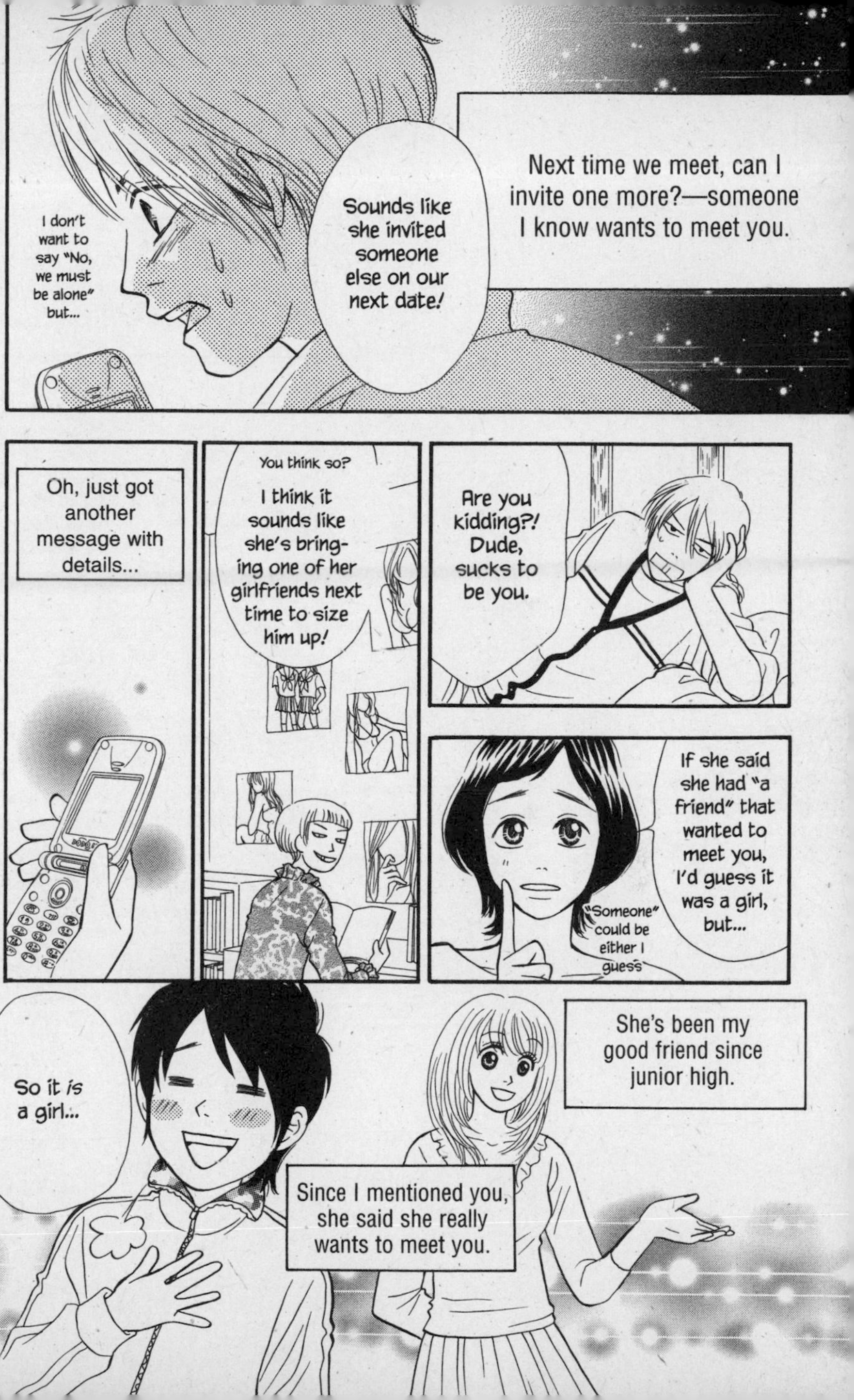
Next time we meet, can I invite one more?—someone I know wants to meet you.
Sounds like she invited someone else on our next date!
I don't want to say "No, we must be alone" but...
Are you kidding?! Dude, sucks to be you.
If she said she had "a friend" that wanted to meet you, I'd guess it was a girl, but...
"Someone" could be either I guess
You think so?
I think it sounds like she's bring-ing one of her girlfriends next time to size him up!
Oh, just got another message with details...
She's been my good friend since junior high.
Since I mentioned you, she said she really wants to meet you.
So it *is* a girl...

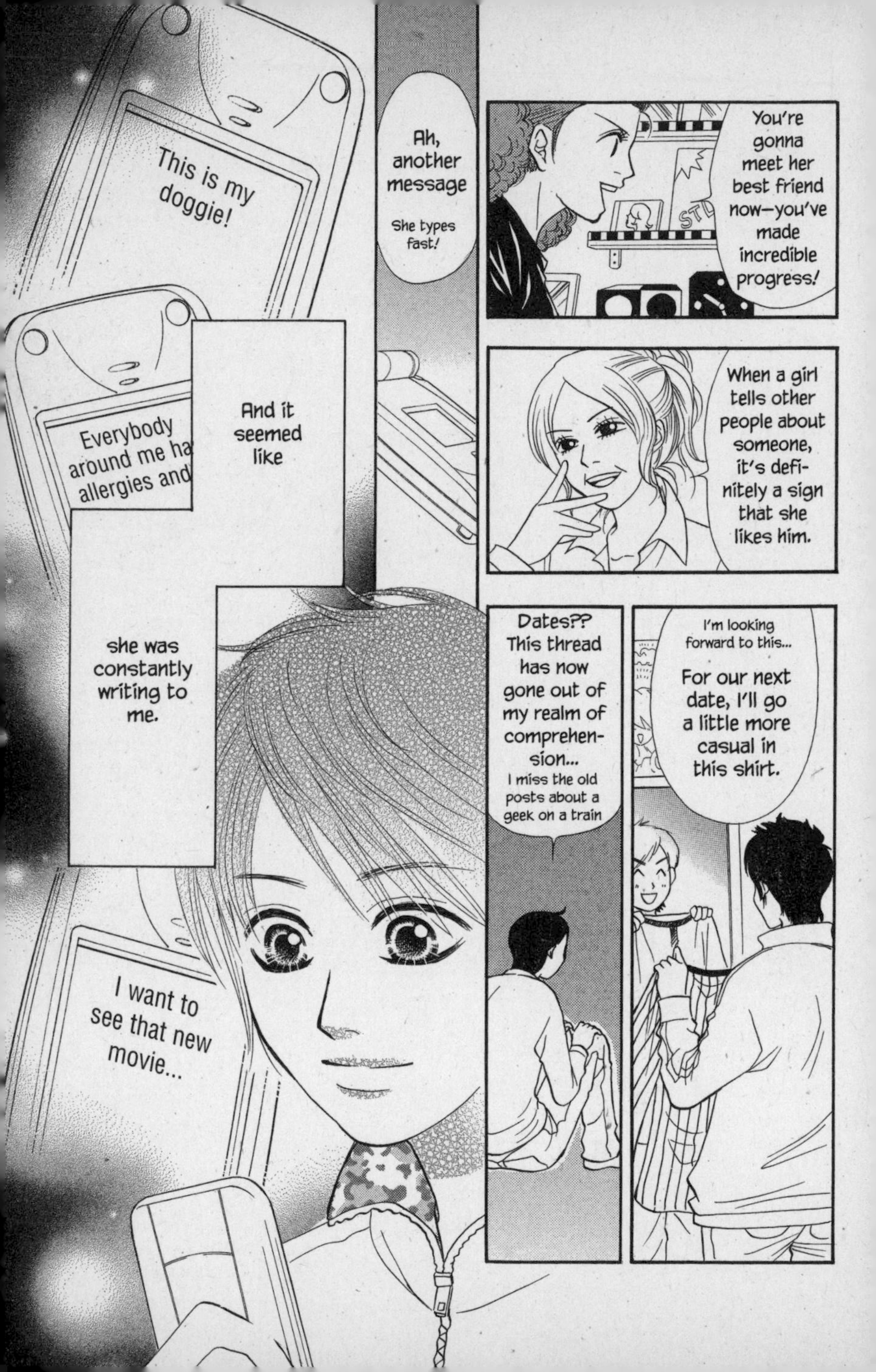
You're gonna meet her best friend now—you've made incredible progress!
When a girl tells other people about someone, it's definitely a sign that she likes him.
I'm looking forward to this...
For our next date, I'll go a little more casual in this shirt.
Dates?? This thread has now gone out of my realm of comprehension...
I miss the old posts about a geek on a train
Ah, another message
She types fast!
This is my doggie!
Everybody around me ha allergies and
And it seemed like
she was constantly writing to me.
I want to see that new movie...

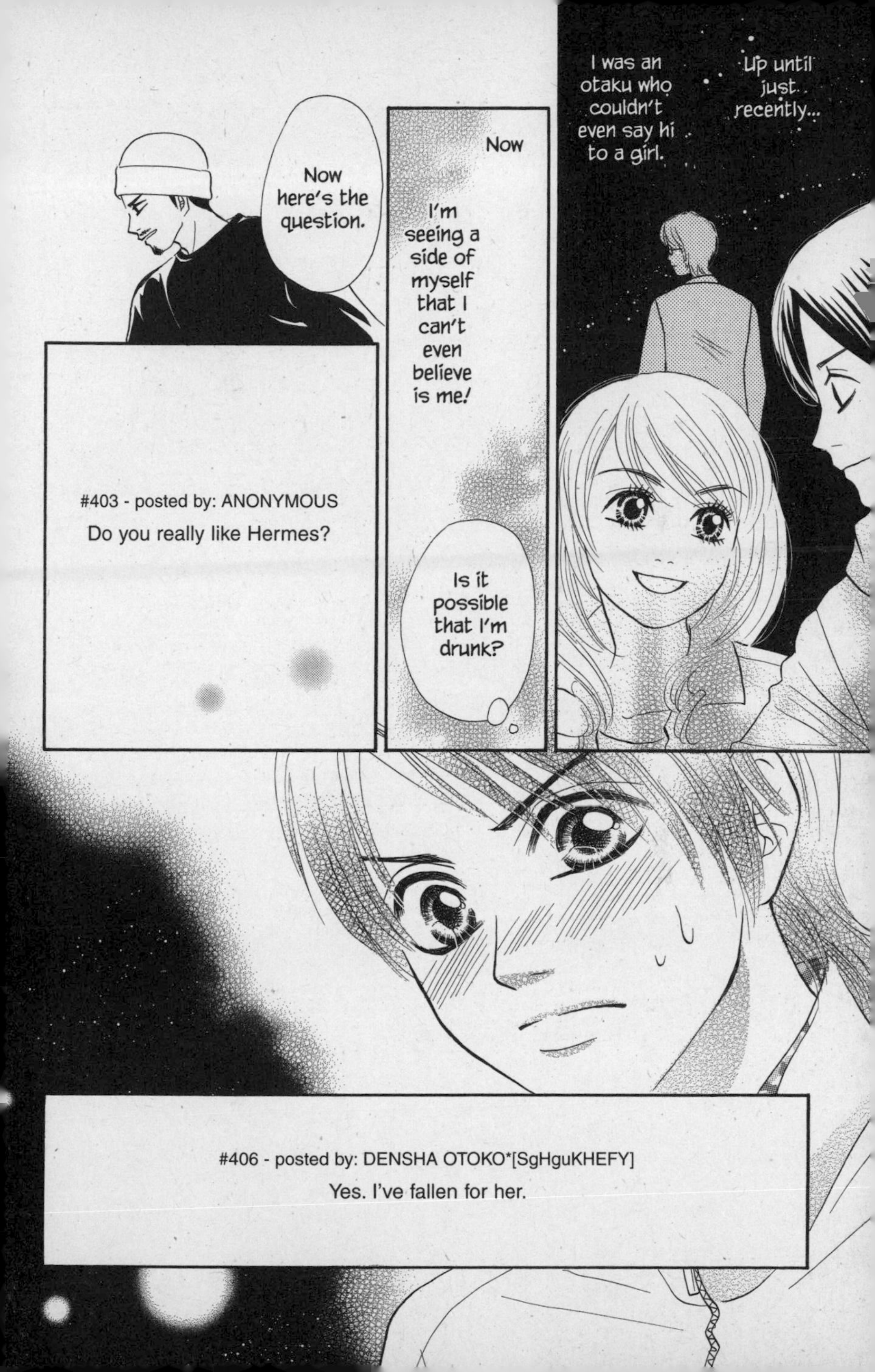
Up until just recently...
I was an otaku who couldn't even say hi to a girl.
Now
I'm seeing a side of myself that I can't even believe is me!
Is it possible that I'm drunk?
Now here's the question.
#403 - posted by: ANONYMOUS
Do you really like Hermes?
#406 - posted by: DENSHA OTOKO*[SgHguKHEFY]
Yes. I've fallen for her.

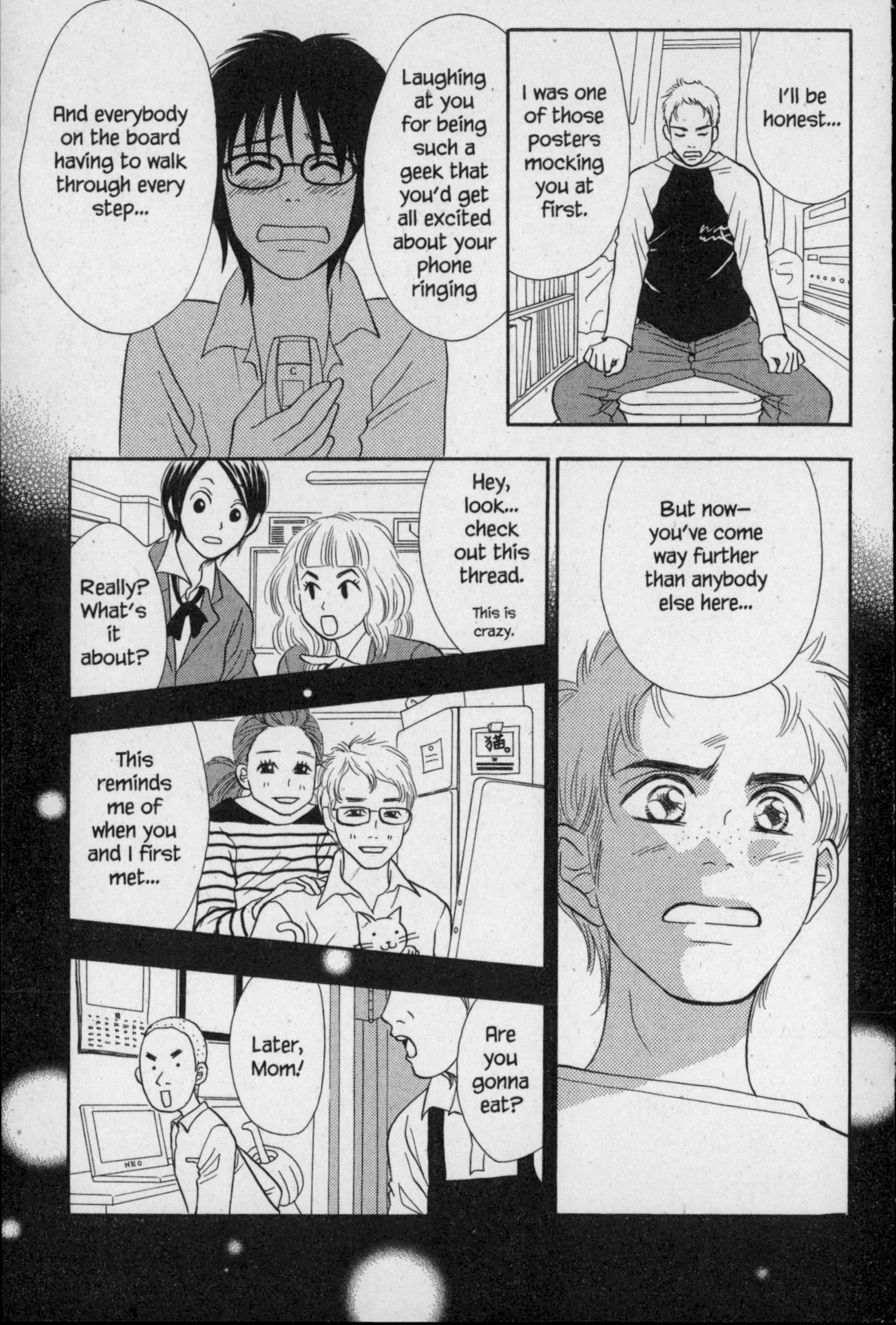
I'll be honest...
I was one of those posters mocking you at first.
Laughing at you for being such a geek that you'd get all excited about your phone ringing
And everybody on the board having to walk through every step...
But now— you've come way further than anybody else here...
Hey, look... check out this thread.
This is crazy.
Really? What's it about?
This reminds me of when you and I first met...
Are you gonna eat?
Later, Mom!

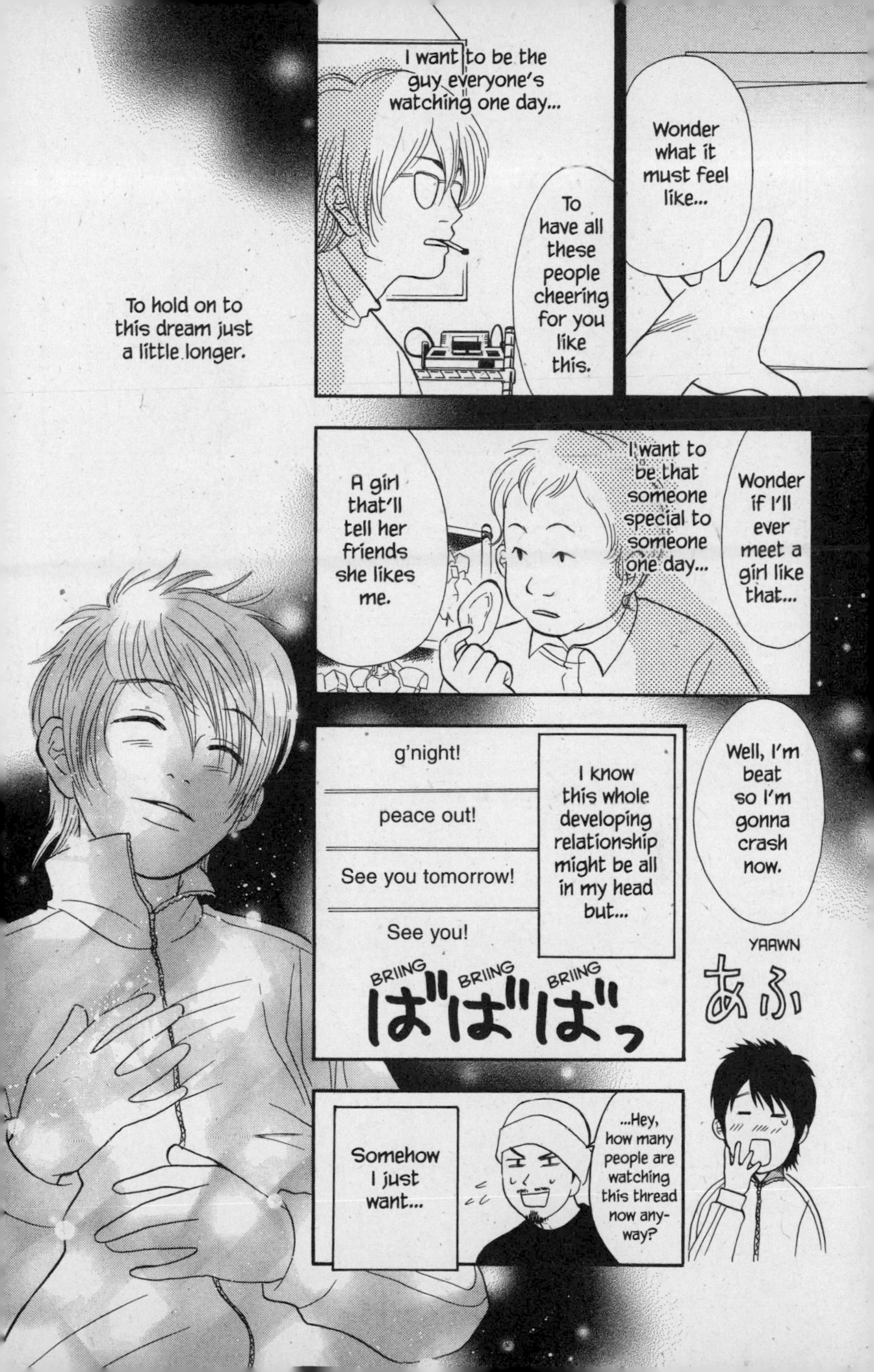

Wonder what it must feel like...
To have all these people cheering for you like this.
I want to be the guy everyone's watching one day...
Wonder if I'll ever meet a girl like that...
I want to be that someone special to someone one day...
A girl that'll tell her friends she likes me.
Well, I'm beat so I'm gonna crash now.
YAAWN
あふ
I know this whole developing relationship might be all in my head but...
g'night!
peace out!
See you tomorrow!
See you!
BRIING BRIING BRIING
ばばばっ
...Hey, how many people are watching this thread now anyway?
Somehow I just want...
To hold on to this dream just a little longer.

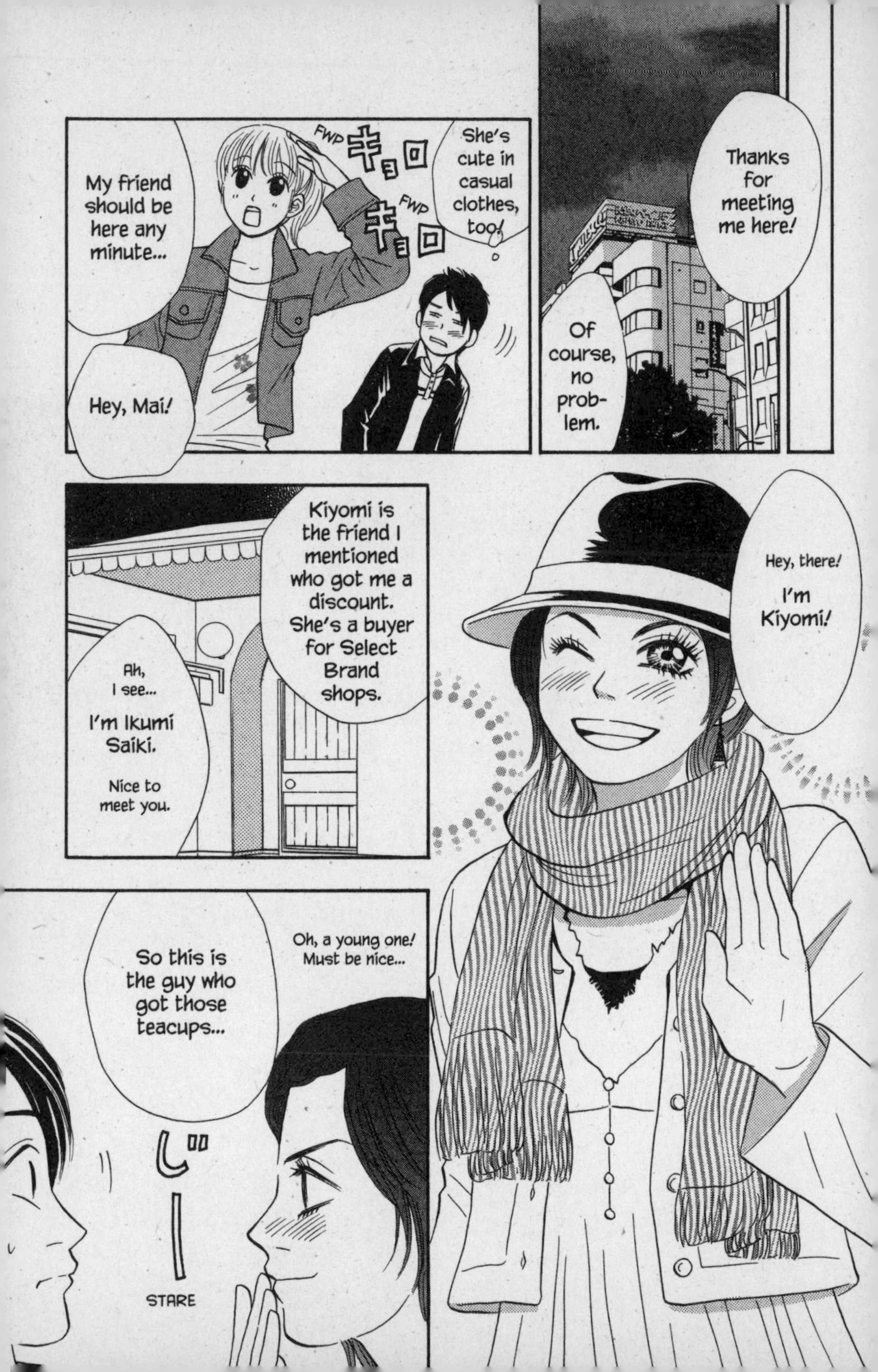

Thanks for meeting me here!
Of course, no problem.
She's cute in casual clothes, too!
FWP キョロ
FWP キョロ
My friend should be here any minute...
Hey, Mai!
Hey, there!
I'm Kiyomi!
Kiyomi is the friend I mentioned who got me a discount. She's a buyer for Select Brand shops.
Ah, I see...
I'm Ikumi Saiki.
Nice to meet you.
Oh, a young one! Must be nice...
So this is the guy who got those teacups...
じー
STARE

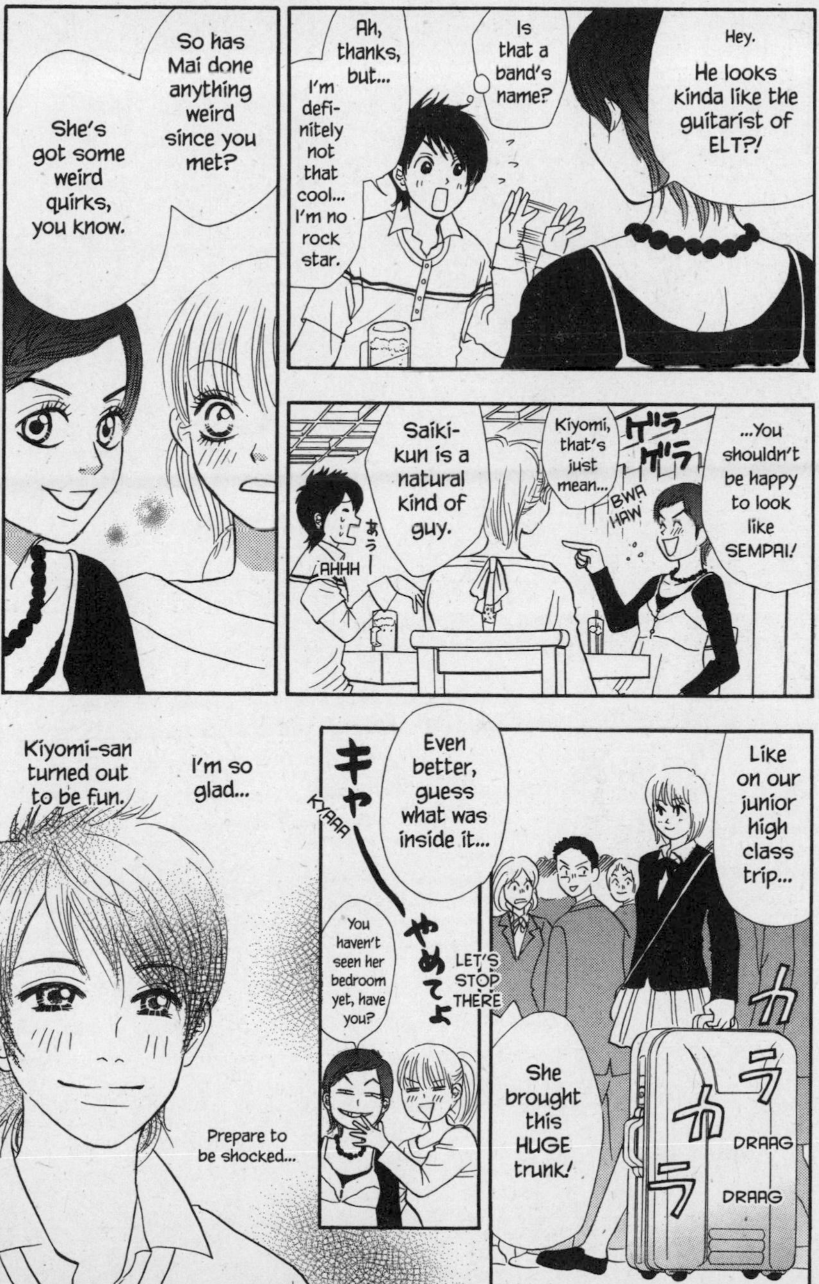
Hey.
He looks kinda like the guitarist of ELT?!
Is that a band's name?
Ah, thanks, but...
I'm definitely not that cool... I'm no rock star.
...You shouldn't be happy to look like SEMPAI!
ゲラゲラ
BWA HAW
Kiyomi, that's just mean...
Saiki-kun is a natural kind of guy.
あらー
AHHH
So has Mai done anything weird since you met?
She's got some weird quirks, you know.
Like on our junior high class trip...
カラカラ
DRAAG DRAAG
She brought this HUGE trunk!
Even better, guess what was inside it...
キャー
KYAAA
やめてよ
LET'S STOP THERE
You haven't seen her bedroom yet, have you?
I'm so glad...
Kiyomi-san turned out to be fun.
Prepare to be shocked...

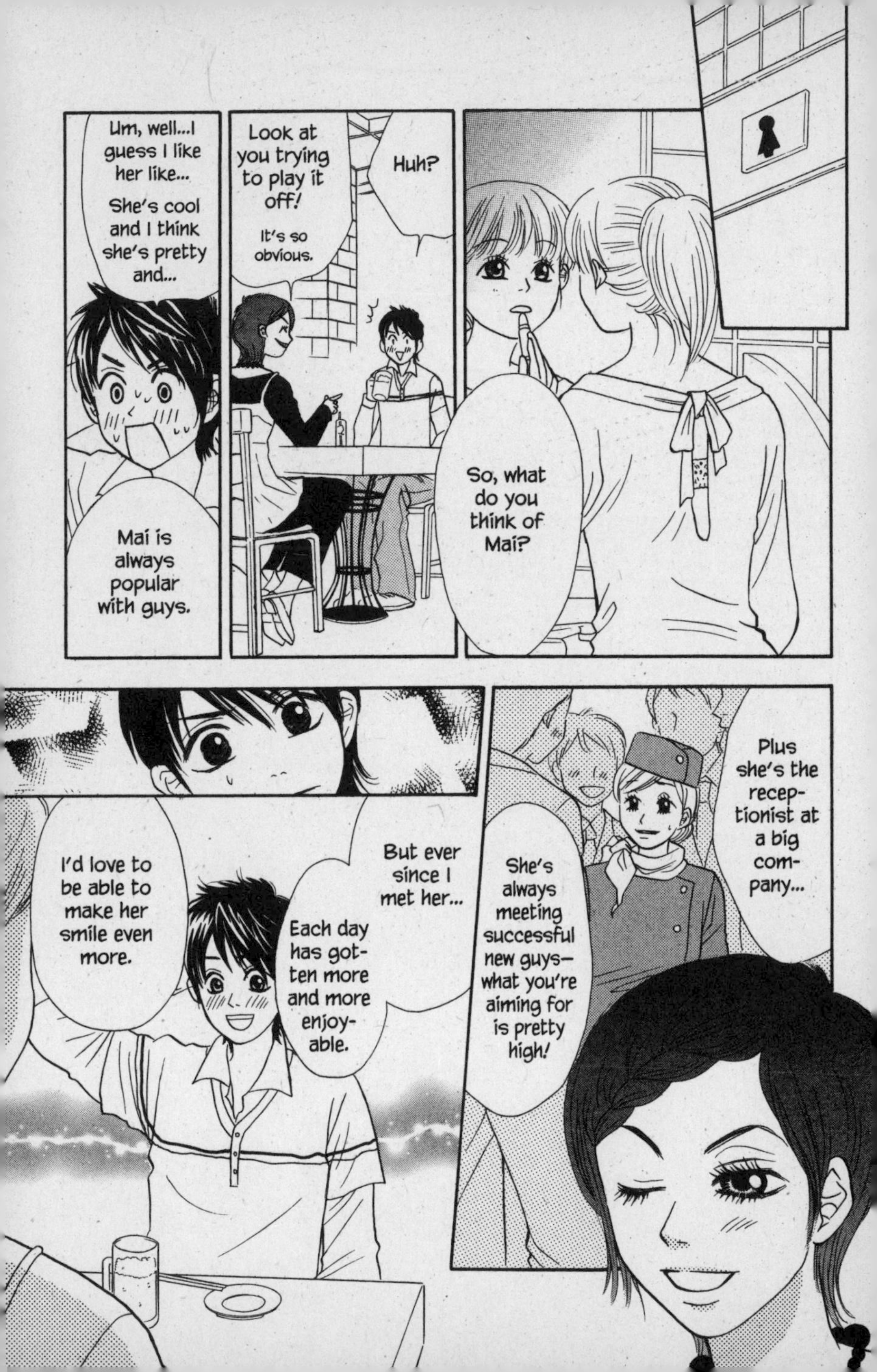
So, what do you think of Mai?
Huh?
Look at you trying to play it off!
It's so obvious.
Um, well...I guess I like her like...
She's cool and I think she's pretty and...
Mai is always popular with guys.
Plus she's the receptionist at a big company...
She's always meeting successful new guys—what you're aiming for is pretty high!
But ever since I met her...
Each day has gotten more and more enjoyable.
I'd love to be able to make her smile even more.

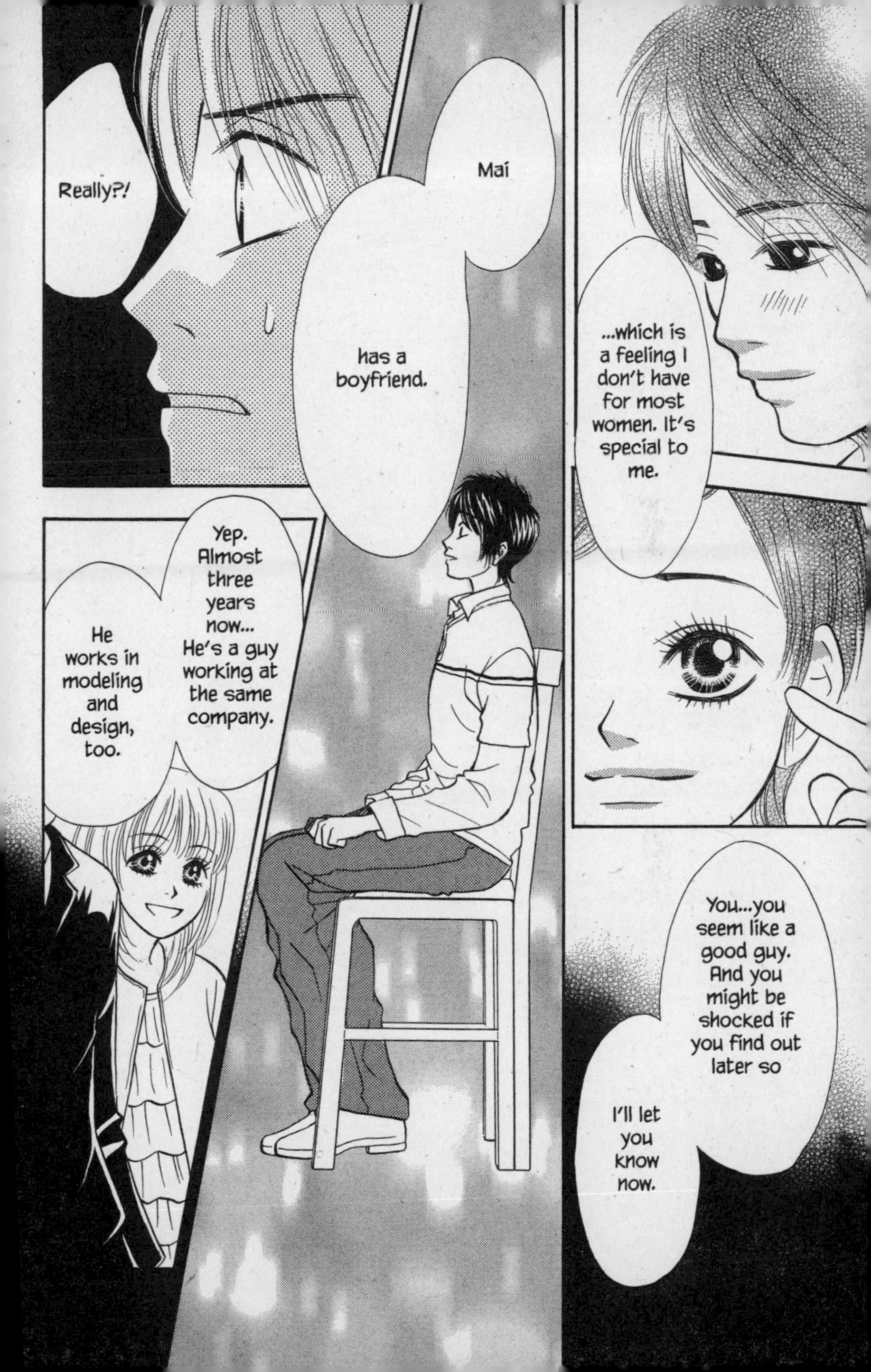
...which is a feeling I don't have for most women. It's special to me.
You...you seem like a good guy. And you might be shocked if you find out later so
I'll let you know now.
Mai
has a boyfriend.
Really?!
Yep. Almost three years now... He's a guy working at the same company.
He works in modeling and design, too.

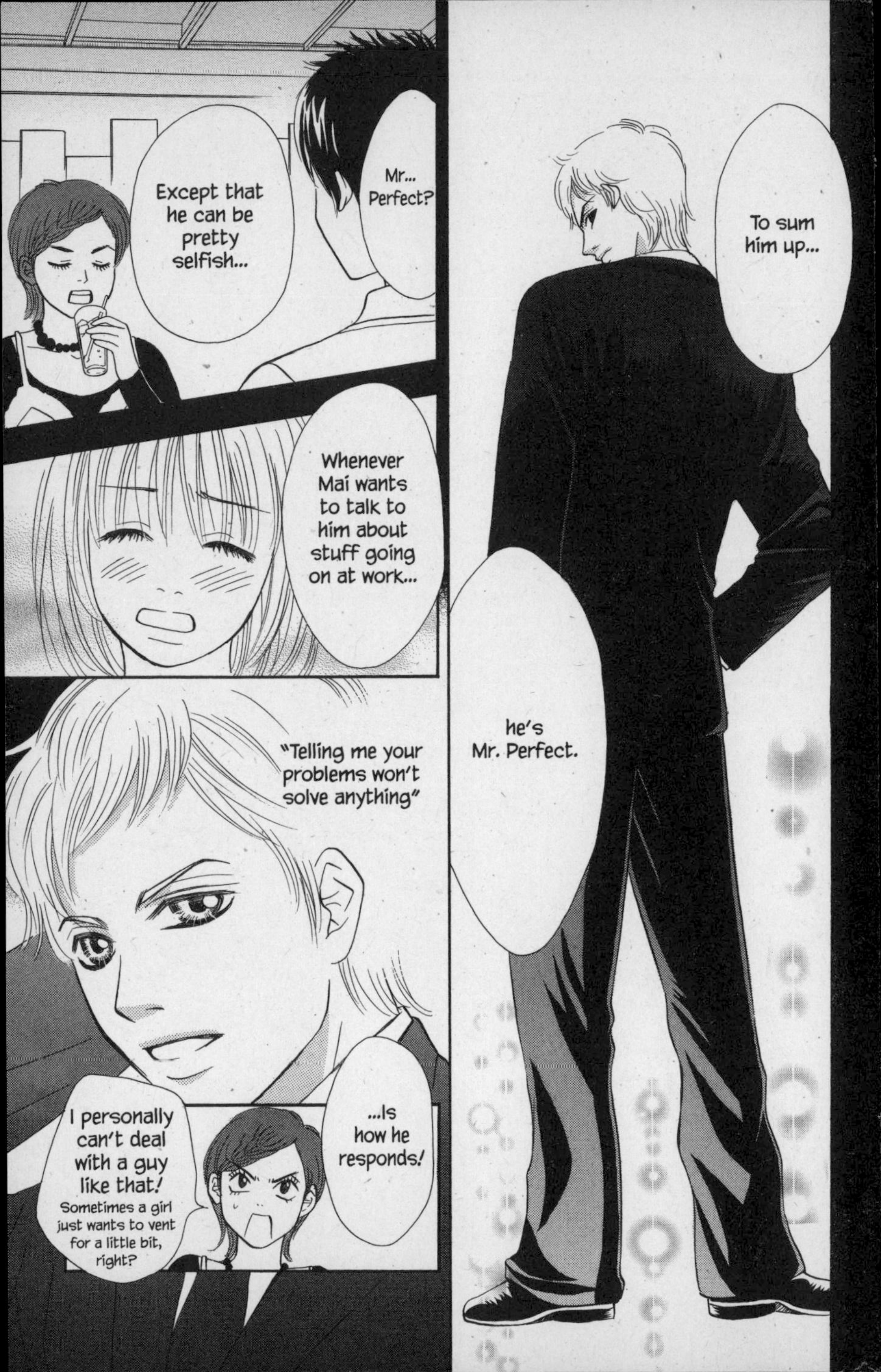
To sum him up...
he's Mr. Perfect.
Mr... Perfect?
Except that he can be pretty selfish...
Whenever Mai wants to talk to him about stuff going on at work...
"Telling me your problems won't solve anything"
...Is how he responds!
I personally can't deal with a guy like that!
Sometimes a girl just wants to vent for a little bit, right?

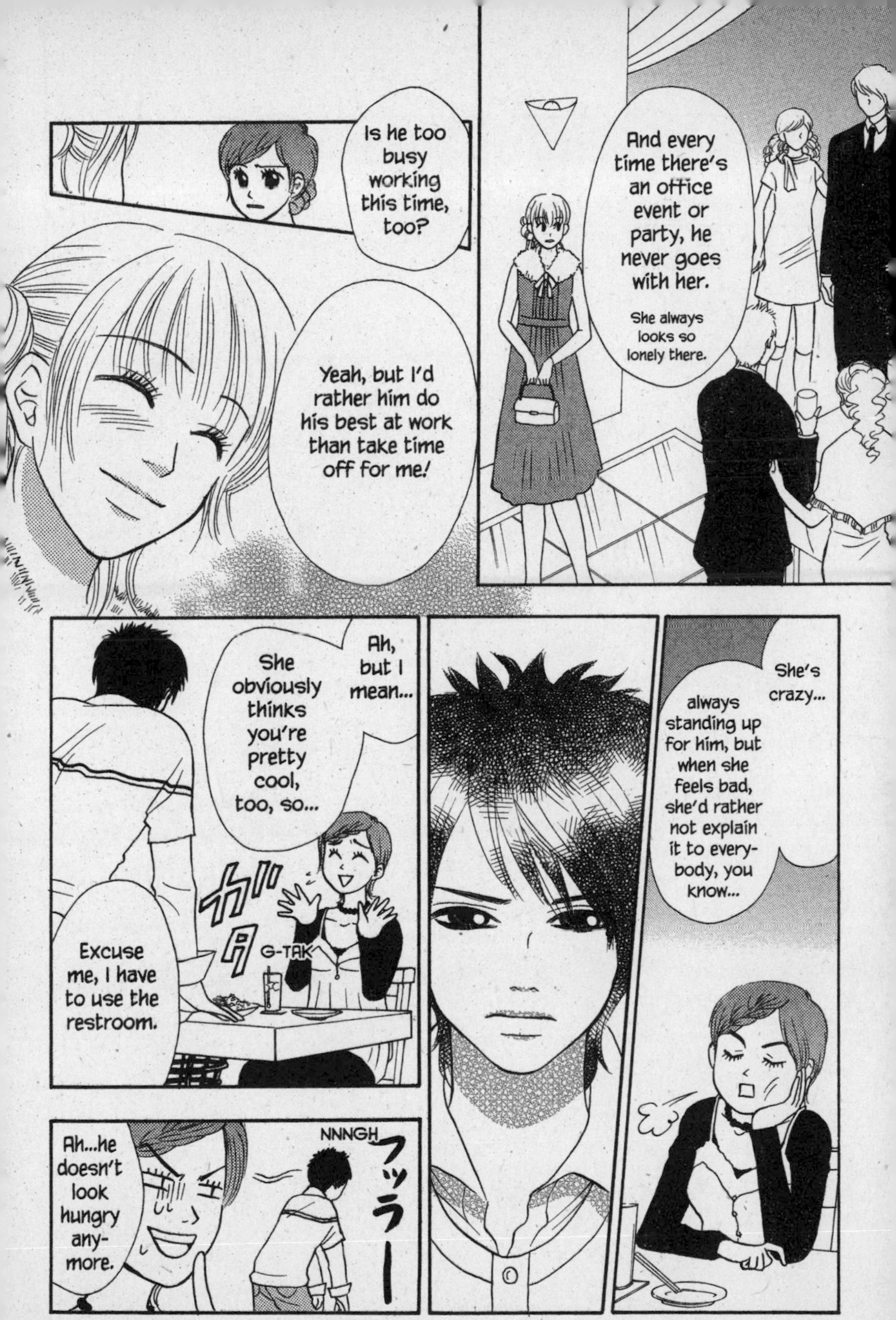
And every time there's an office event or party, he never goes with her.
She always looks so lonely there.
Is he too busy working this time, too?
Yeah, but I'd rather him do his best at work than take time off for me!
She's crazy...
always standing up for him, but when she feels bad, she'd rather not explain it to every-body, you know...
Ah, but I mean...
She obviously thinks you're pretty cool, too, so...
ガタ
G-TAK
Excuse me, I have to use the restroom.
NNNGH
フッラー
Ah...he doesn't look hungry any-more.

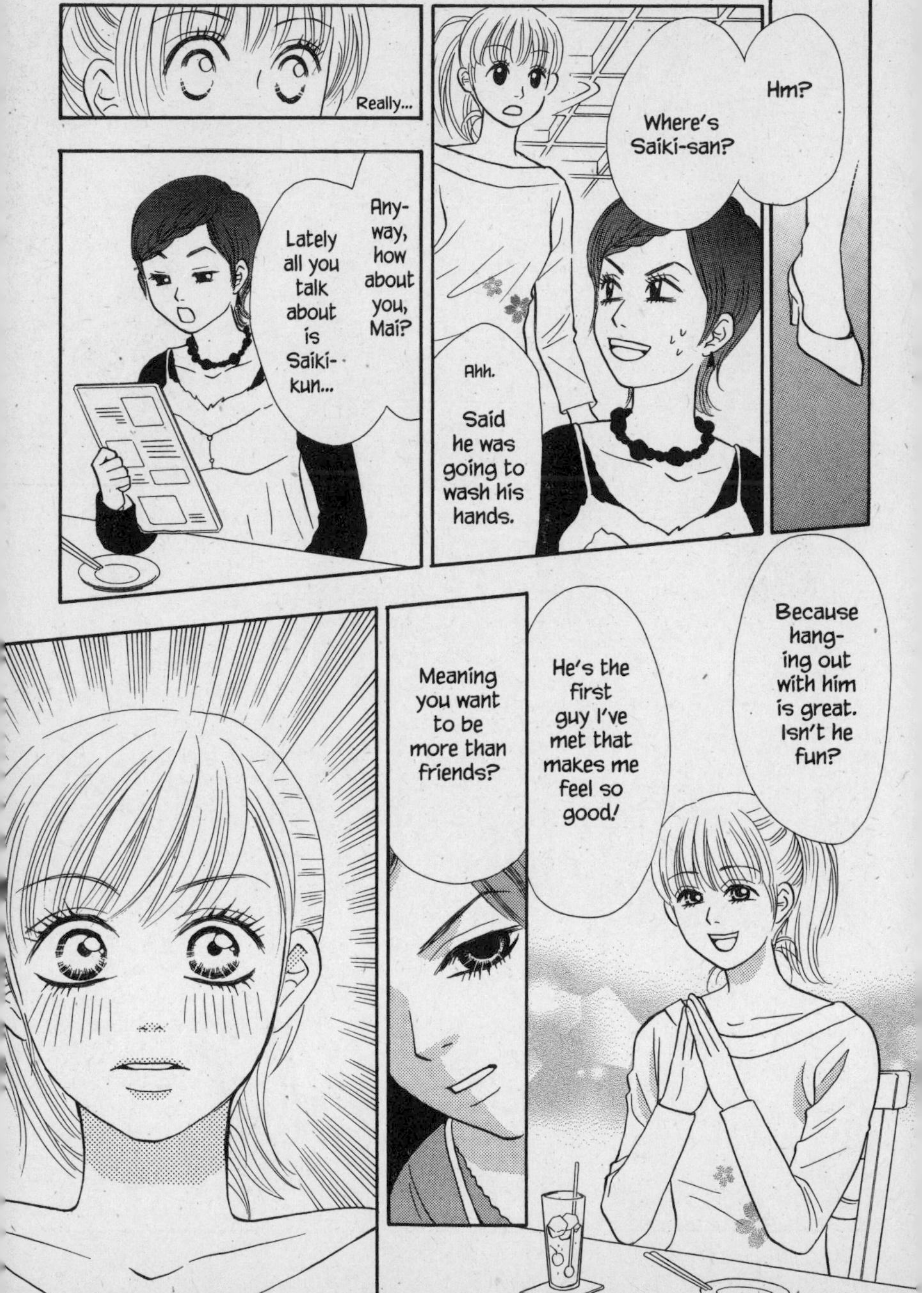
Hm?
Where's Saiki-san?
Ahh.
Said he was going to wash his hands.
Really...
Any-way, how about you, Mai?
Lately all you talk about is Saiki-kun...
Because hang-ing out with him is great. Isn't he fun?
He's the first guy I've met that makes me feel so good!
Meaning you want to be more than friends?

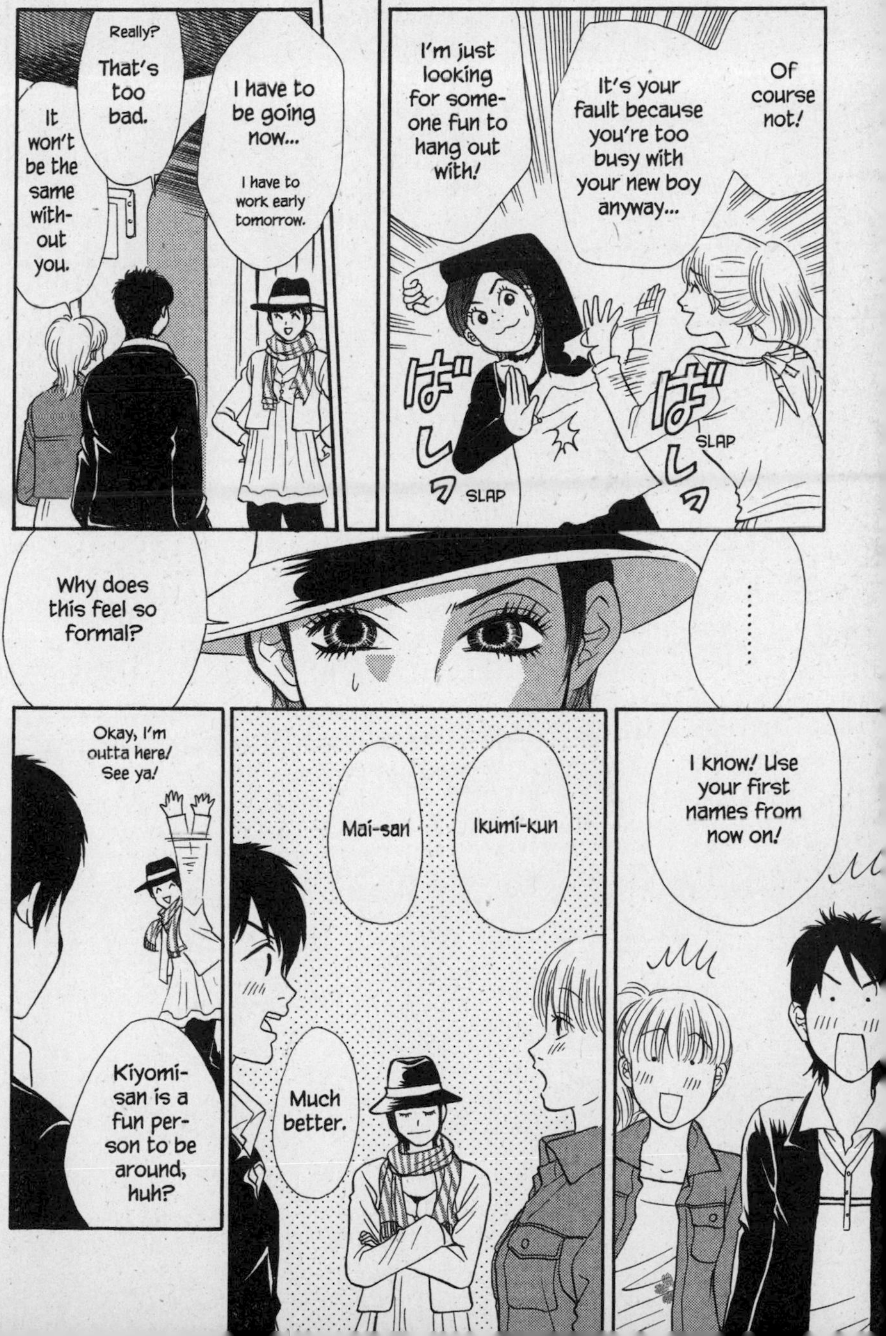
Of course not!
It's your fault because you're too busy with your new boy anyway...
I'm just looking for some-one fun to hang out with!
ばしっ
SLAP
ばしっ
SLAP
I have to be going now...
I have to work early tomorrow.
Really?
That's too bad.
It won't be the same with-out you.
......
Why does this feel so formal?
I know! Use your first names from now on!
Ikumi-kun
Mai-san
Much better.
Okay, I'm outta here! See ya!
Kiyomi-san is a fun per-son to be around, huh?

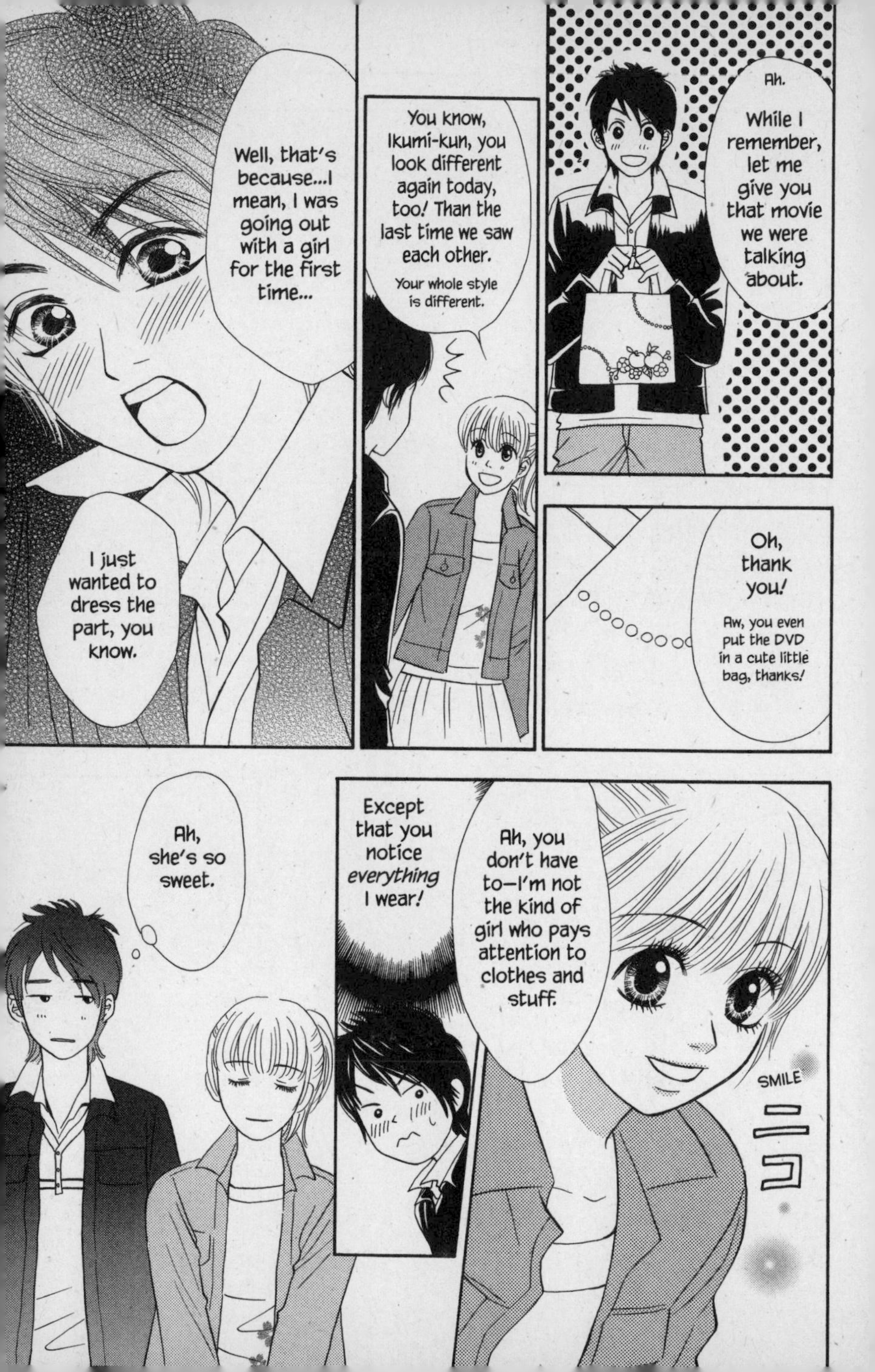
Ah.
While I remember, let me give you that movie we were talking about.
Oh, thank you!
Aw, you even put the DVD in a cute little bag, thanks!
You know, Ikumi-kun, you look different again today, too! Than the last time we saw each other.
Your whole style is different.
Well, that's because...I mean, I was going out with a girl for the first time...
I just wanted to dress the part, you know.
Ah, you don't have to—I'm not the kind of girl who pays attention to clothes and stuff.
Except that you notice *everything* I wear!
SMILE
Ah, she's so sweet.

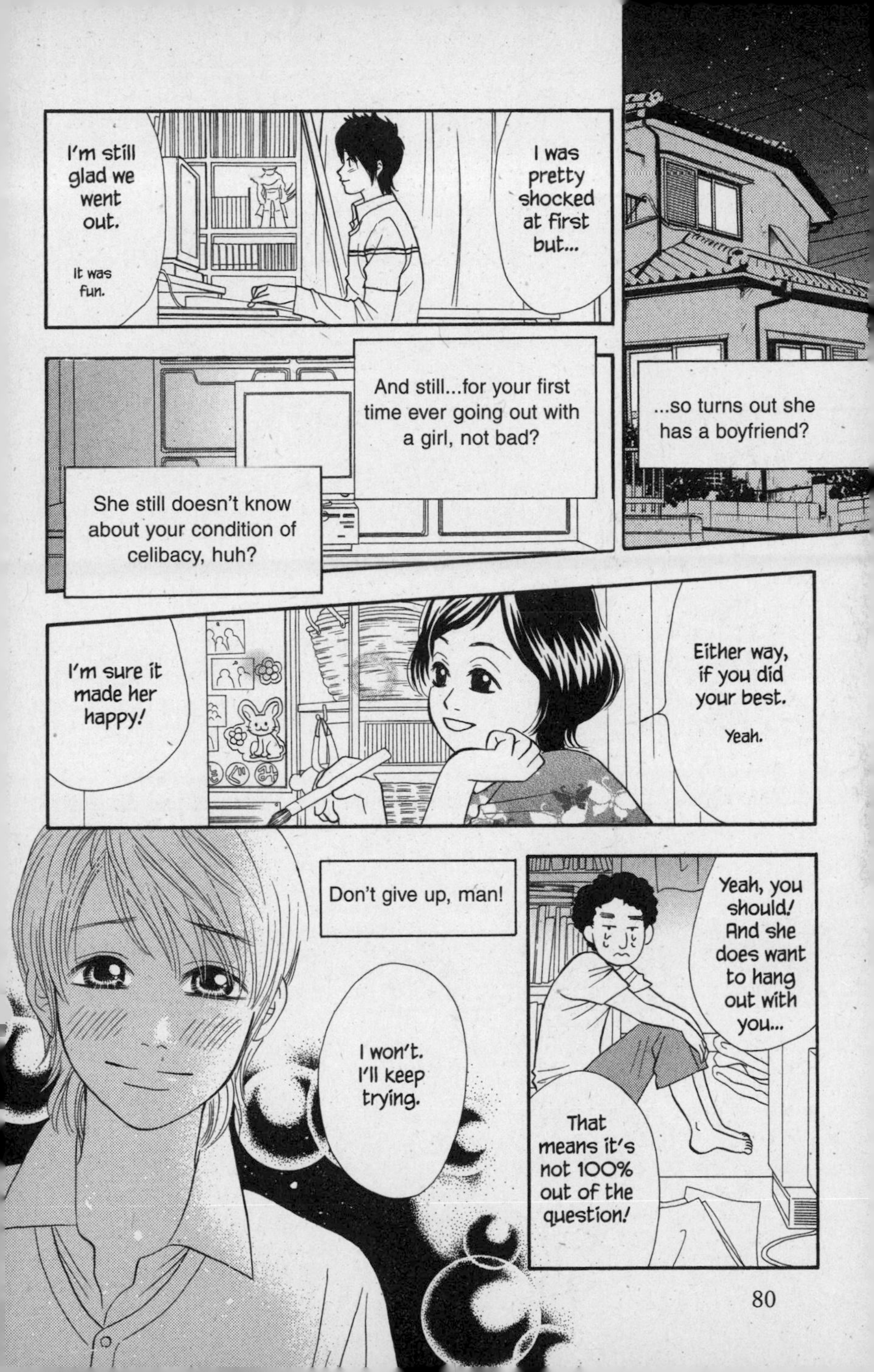

...so turns out she has a boyfriend?
I was pretty shocked at first but...
I'm still glad we went out.
It was fun.
And still...for your first time ever going out with a girl, not bad?
She still doesn't know about your condition of celibacy, huh?
Either way, if you did your best.
Yeah.
I'm sure it made her happy!
Yeah, you should! And she does want to hang out with you...
That means it's not 100% out of the question!
Don't give up, man!
I won't. I'll keep trying.

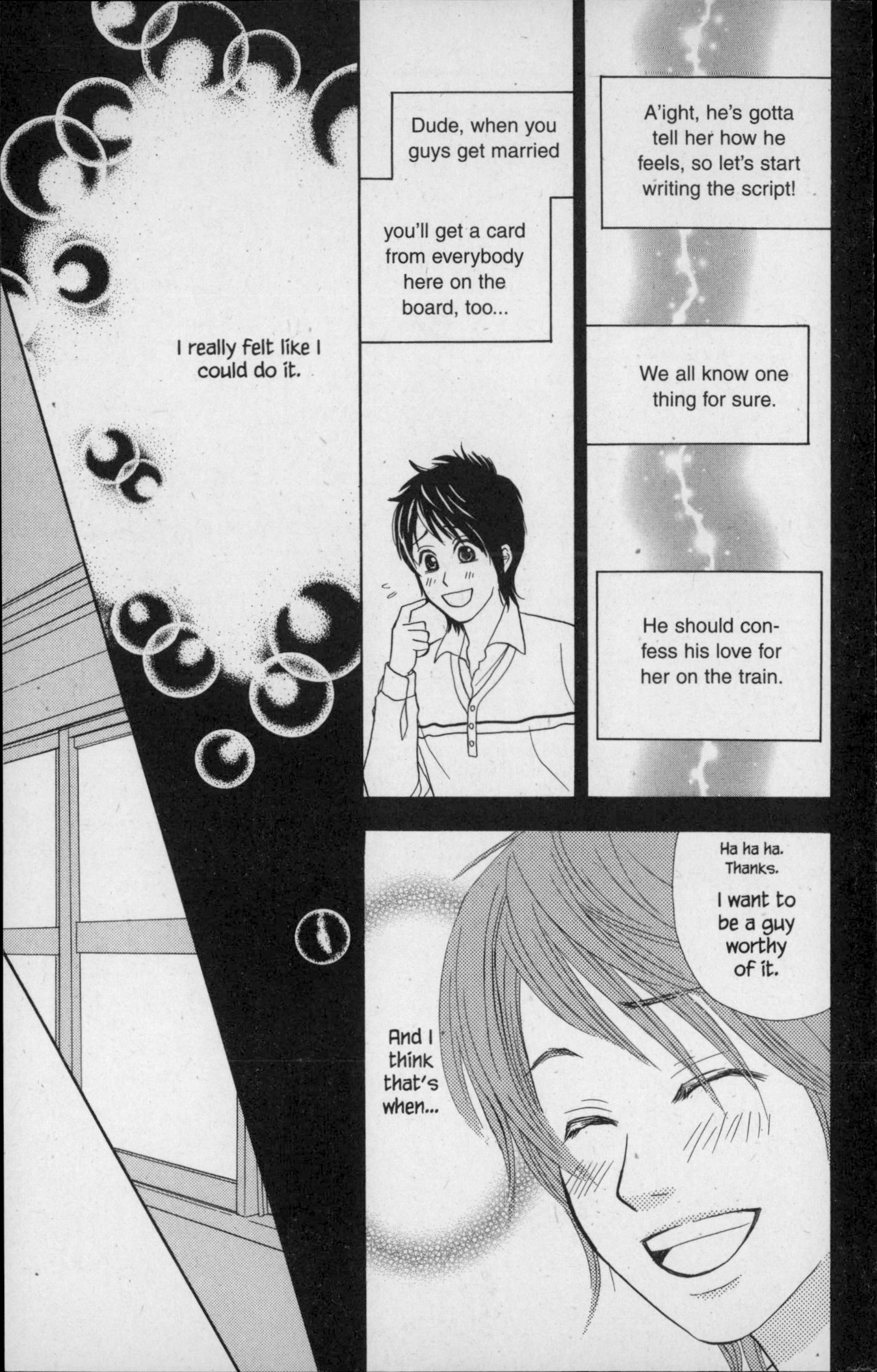
A'ight, he's gotta tell her how he feels, so let's start writing the script!
We all know one thing for sure.
He should confess his love for her on the train.
Dude, when you guys get married
you'll get a card from everybody here on the board, too...
Ha ha ha. Thanks.
I want to be a guy worthy of it.
And I think that's when...
I really felt like I could do it.

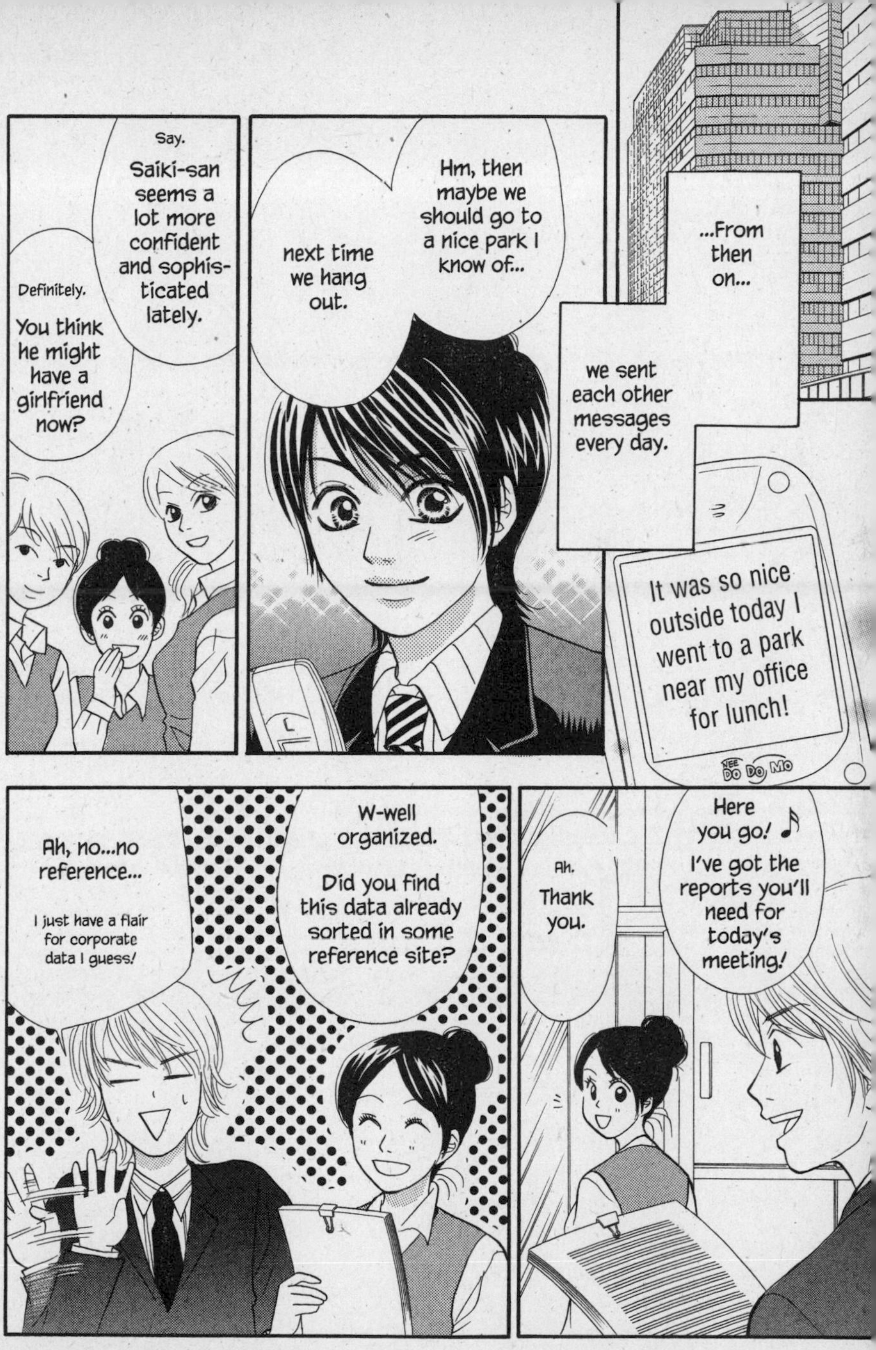
...From then on...
we sent each other messages every day.
It was so nice outside today I went to a park near my office for lunch!
Hm, then maybe we should go to a nice park I know of...
next time we hang out.
Say.
Saiki-san seems a lot more confident and sophisticated lately.
Definitely.
You think he might have a girlfriend now?
Here you go! ♪
I've got the reports you'll need for today's meeting!
Ah.
Thank you.
W-well organized.
Did you find this data already sorted in some reference site?
Ah, no...no reference...
I just have a flair for corporate data I guess!

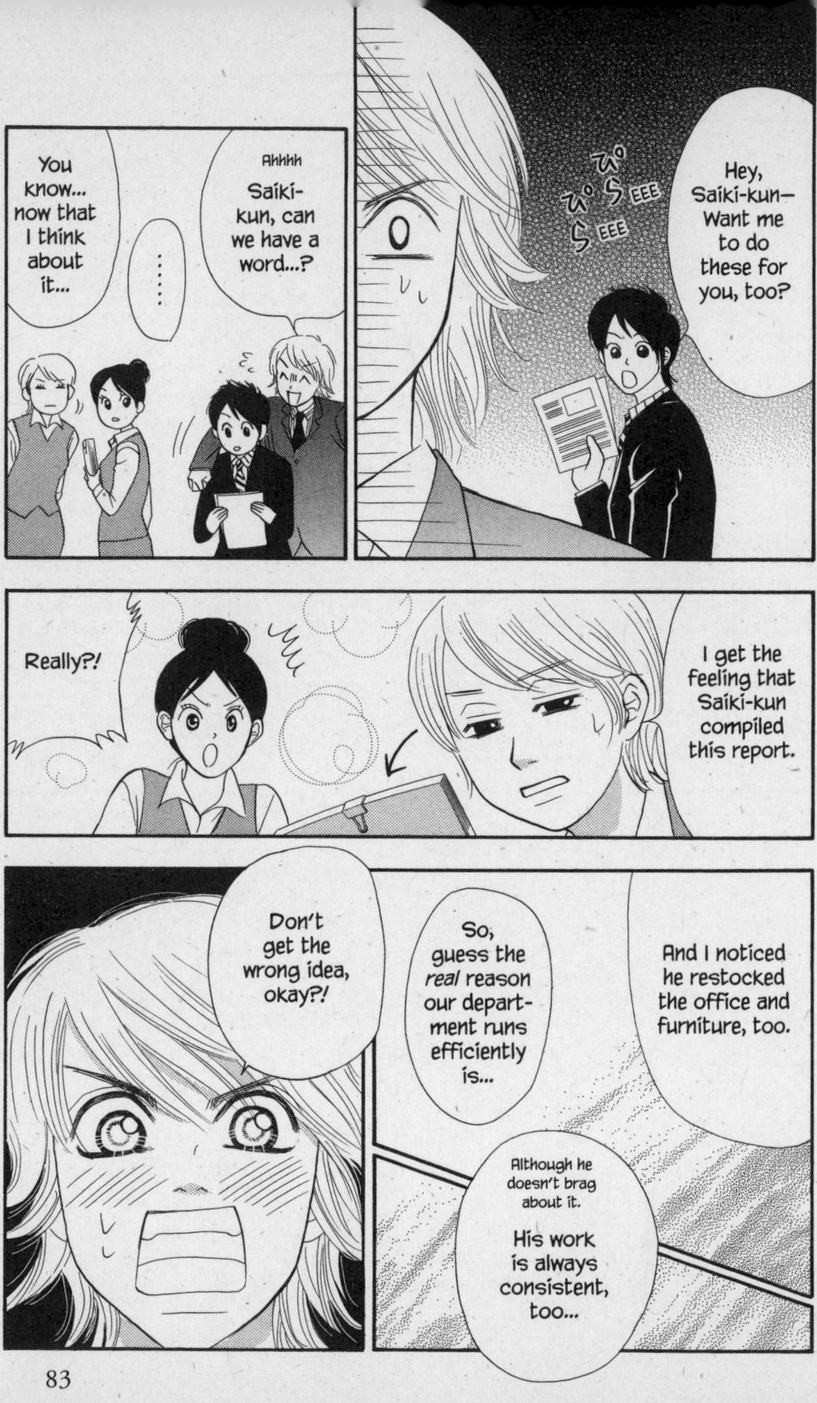
Hey, Saiki-kun— Want me to do these for you, too?
Ahhhh
Saiki-kun, can we have a word...?
......
You know... now that I think about it...
I get the feeling that Saiki-kun compiled this report.
Really?!
And I noticed he restocked the office and furniture, too.
So, guess the *real* reason our department runs efficiently is...
Although he doesn't brag about it.
His work is always consistent, too...
Don't get the wrong idea, okay?!

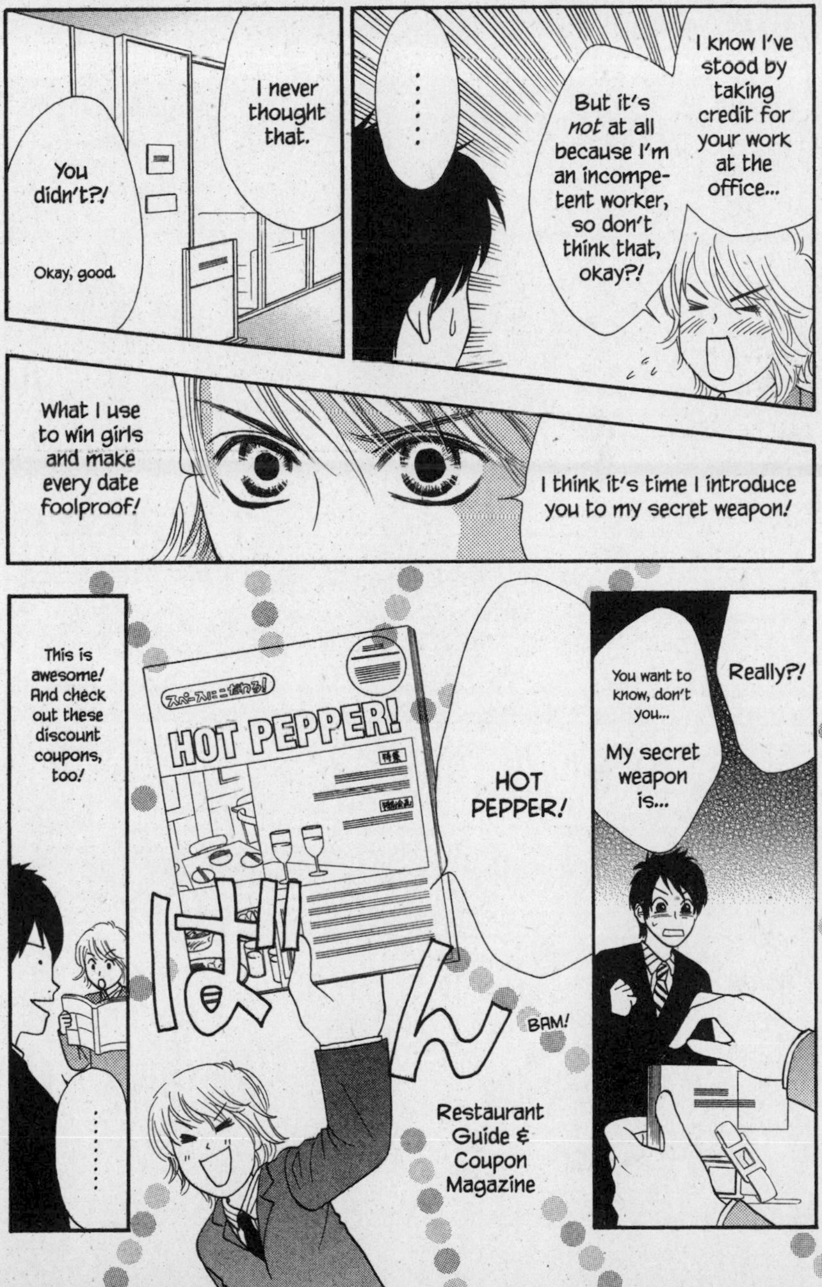
I know I've stood by taking credit for your work at the office...
But it's *not* at all because I'm an incompetent worker, so don't think that, okay?!
......
I never thought that.
You didn't?!
Okay, good.
I think it's time I introduce you to my secret weapon!
What I use to win girls and make every date foolproof!
Really?!
You want to know, don't you...
My secret weapon is...
HOT PEPPER!
HOT PEPPER!
ばん
BAM!
Restaurant Guide & Coupon Magazine
This is awesome! And check out these discount coupons, too!
......

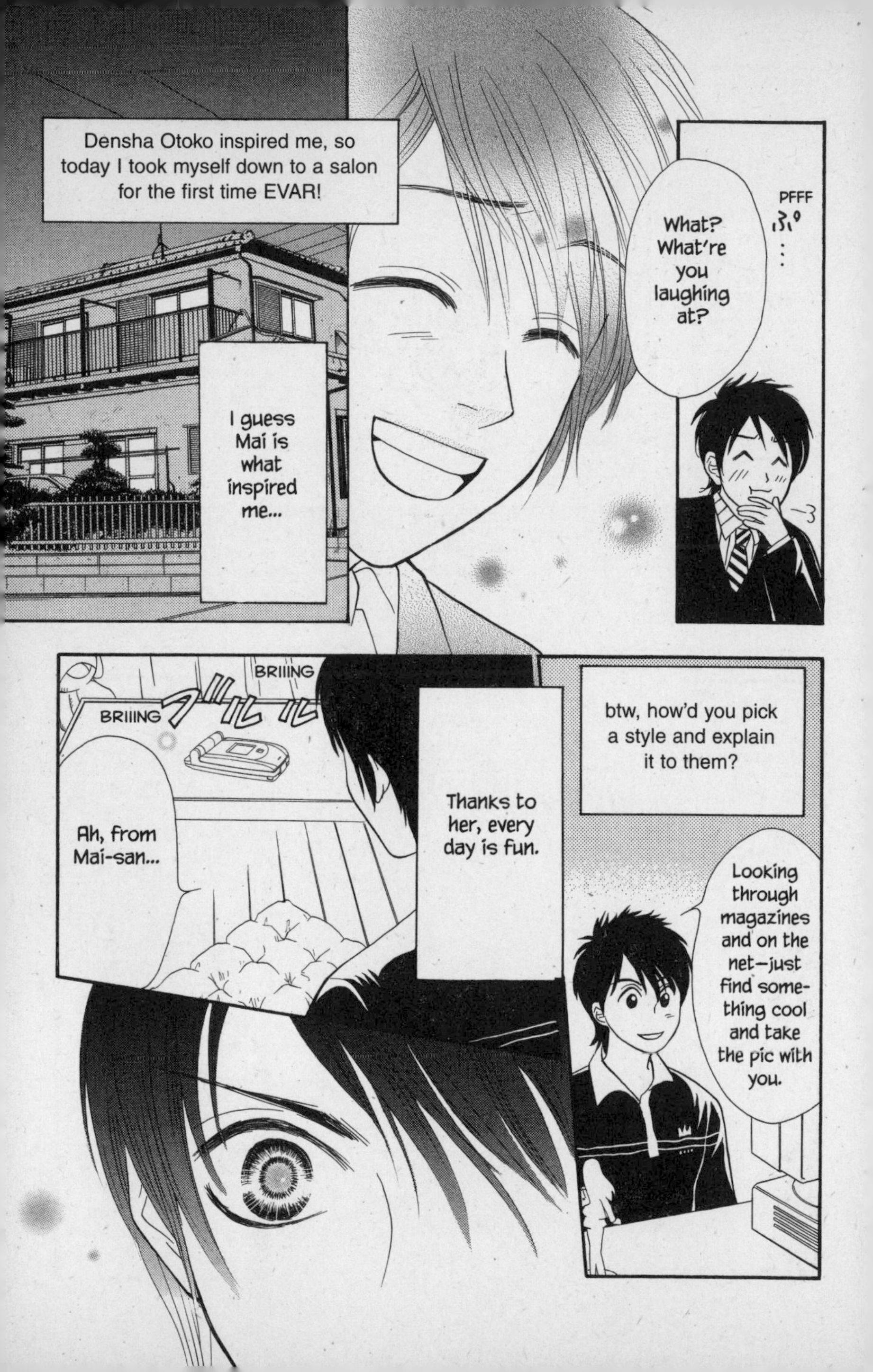
PFFF
ふっ…
What? What're you laughing at?
Densha Otoko inspired me, so today I took myself down to a salon for the first time EVAR!
I guess Mai is what inspired me...
btw, how'd you pick a style and explain it to them?
Looking through magazines and on the net—just find something cool and take the pic with you.
Thanks to her, every day is fun.
BRIIING
BRIIING
ブルル
Ah, from Mai-san...

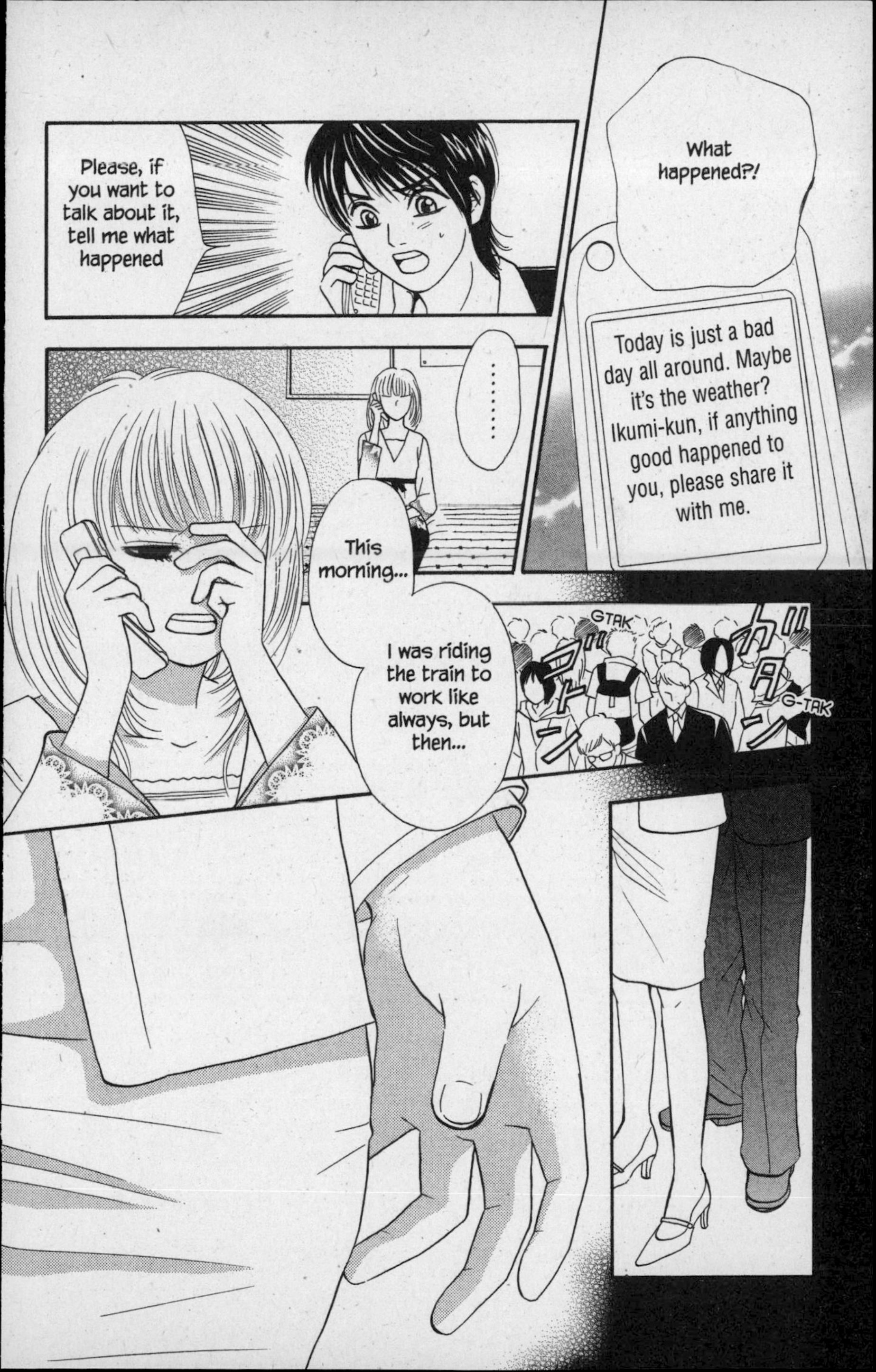
What happened?!
Today is just a bad day all around. Maybe it's the weather? Ikumi-kun, if anything good happened to you, please share it with me.
Please, if you want to talk about it, tell me what happened
......
This morning...
I was riding the train to work like always, but then...
GTAK
G-TAK

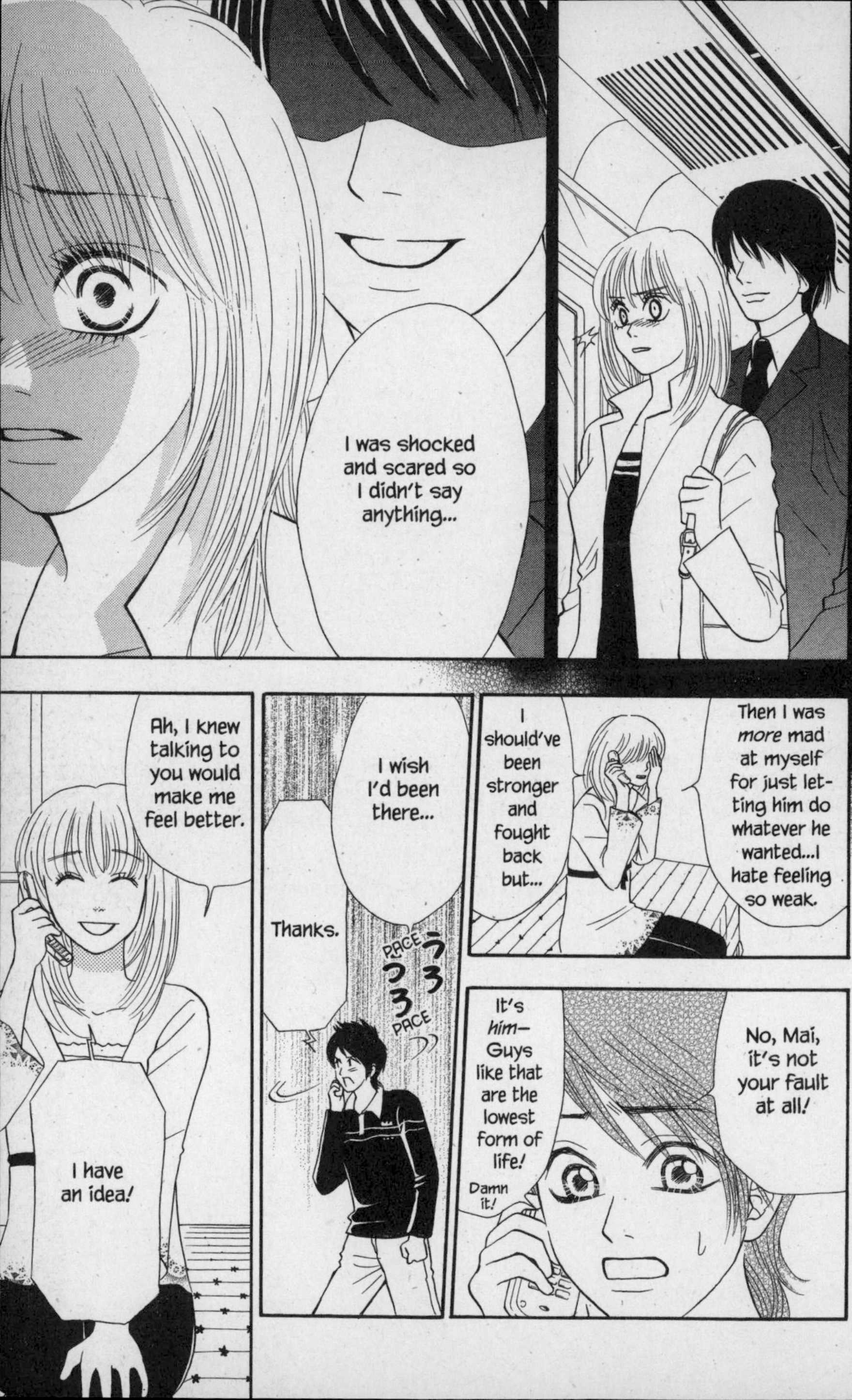
I was shocked and scared so I didn't say anything...
Then I was *more* mad at myself for just letting him do whatever he wanted...I hate feeling so weak.
I should've been stronger and fought back but...
No, Mai, it's not your fault at all!
It's *him*— Guys like that are the lowest form of life!
Damn it!
I wish I'd been there...
Thanks.
うろうろ
PACE PACE
Ah, I knew talking to you would make me feel better.
I have an idea!

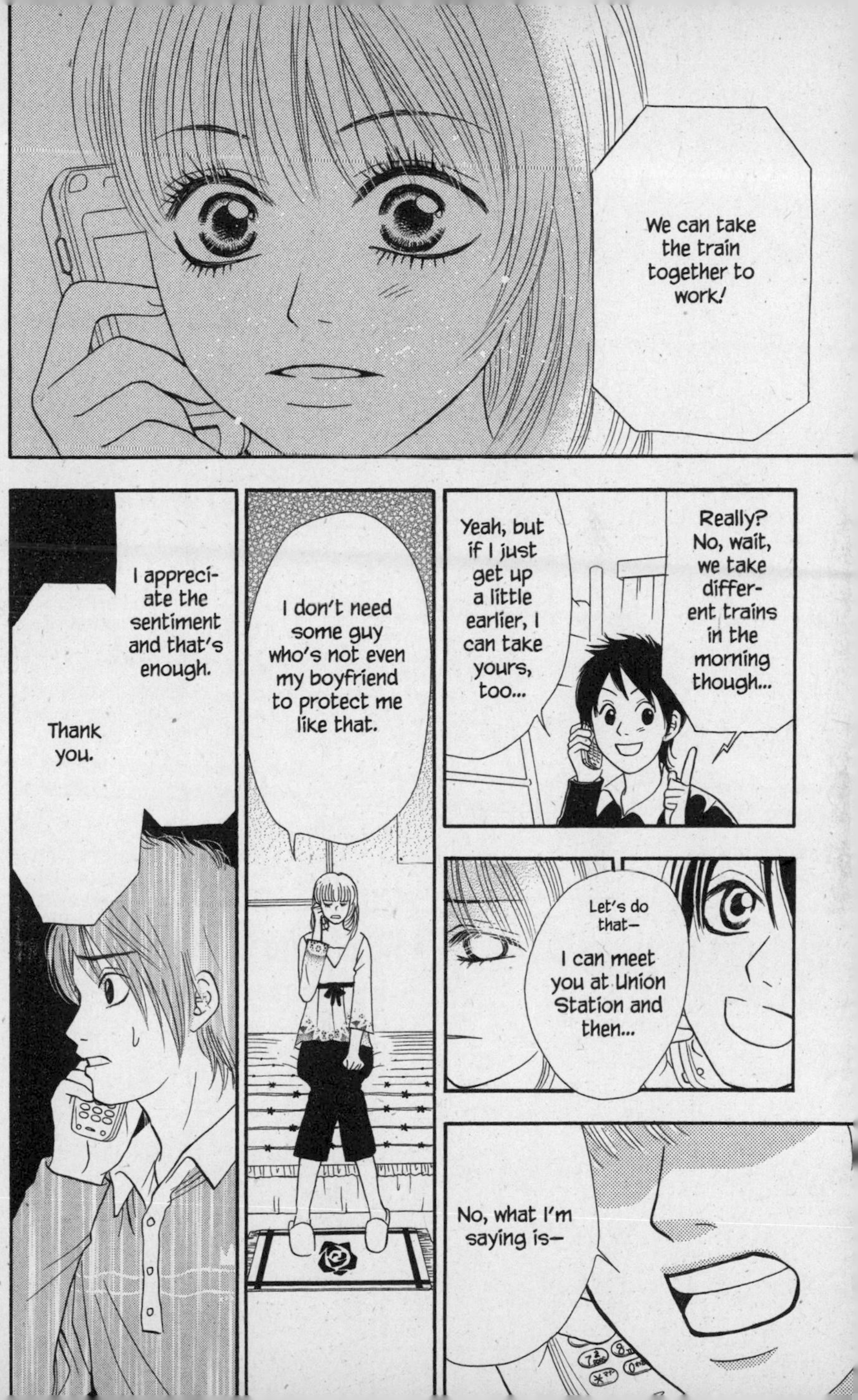
We can take the train together to work!
Really? No, wait, we take different trains in the morning though...
Yeah, but if I just get up a little earlier, I can take yours, too...
Let's do that—
I can meet you at Union Station and then...
No, what I'm saying is—
I don't need some guy who's not even my boyfriend to protect me like that.
I appreciate the sentiment and that's enough.
Thank you.

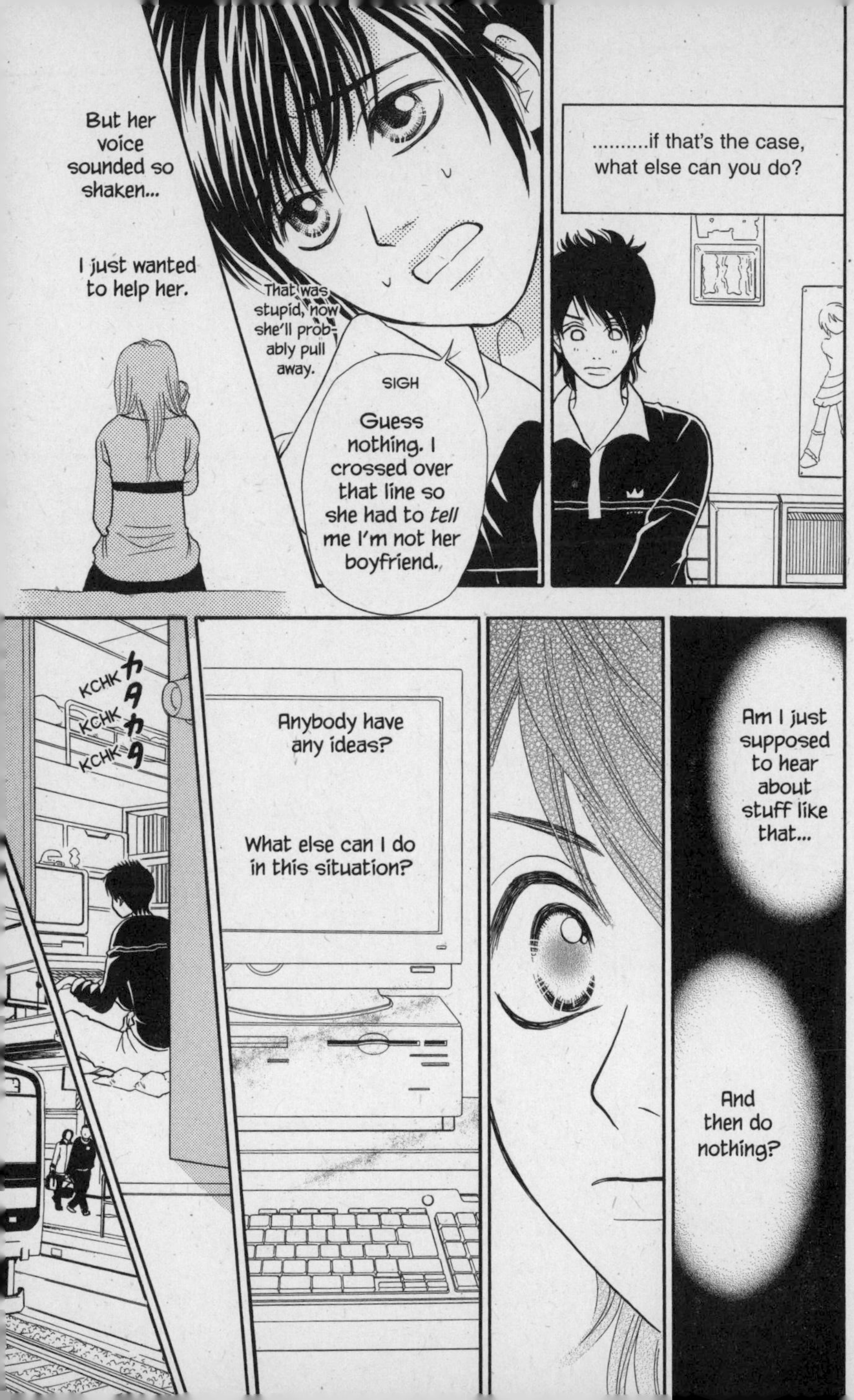
..........if that's the case, what else can you do?
That was stupid, now she'll probably pull away.
SIGH
Guess nothing. I crossed over that line so she had to *tell* me I'm not her boyfriend.
But her voice sounded so shaken...
I just wanted to help her.
Am I just supposed to hear about stuff like that...
And then do nothing?
Anybody have any ideas?
What else can I do in this situation?
KCHK KCHK KCHK
カタカタ

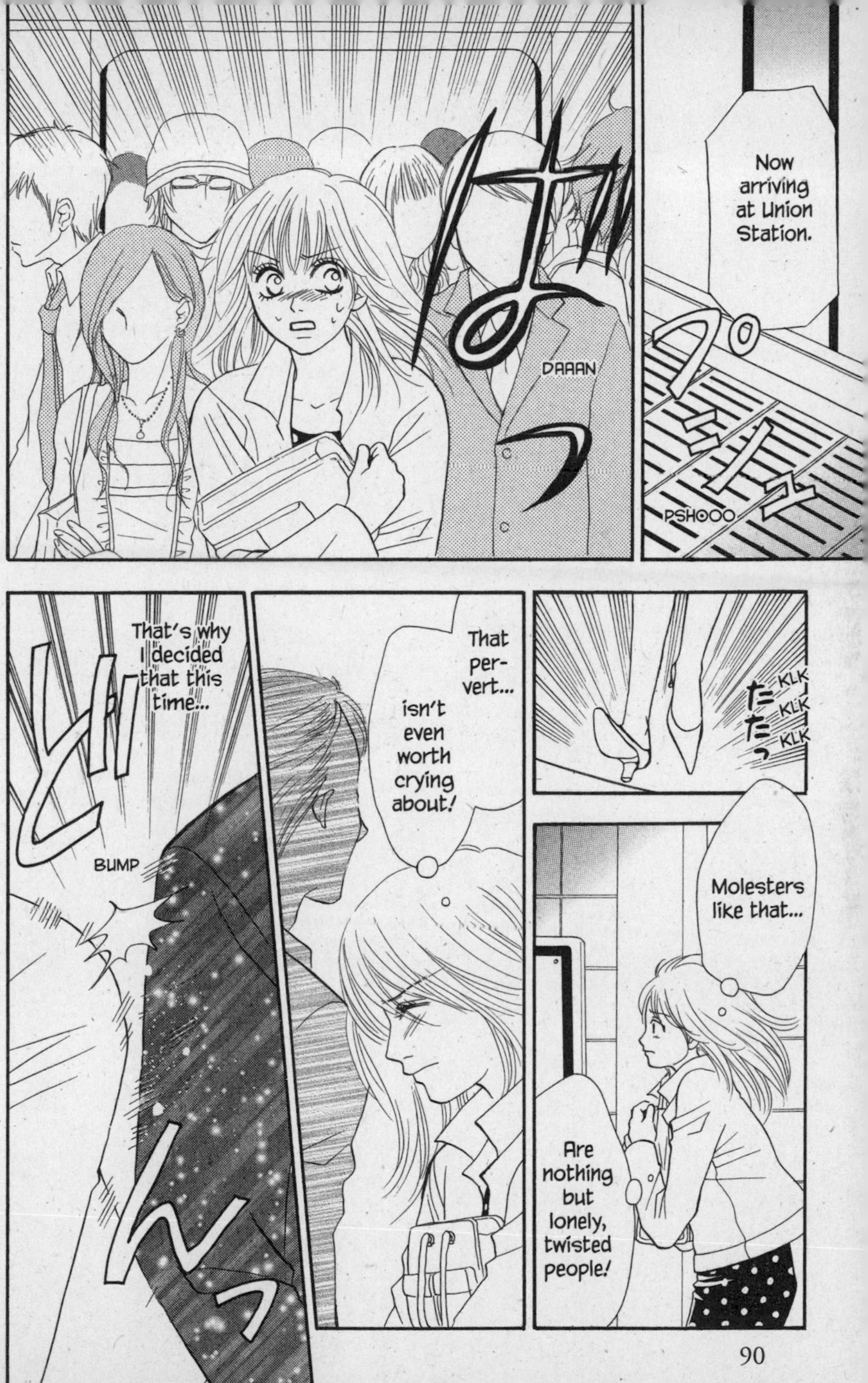
Now arriving at Union Station.
PSHOOO
DAAAN
たたっ
KLK KLK KLK
Molesters like that...
Are nothing but lonely, twisted people!
That per-vert...
isn't even worth crying about!
That's why I decided that this time...
BUMP

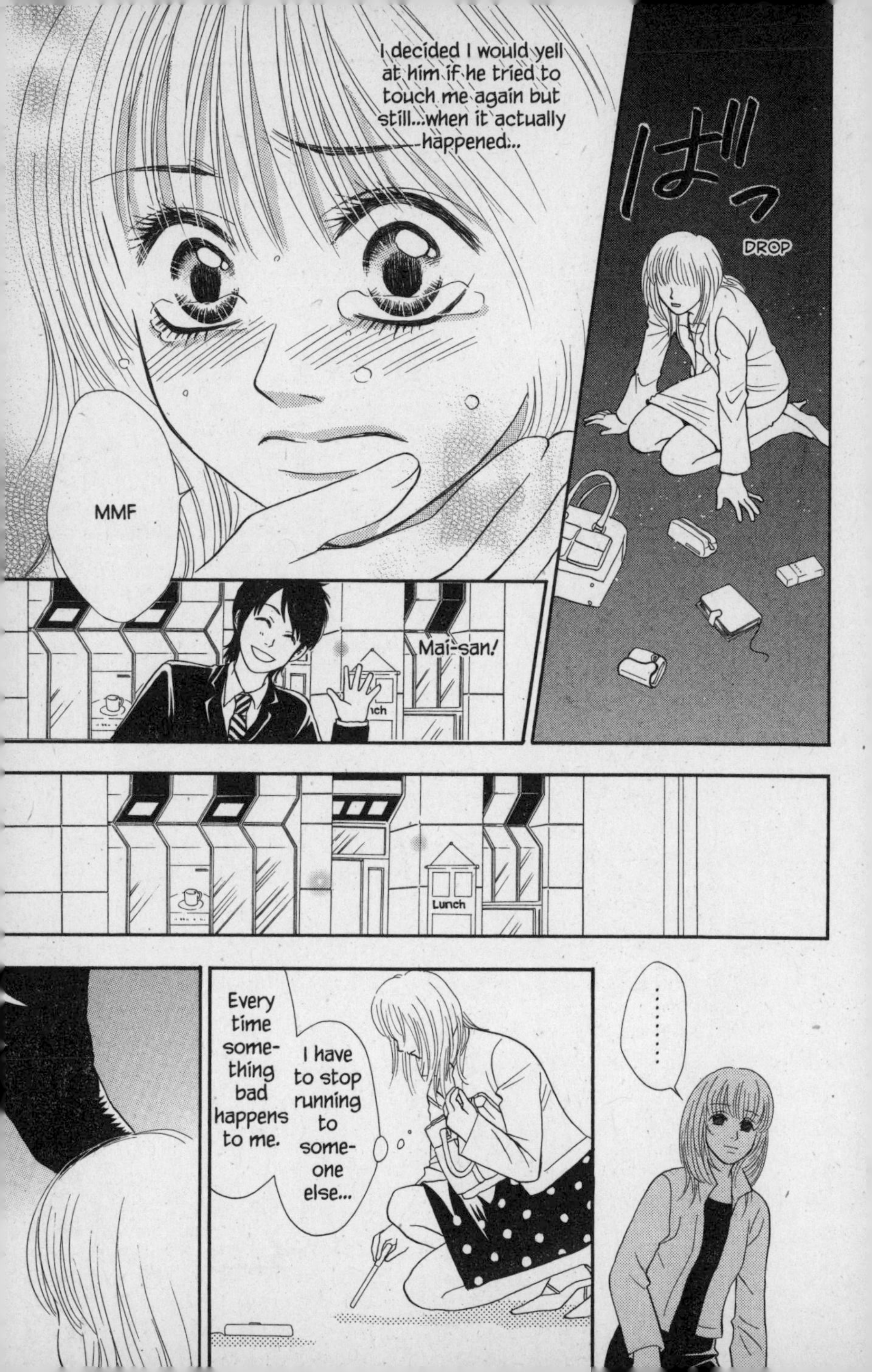
ばっ
DROP
I decided I would yell at him if he tried to touch me again but still...when it actually happened...
MMF
Mai-san!
Lunch
......
I have to stop running to someone else...
Every time something bad happens to me.

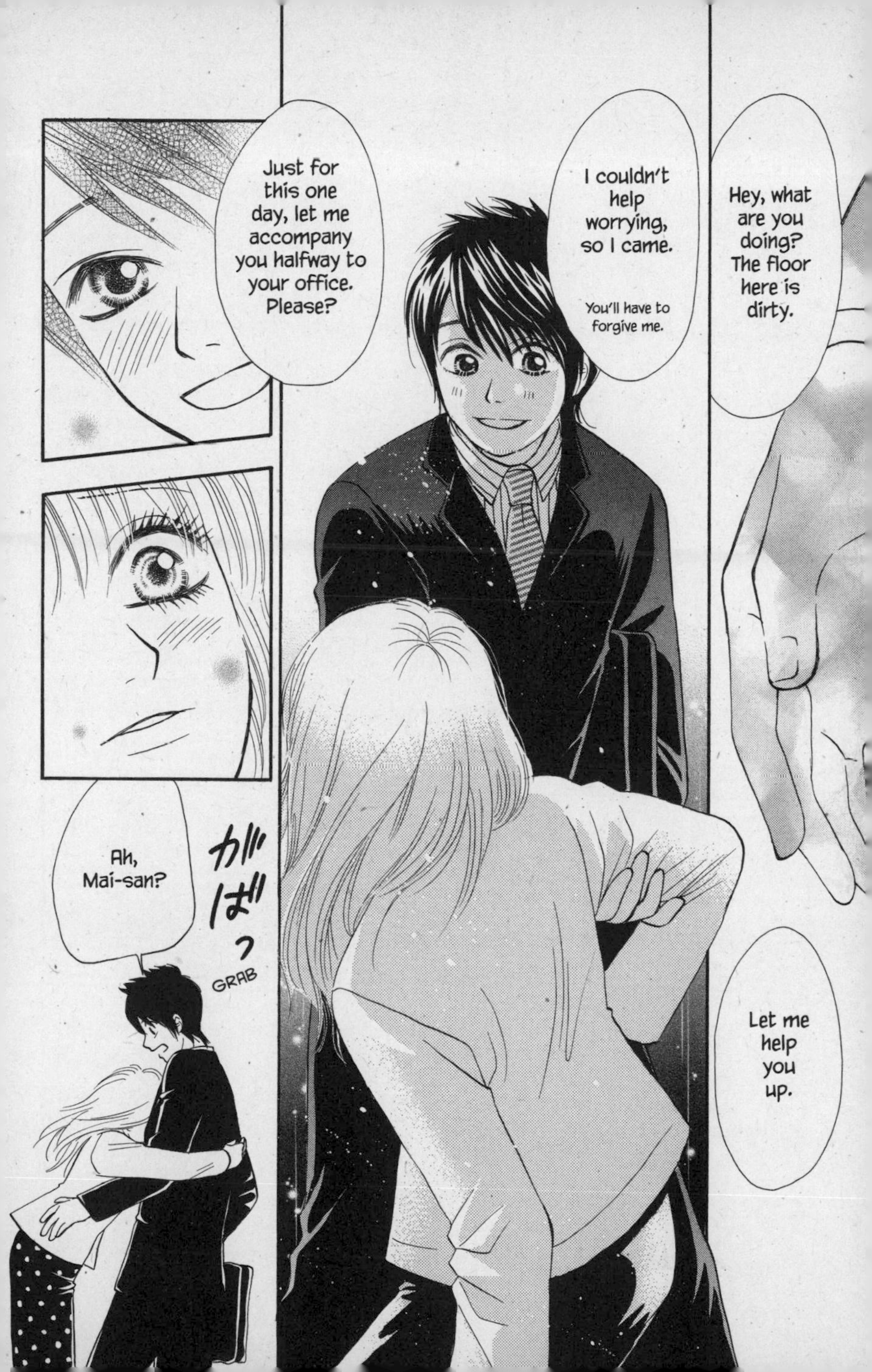
Hey, what are you doing? The floor here is dirty.
Let me help you up.
I couldn't help worrying, so I came.
You'll have to forgive me.
Just for this one day, let me accompany you halfway to your office. Please?
がばっ
GRAB
Ah, Mai-san?

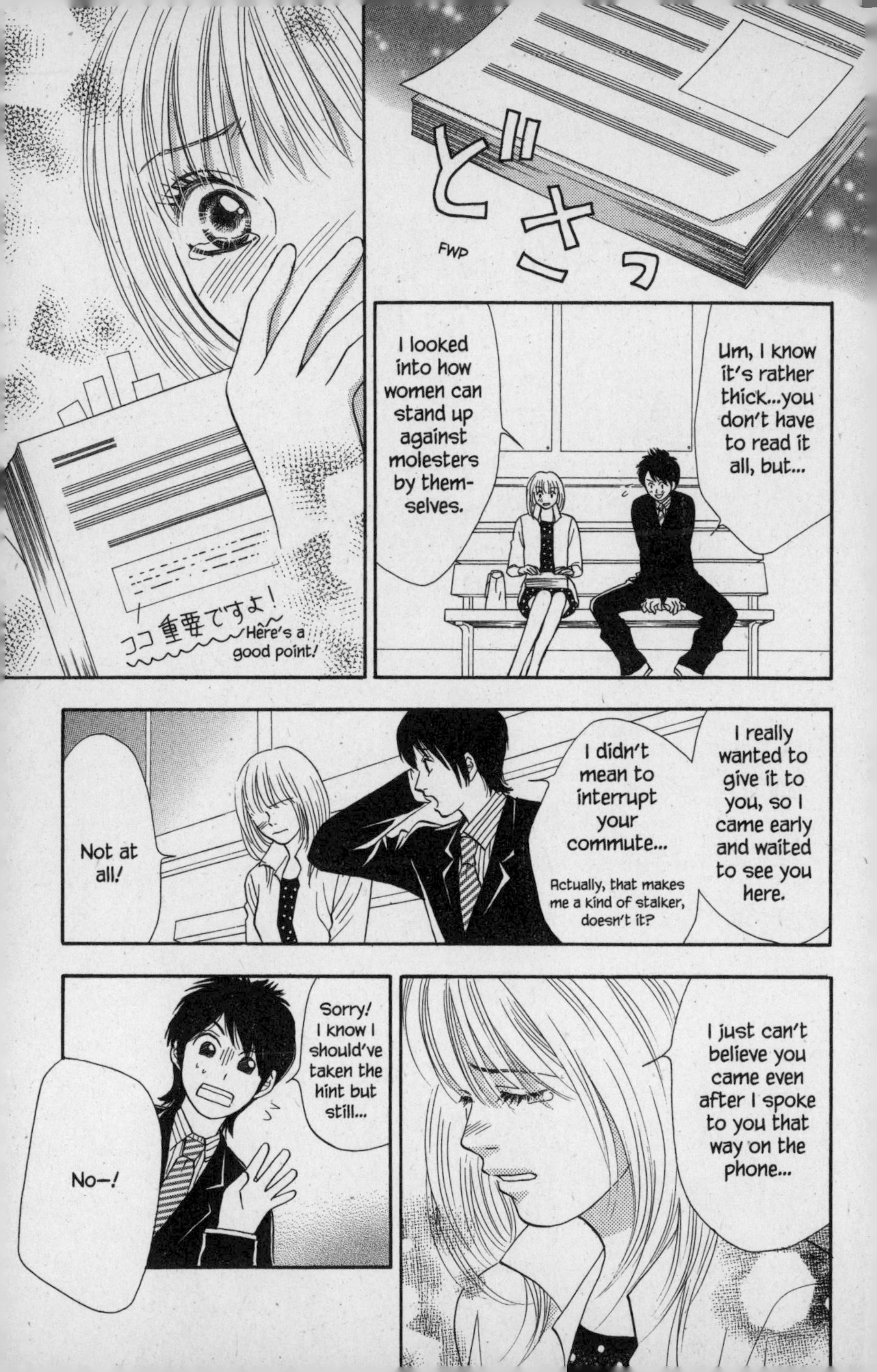
どさっ
FWP
Um, I know it's rather thick...you don't have to read it all, but...
I looked into how women can stand up against molesters by themselves.
ココ重要ですよ!
Here's a good point!
I really wanted to give it to you, so I came early and waited to see you here.
I didn't mean to interrupt your commute...
Actually, that makes me a kind of stalker, doesn't it?
Not at all!
I just can't believe you came even after I spoke to you that way on the phone...
Sorry! I know I should've taken the hint but still...
No—!

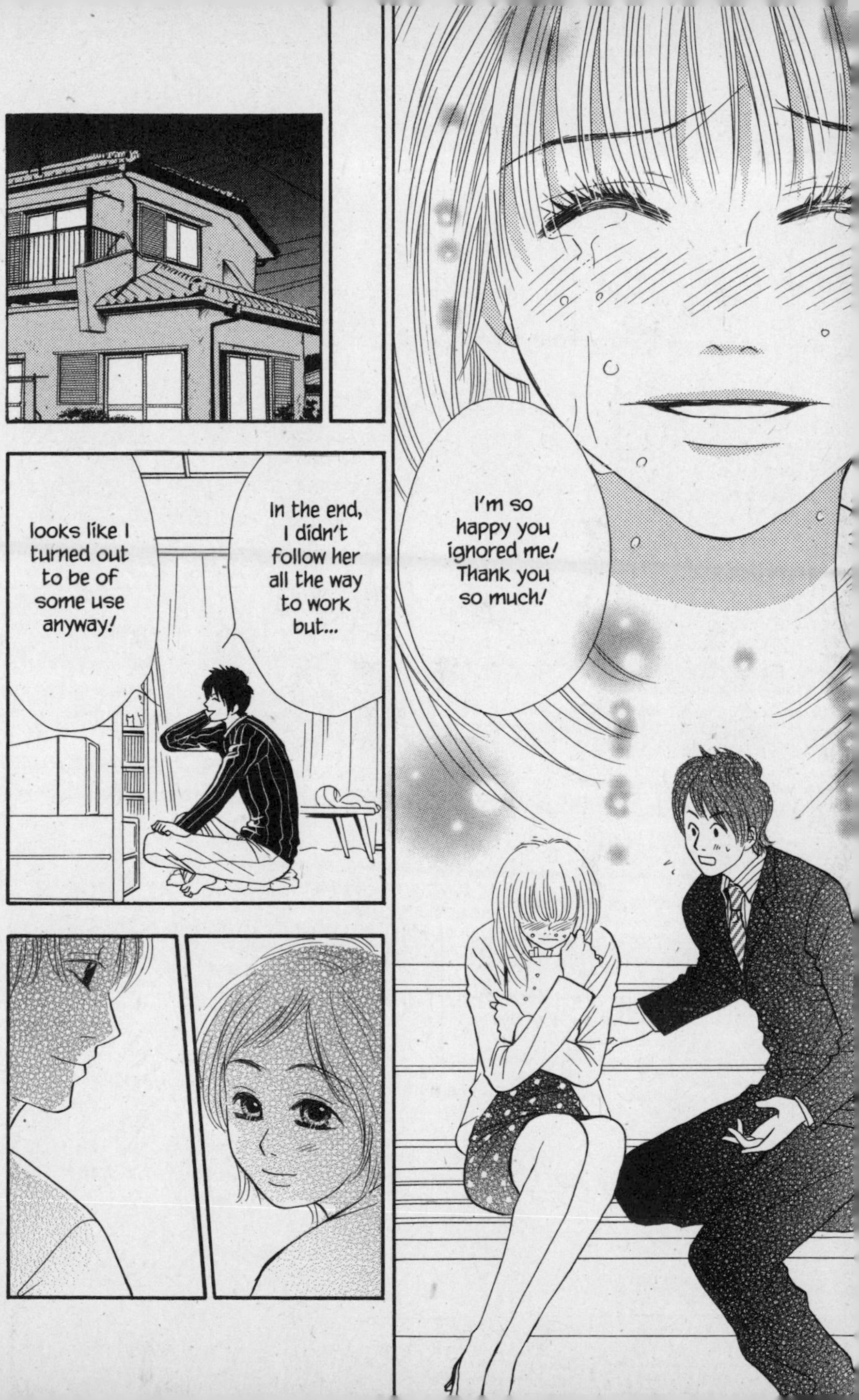
I'm so happy you ignored me! Thank you so much!
In the end, I didn't follow her all the way to work but...
looks like I turned out to be of some use anyway!

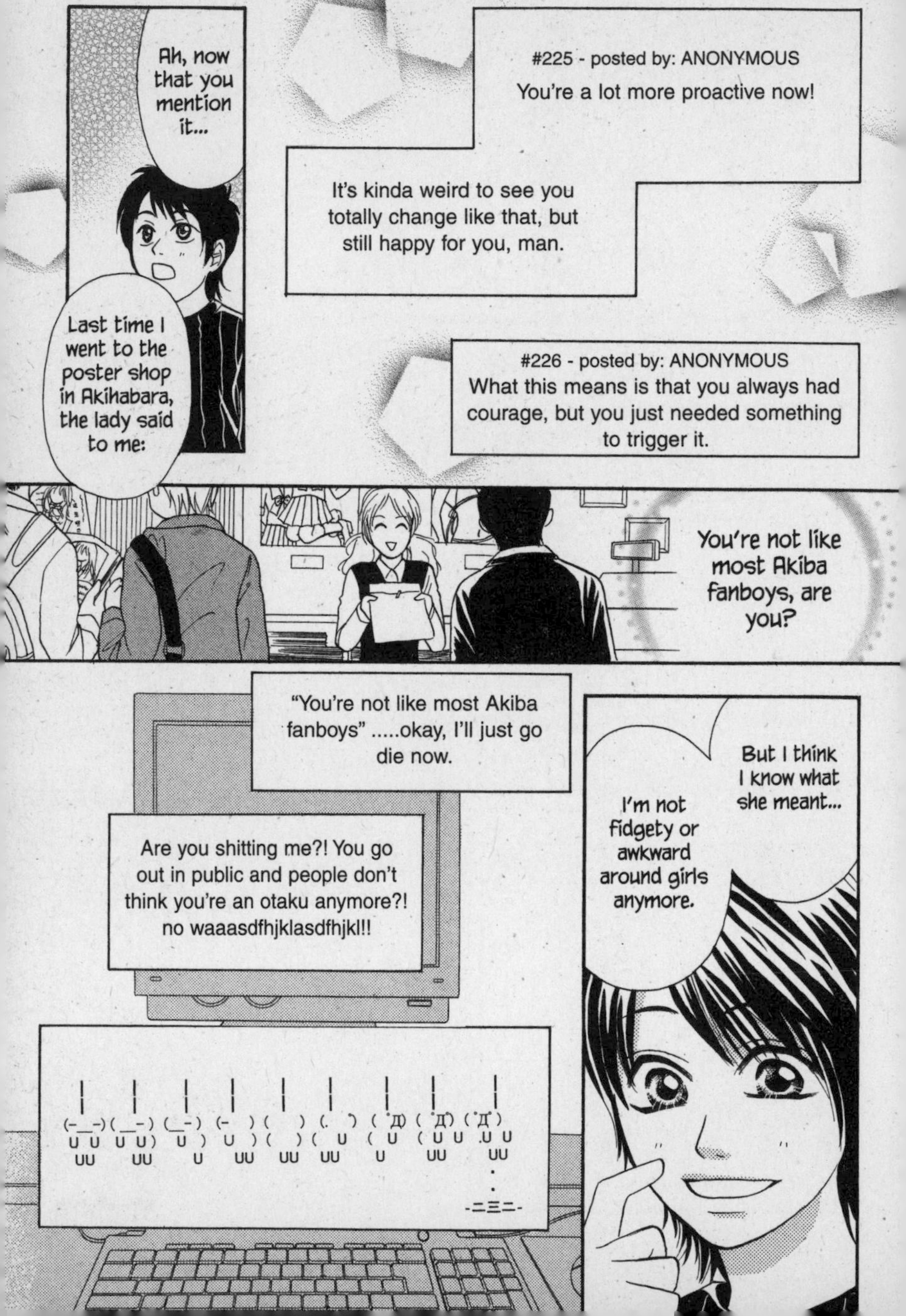
#225 - posted by: ANONYMOUS
You're a lot more proactive now!
It's kinda weird to see you totally change like that, but still happy for you, man.
#226 - posted by: ANONYMOUS
What this means is that you always had courage, but you just needed something to trigger it.
Ah, now that you mention it...
Last time I went to the poster shop in Akihabara, the lady said to me:
You're not like most Akiba fanboys, are you?
But I think I know what she meant...
I'm not fidgety or awkward around girls anymore.
"You're not like most Akiba fanboys" .....okay, I'll just go die now.
Are you shitting me?! You go out in public and people don't think you're an otaku anymore?! no waaasdfhjklasdfhjkl!!

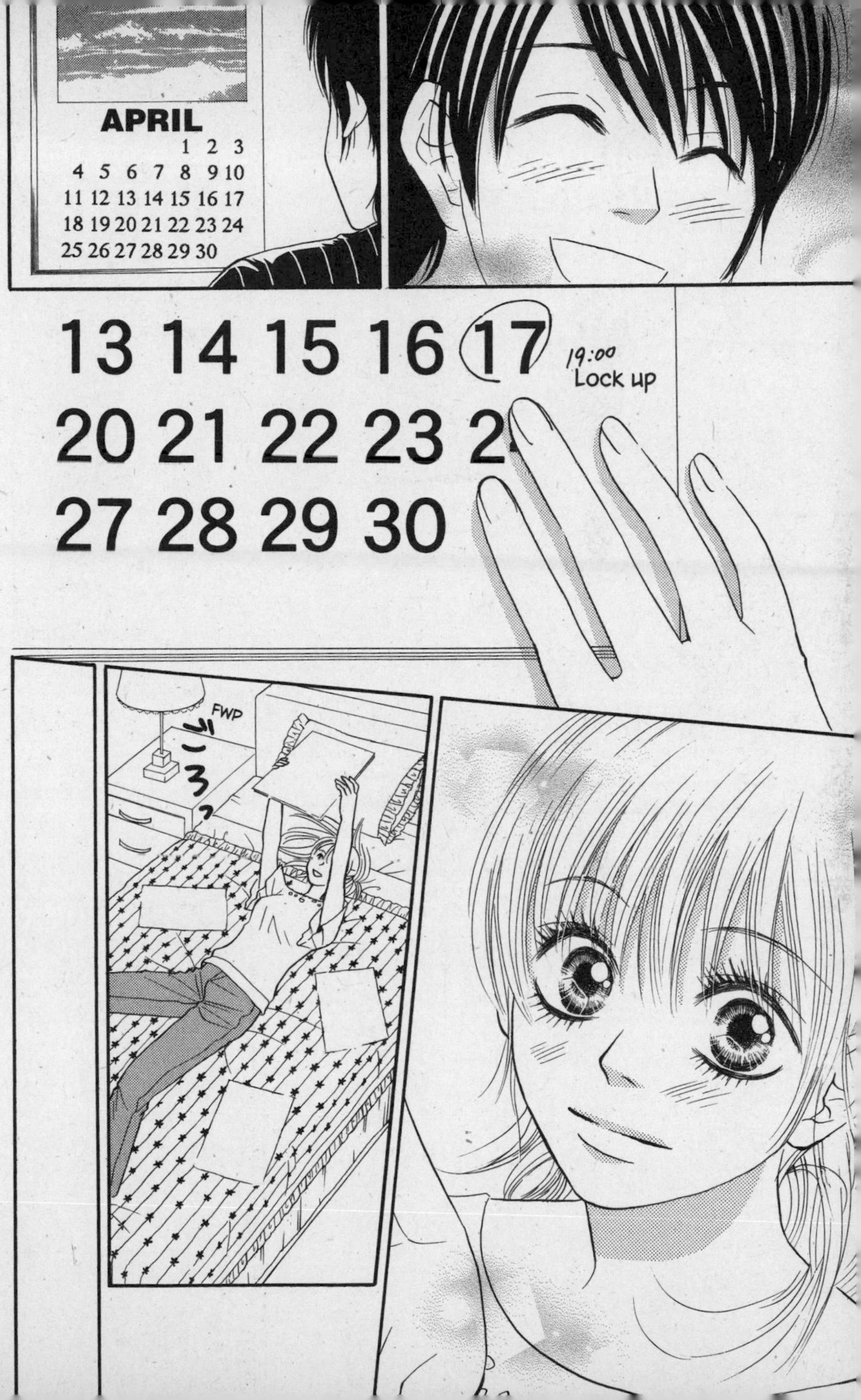
APRIL
1 2 3
4 5 6 7 8 9 10
11 12 13 14 15 16 17
18 19 20 21 22 23 24
25 26 27 28 29 30
13 14 15 16 17
20 21 22 23 24
27 28 29 30
19:00
Lock up
FWP

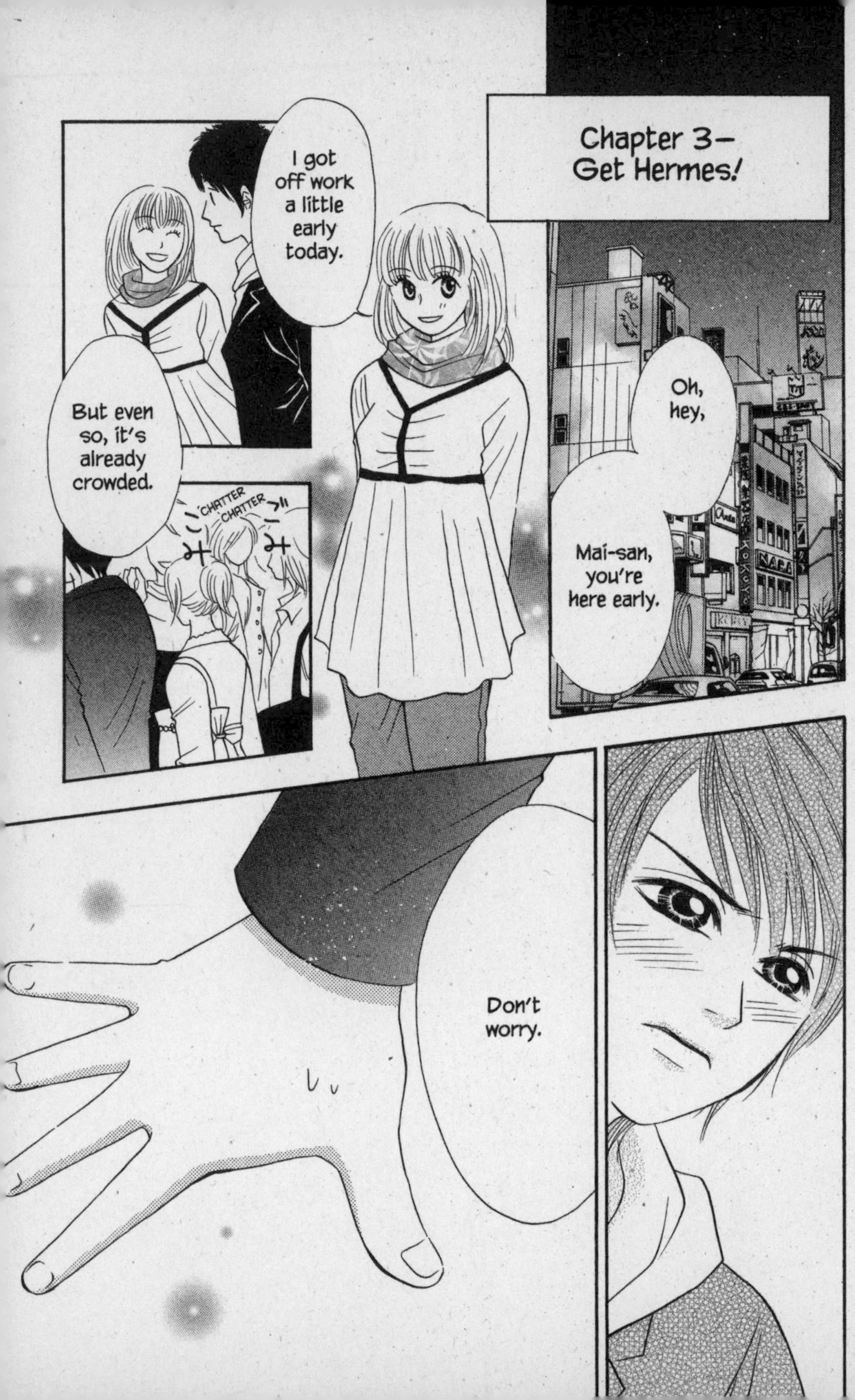
Chapter 3—
Get Hermes!
Oh, hey,
Mai-san, you're here early.
I got off work a little early today.
But even so, it's already crowded.
CHATTER CHATTER
Don't worry.

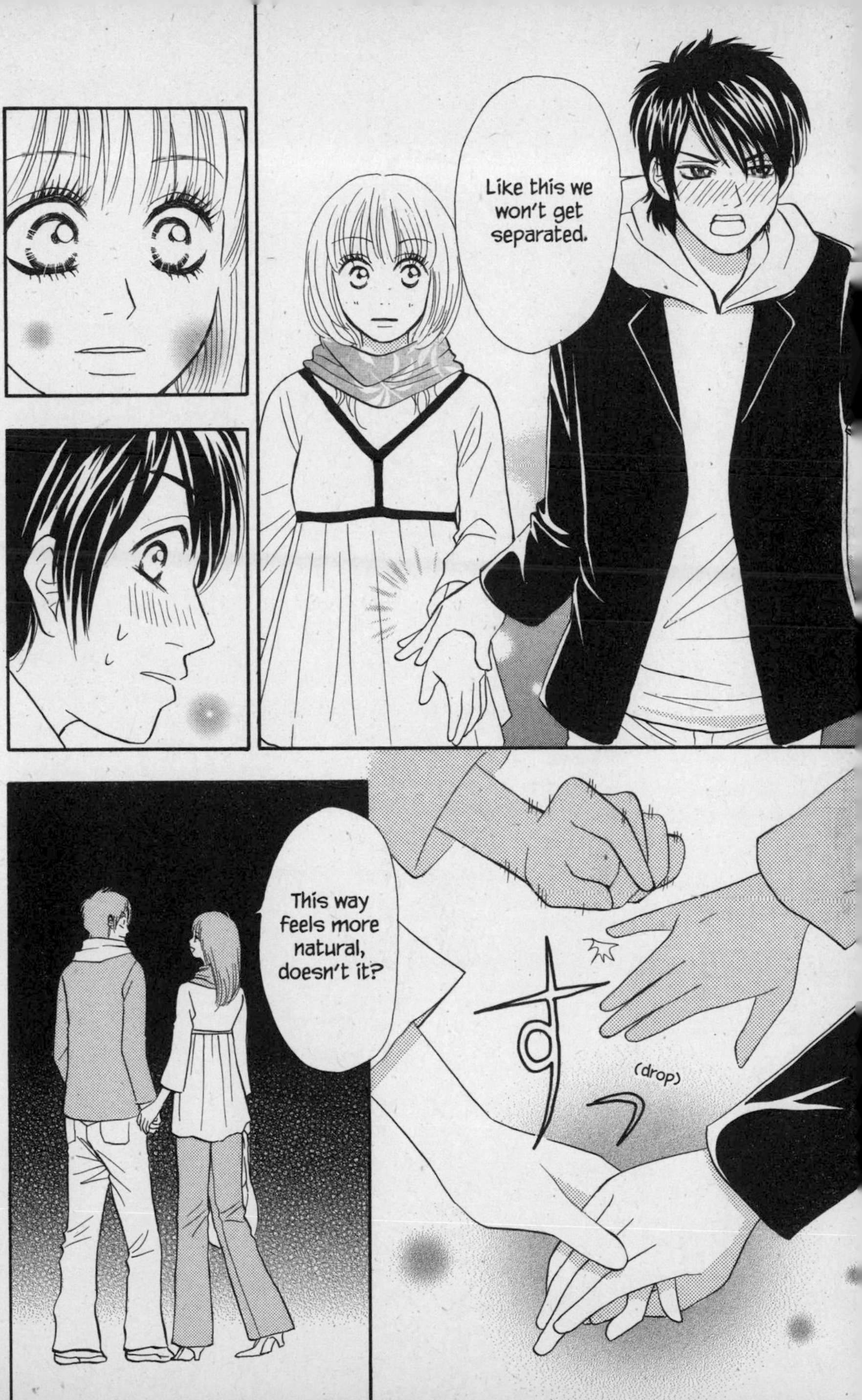

Like this we won't get separated.
す
(drop)
This way feels more natural, doesn't it?

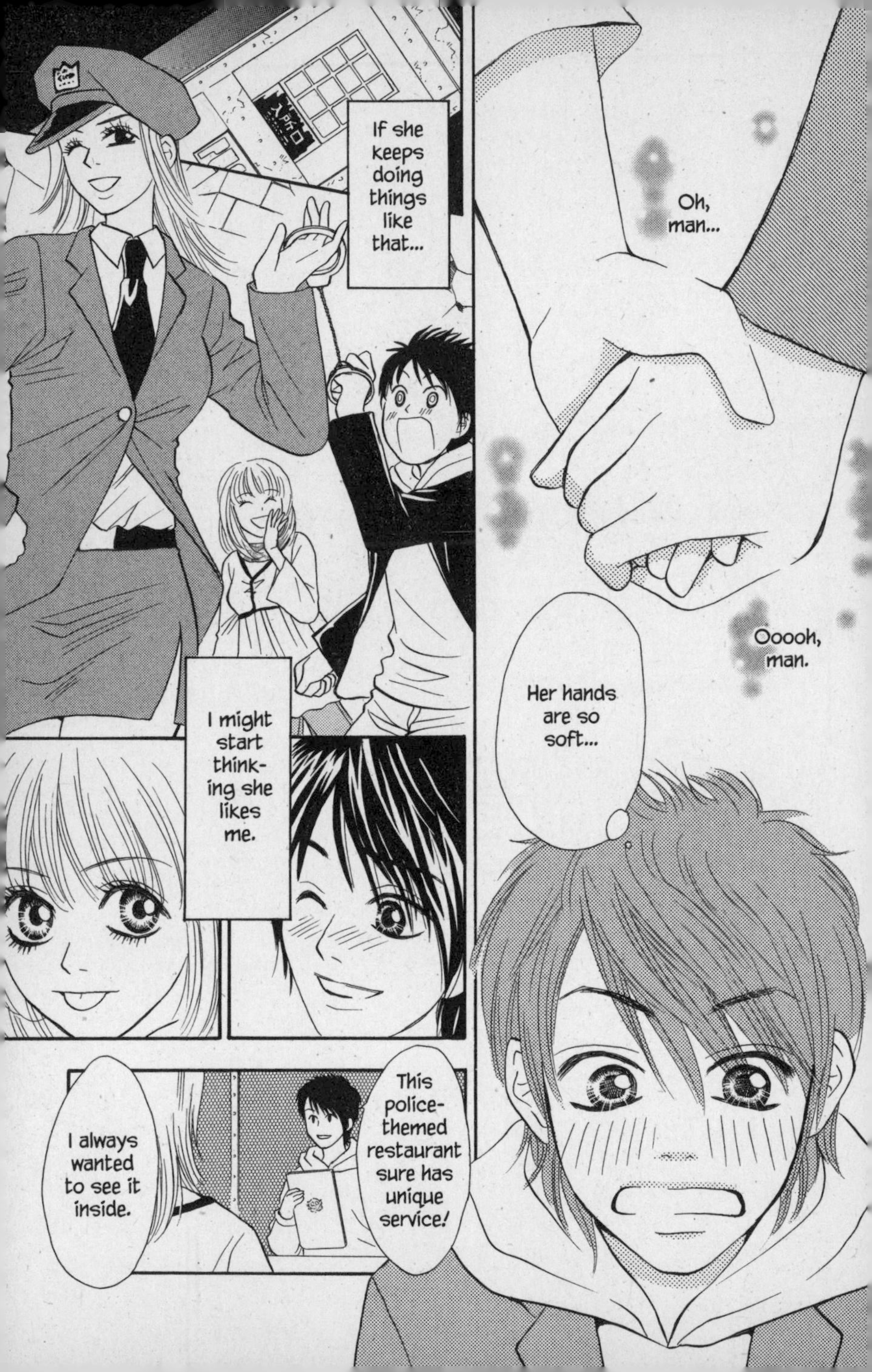

Oh, man...
Ooooh, man.
Her hands are so soft...
If she keeps doing things like that...
I might start think-ing she likes me.
This police-themed restaurant sure has unique service!
I always wanted to see it inside.

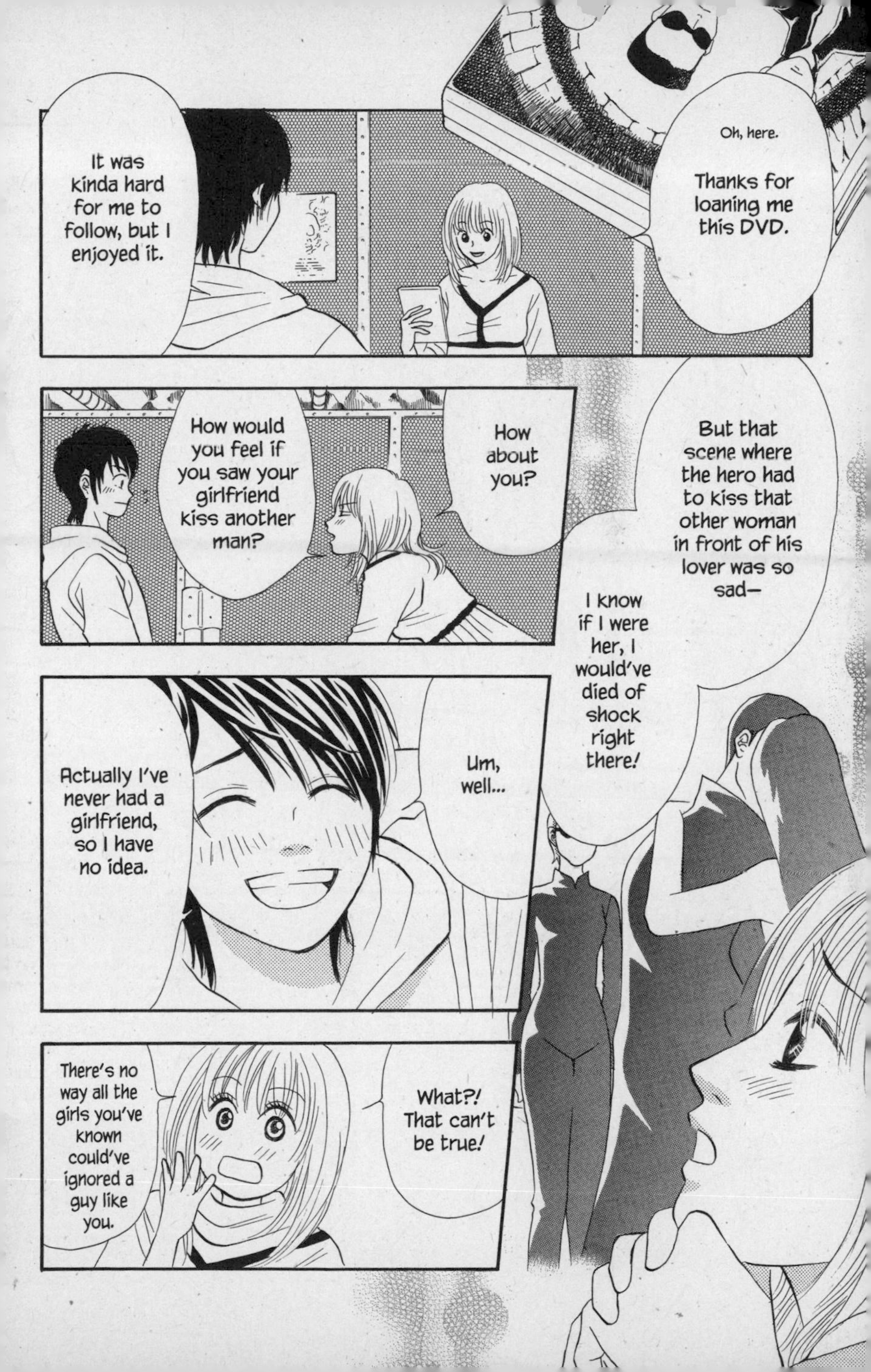

Oh, here.
Thanks for loaning me this DVD.
It was kinda hard for me to follow, but I enjoyed it.
But that scene where the hero had to kiss that other woman in front of his lover was so sad—
I know if I were her, I would've died of shock right there!
How about you?
How would you feel if you saw your girlfriend kiss another man?
Um, well...
Actually I've never had a girlfriend, so I have no idea.
What?! That can't be true!
There's no way all the girls you've known could've ignored a guy like you.

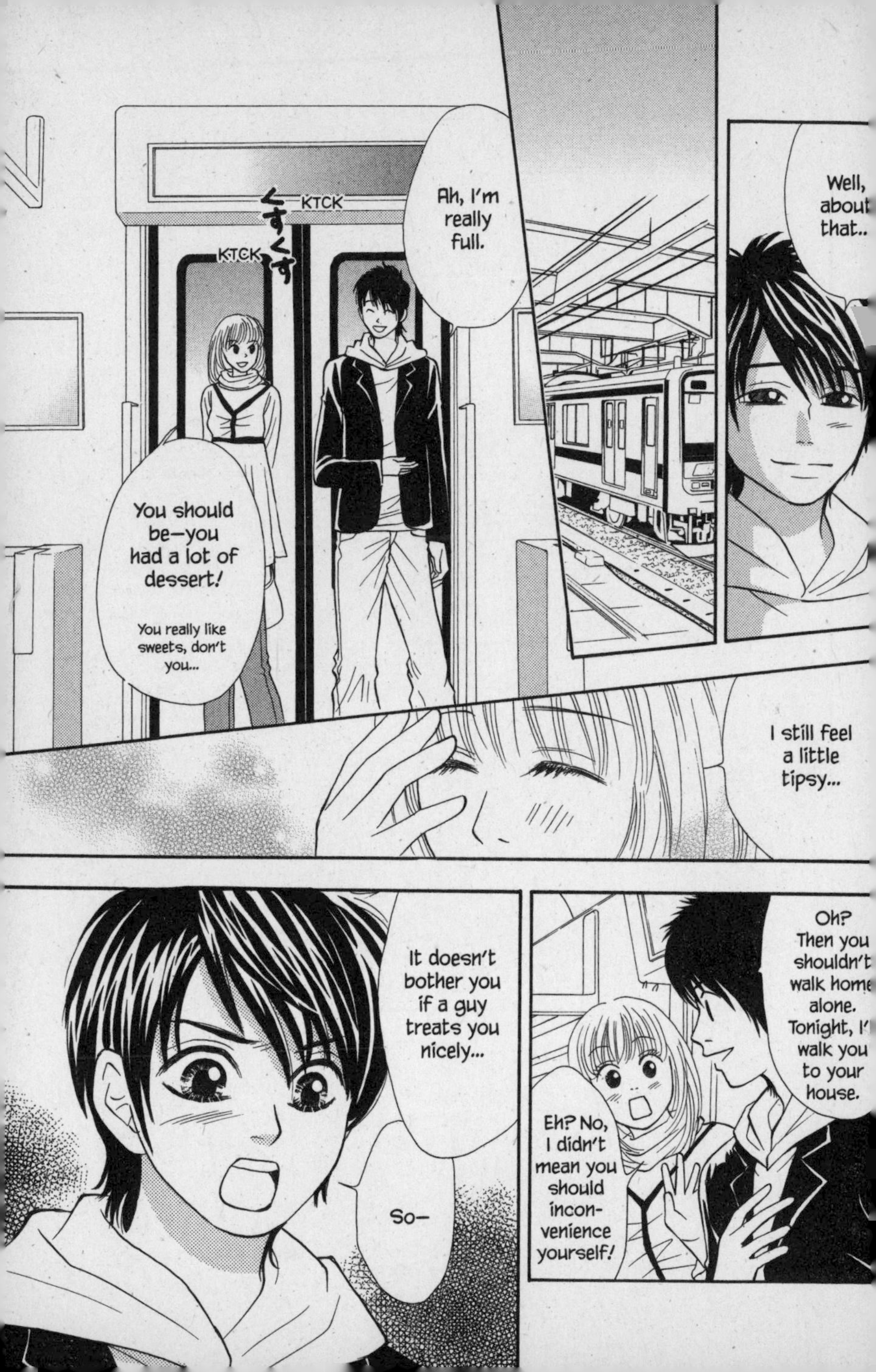
Well, about that...
Ah, I'm really full.
KTCK
KTCK
くすくす
You should be—you had a lot of dessert!
You really like sweets, don't you...
I still feel a little tipsy...
Oh? Then you shouldn't walk home alone. Tonight, I' walk you to your house.
Eh? No, I didn't mean you should incon-venience yourself!
It doesn't bother you if a guy treats you nicely...
So—

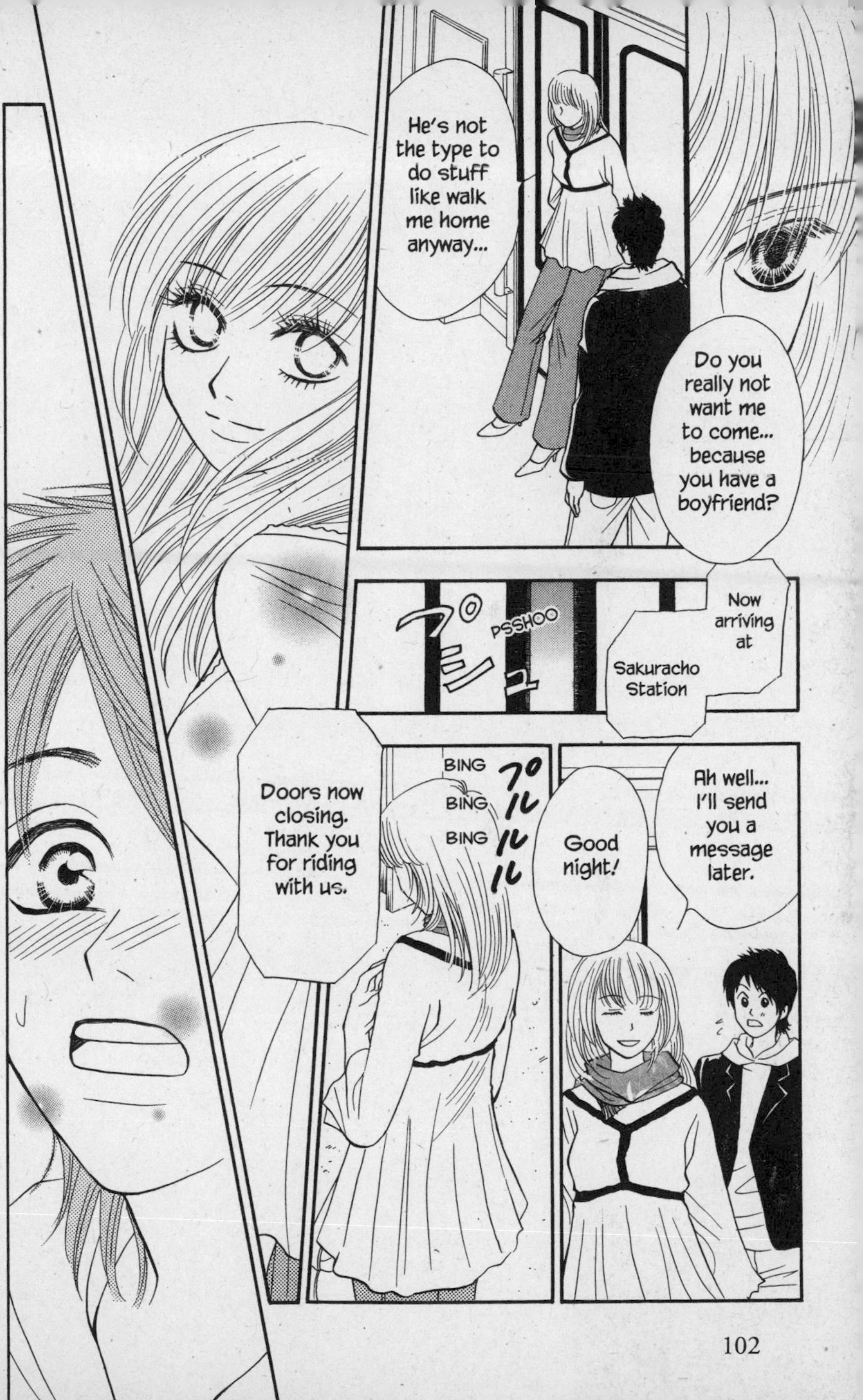
He's not the type to do stuff like walk me home anyway...
Do you really not want me to come... because you have a boyfriend?
Now arriving at
Sakuracho Station
PSSHOO
Ah well... I'll send you a message later.
Good night!
BING
BING
BING
Doors now closing. Thank you for riding with us.

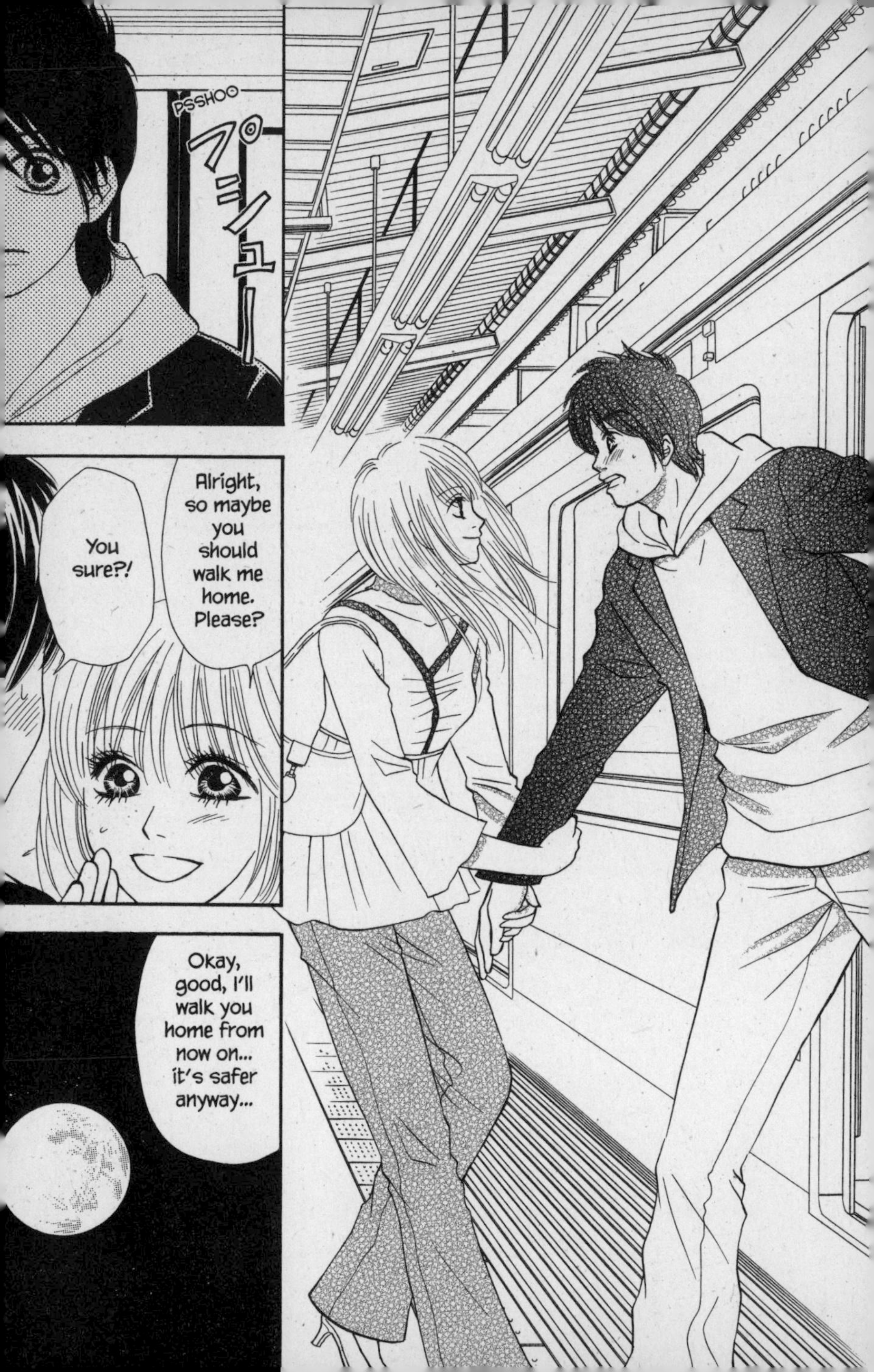
PSSHOO
プシュー
Alright, so maybe you should walk me home. Please?
You sure?!
Okay, good, I'll walk you home from now on... it's safer anyway...

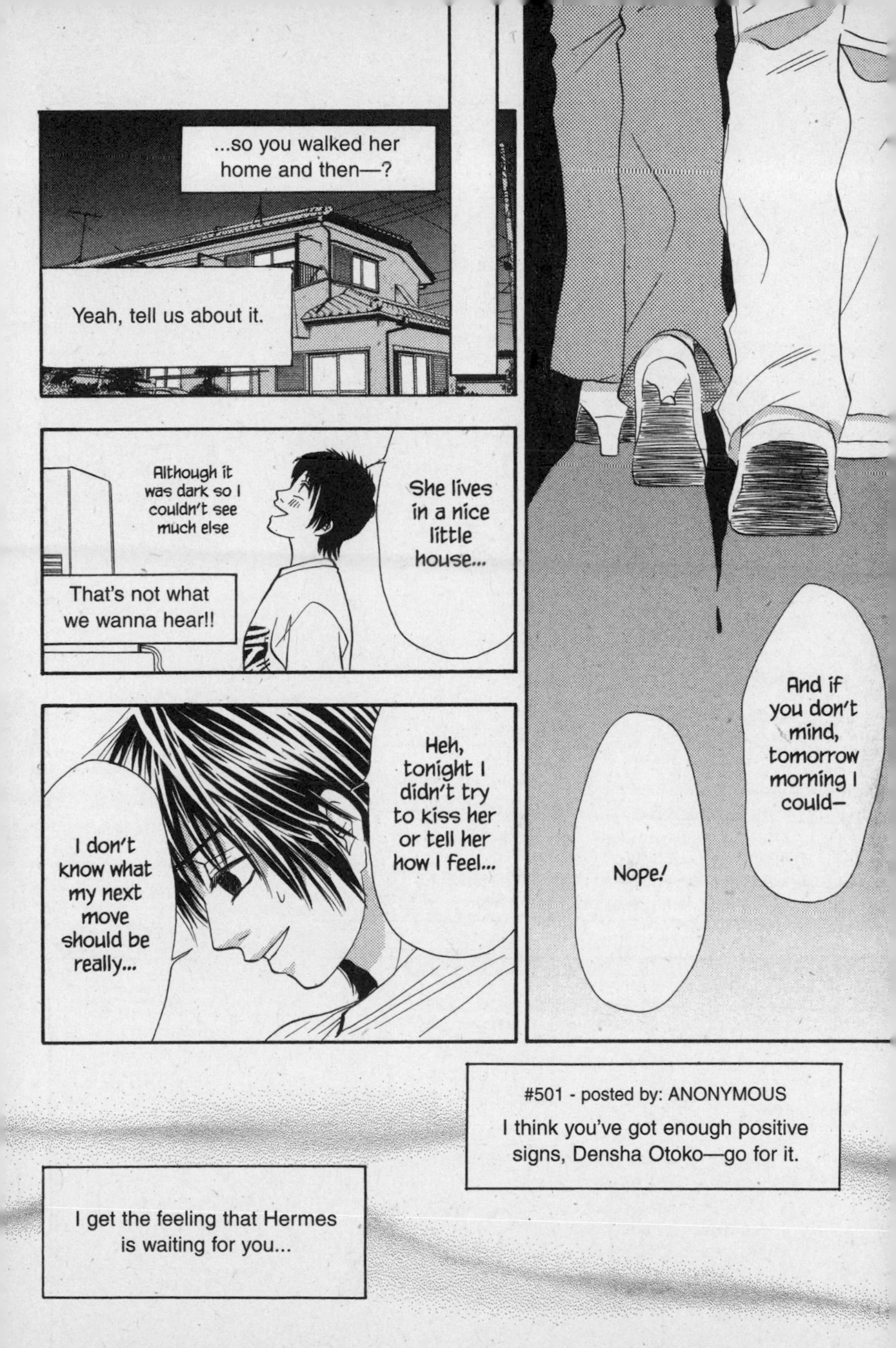
And if you don't mind, tomorrow morning I could–
Nope!
...so you walked her home and then—?
Yeah, tell us about it.
She lives in a nice little house...
Although it was dark so I couldn't see much else
That's not what we wanna hear!!
Heh, tonight I didn't try to kiss her or tell her how I feel...
I don't know what my next move should be really...
#501 - posted by: ANONYMOUS
I think you've got enough positive signs, Densha Otoko—go for it.
I get the feeling that Hermes is waiting for you...

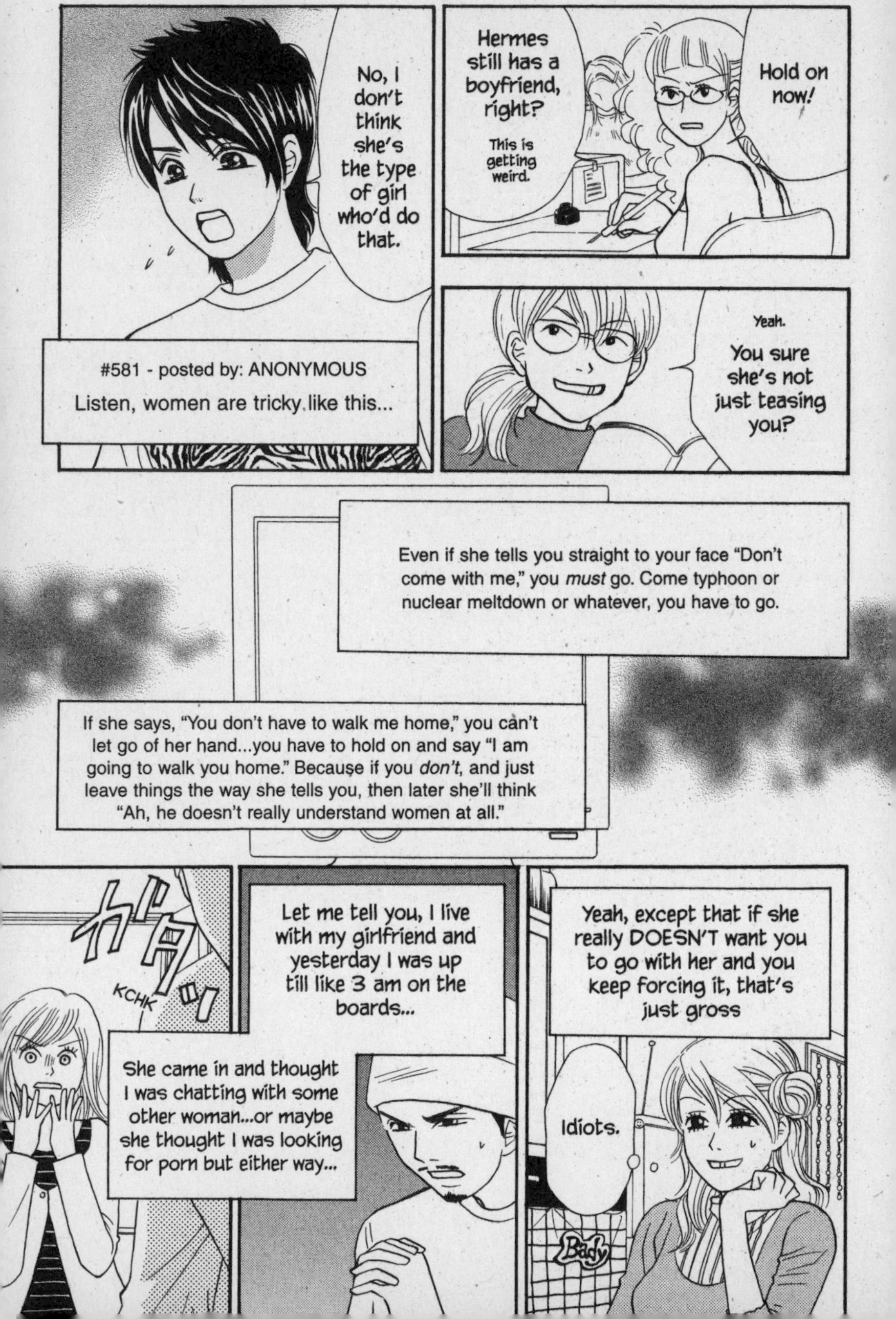
Hold on now!
Hermes still has a boyfriend, right?
This is getting weird.
Yeah.
You sure she's not just teasing you?
No, I don't think she's the type of girl who'd do that.
#581 - posted by: ANONYMOUS
Listen, women are tricky like this...
Even if she tells you straight to your face "Don't come with me," you *must* go. Come typhoon or nuclear meltdown or whatever, you have to go.
If she says, "You don't have to walk me home," you can't let go of her hand...you have to hold on and say "I am going to walk you home." Because if you *don't*, and just leave things the way she tells you, then later she'll think "Ah, he doesn't really understand women at all."
Yeah, except that if she really DOESN'T want you to go with her and you keep forcing it, that's just gross
Idiots.
Bady
Let me tell you, I live with my girlfriend and yesterday I was up till like 3 am on the boards...
She came in and thought I was chatting with some other woman...or maybe she thought I was looking for porn but either way...
KCHK

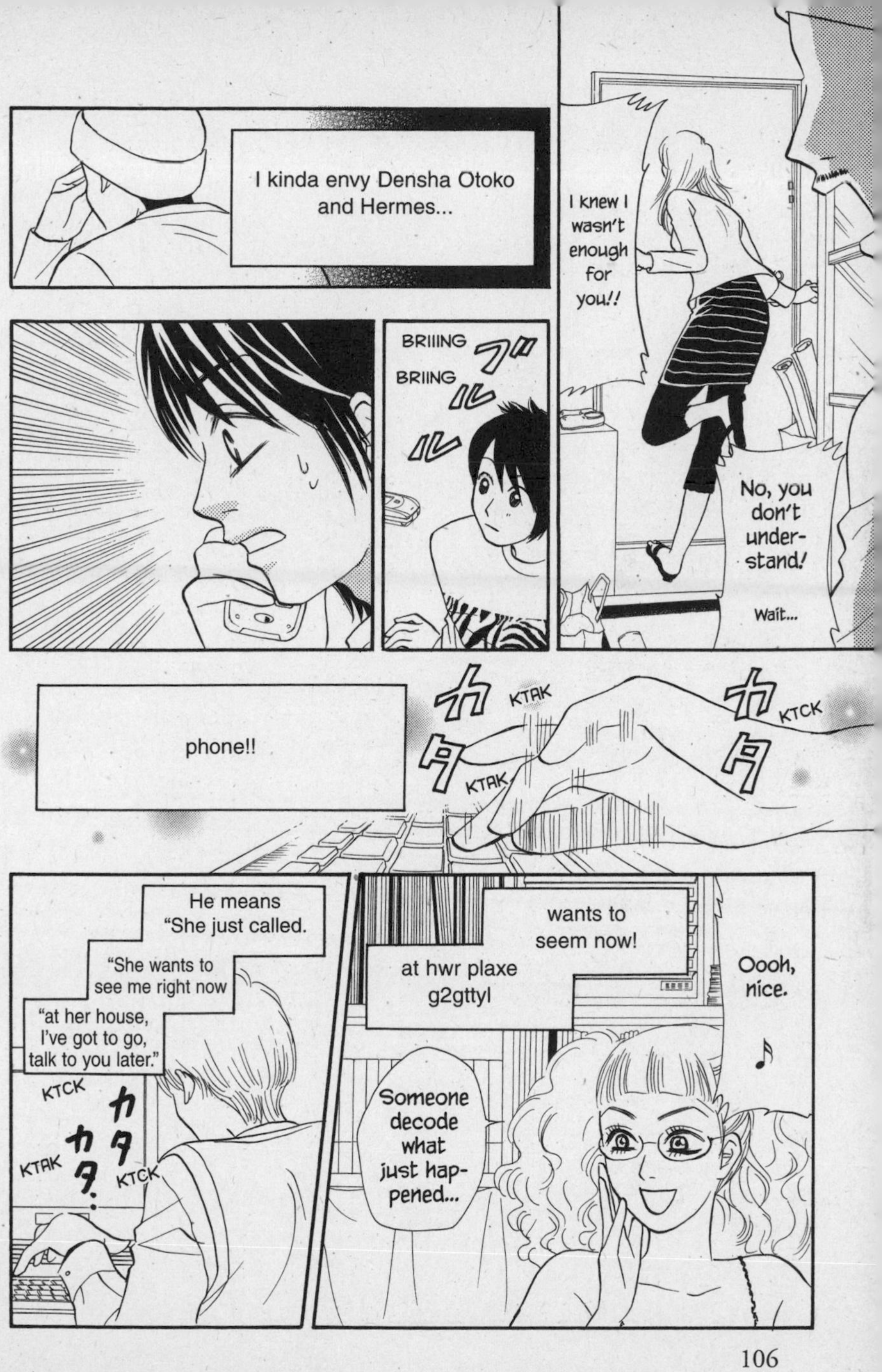
I knew I wasn't enough for you!!
No, you don't understand!
Wait...
I kinda envy Densha Otoko and Hermes...
BRIIING
BRIING
ブルル
KTCK
カタ
KTAK
カタ
KTAK
phone!!
wants to seem now!
at hwr plaxe g2gttyl
Oooh, nice.
Someone decode what just happened...
He means "She just called.
"She wants to see me right now
"at her house, I've got to go, talk to you later."
KTCK
カタ
カタ
KTAK
KTCK

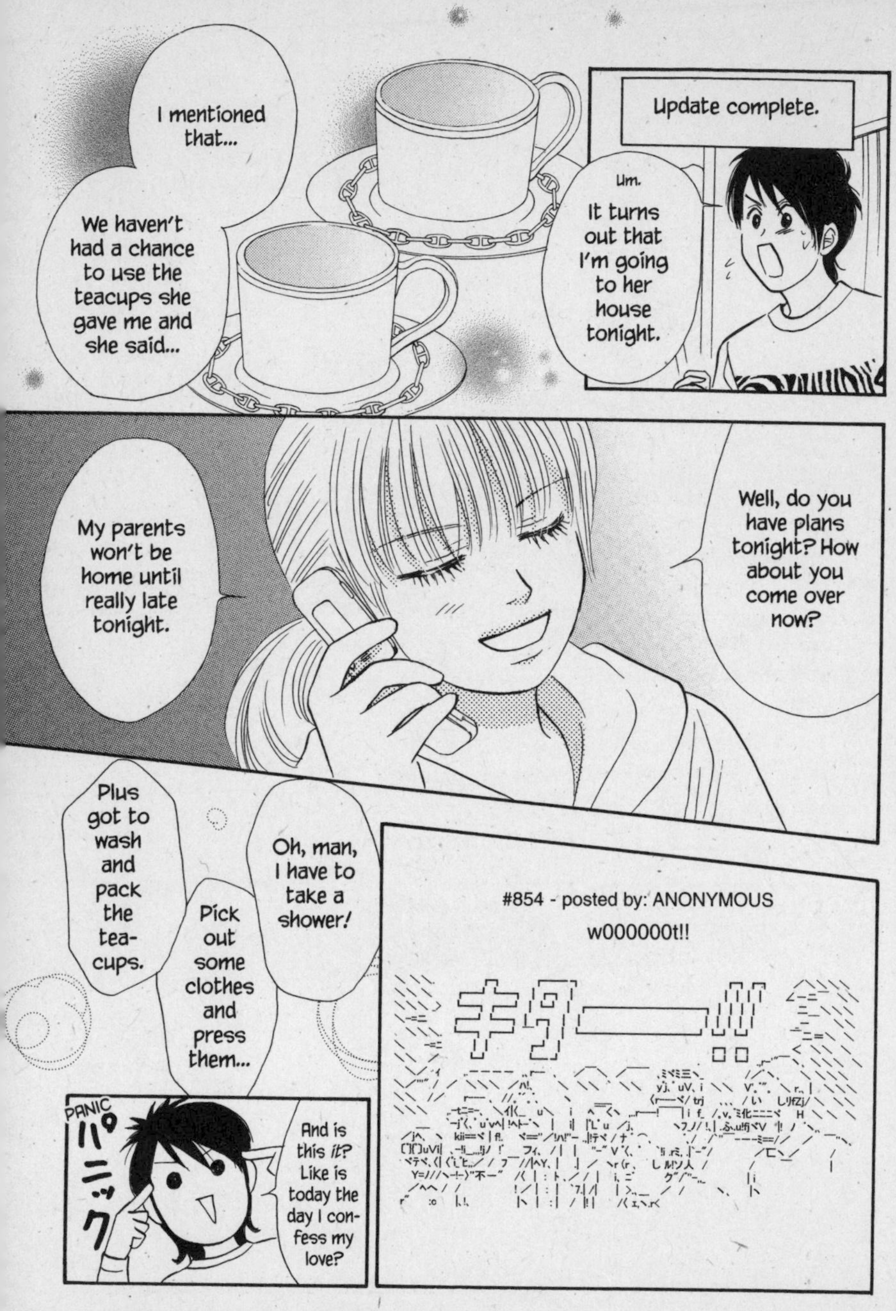
Update complete.
Um. It turns out that I'm going to her house tonight.
I mentioned that...
We haven't had a chance to use the teacups she gave me and she said...
Well, do you have plans tonight? How about you come over now?
My parents won't be home until really late tonight.
#854 - posted by: ANONYMOUS
w000000t!!
Oh, man, I have to take a shower!
Pick out some clothes and press them...
Plus got to wash and pack the tea-cups.
And is this it? Like is today the day I confess my love?
PANIC
パニック

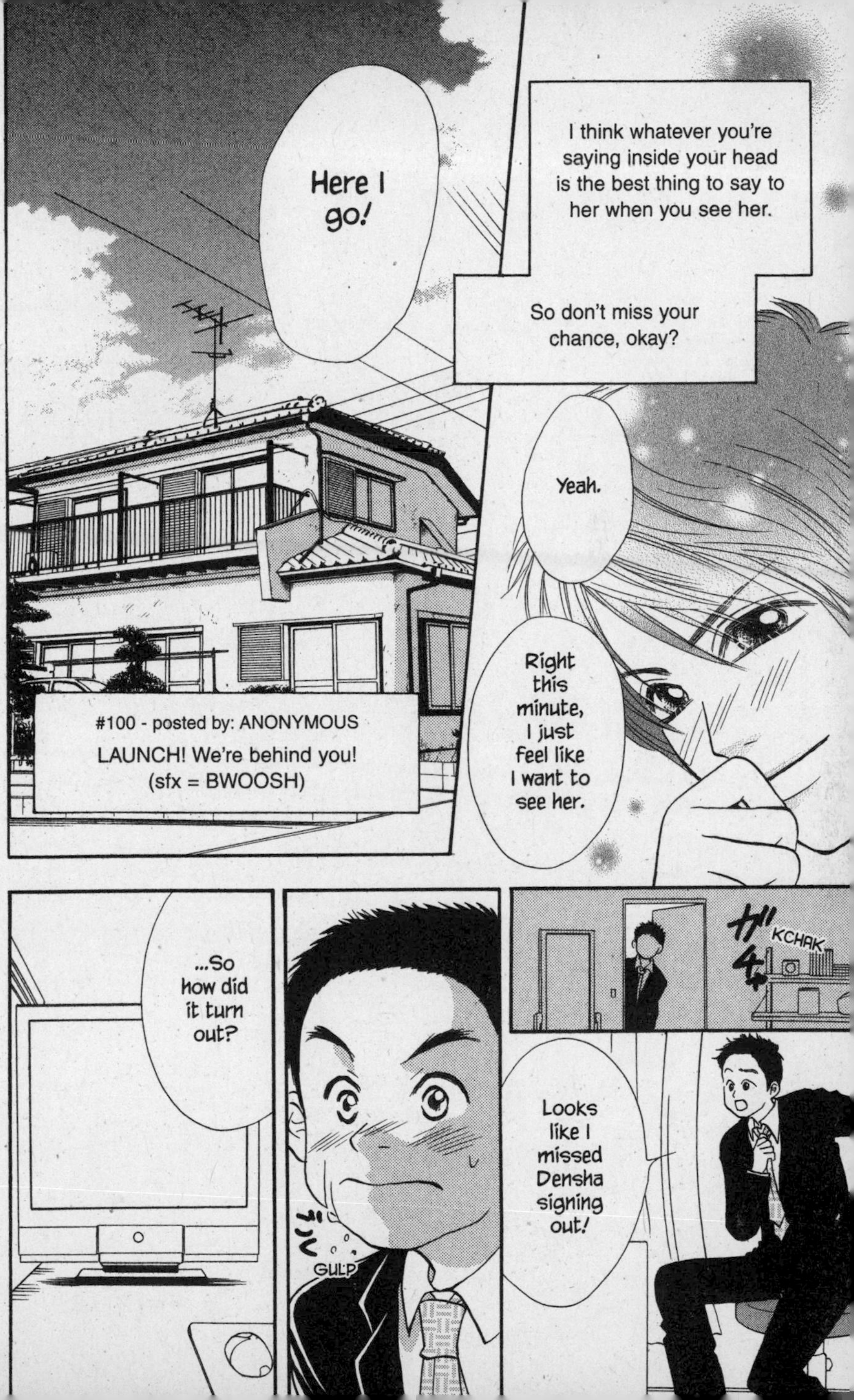
I think whatever you're saying inside your head is the best thing to say to her when you see her.
So don't miss your chance, okay?
Yeah.
Right this minute, I just feel like I want to see her.
Here I go!
#100 - posted by: ANONYMOUS
LAUNCH! We're behind you!
(sfx = BWOOSH)
KCHAK
Looks like I missed Densha signing out!
GULP
...So how did it turn out?

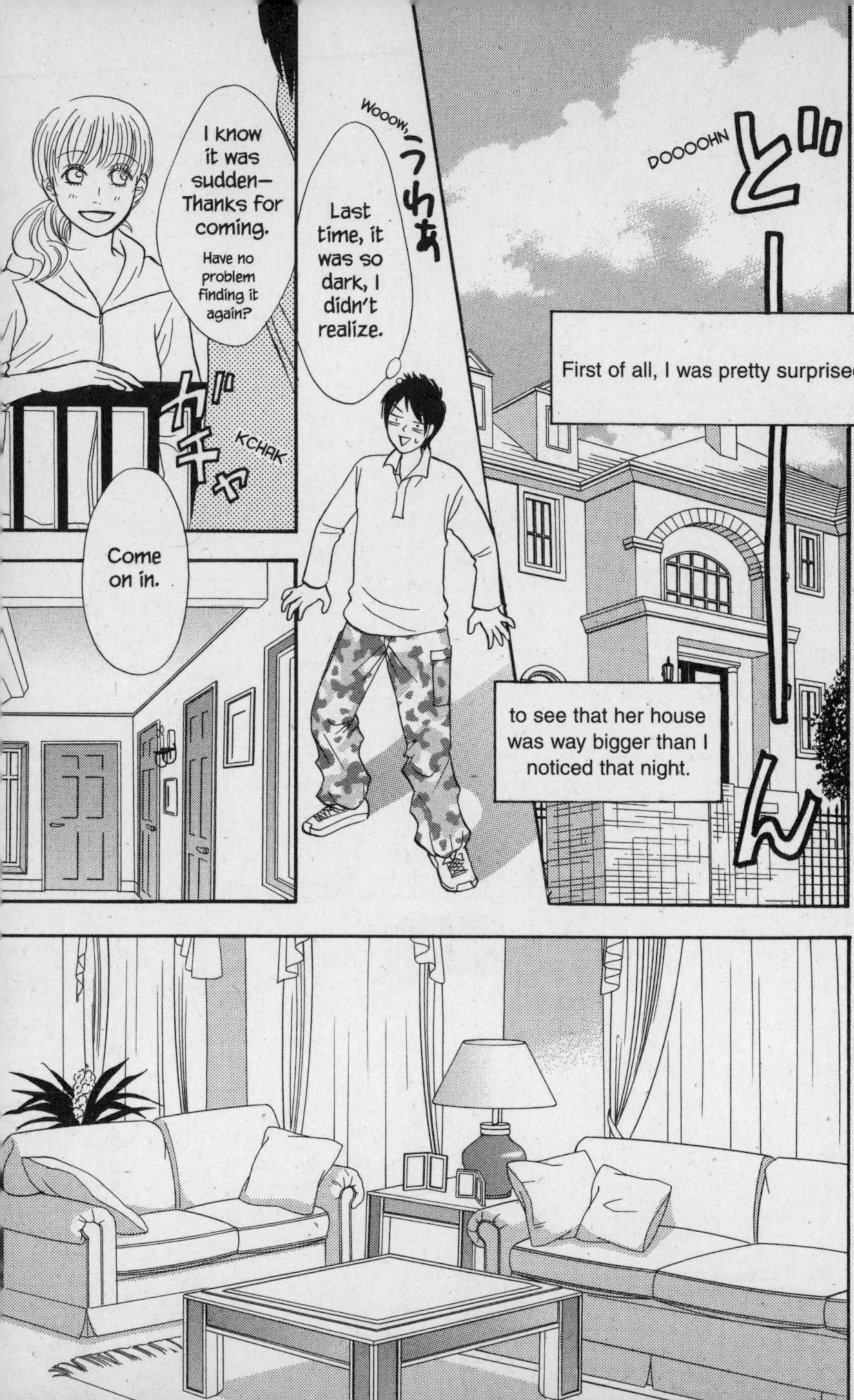
DOOOOHN
どーん
First of all, I was pretty surprised
to see that her house was way bigger than I noticed that night.
WOOOW,
うわあ
Last time, it was so dark, I didn't realize.
I know it was sudden— Thanks for coming.
Have no problem finding it again?
KCHAK
ガチャ
Come on in.

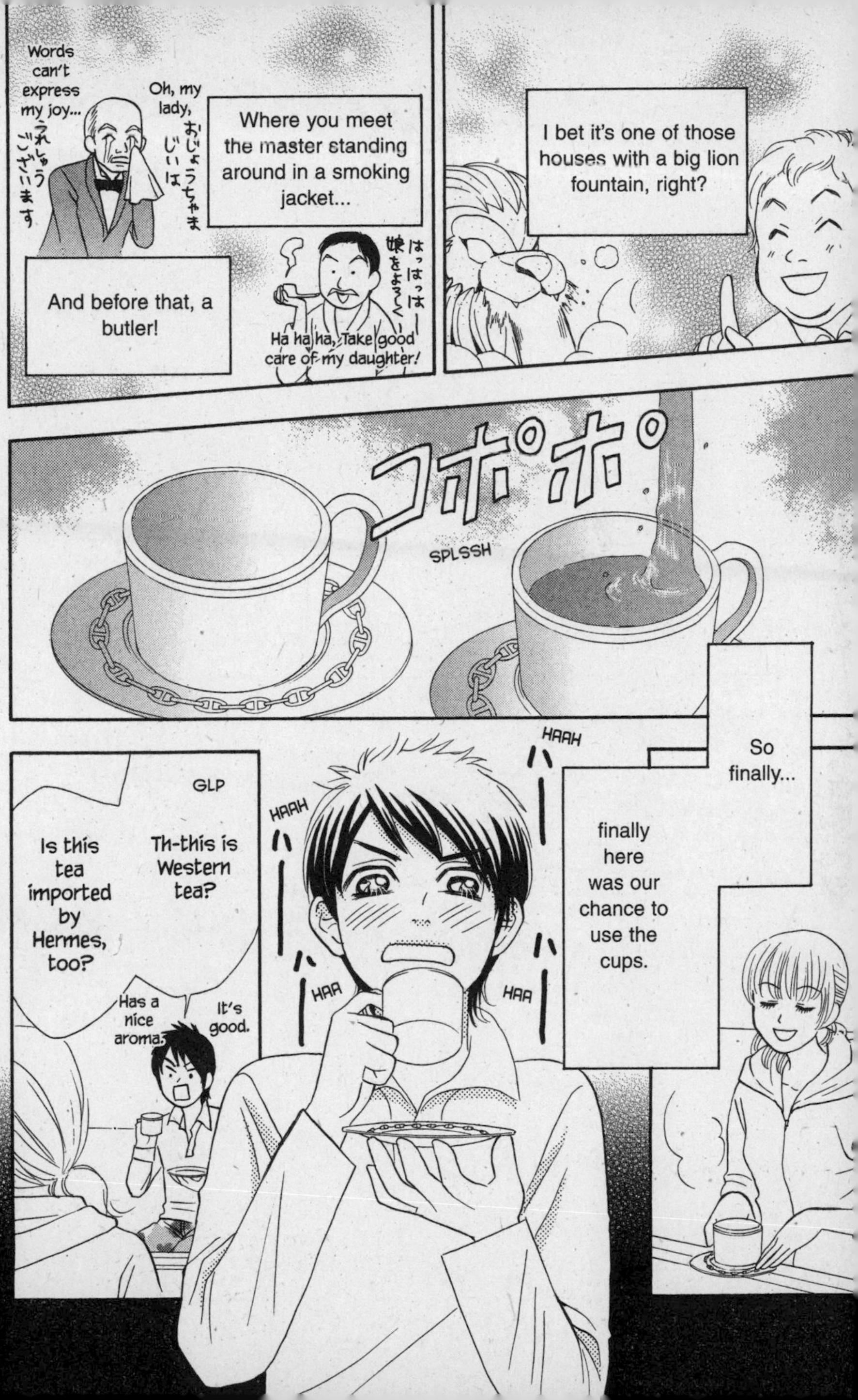
I bet it's one of those houses with a big lion fountain, right?
Where you meet the master standing around in a smoking jacket...
はっはっは 娘をよろしく
Ha ha ha, Take good care of my daughter!
Oh, my lady,
おじょうちゃま じいは
Words can't express my joy...
うれしゅうございます
And before that, a butler!
コポポ
SPLSSH
So finally...
finally here was our chance to use the cups.
ハー
HAAH
ハー
HAA
ハー
HAAH
ハー
HAA
GLP
Th-this is Western tea?
Is this tea imported by Hermes, too?
It's good.
Has a nice aroma.

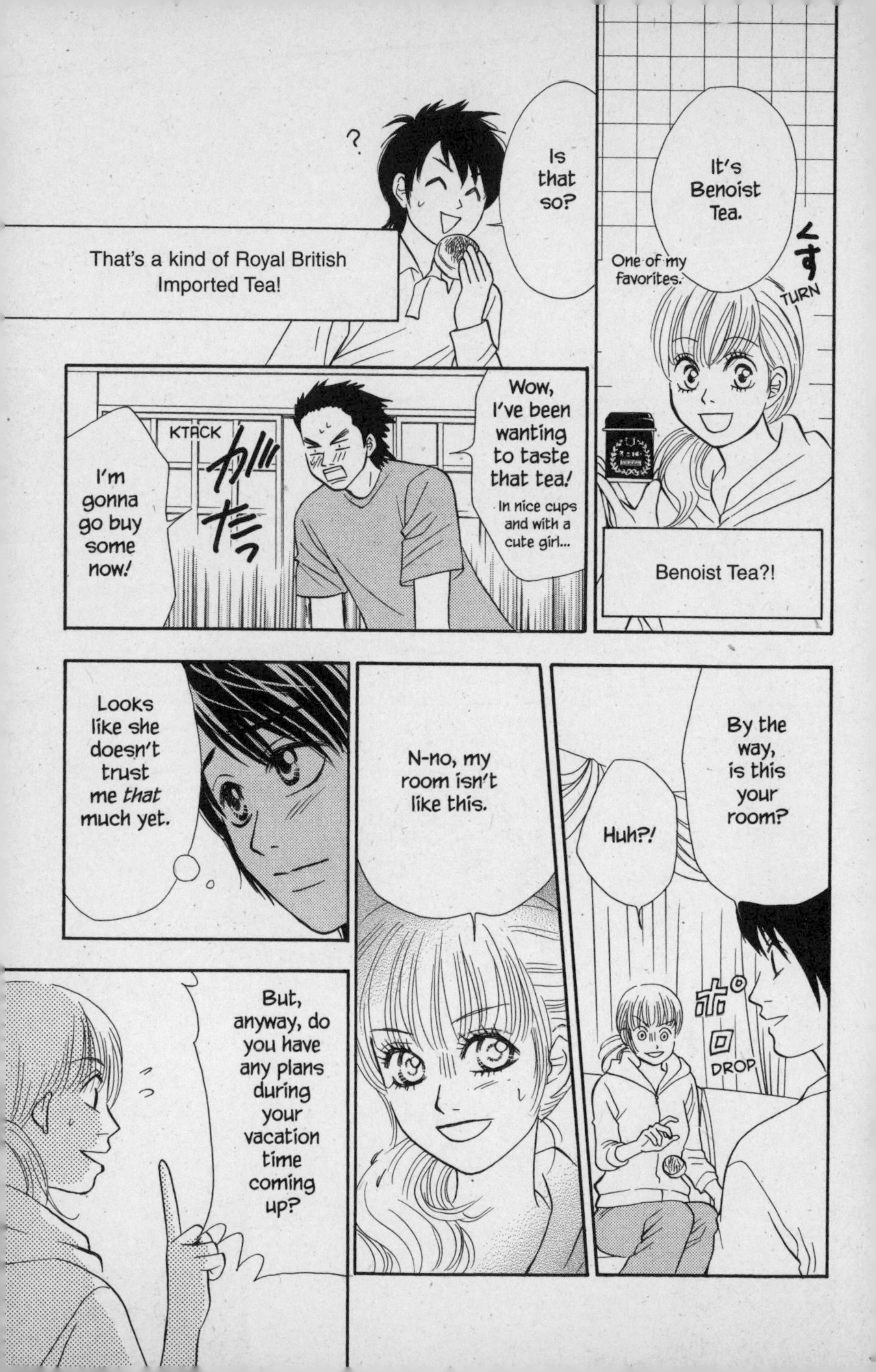
It's Benoist Tea.
One of my favorites.
TURN
Benoist Tea?!
Is that so?
That's a kind of Royal British Imported Tea!
Wow, I've been wanting to taste that tea!
In nice cups and with a cute girl...
KTACK
I'm gonna go buy some now!
By the way, is this your room?
Huh?!
DROP
N-no, my room isn't like this.
Looks like she doesn't trust me *that* much yet.
But, anyway, do you have any plans during your vacation time coming up?

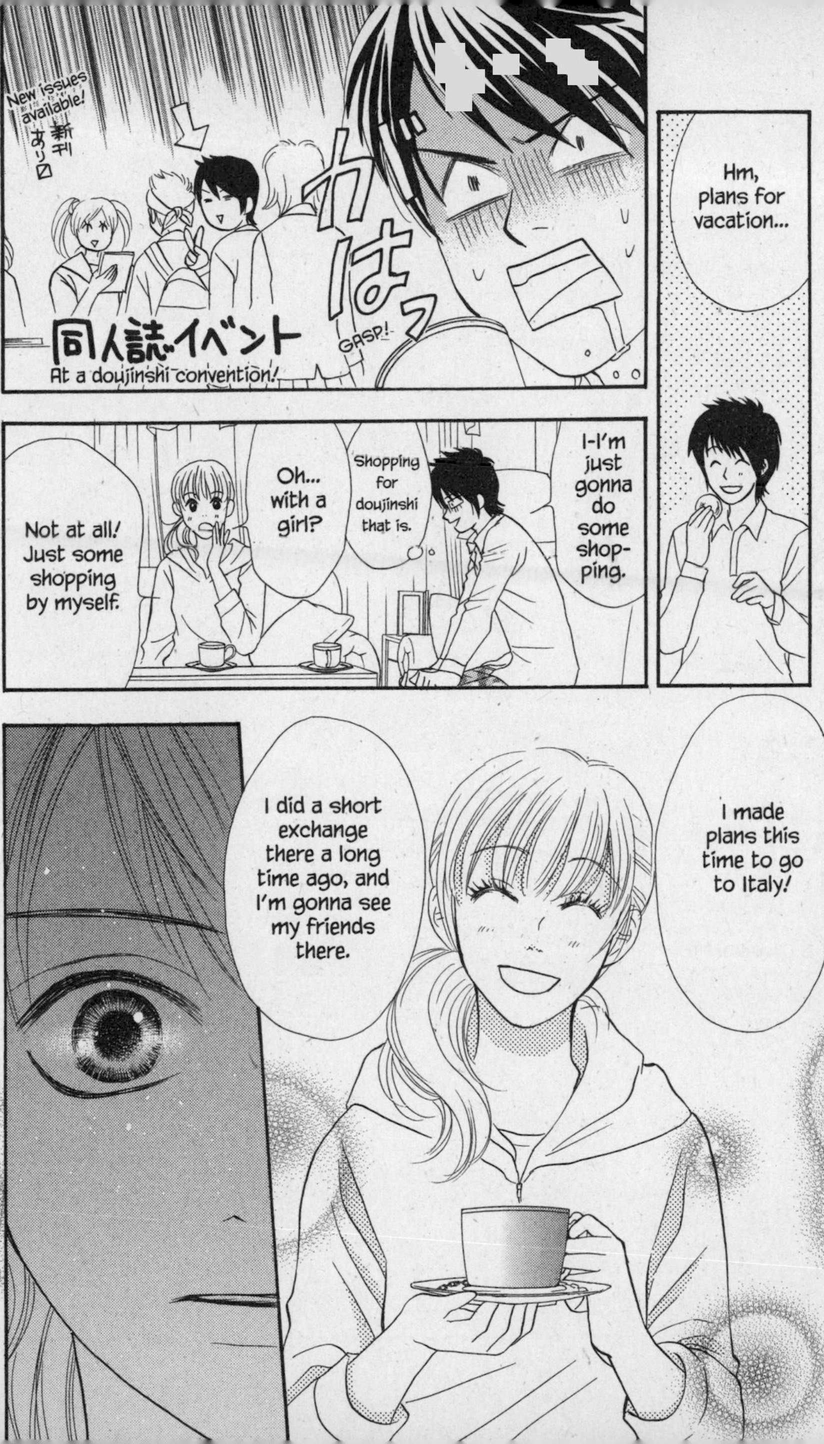
Hm, plans for vacation...
New issues available!
新刊あり
わはっ
GASP!
同人誌イベント
At a doujinshi convention!
I-I'm just gonna do some shop-ping.
Shopping for doujinshi that is.
Oh... with a girl?
Not at all! Just some shopping by myself.
I made plans this time to go to Italy!
I did a short exchange there a long time ago, and I'm gonna see my friends there.

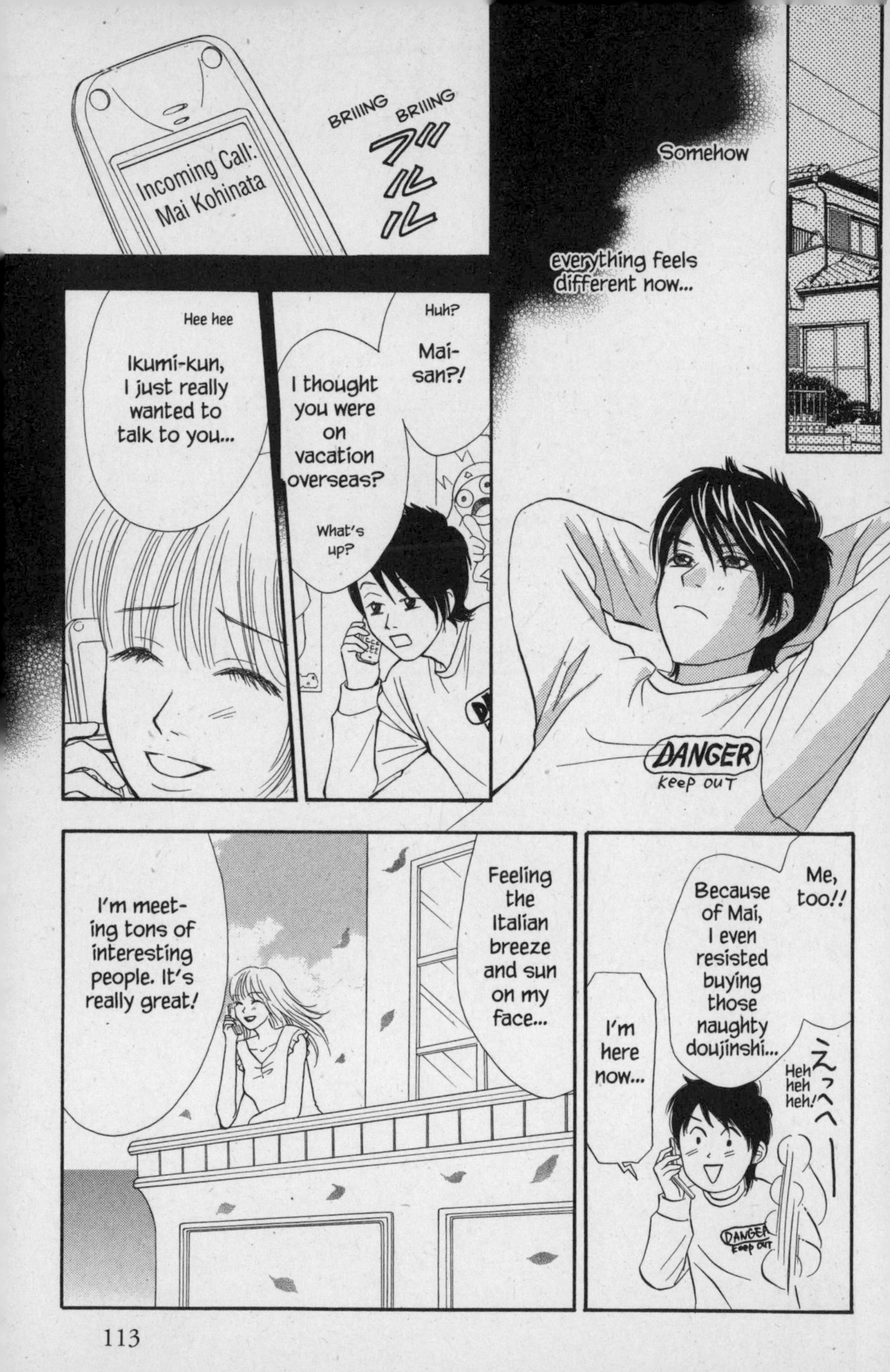
Somehow
everything feels different now...
Incoming Call: Mai Kohinata
BRIIING BRIIING
ブルル
DANGER keep out
Huh?
Mai-san?!
I thought you were on vacation overseas?
What's up?
Hee hee
Ikumi-kun, I just really wanted to talk to you...
Me, too!!
Because of Mai, I even resisted buying those naughty doujinshi...
えっへへー
Heh heh heh!
I'm here now...
DANGER keep out
Feeling the Italian breeze and sun on my face...
I'm meeting tons of interesting people. It's really great!

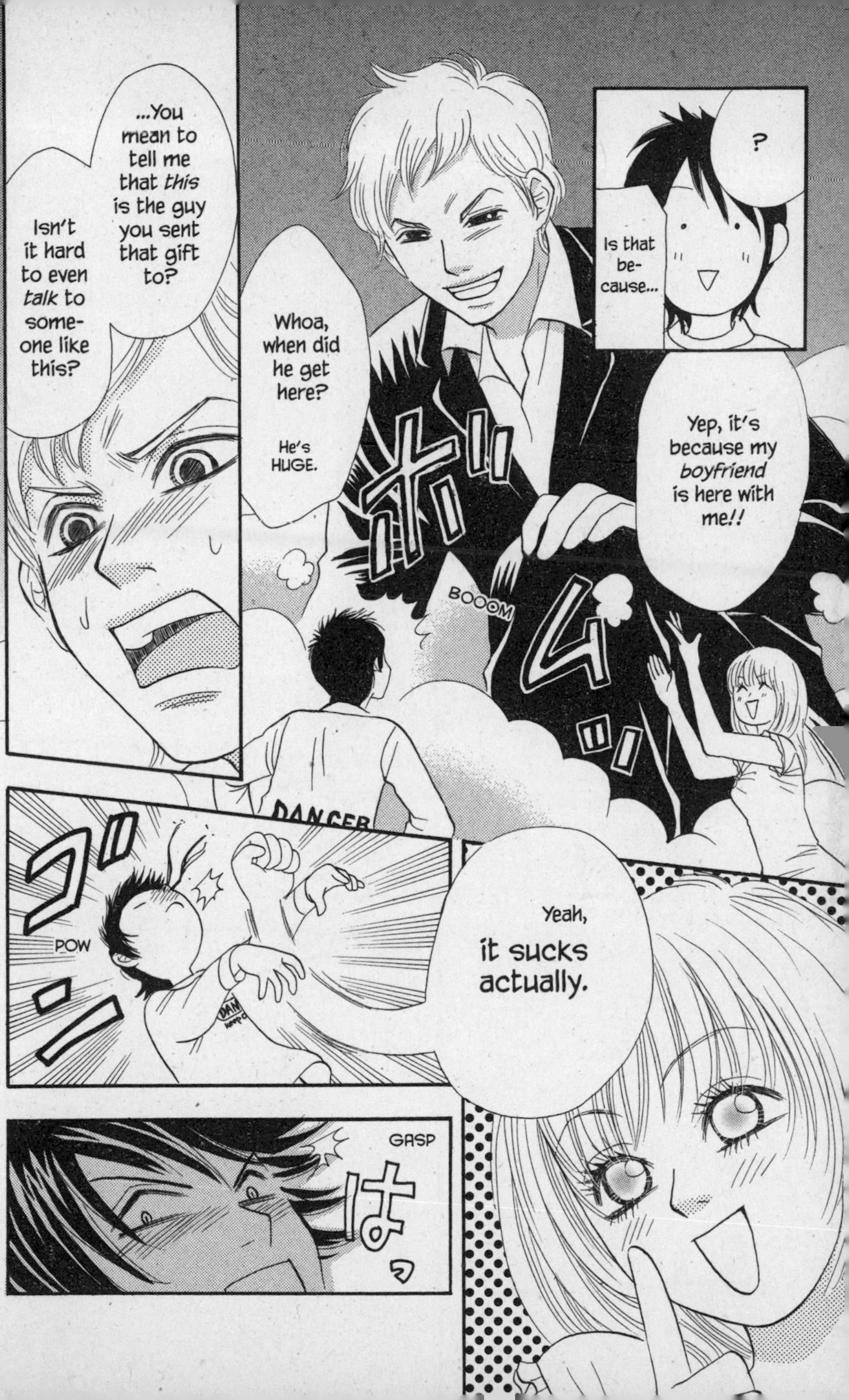

?
Is that be-cause...
Yep, it's because my *boyfriend* is here with me!!
BOOOM
Whoa, when did he get here?
He's HUGE.
DANCER
...You mean to tell me that *this* is the guy you sent that gift to?
Isn't it hard to even *talk* to some-one like this?
Yeah, it sucks actually.
POW
GASP

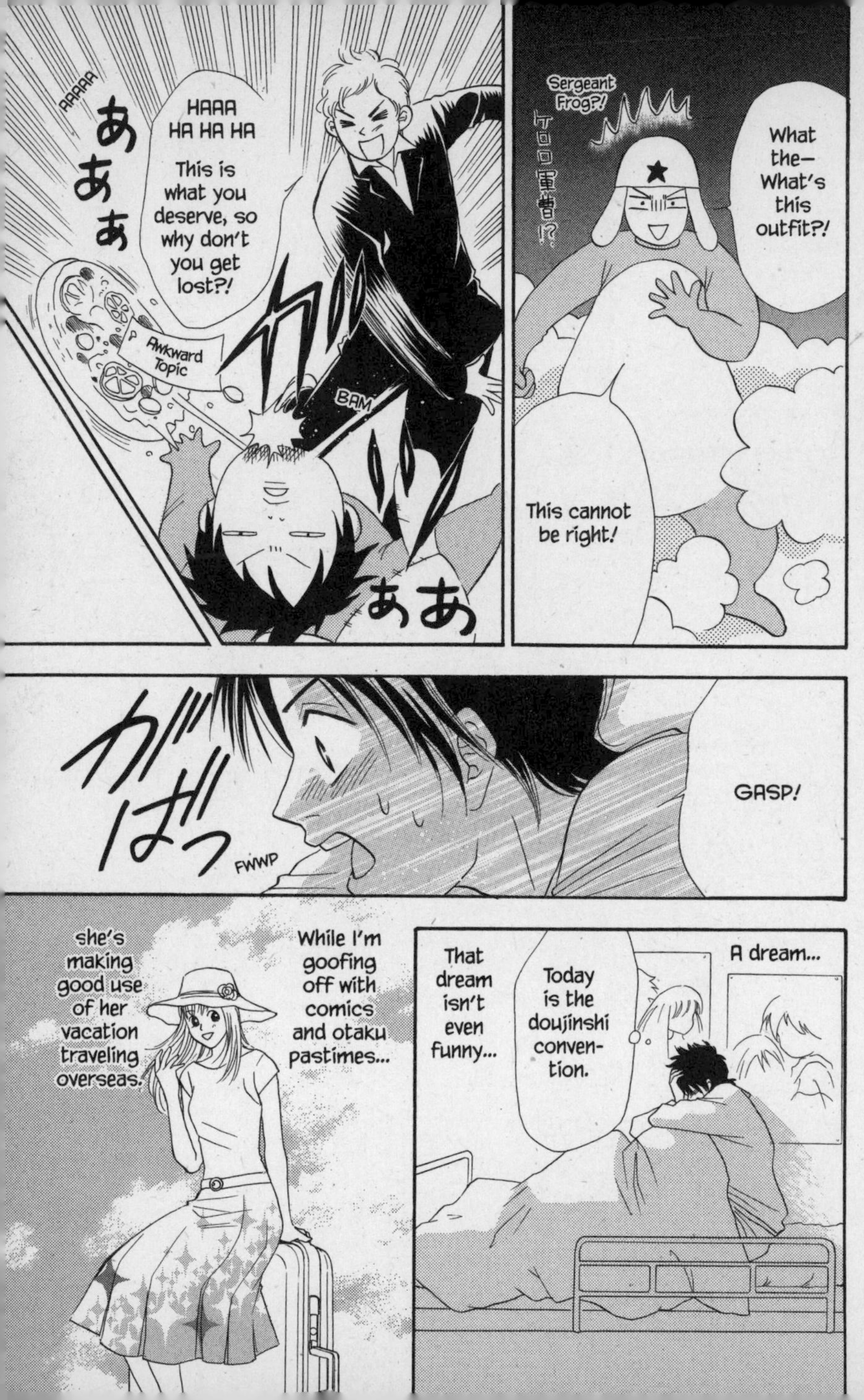
Sergeant Frog?!
ケロロ軍曹!?
What the— What's this outfit?!
This cannot be right!
AAAAA
あああ
HAAA HA HA HA
This is what you deserve, so why don't you get lost?!
Awkward Topic
BAM
ああ
GASP!
がばっ
FWWP
A dream...
Today is the doujinshi convention.
That dream isn't even funny...
While I'm goofing off with comics and otaku pastimes...
she's making good use of her vacation traveling overseas.

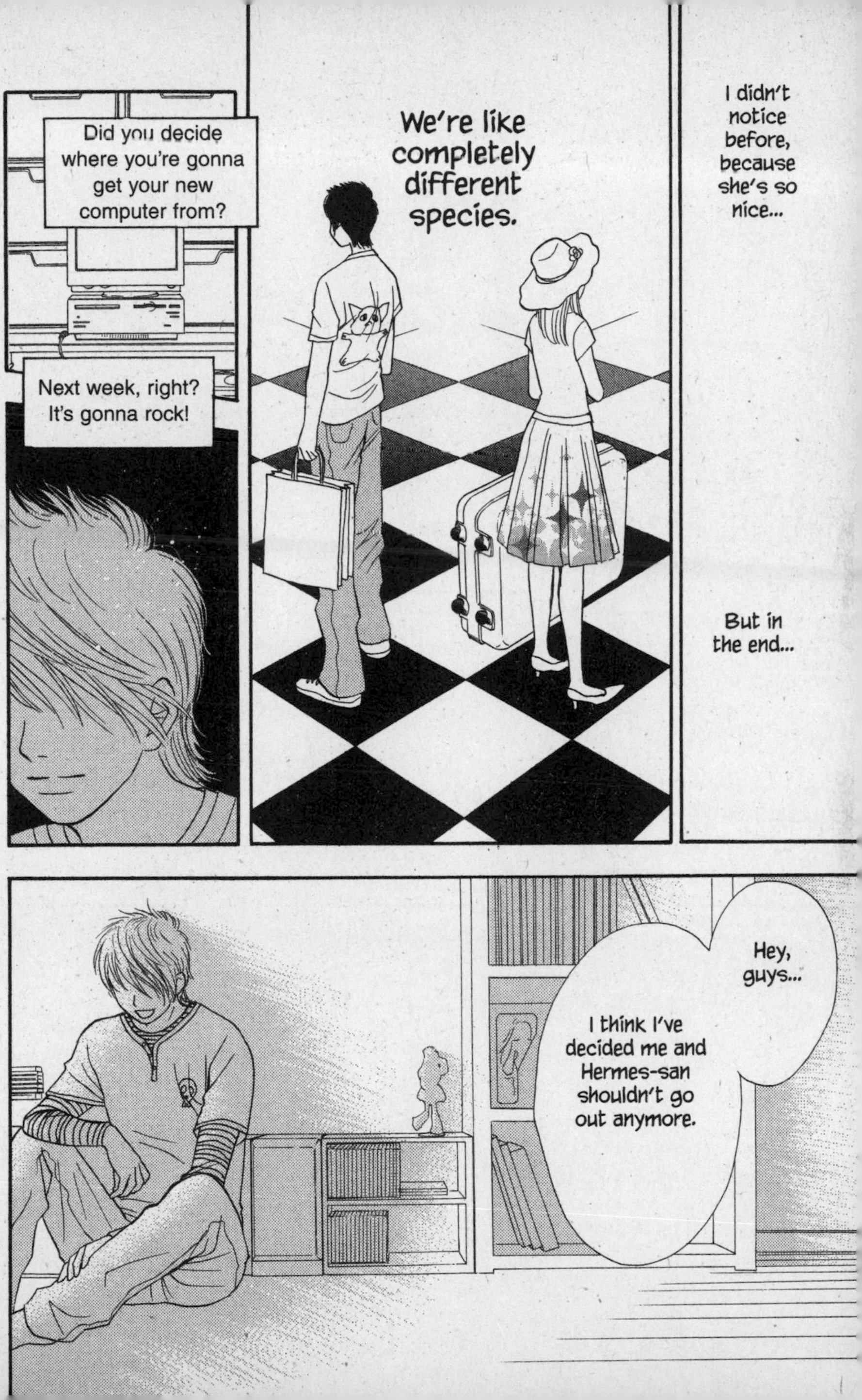
I didn't notice before, because she's so nice...
But in the end...
We're like completely different species.
Did you decide where you're gonna get your new computer from?
Next week, right? It's gonna rock!
Hey, guys...
I think I've decided me and Hermes-san shouldn't go out anymore.

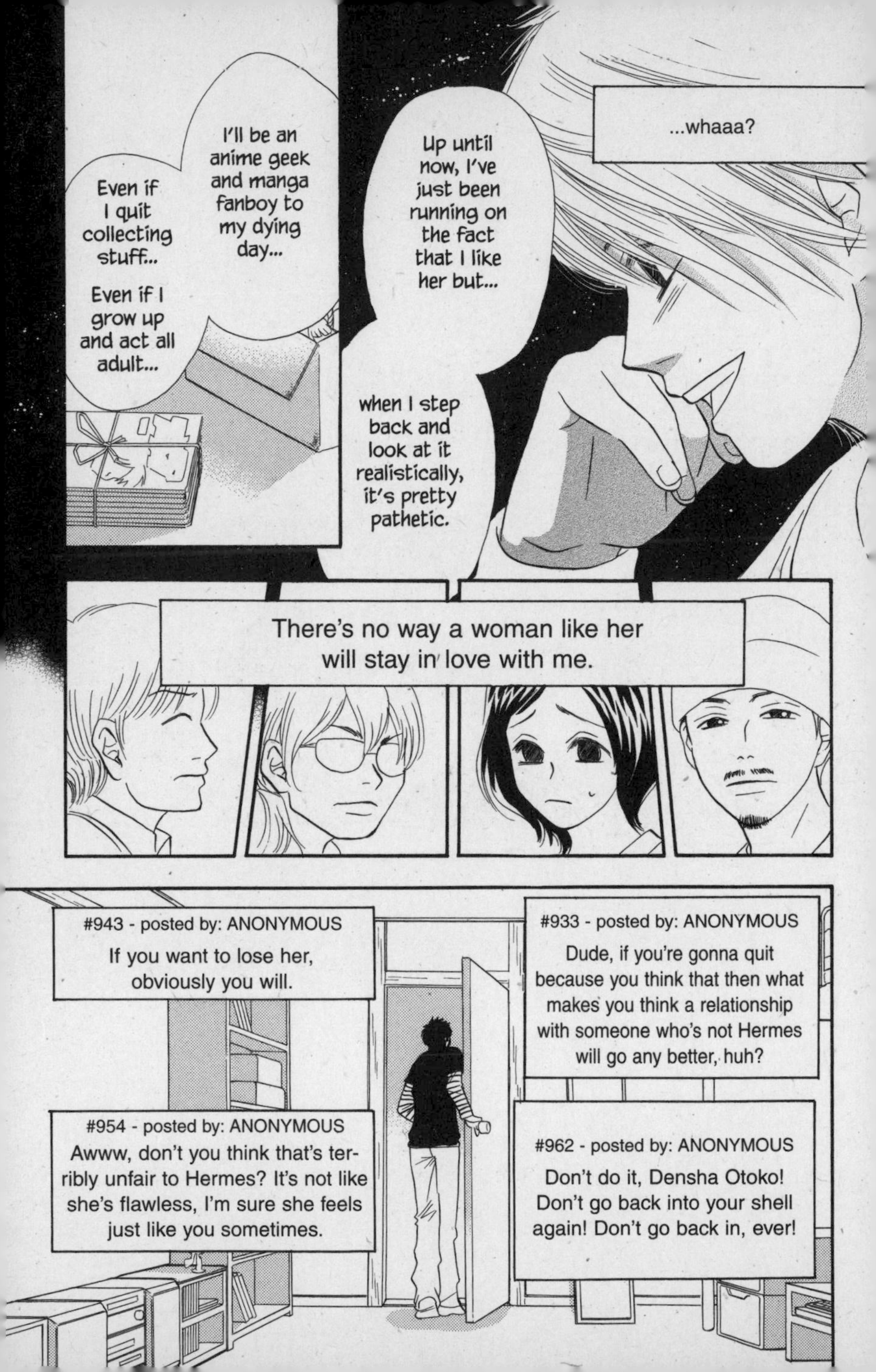
...whaaa?
Up until now, I've just been running on the fact that I like her but...
when I step back and look at it realistically, it's pretty pathetic.
I'll be an anime geek and manga fanboy to my dying day...
Even if I quit collecting stuff...
Even if I grow up and act all adult...
There's no way a woman like her will stay in love with me.
#933 - posted by: ANONYMOUS
Dude, if you're gonna quit because you think that then what makes you think a relationship with someone who's not Hermes will go any better, huh?
#943 - posted by: ANONYMOUS
If you want to lose her, obviously you will.
#962 - posted by: ANONYMOUS
Don't do it, Densha Otoko! Don't go back into your shell again! Don't go back in, ever!
#954 - posted by: ANONYMOUS
Awww, don't you think that's terribly unfair to Hermes? It's not like she's flawless, I'm sure she feels just like you sometimes.

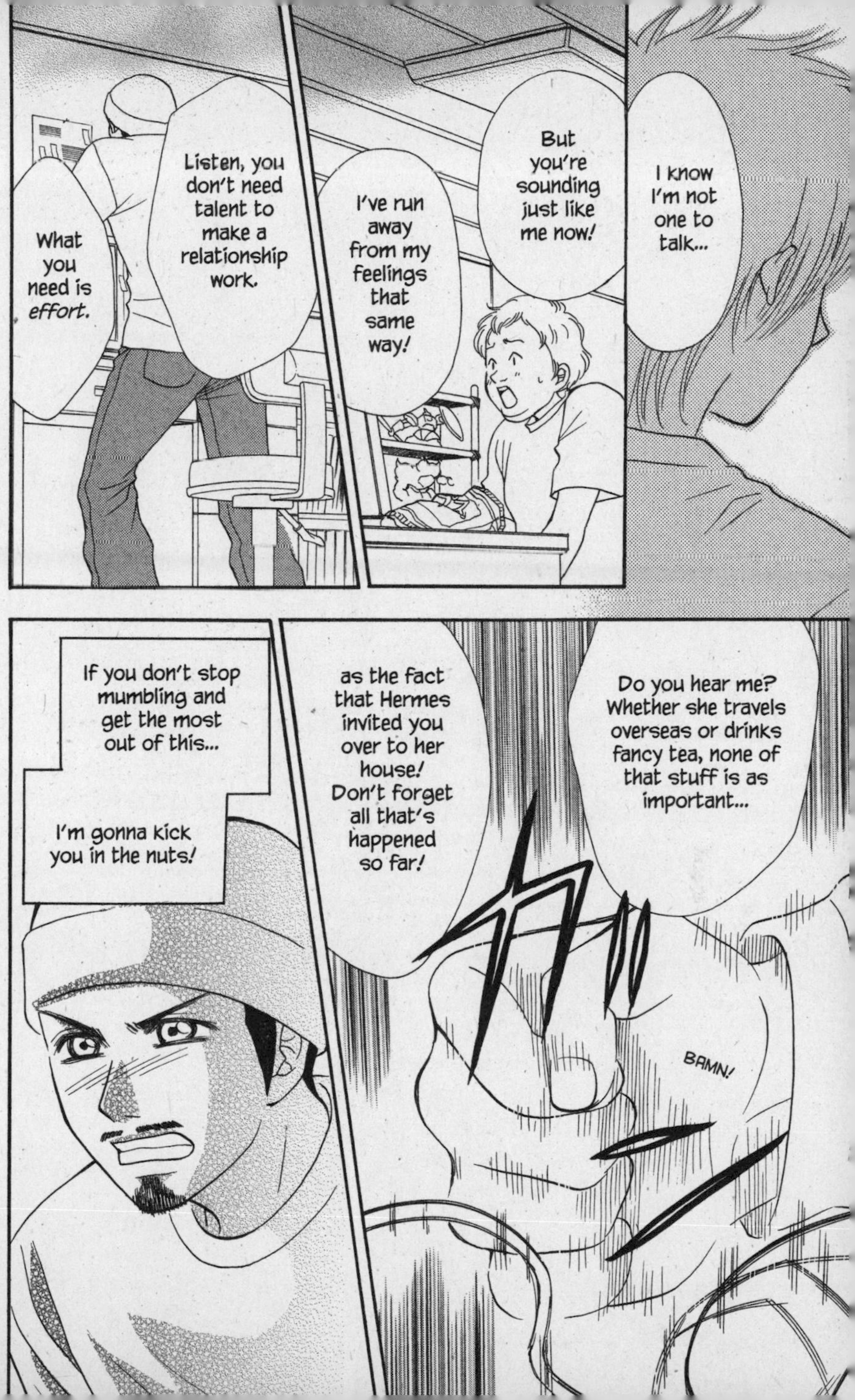
I know I'm not one to talk...
But you're sounding just like me now!
I've run away from my feelings that same way!
Listen, you don't need talent to make a relationship work.
What you need is *effort*.
Do you hear me? Whether she travels overseas or drinks fancy tea, none of that stuff is as important...
as the fact that Hermes invited you over to her house! Don't forget all that's happened so far!
BAMN!
If you don't stop mumbling and get the most out of this...
I'm gonna kick you in the nuts!

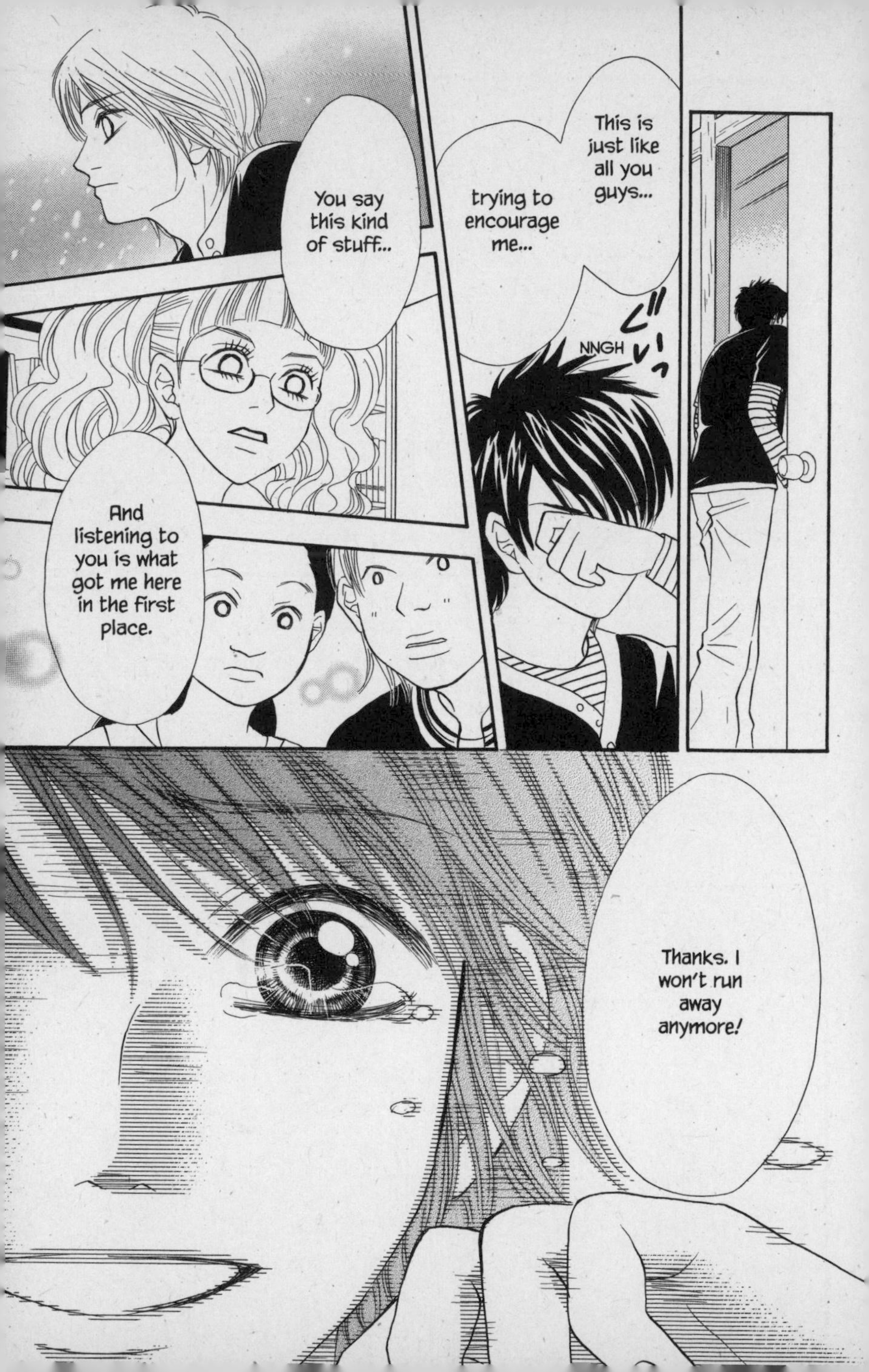
This is just like all you guys...
trying to encourage me...
NNGH
You say this kind of stuff...
And listening to you is what got me here in the first place.
Thanks. I won't run away anymore!

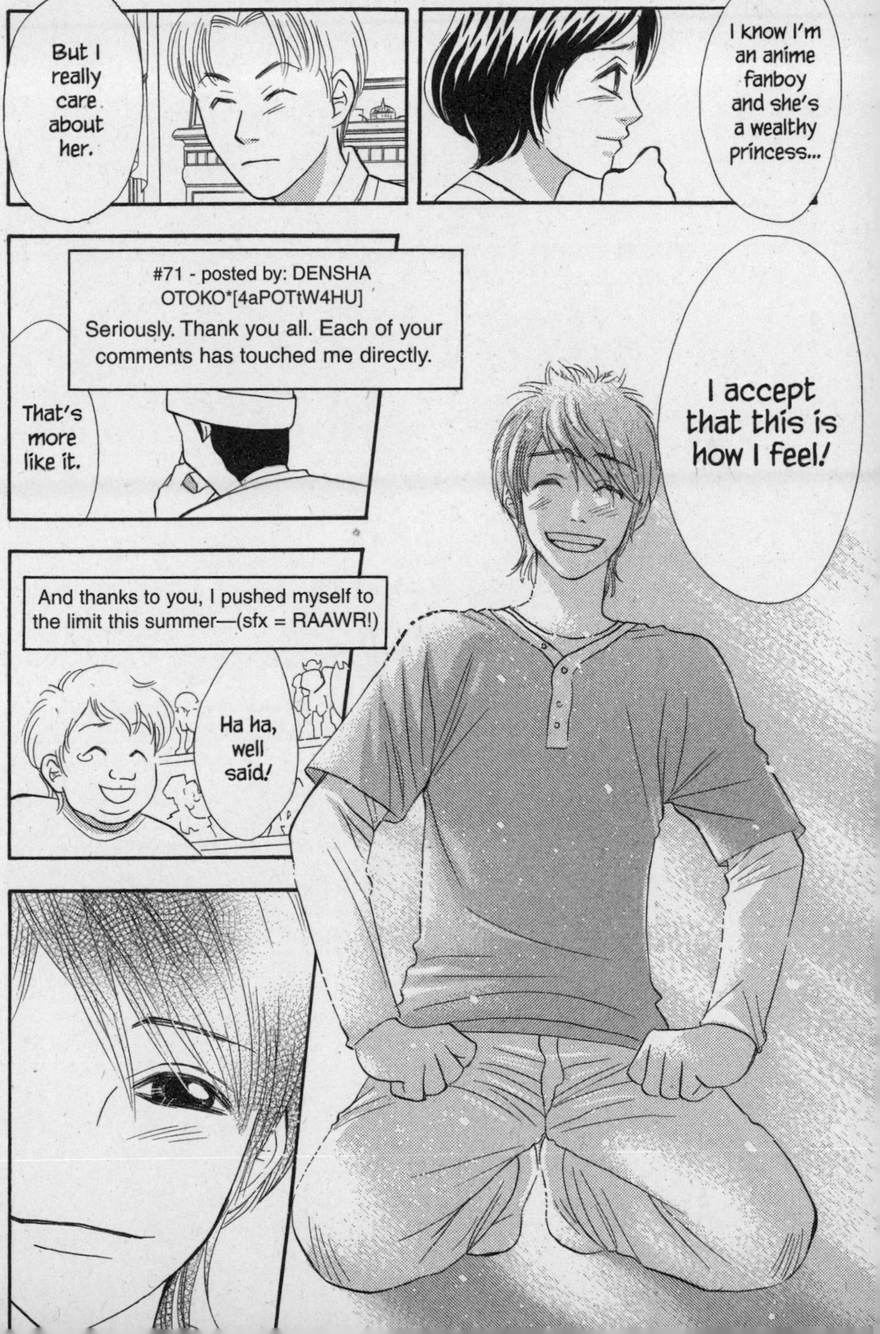
I know I'm an anime fanboy and she's a wealthy princess...
But I really care about her.
I accept that this is how I feel!
#71 - posted by: DENSHA OTOKO*[4aPOTtW4HU]
Seriously. Thank you all. Each of your comments has touched me directly.
That's more like it.
And thanks to you, I pushed myself to the limit this summer—(sfx = RAAWR!)
Ha ha, well said!

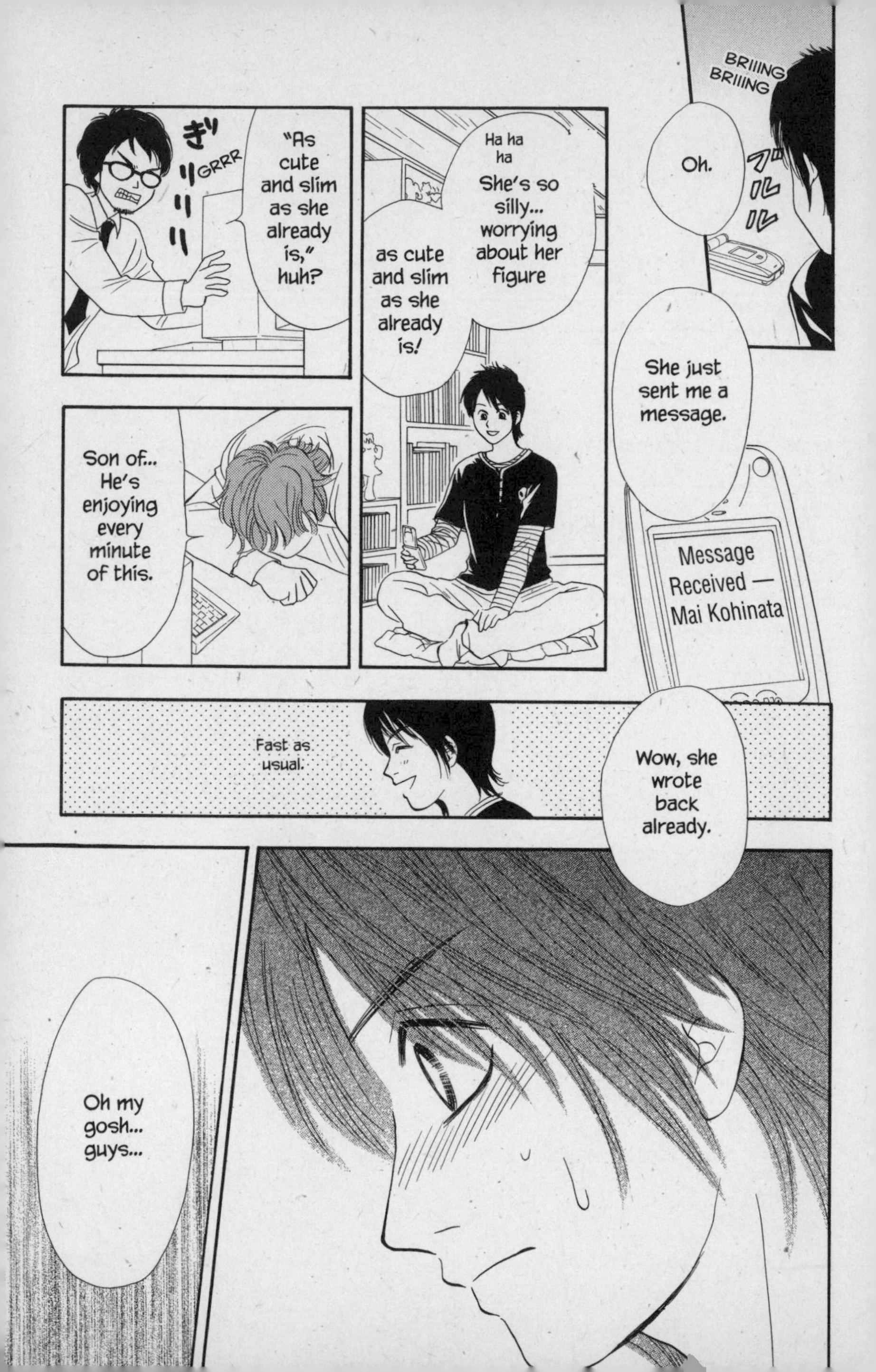
BRIIING BRIIING
ブルル
Oh.
She just sent me a message.
Message Received — Mai Kohinata
Ha ha ha
She's so silly... worrying about her figure
as cute and slim as she already is!
ぎりりり GRRR
"As cute and slim as she already is," huh?
Son of... He's enjoying every minute of this.
Wow, she wrote back already.
Fast as usual.
Oh my gosh... guys...

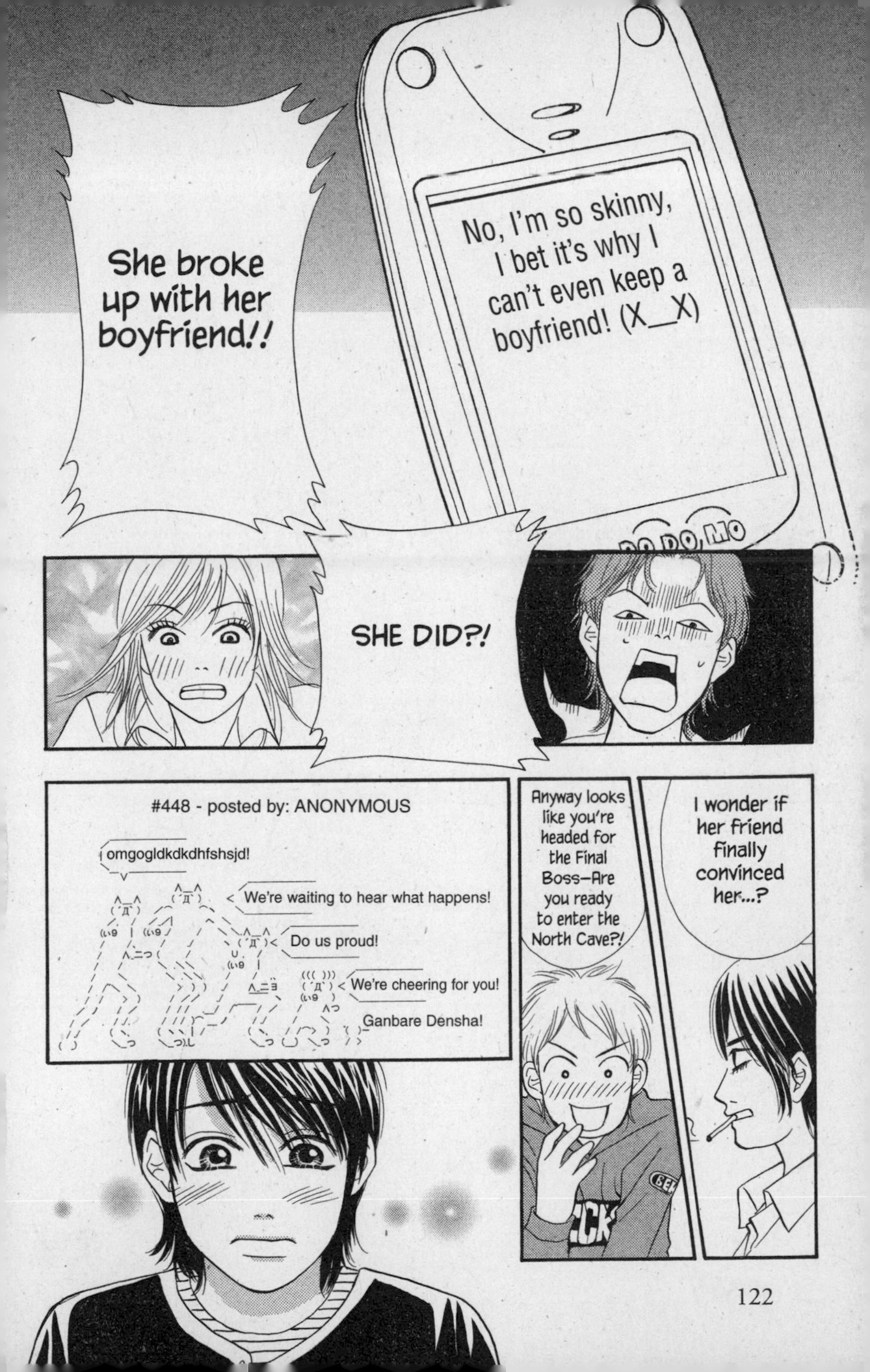
No, I'm so skinny, I bet it's why I can't even keep a boyfriend! (X_X)
DO DO MO
She broke up with her boyfriend!!
SHE DID?!
I wonder if her friend finally convinced her...?
Anyway looks like you're headed for the Final Boss—Are you ready to enter the North Cave?!
#448 - posted by: ANONYMOUS
omgogldkdkdhfshsjd!
We're waiting to hear what happens!
Do us proud!
We're cheering for you!
Ganbare Densha!

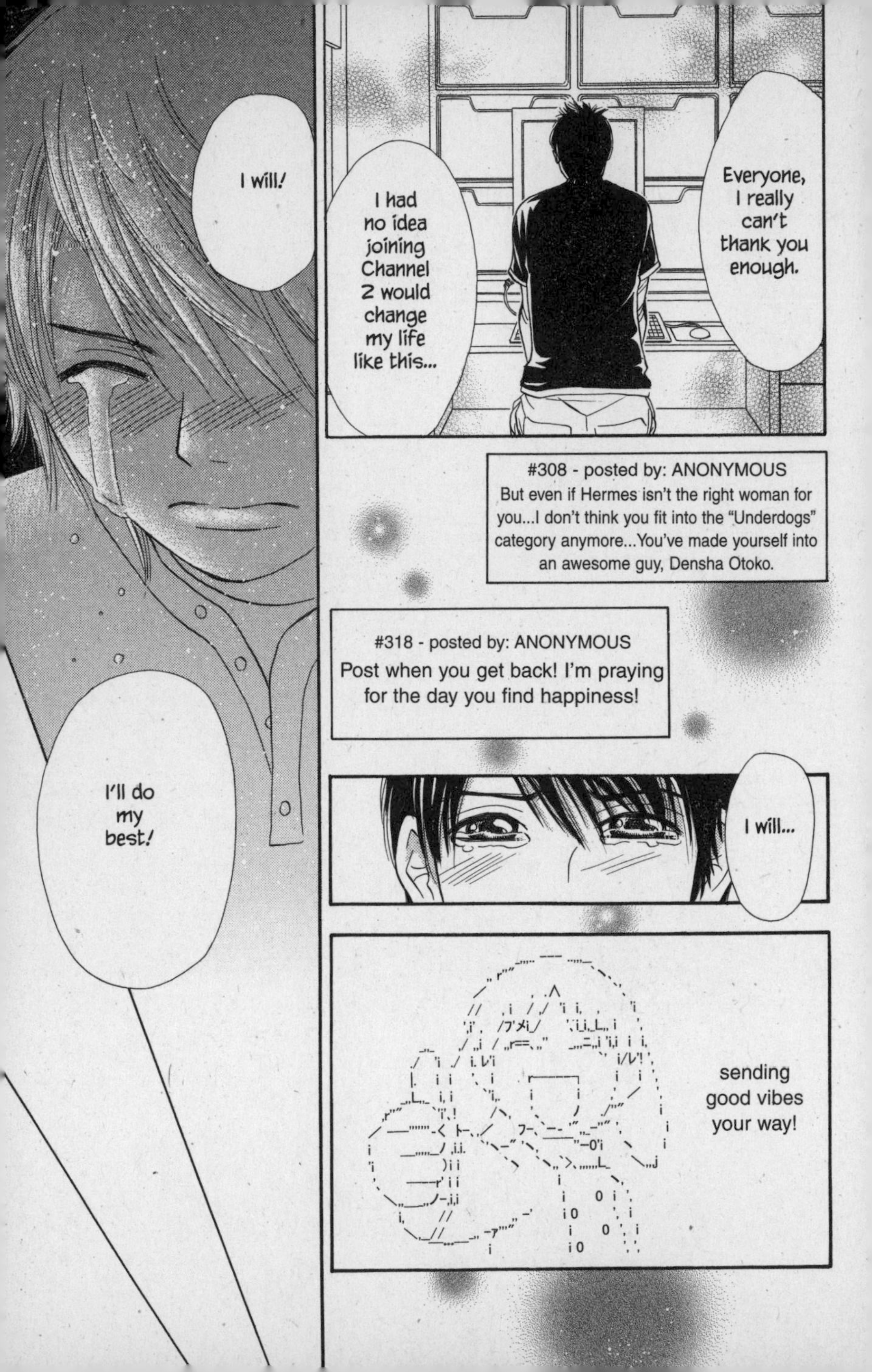
Everyone, I really can't thank you enough.
I had no idea joining Channel 2 would change my life like this...
#308 - posted by: ANONYMOUS
But even if Hermes isn't the right woman for you...I don't think you fit into the "Underdogs" category anymore...You've made yourself into an awesome guy, Densha Otoko.
#318 - posted by: ANONYMOUS
Post when you get back! I'm praying for the day you find happiness!
I will...
sending good vibes your way!
I will!
I'll do my best!

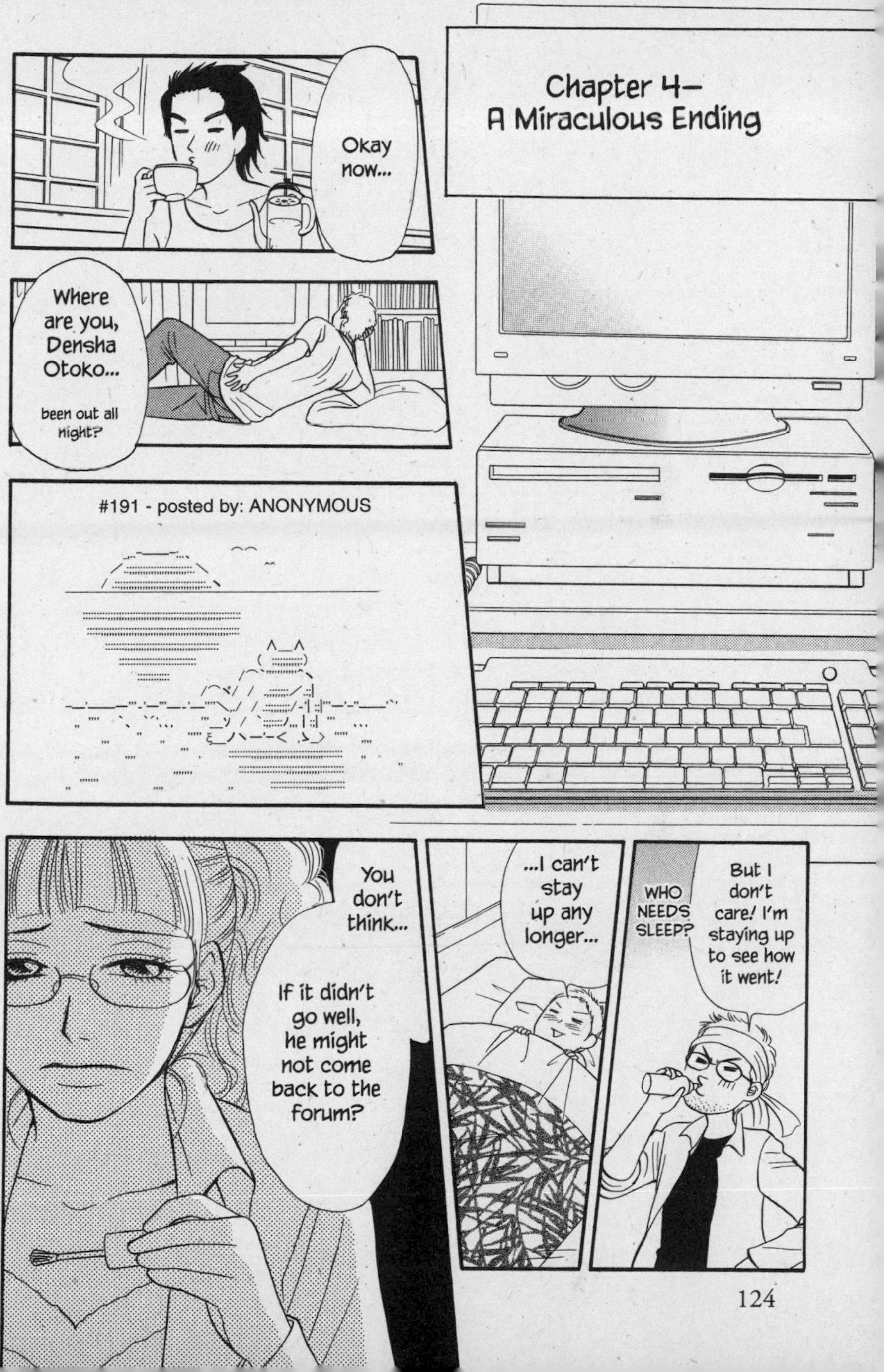
Chapter 4—
A Miraculous Ending
Okay now...
Where are you, Densha Otoko...
been out all night?
#191 - posted by: ANONYMOUS
But I don't care! I'm staying up to see how it went!
WHO NEEDS SLEEP?
...I can't stay up any longer...
You don't think...
If it didn't go well, he might not come back to the forum?

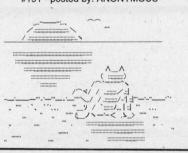

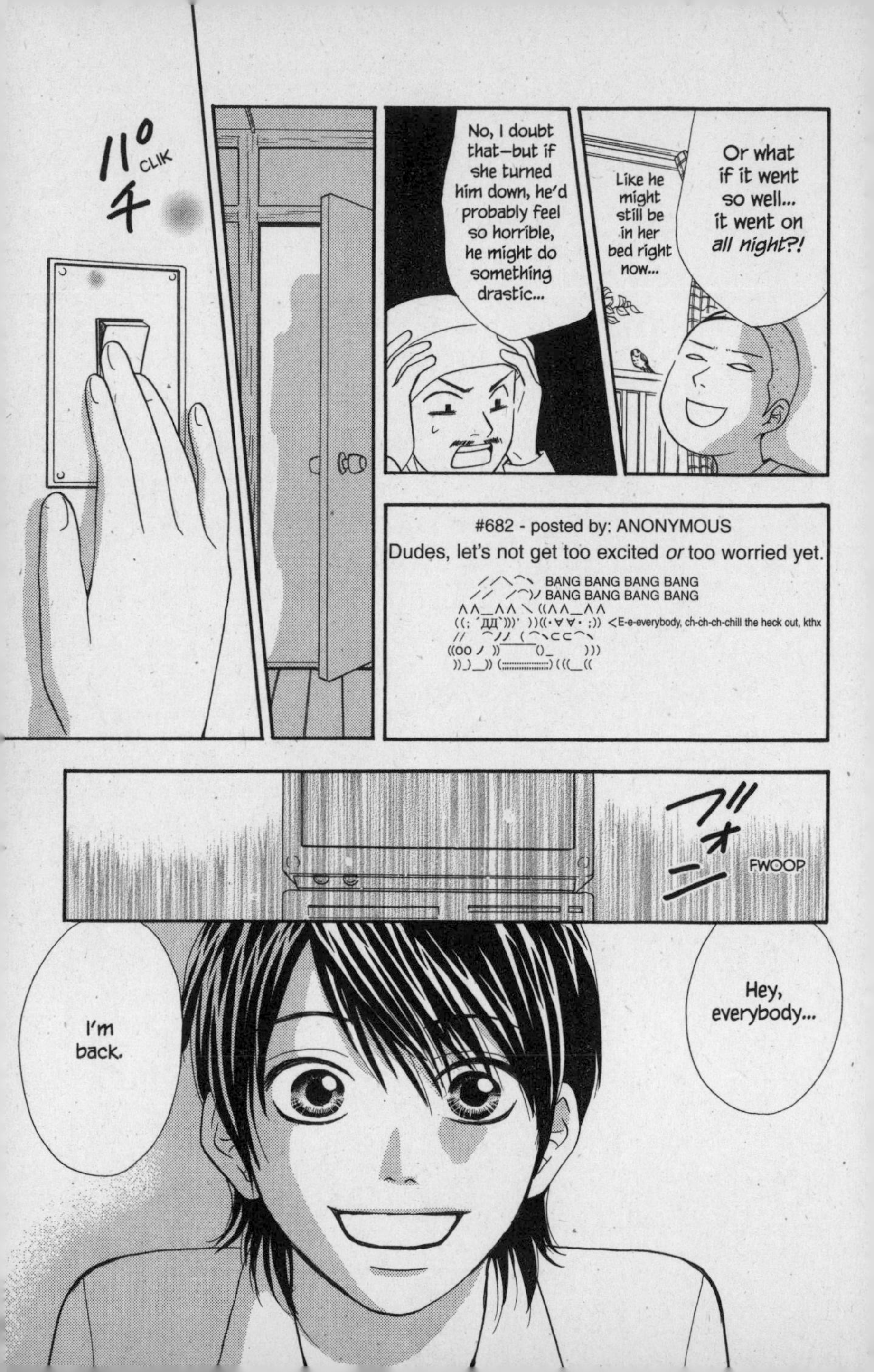
Or what if it went so well... it went on *all night?!*
Like he might still be in her bed right now...
No, I doubt that—but if she turned him down, he'd probably feel so horrible, he might do something drastic...
#682 - posted by: ANONYMOUS
Dudes, let's not get too excited *or* too worried yet.
BANG BANG BANG BANG
BANG BANG BANG BANG
<E-e-everybody, ch-ch-ch-chill the heck out, kthx
CLIK
FWOOP
Hey, everybody...
I'm back.

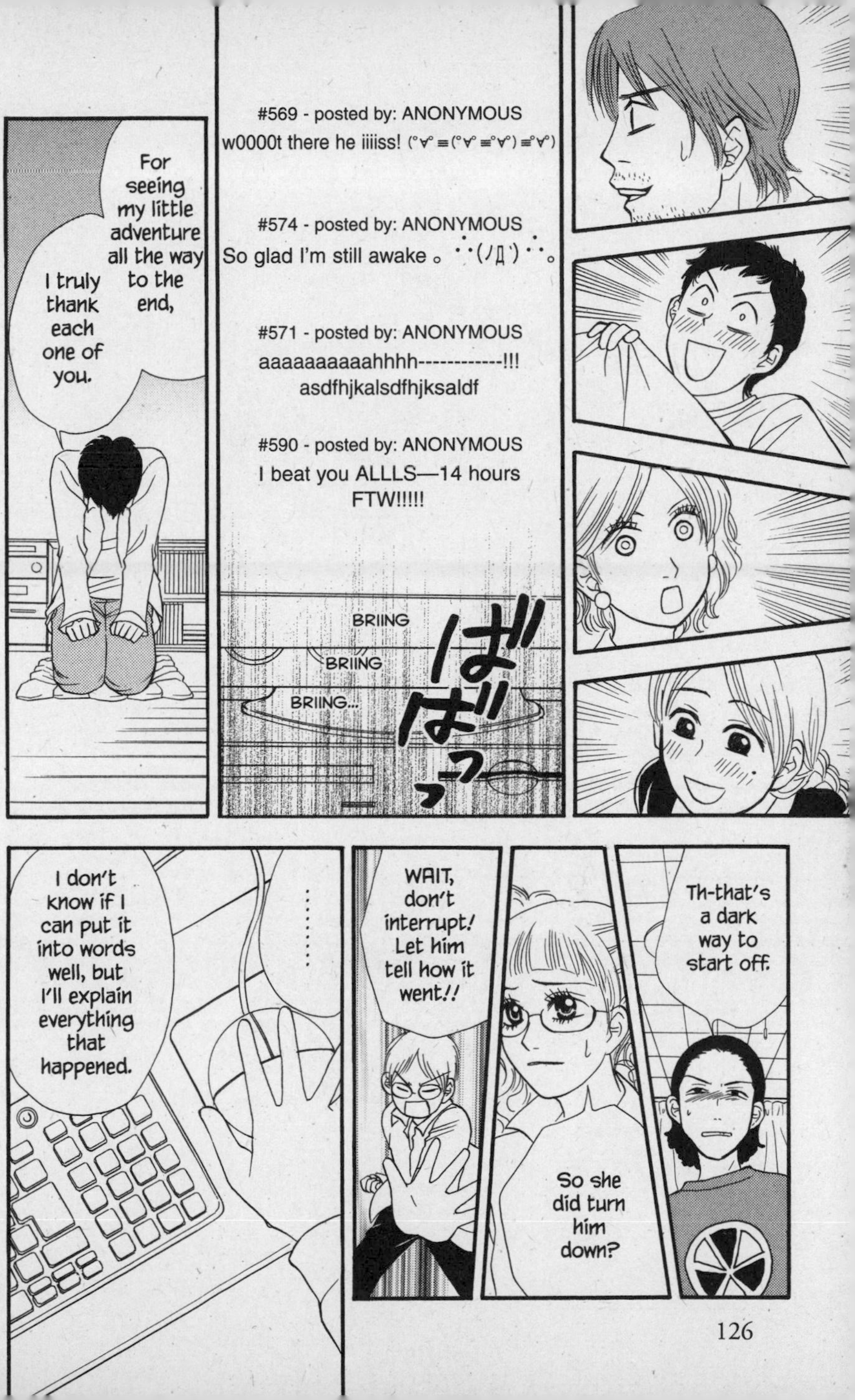
#569 - posted by: ANONYMOUS
w0000t there he iiiiss! (°∀°≡(°∀°≡°∀°)≡°∀°)
#574 - posted by: ANONYMOUS
So glad I'm still awake 。·:·(ﾉД`)·:·。
#571 - posted by: ANONYMOUS
aaaaaaaaaahhhh------------!!!
asdfhjkalsdfhjksaldf
#590 - posted by: ANONYMOUS
I beat you ALLLS—14 hours FTW!!!!!
BRIING
BRIING
BRIING...
ばばっ
For seeing my little adventure all the way to the end,
I truly thank each one of you.
Th-that's a dark way to start off.
So she did turn him down?
WAIT, don't interrupt! Let him tell how it went!!
....
I don't know if I can put it into words well, but I'll explain everything that happened.

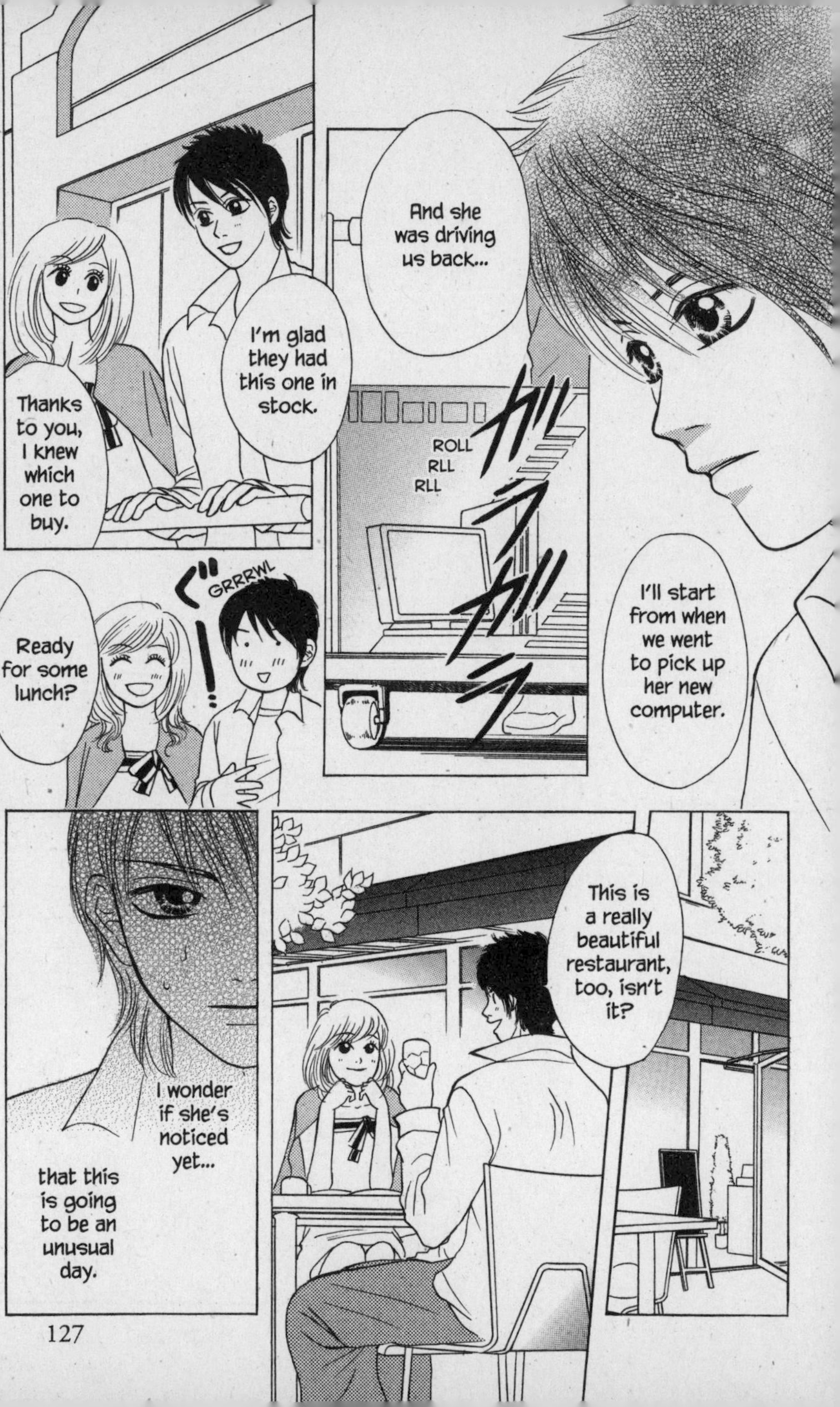
I'll start from when we went to pick up her new computer.
ROLL
RLL
RLL
And she was driving us back...
I'm glad they had this one in stock.
Thanks to you, I knew which one to buy.
GRRRWL
Ready for some lunch?
This is a really beautiful restaurant, too, isn't it?
I wonder if she's noticed yet...
that this is going to be an unusual day.

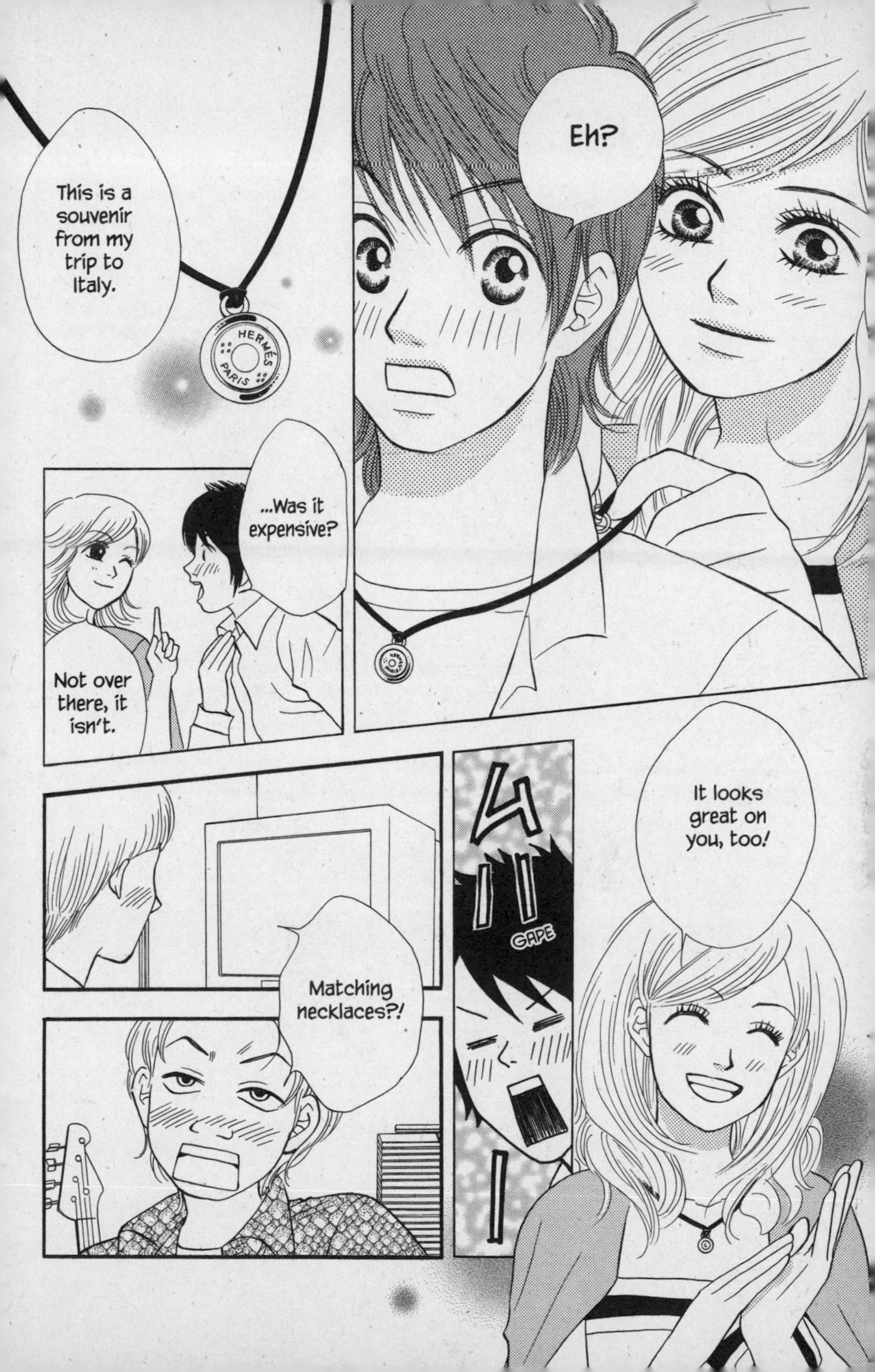
Eh?
This is a souvenir from my trip to Italy.
HERMÈS PARIS
...Was it expensive?
Not over there, it isn't.
It looks great on you, too!
GAPE
Matching necklaces?!

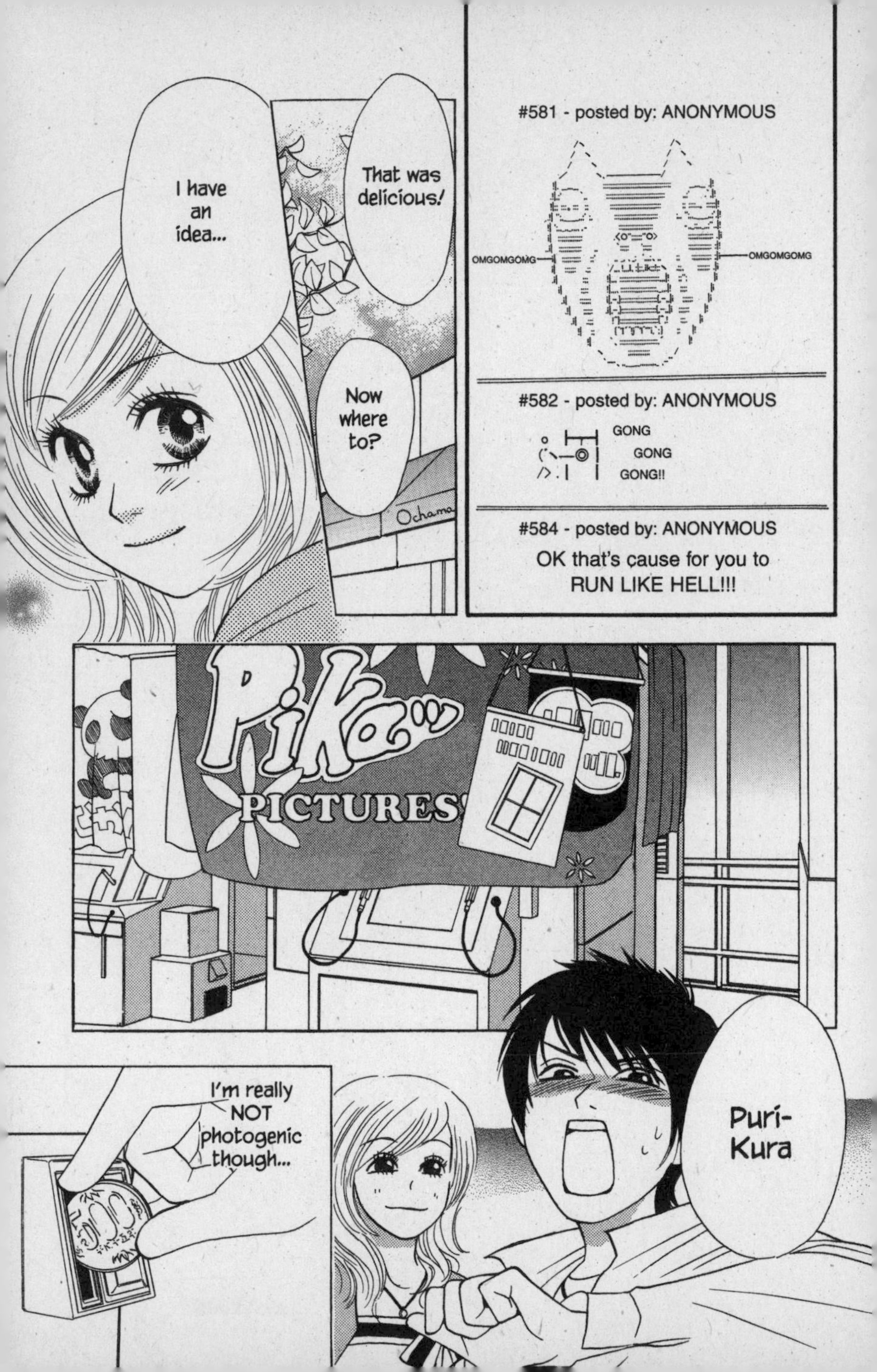
#581 - posted by: ANONYMOUS
OMGOMGOMG
OMGOMGOMG
#582 - posted by: ANONYMOUS
GONG
GONG
GONG!!
#584 - posted by: ANONYMOUS
OK that's cause for you to RUN LIKE HELL!!!
That was delicious!
Now where to?
Ochama
I have an idea...
Pika
PICTURES!
Puri-Kura
I'm really NOT photogenic though...

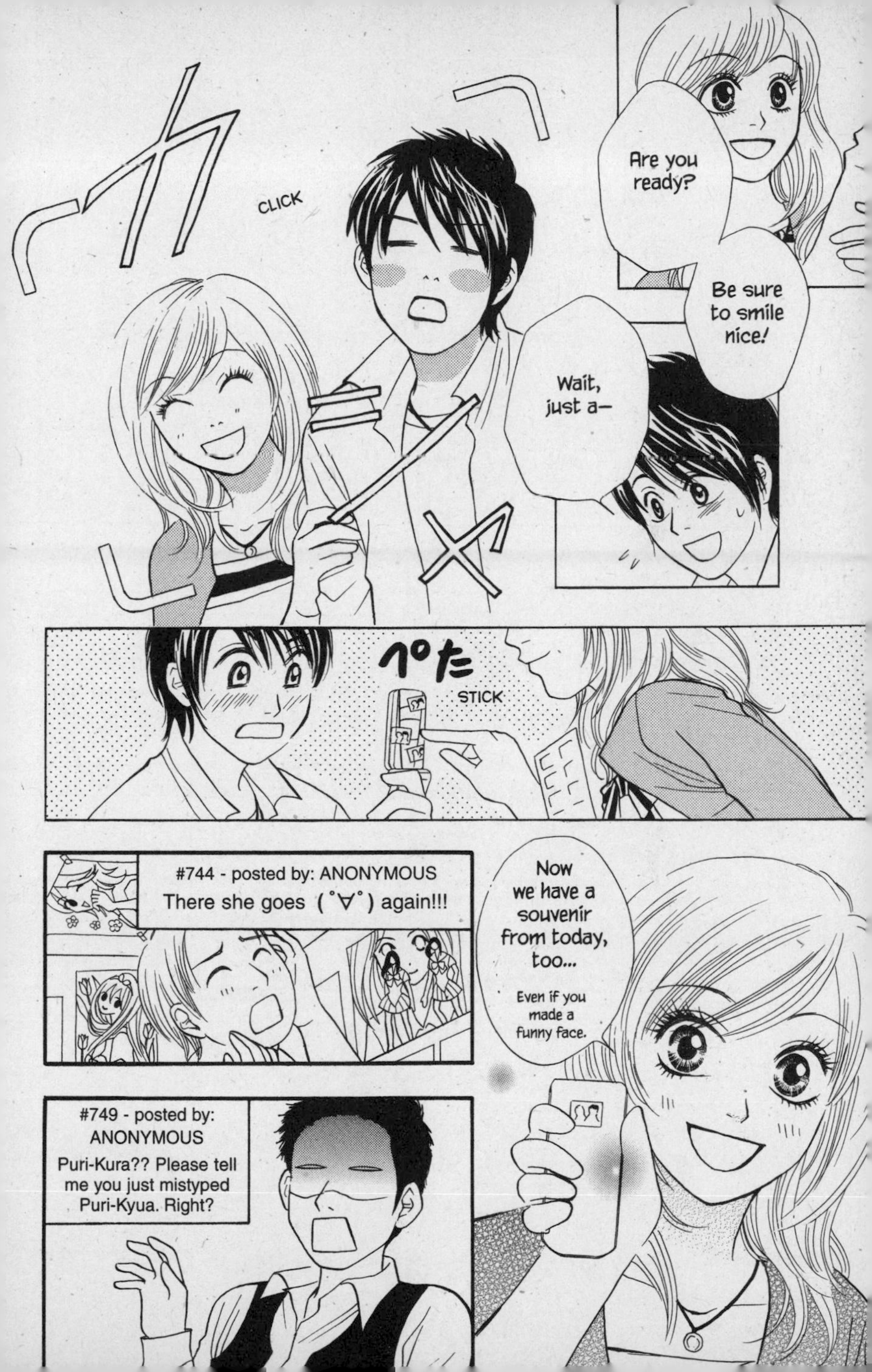
Are you ready?
Be sure to smile nice!
Wait, just a—
CLICK
ぺた
STICK
Now we have a souvenir from today, too...
Even if you made a funny face.
#744 - posted by: ANONYMOUS
There she goes (ﾟ∀ﾟ) again!!!
#749 - posted by: ANONYMOUS
Puri-Kura?? Please tell me you just mistyped Puri-Kyua. Right?

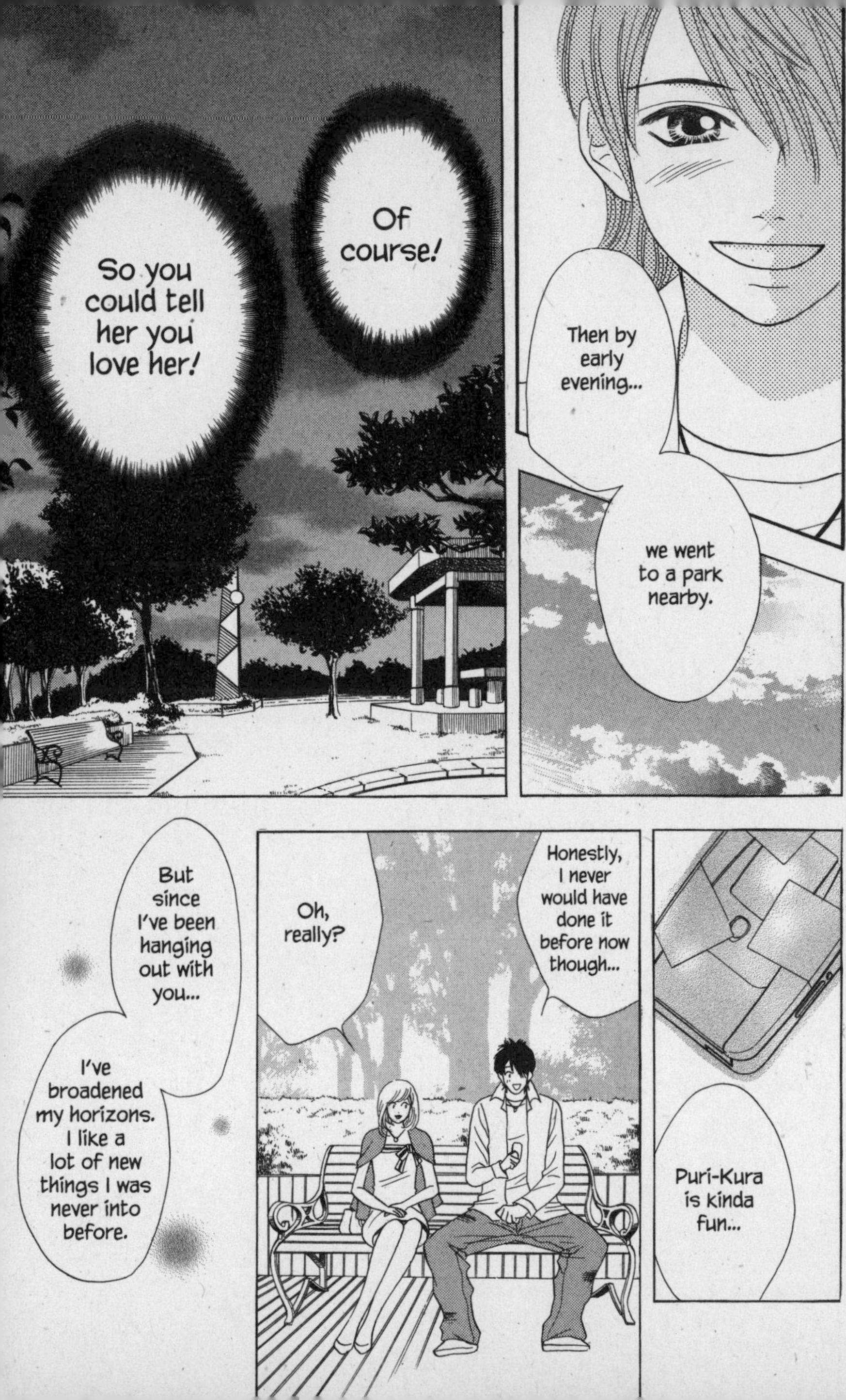
Then by early evening...
we went to a park nearby.
Of course!
So you could tell her you love her!
Puri-Kura is kinda fun...
Honestly, I never would have done it before now though...
Oh, really?
But since I've been hanging out with you...
I've broadened my horizons. I like a lot of new things I was never into before.

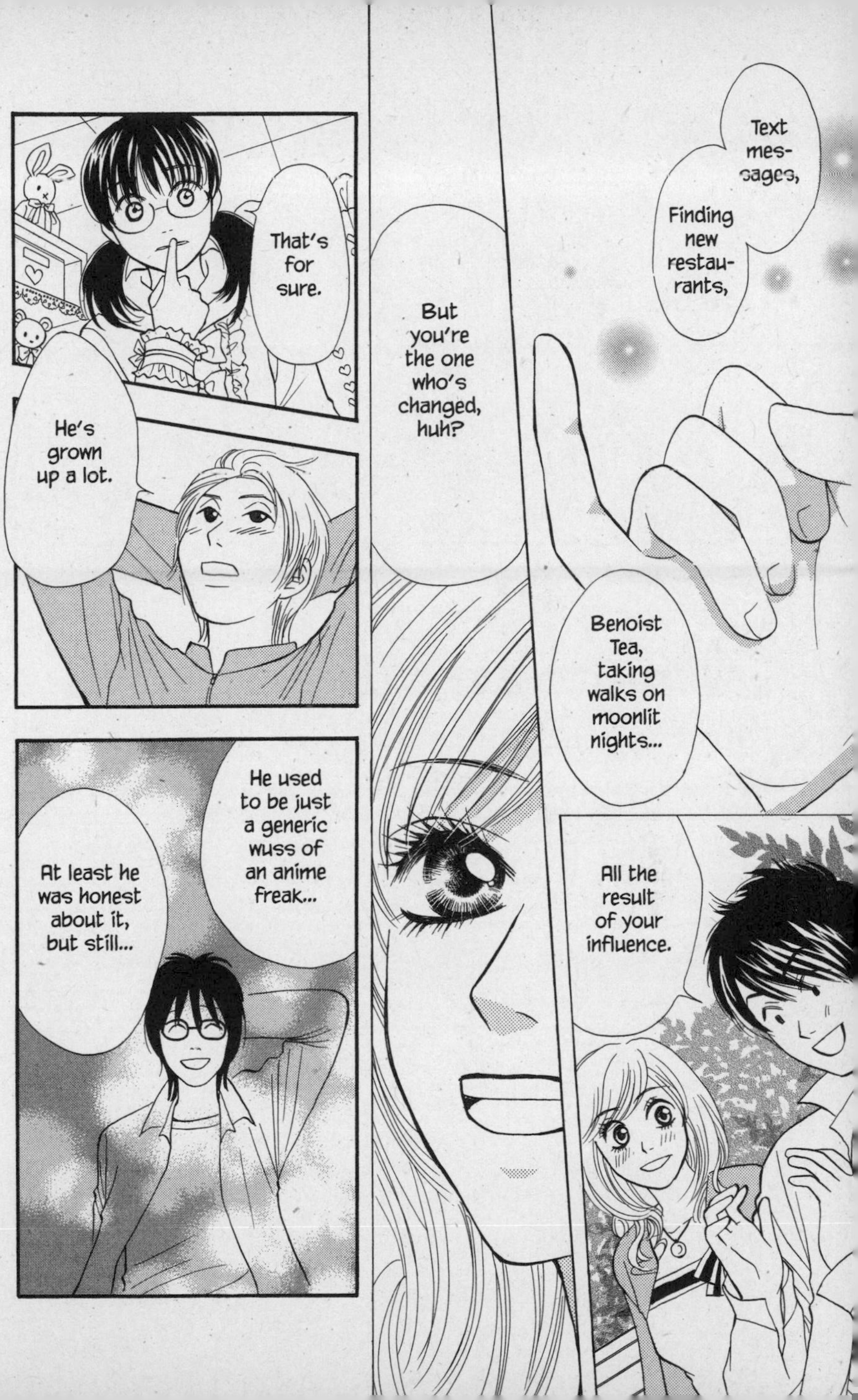
Text messages,
Finding new restaurants,
Benoist Tea, taking walks on moonlit nights...
All the result of your influence.
But you're the one who's changed, huh?
That's for sure.
He's grown up a lot.
He used to be just a generic wuss of an anime freak...
At least he was honest about it, but still...

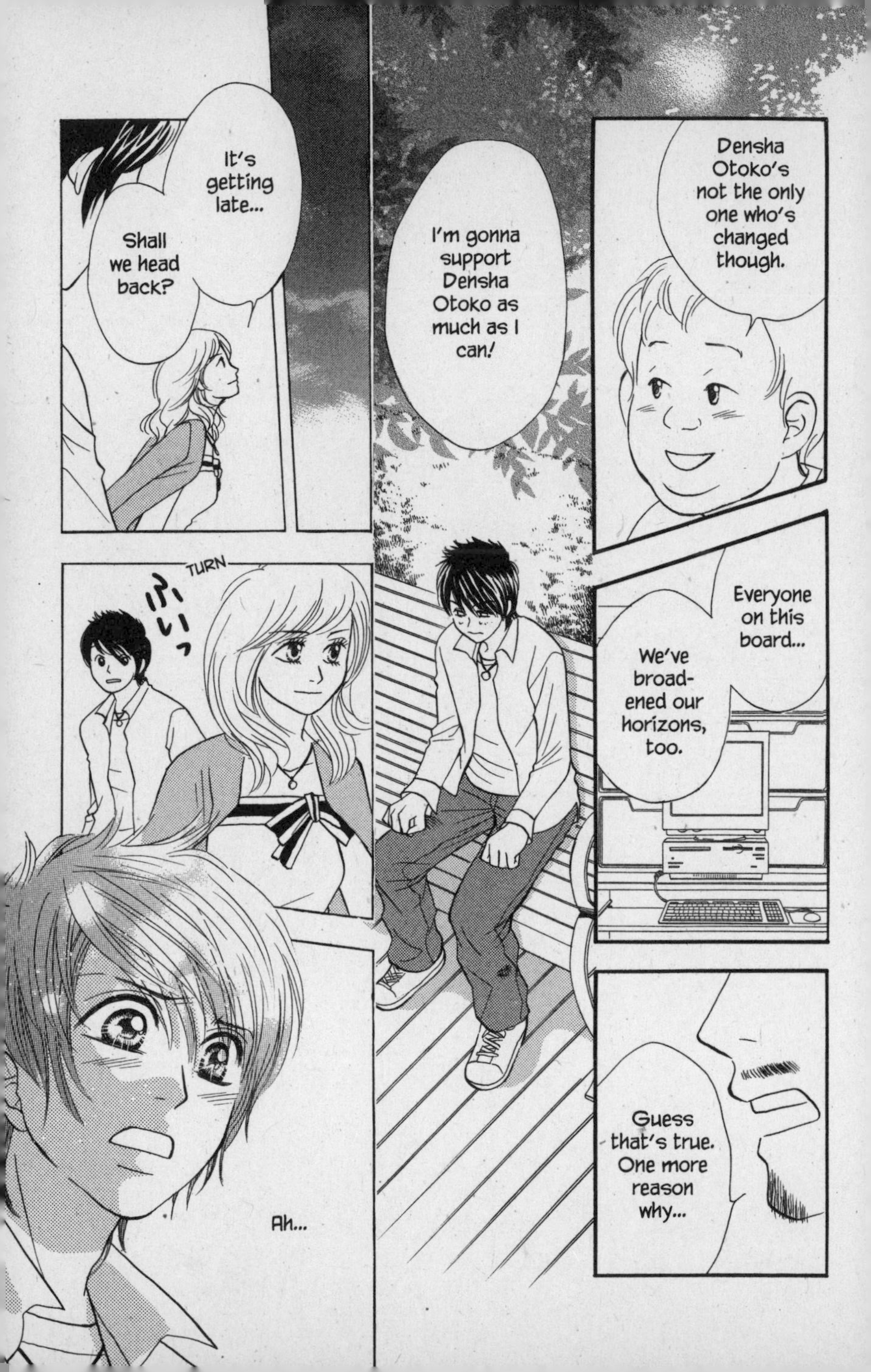
Densha Otoko's not the only one who's changed though.
Everyone on this board...
We've broad-ened our horizons, too.
Guess that's true. One more reason why...
I'm gonna support Densha Otoko as much as I can!
It's getting late...
Shall we head back?
TURN
ふいっ
Ah...

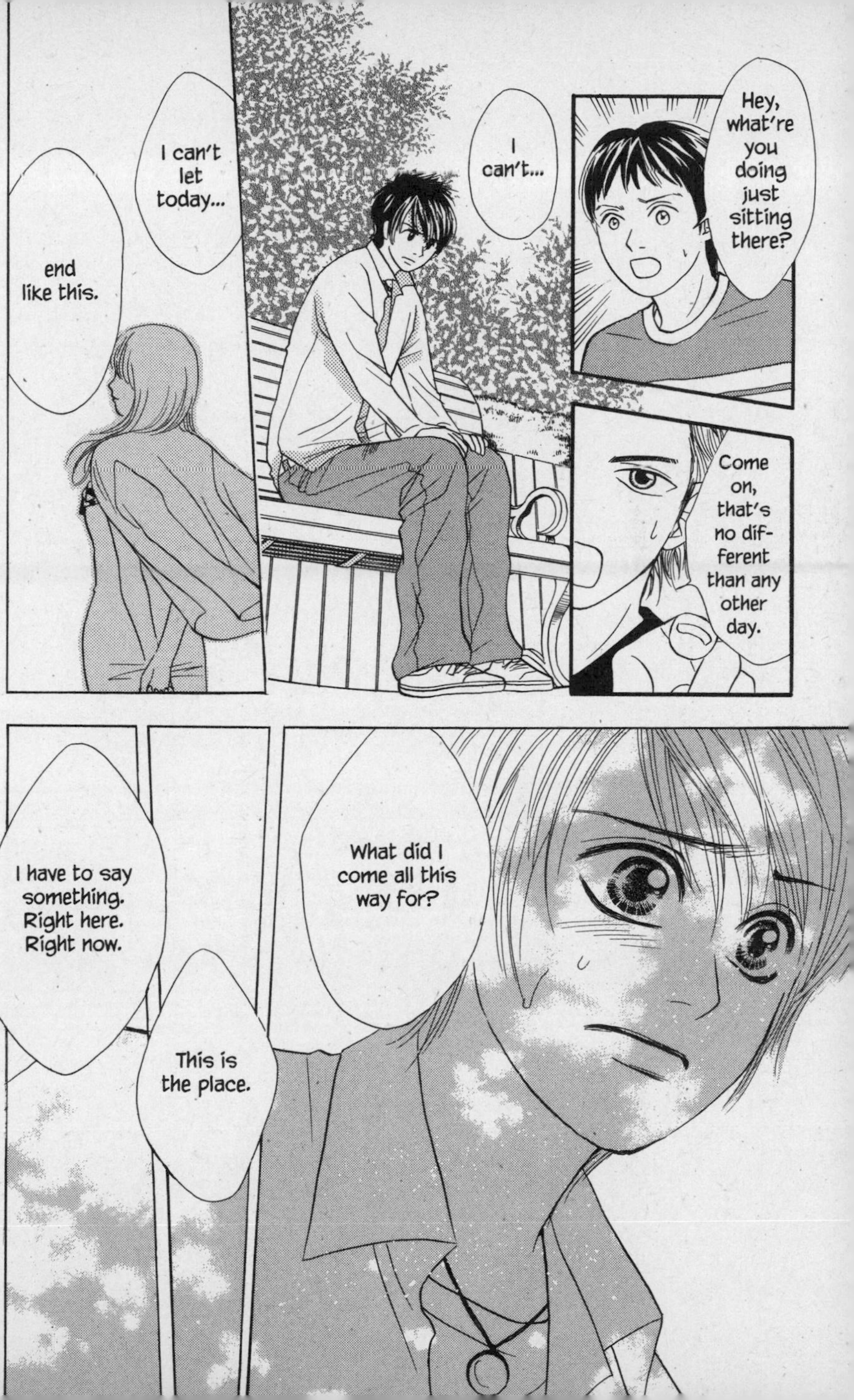
Hey, what're you doing just sitting there?
Come on, that's no different than any other day.
I can't...
I can't let today...
end like this.
What did I come all this way for?
This is the place.
I have to say something. Right here. Right now.

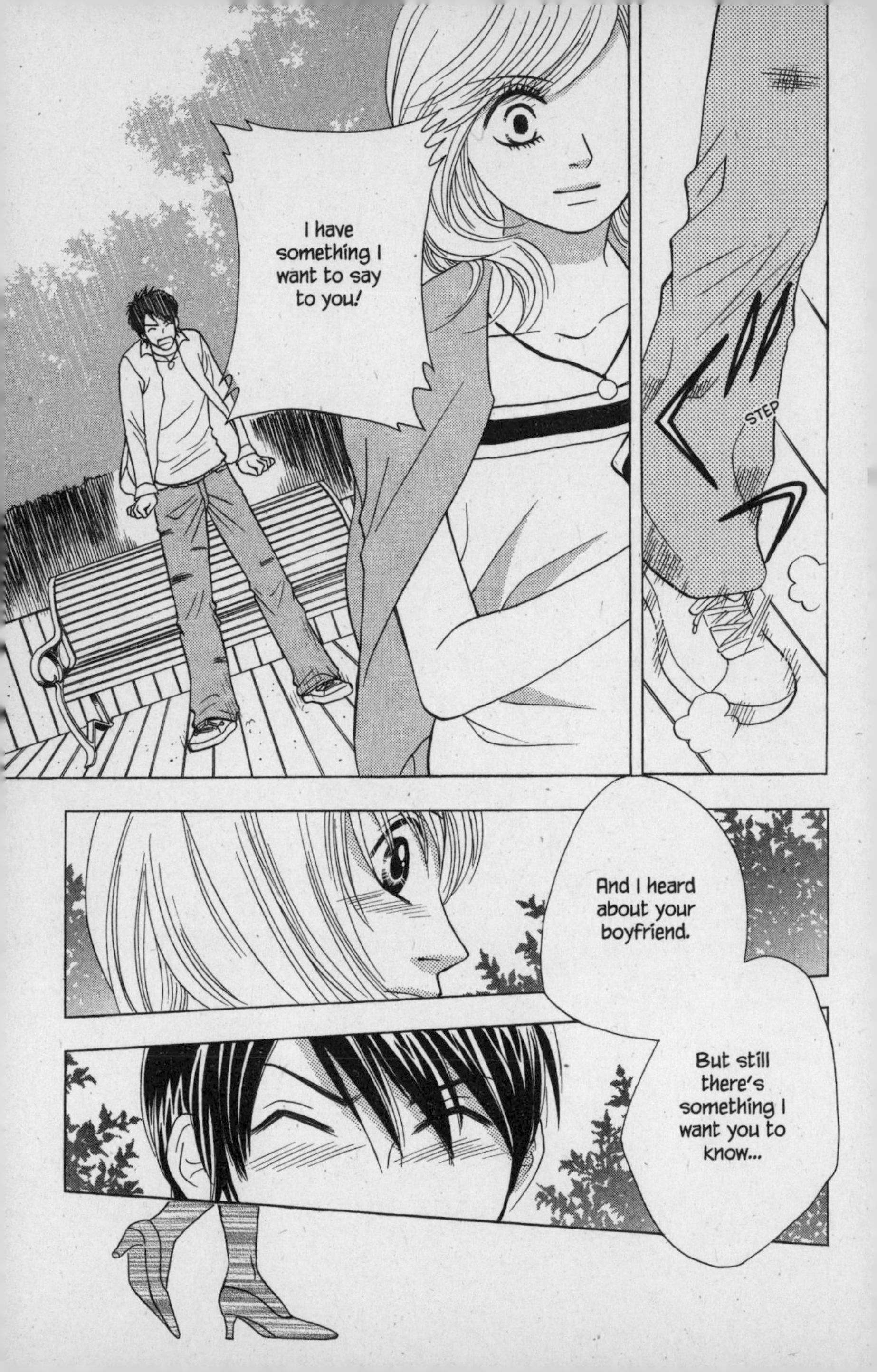
STEP
I have something I want to say to you!
And I heard about your boyfriend.
But still there's something I want you to know...

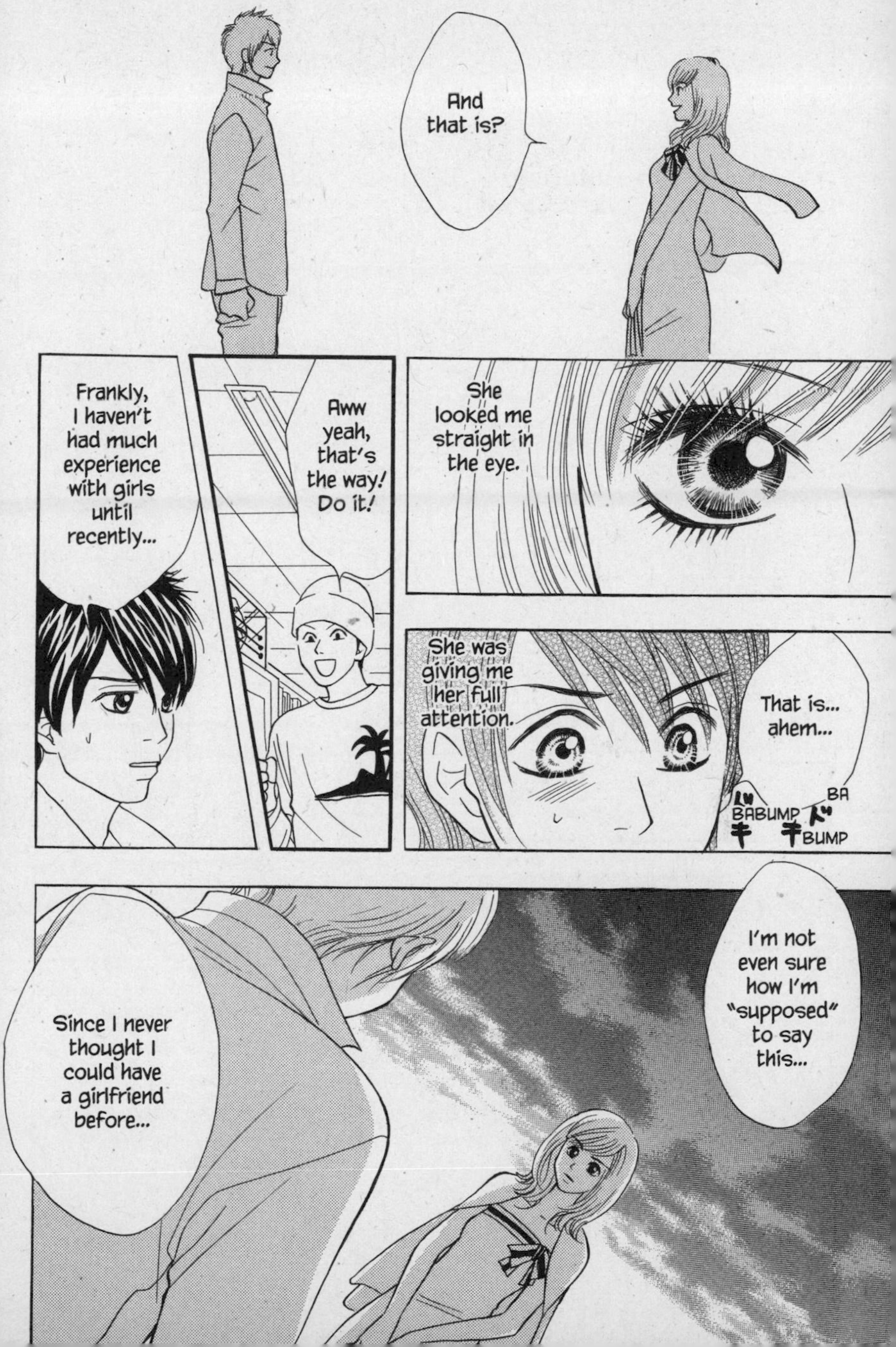
And that is?
She looked me straight in the eye.
She was giving me her full attention.
That is... ahem...
BABUMP
BA BUMP
Aww yeah, that's the way! Do it!
Frankly, I haven't had much experience with girls until recently...
I'm not even sure how I'm "supposed" to say this...
Since I never thought I could have a girlfriend before...

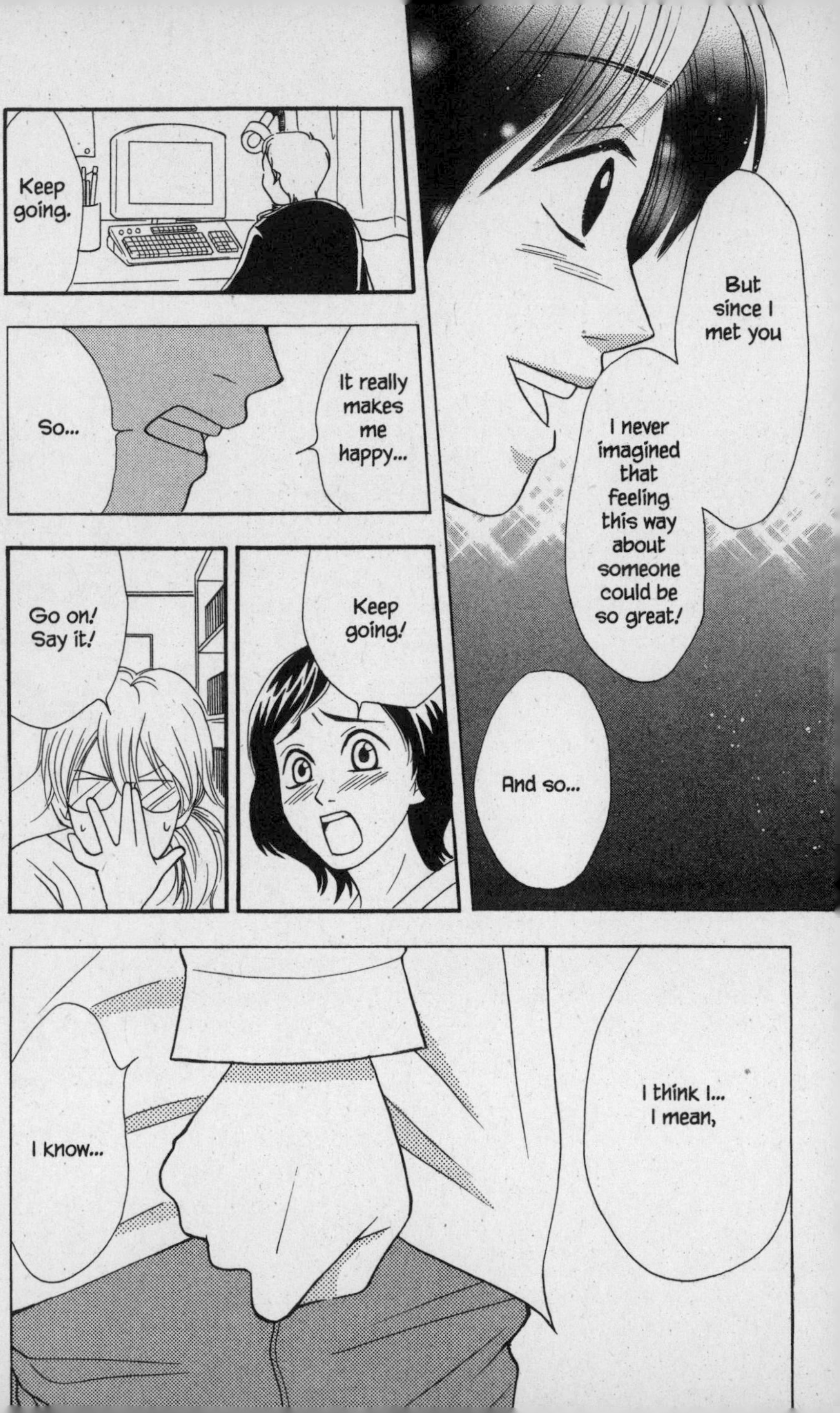
But since I met you
I never imagined that feeling this way about someone could be so great!
And so...
Keep going.
It really makes me happy...
So...
Keep going!
Go on! Say it!
I think I... I mean,
I know...

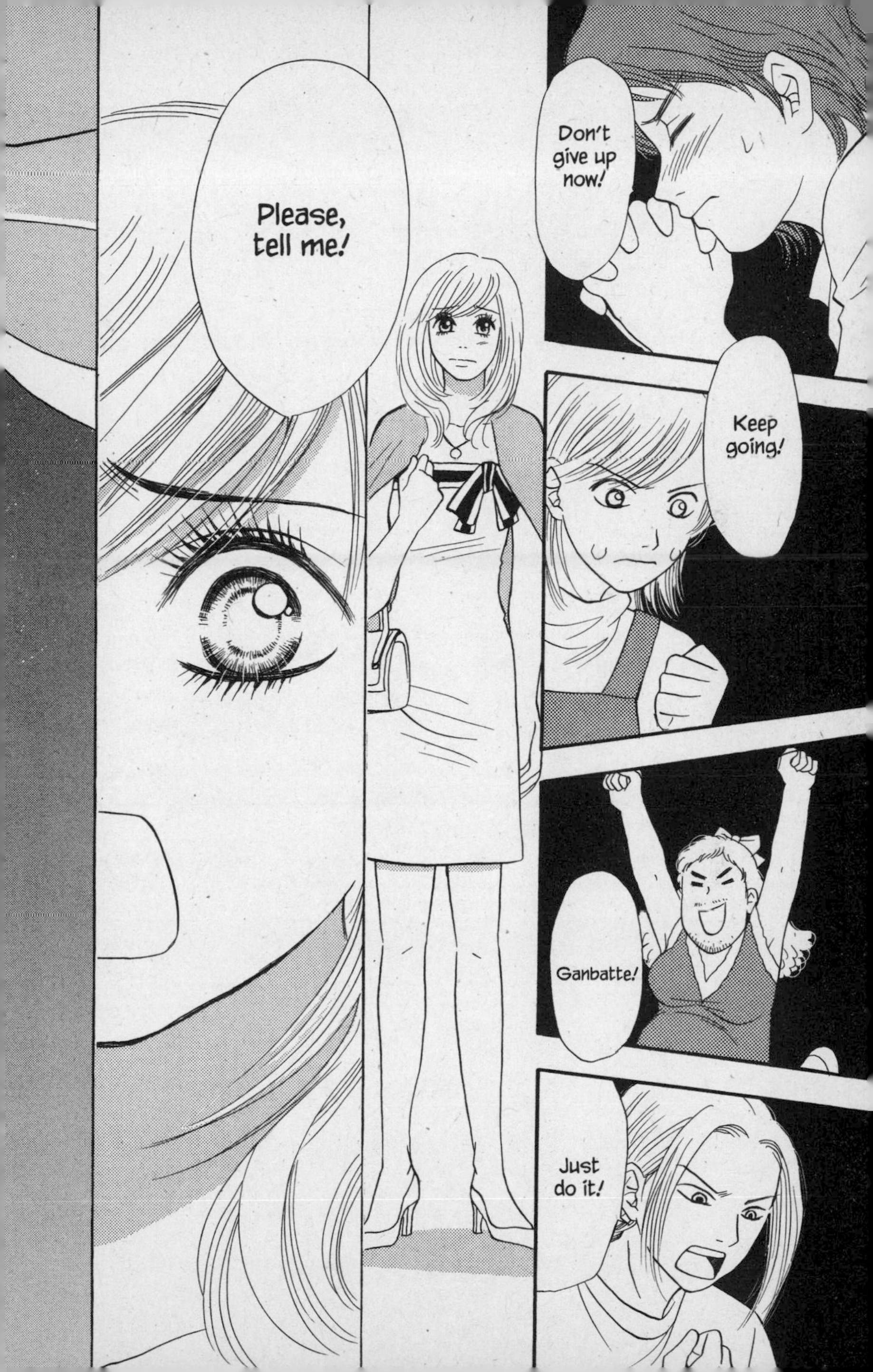
Don't give up now!
Keep going!
Ganbatte!
Just do it!
Please, tell me!

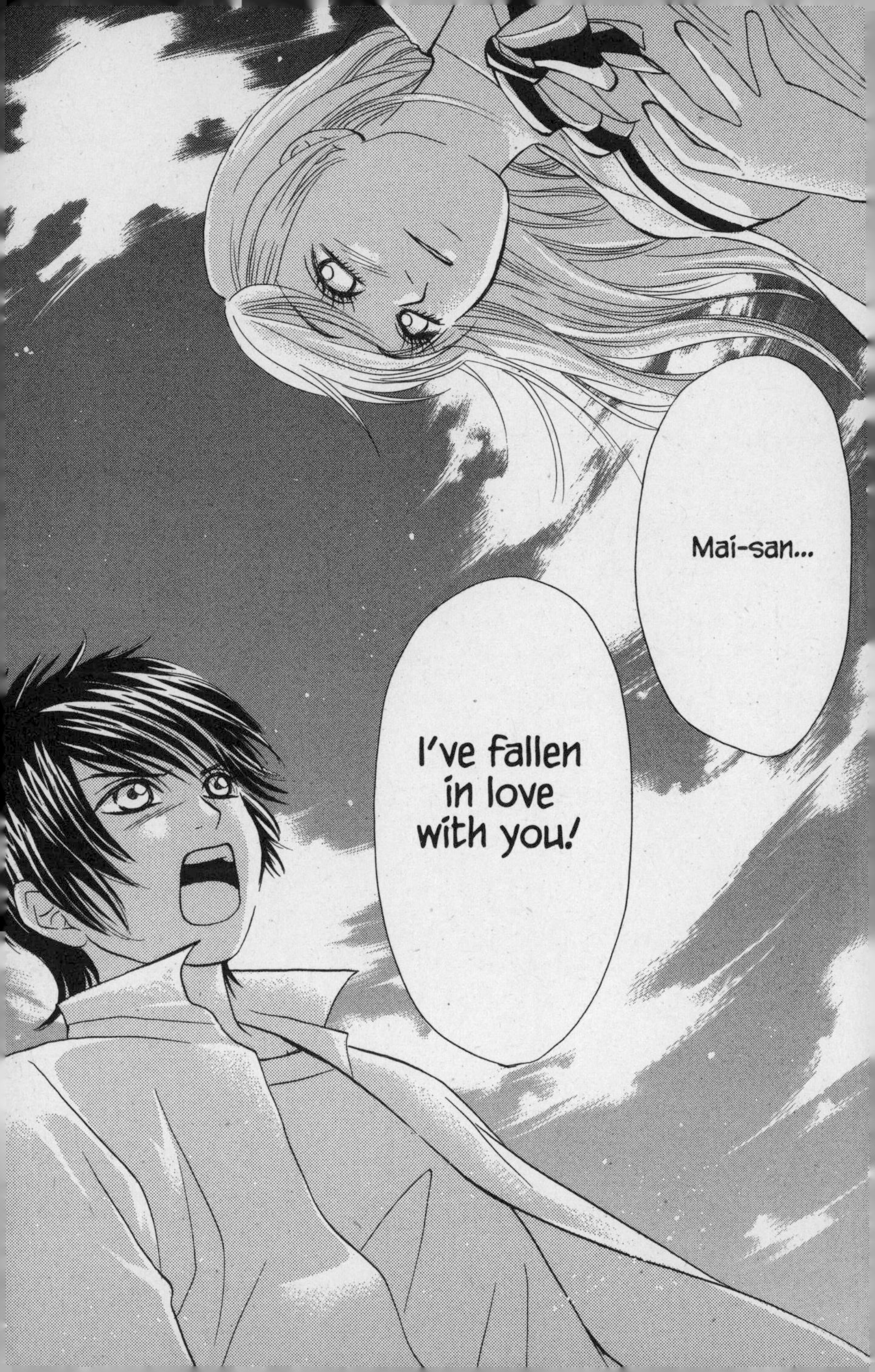
Mai-san...
I've fallen in love with you!

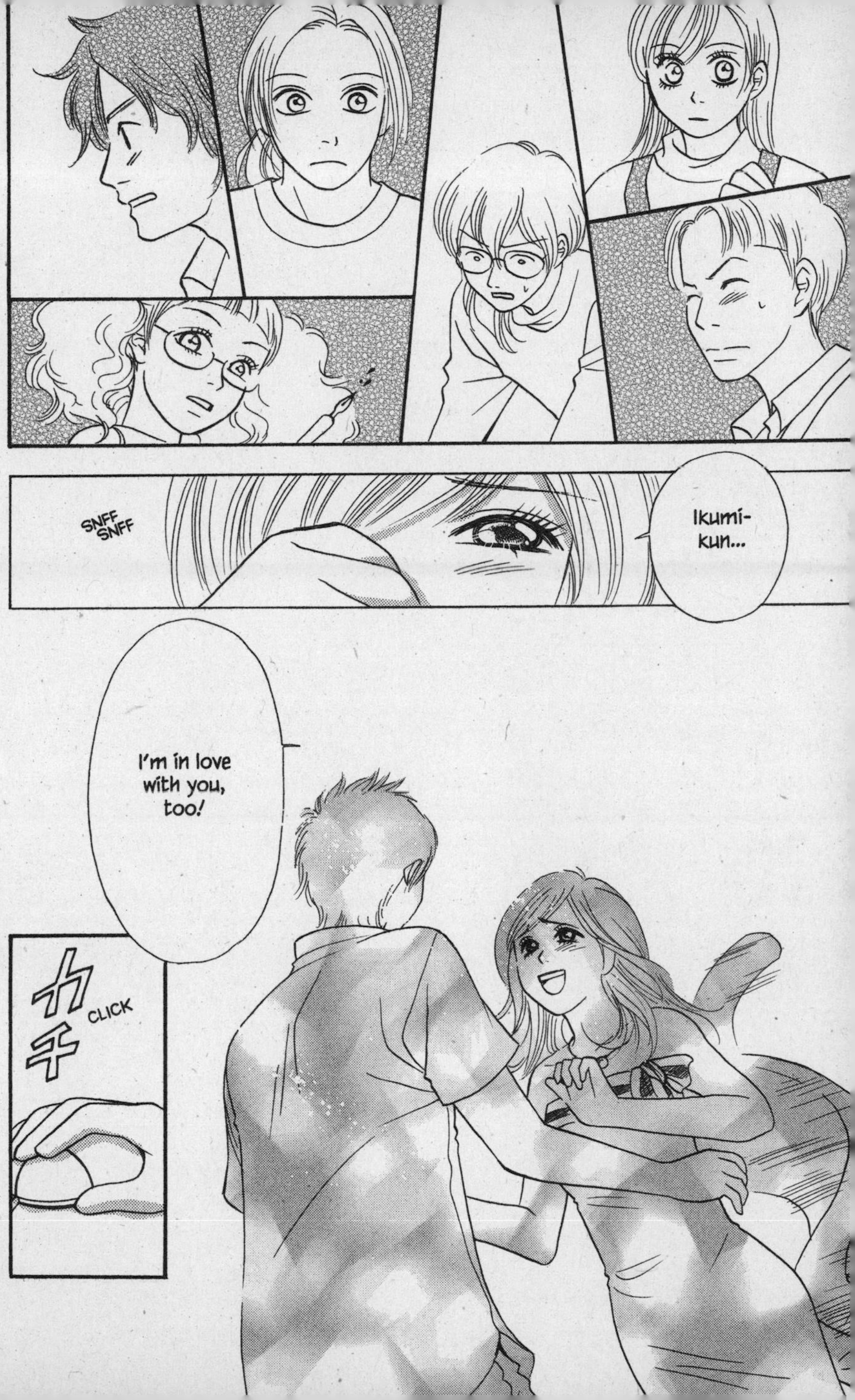
Ikumi-kun...
SNFF SNFF
I'm in love with you, too!
カチ
CLICK

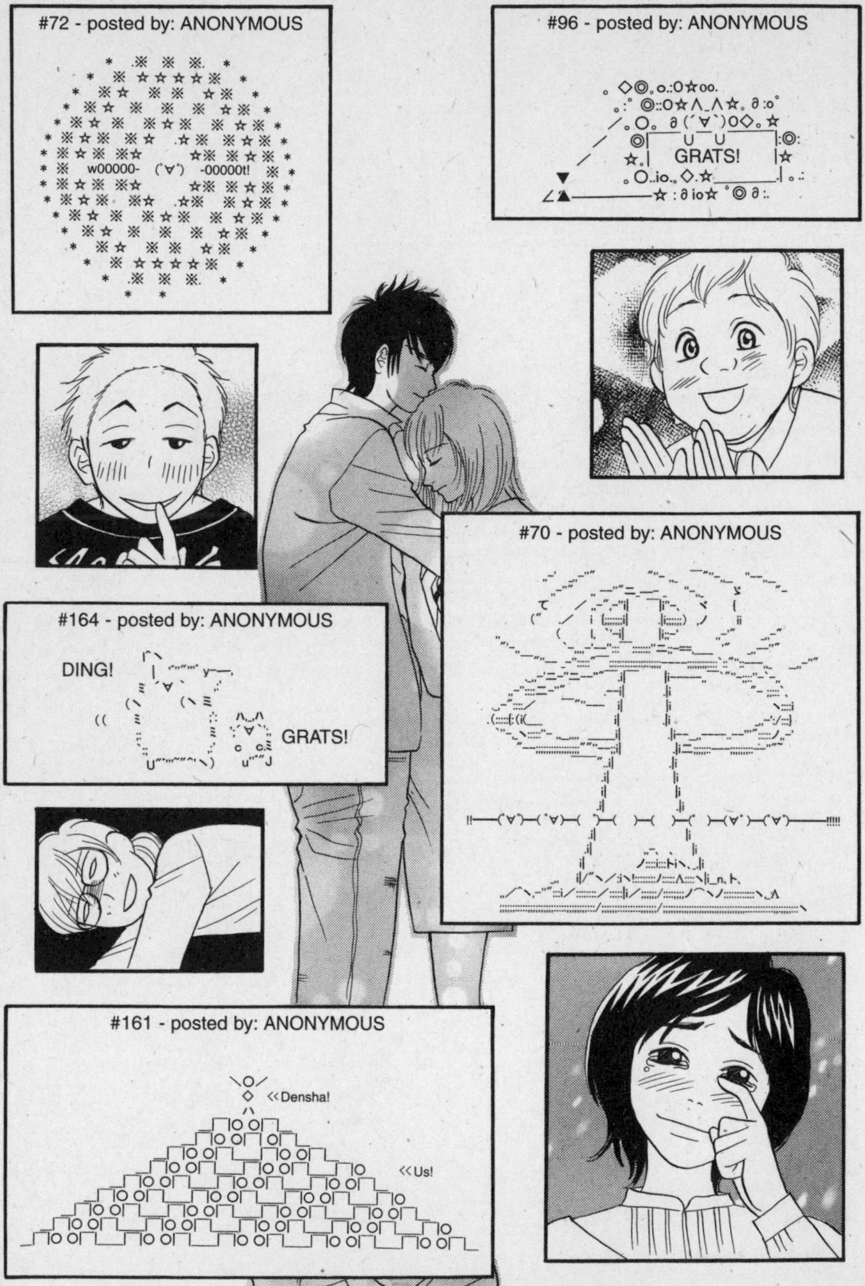
#96 - posted by: ANONYMOUS
GRATS!
#72 - posted by: ANONYMOUS
w00000- (ﾟ∀ﾟ) -00000t!
#70 - posted by: ANONYMOUS
#164 - posted by: ANONYMOUS
DING!
GRATS!
#161 - posted by: ANONYMOUS
<<Densha!
<<Us!

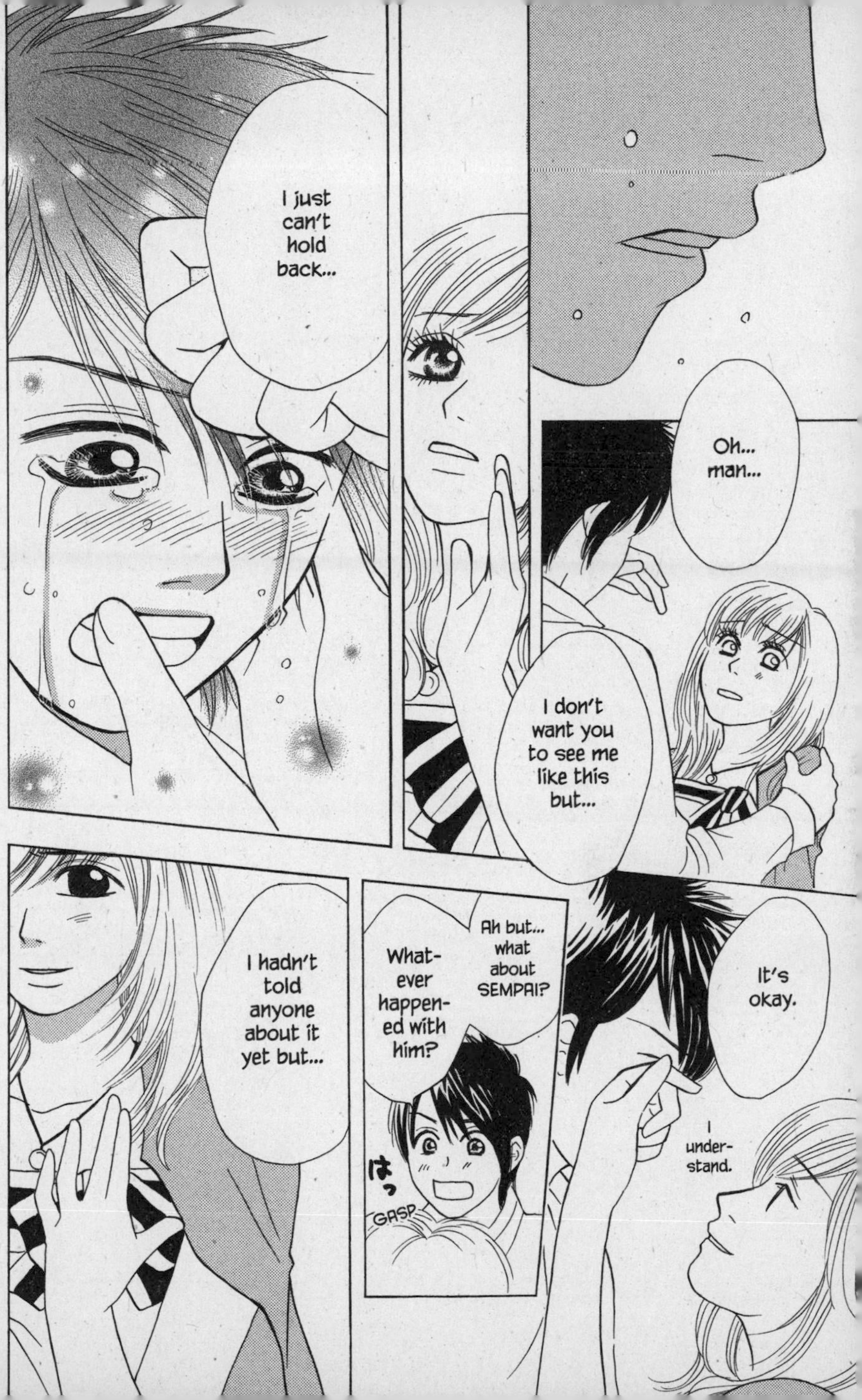
Oh... man...
I don't want you to see me like this but...
I just can't hold back...
It's okay.
I under-stand.
Ah but... what about SEMPAI?
What-ever happen-ed with him?
はっ
GASP
I hadn't told anyone about it yet but...

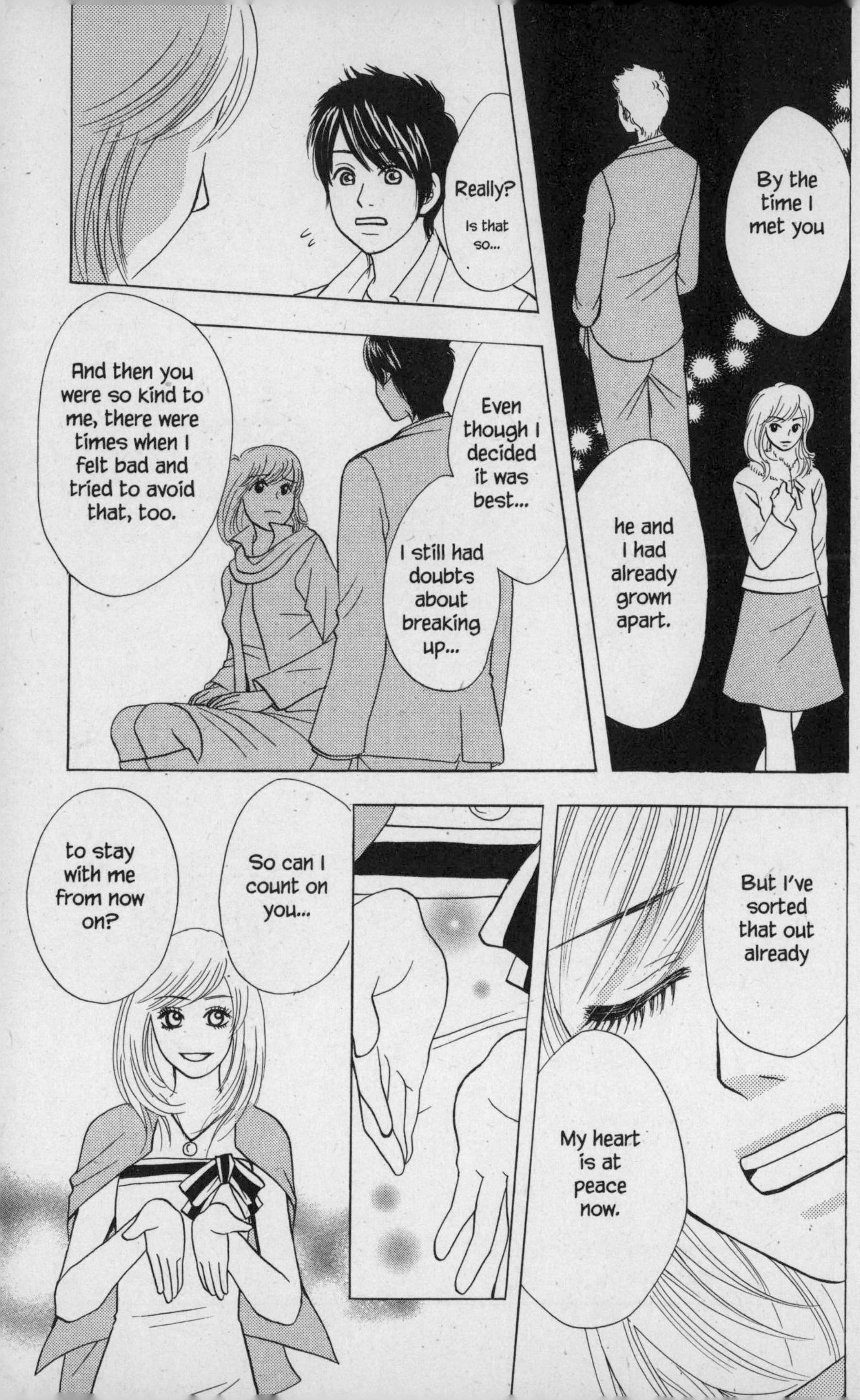
By the time I met you
he and I had already grown apart.
Really?
Is that so...
Even though I decided it was best...
I still had doubts about breaking up...
And then you were so kind to me, there were times when I felt bad and tried to avoid that, too.
But I've sorted that out already
My heart is at peace now.
So can I count on you...
to stay with me from now on?

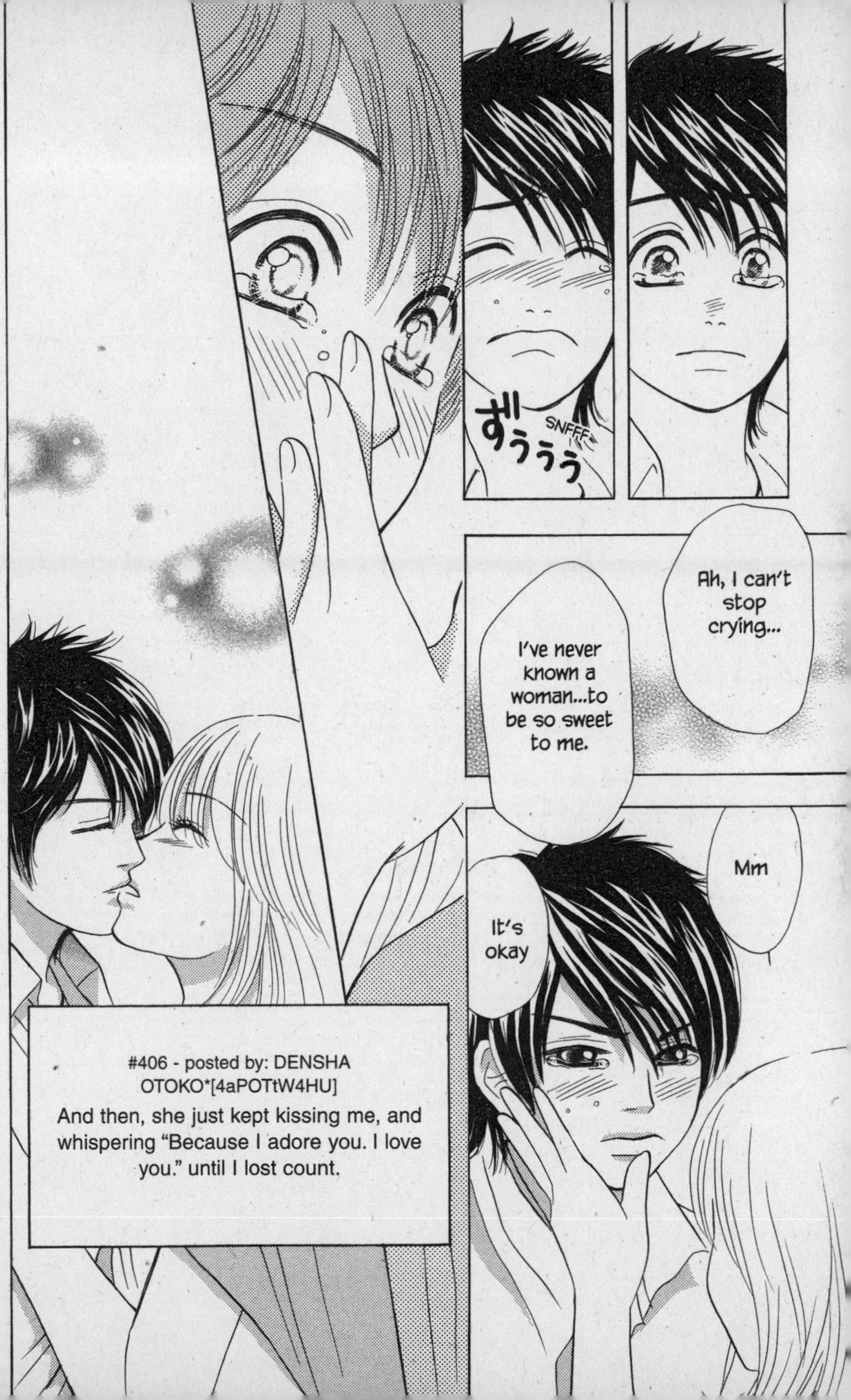
ずううう
SNFFF
Ah, I can't stop crying...
I've never known a woman...to be so sweet to me.
Mm
It's okay
#406 - posted by: DENSHA OTOKO*[4aPOTtW4HU]
And then, she just kept kissing me, and whispering "Because I adore you. I love you." until I lost count.

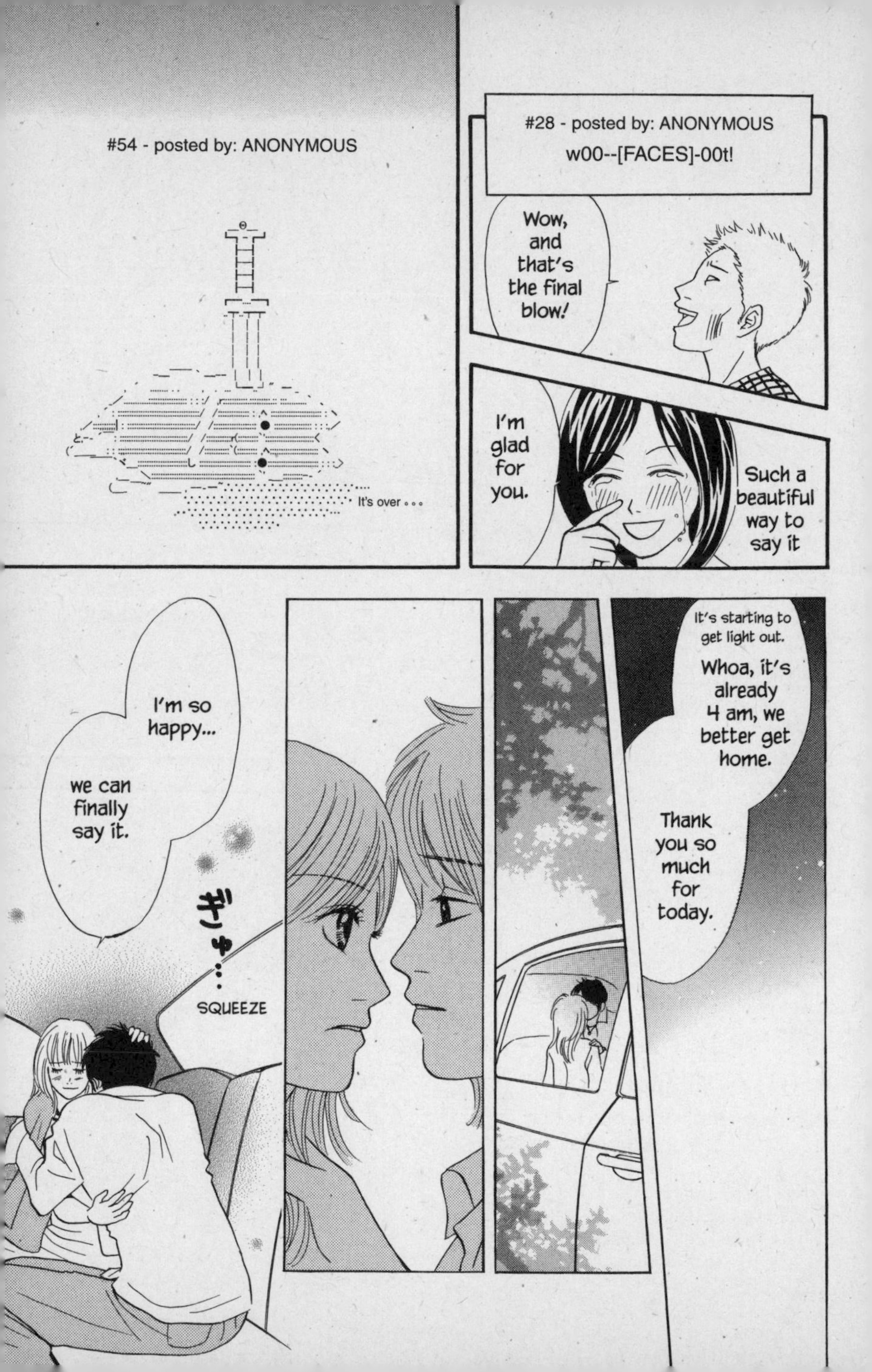
#28 - posted by: ANONYMOUS
w00--[FACES]-00t!
Wow, and that's the final blow!
I'm glad for you.
Such a beautiful way to say it
#54 - posted by: ANONYMOUS
It's over . . .
It's starting to get light out.
Whoa, it's already 4 am, we better get home.
Thank you so much for today.
I'm so happy...
we can finally say it.
ギュ…
SQUEEZE

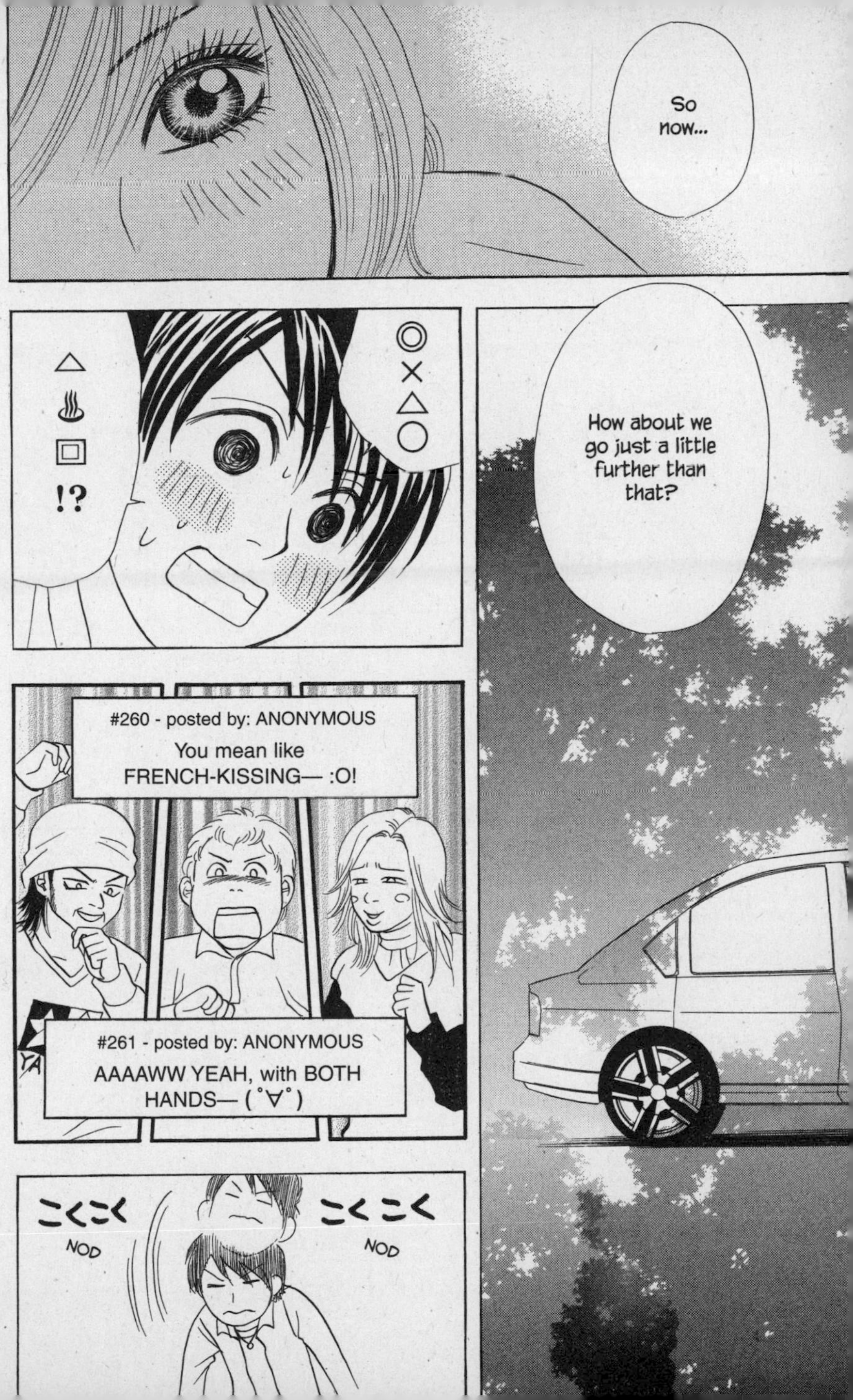

So now...
How about we go just a little further than that?
◎×△○
△ ♨ □ !?
#260 - posted by: ANONYMOUS
You mean like FRENCH-KISSING— :O!
#261 - posted by: ANONYMOUS
AAAAWW YEAH, with BOTH HANDS— (ﾟ∀ﾟ)
こくこく
NOD
こくこく
NOD

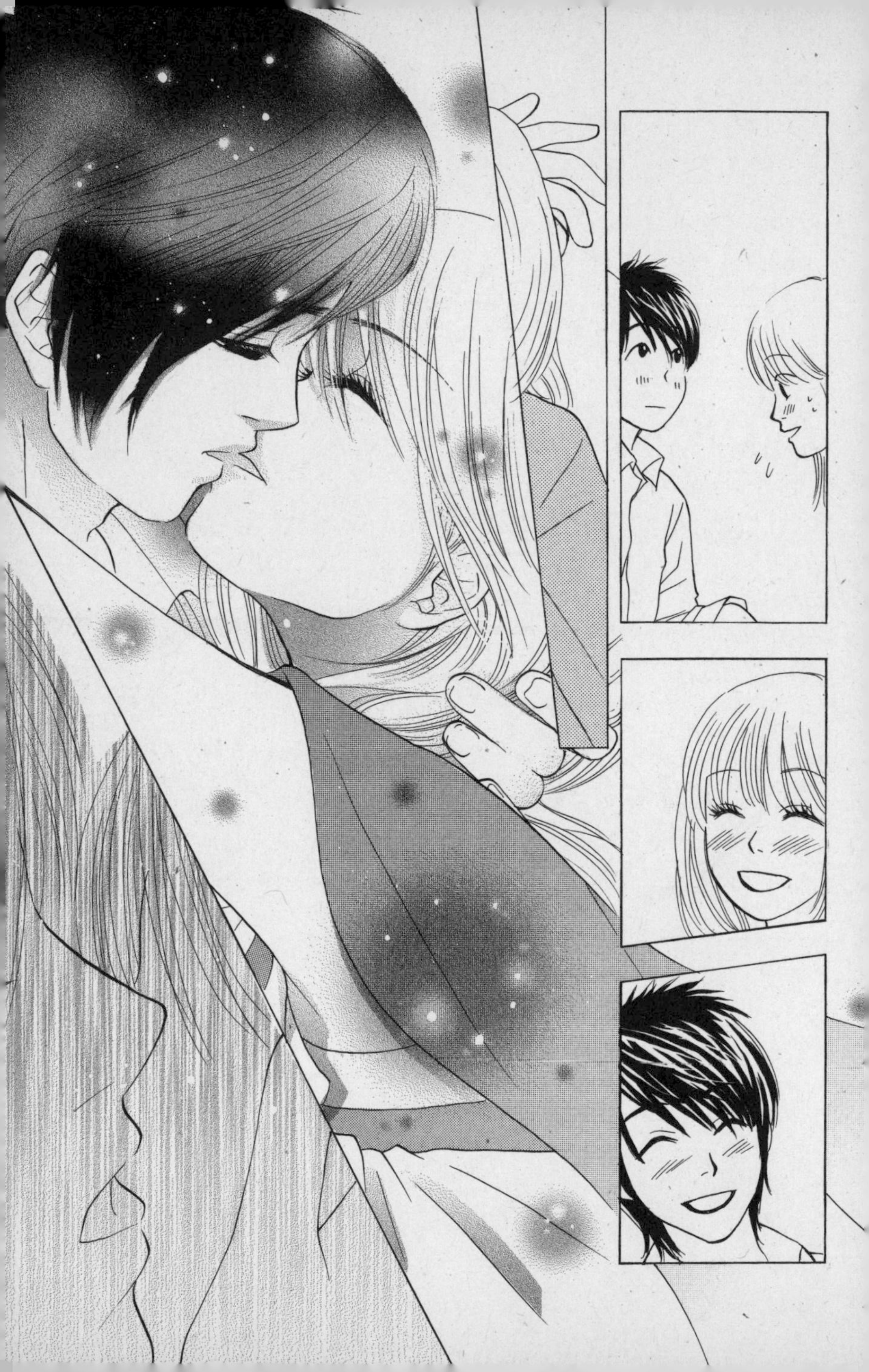

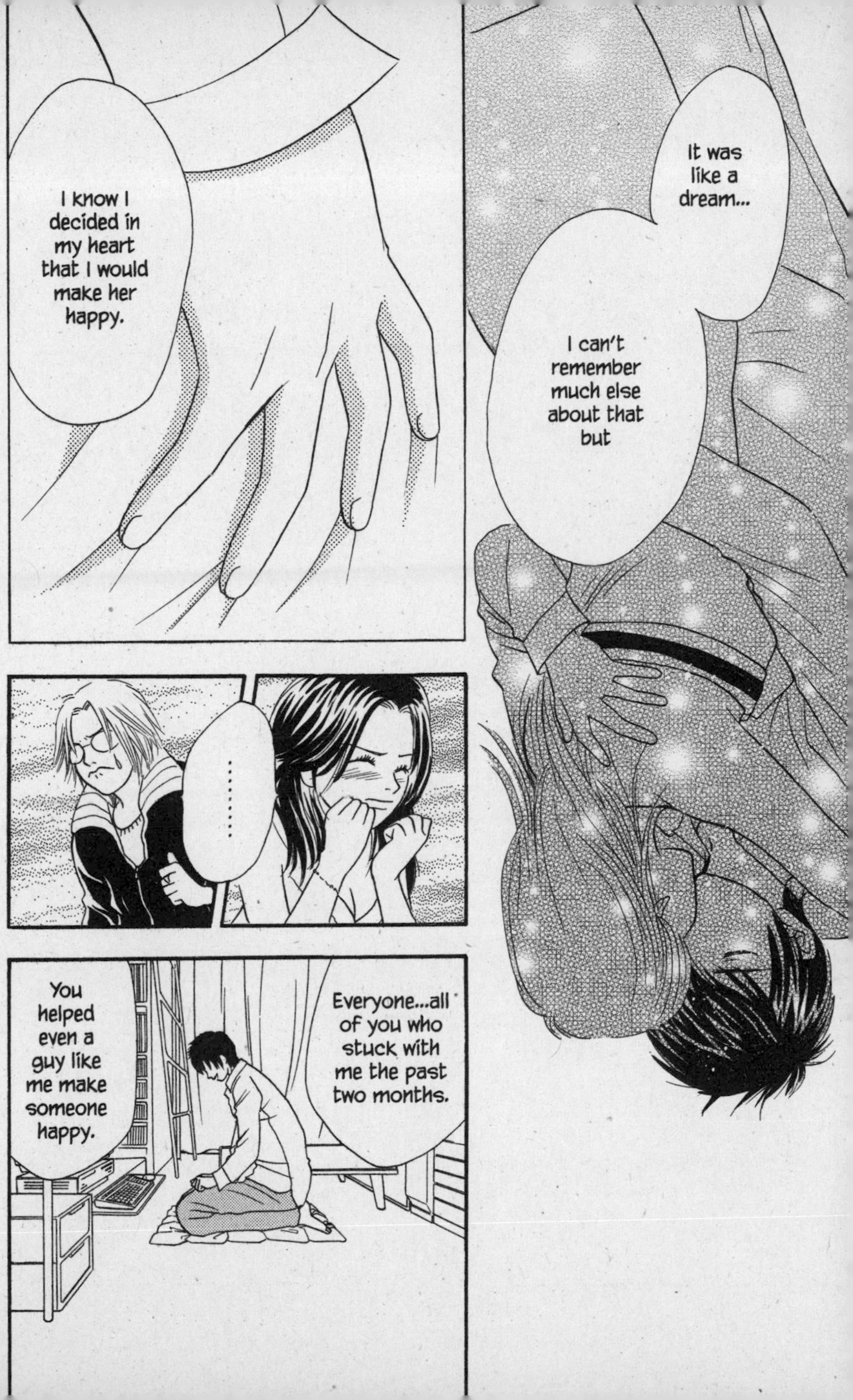
It was like a dream...
I can't remember much else about that but
I know I decided in my heart that I would make her happy.
......
Everyone...all of you who stuck with me the past two months.
You helped even a guy like me make someone happy.

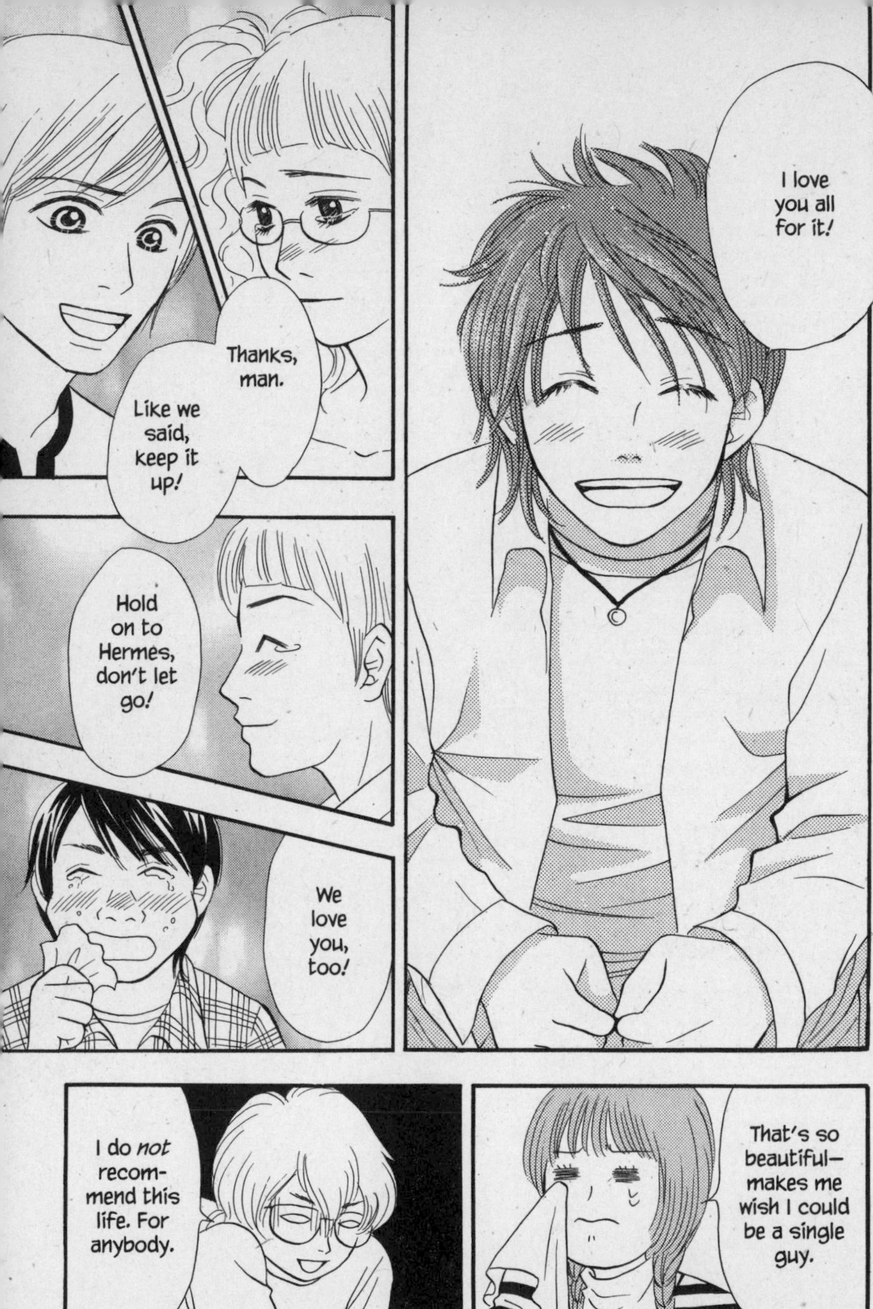
I love you all for it!
Thanks, man.
Like we said, keep it up!
Hold on to Hermes, don't let go!
We love you, too!
That's so beautiful—makes me wish I could be a single guy.
I do *not* recommend this life. For anybody.

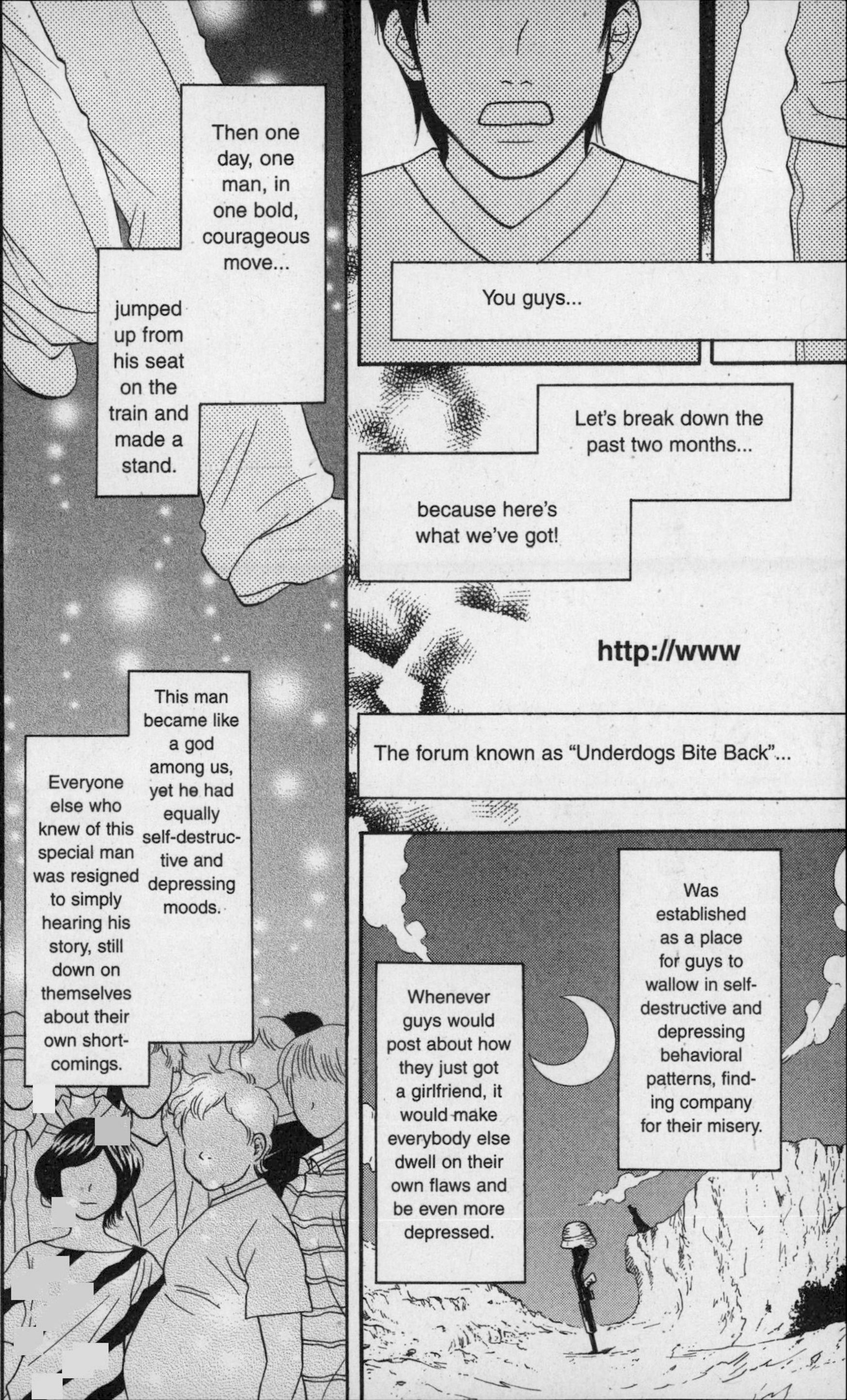
You guys...
Let's break down the past two months...
because here's what we've got!
http://www
The forum known as "Underdogs Bite Back"...
Was established as a place for guys to wallow in self-destructive and depressing behavioral patterns, finding company for their misery.
Whenever guys would post about how they just got a girlfriend, it would make everybody else dwell on their own flaws and be even more depressed.
Then one day, one man, in one bold, courageous move...
jumped up from his seat on the train and made a stand.
This man became like a god among us, yet he had equally self-destructive and depressing moods.
Everyone else who knew of this special man was resigned to simply hearing his story, still down on themselves about their own shortcomings.

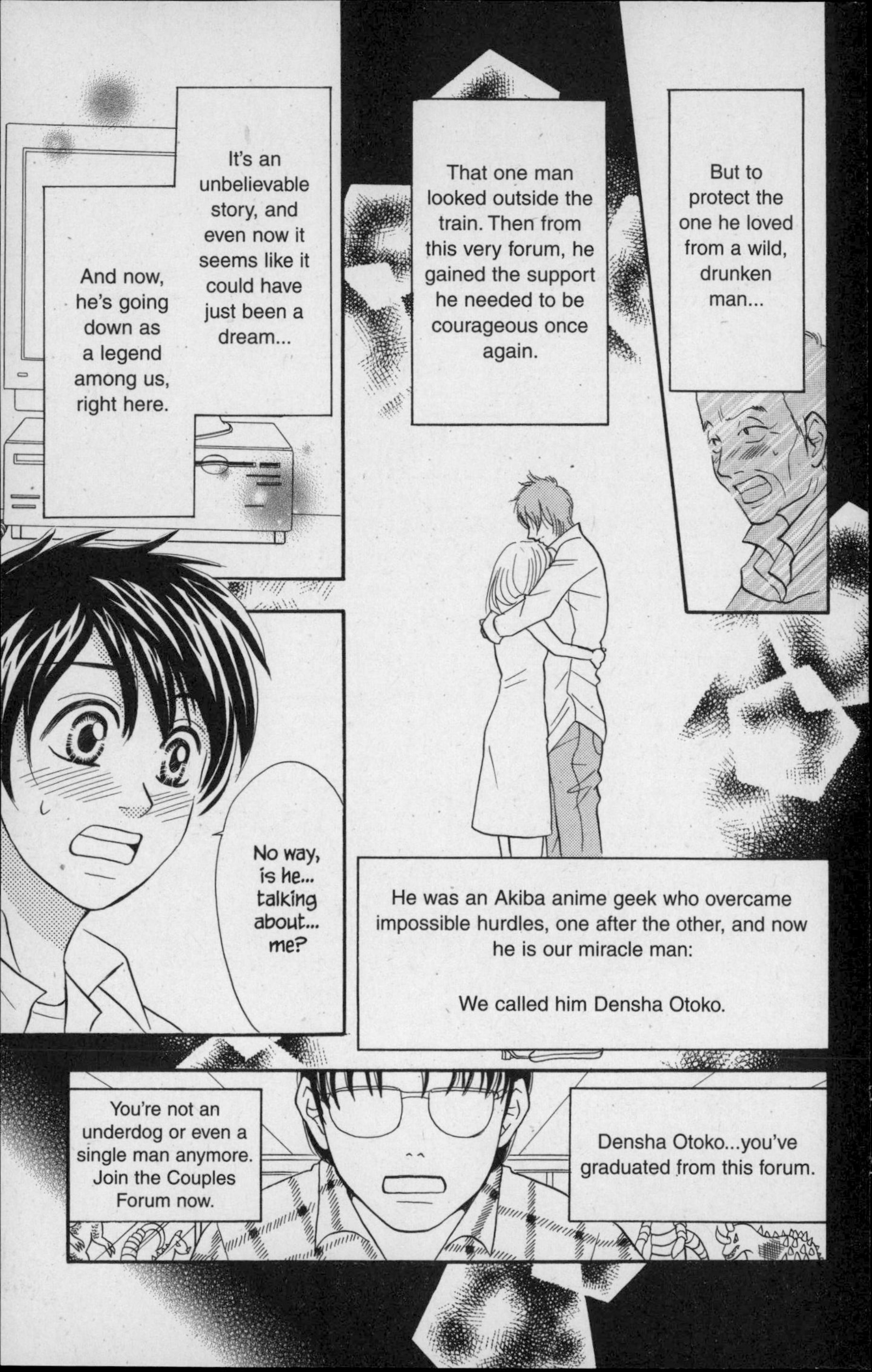
But to protect the one he loved from a wild, drunken man...
That one man looked outside the train. Then from this very forum, he gained the support he needed to be courageous once again.
He was an Akiba anime geek who overcame impossible hurdles, one after the other, and now he is our miracle man:
We called him Densha Otoko.
It's an unbelievable story, and even now it seems like it could have just been a dream...
And now, he's going down as a legend among us, right here.
No way, is he... talking about... me?
Densha Otoko...you've graduated from this forum.
You're not an underdog or even a single man anymore. Join the Couples Forum now.

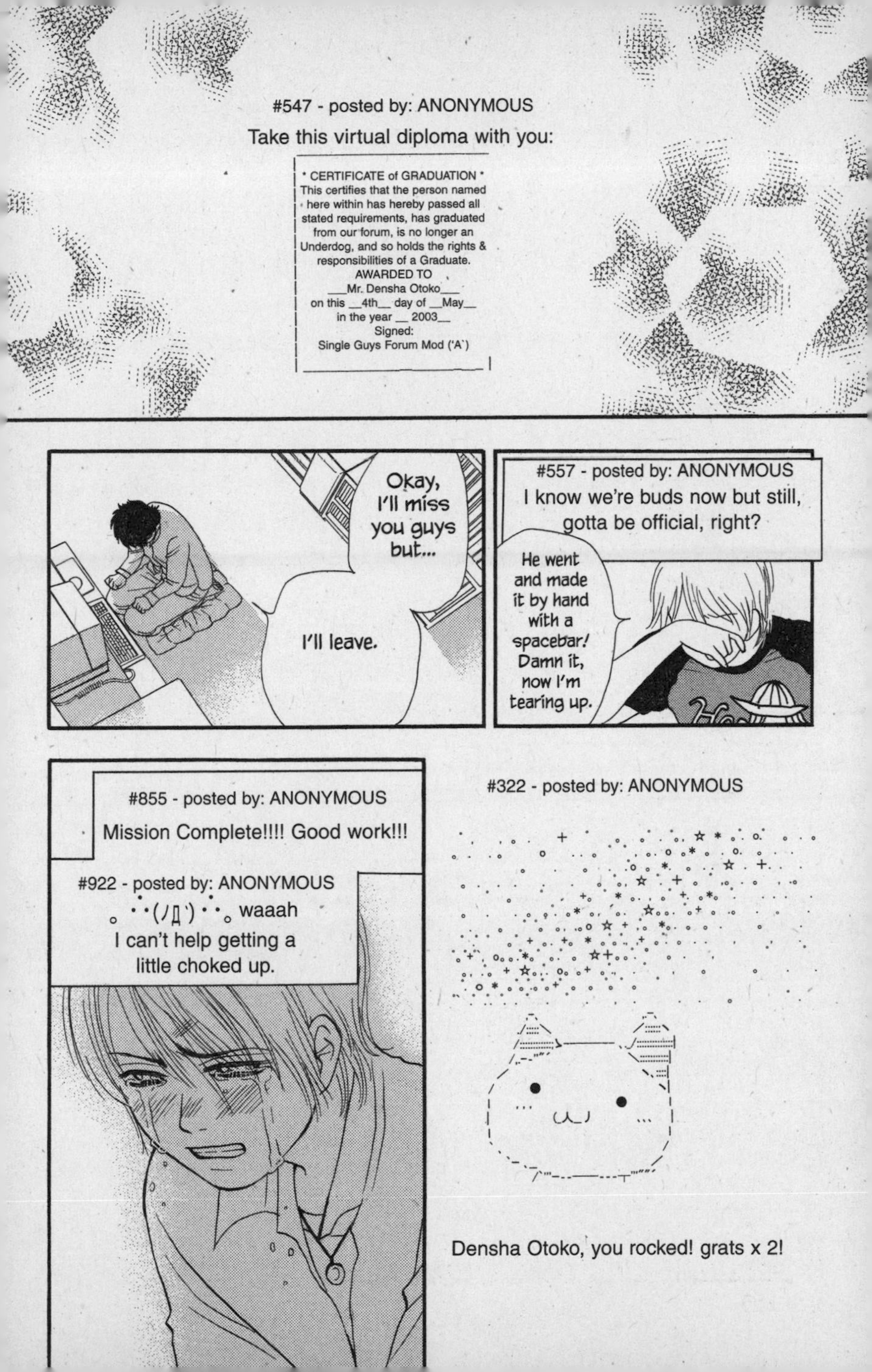
#547 - posted by: ANONYMOUS
Take this virtual diploma with you:
* CERTIFICATE of GRADUATION *
This certifies that the person named here within has hereby passed all stated requirements, has graduated from our forum, is no longer an Underdog, and so holds the rights & responsibilities of a Graduate.
AWARDED TO
___Mr. Densha Otoko___
on this __4th__ day of __May__
in the year __ 2003__
Signed:
Single Guys Forum Mod ('A')
#557 - posted by: ANONYMOUS
I know we're buds now but still, gotta be official, right?
He went and made it by hand with a spacebar! Damn it, now I'm tearing up.
Okay, I'll miss you guys but...
I'll leave.
#322 - posted by: ANONYMOUS
Densha Otoko, you rocked! grats x 2!
#855 - posted by: ANONYMOUS
Mission Complete!!!! Good work!!!
#922 - posted by: ANONYMOUS
。・゚・(ﾉД`)・゚・。 waaah
I can't help getting a little choked up.

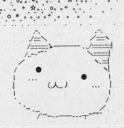

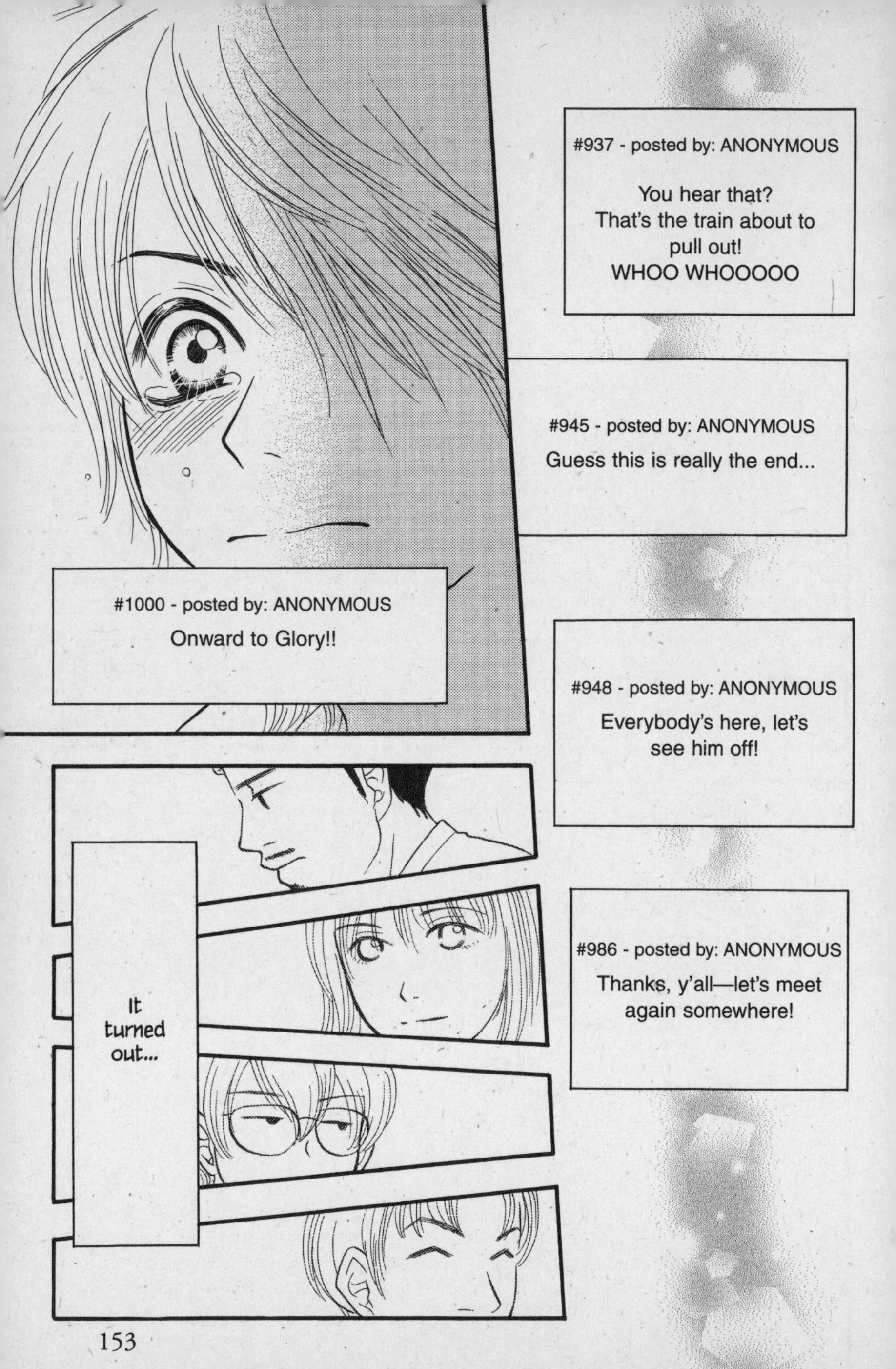
#937 - posted by: ANONYMOUS
You hear that? That's the train about to pull out! WHOO WHOOOOO
#945 - posted by: ANONYMOUS
Guess this is really the end...
#948 - posted by: ANONYMOUS
Everybody's here, let's see him off!
#986 - posted by: ANONYMOUS
Thanks, y'all—let's meet again somewhere!
#1000 - posted by: ANONYMOUS
Onward to Glory!!
It turned out...

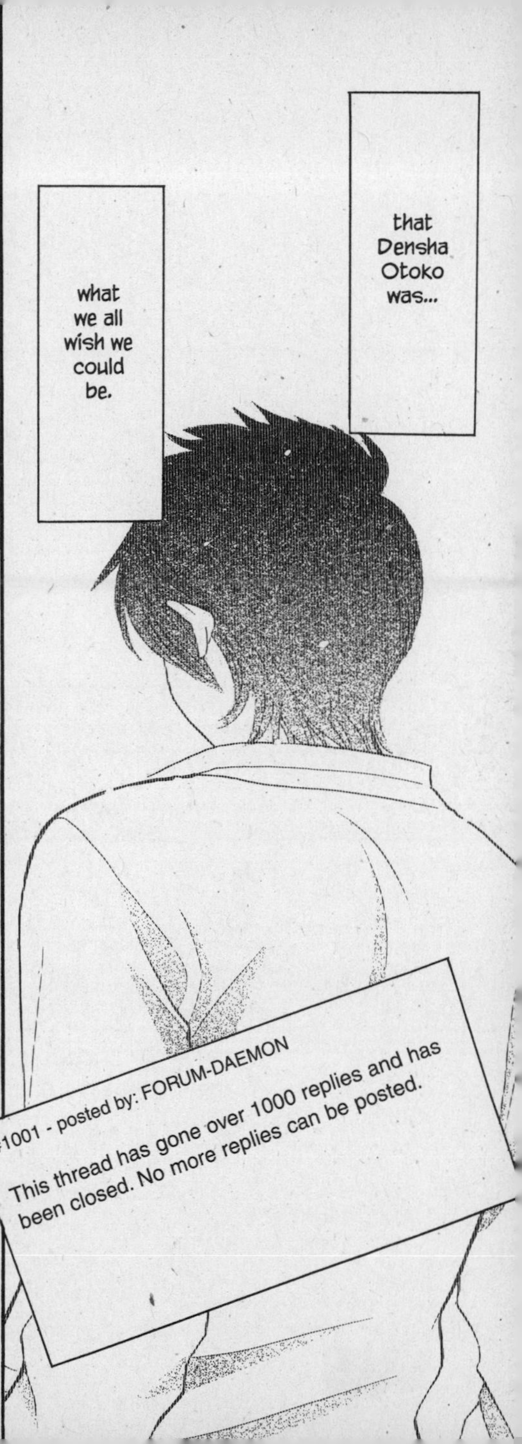
that Densha Otoko was...
what we all wish we could be.
#1001 - posted by: FORUM-DAEMON
This thread has gone over 1000 replies and has been closed. No more replies can be posted.
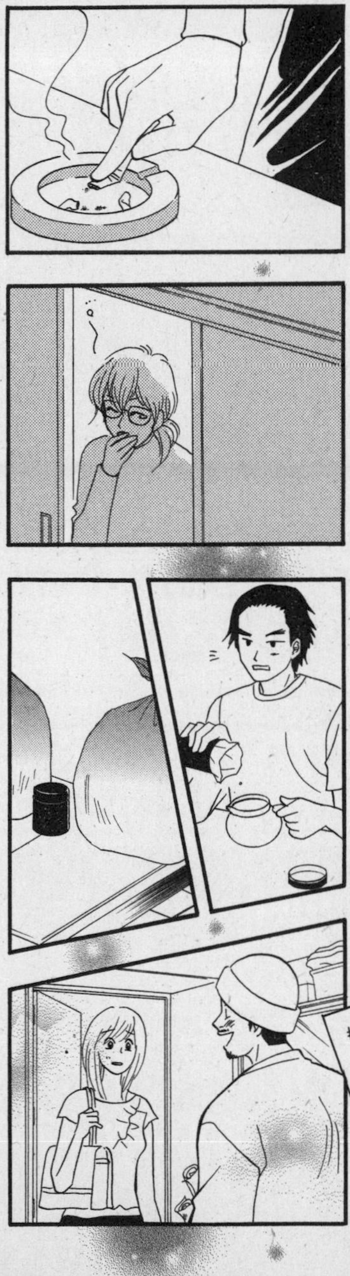

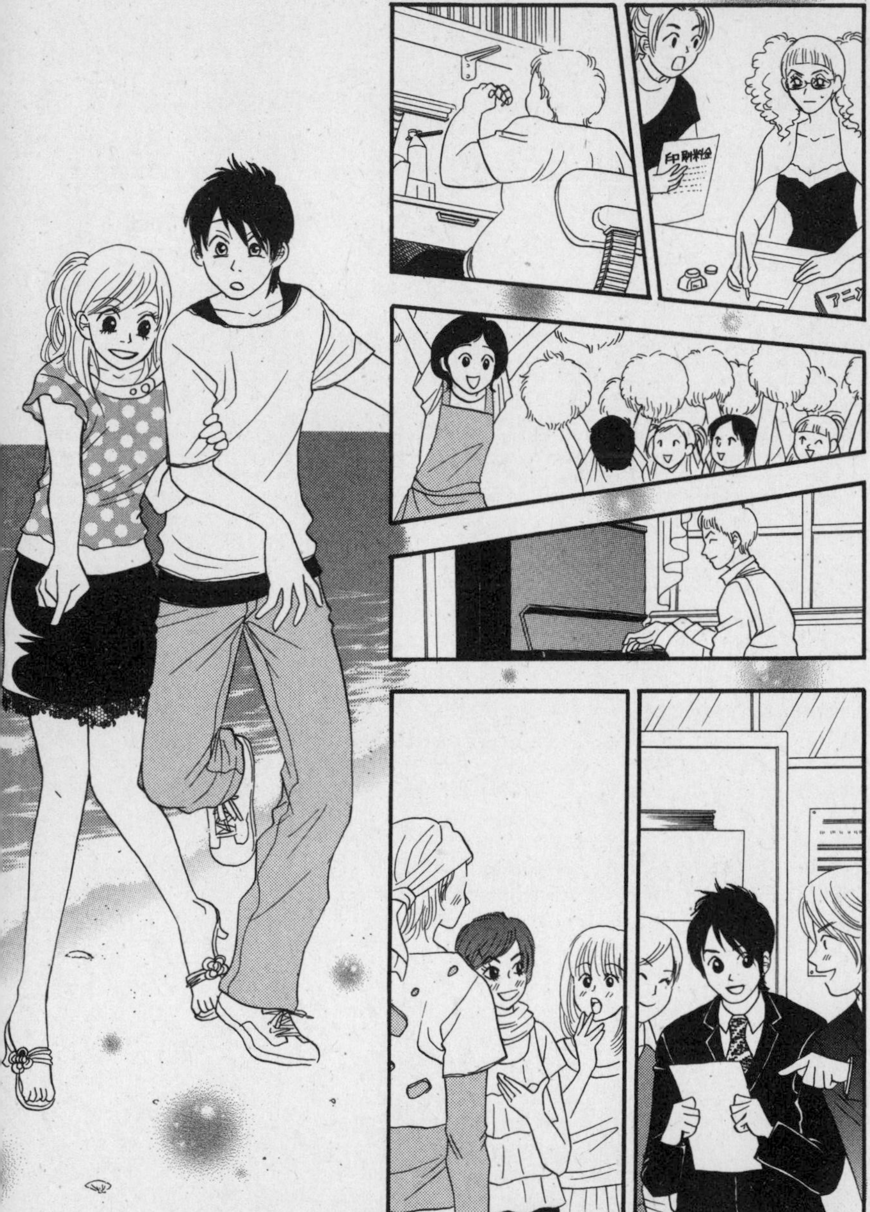
印刷料金

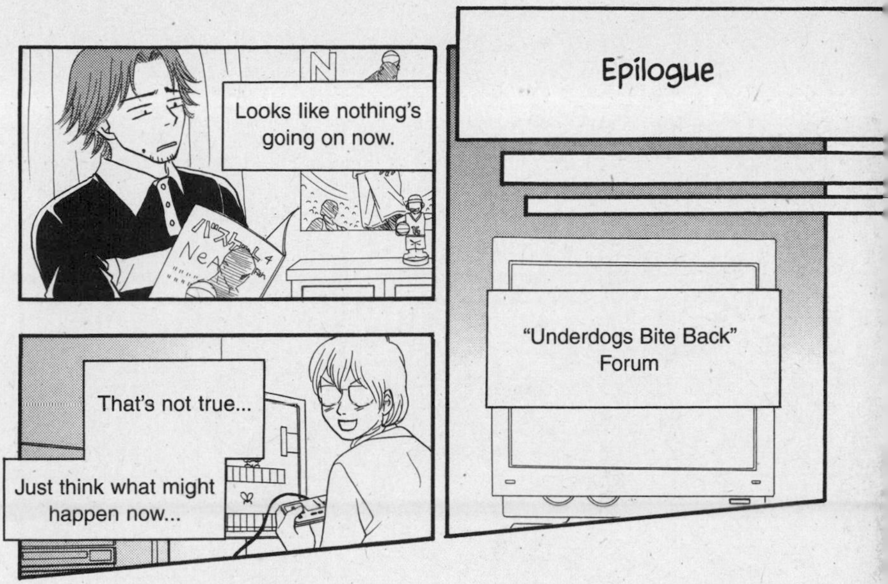
Epilogue
"Underdogs Bite Back" Forum
Looks like nothing's going on now.
That's not true...
Just think what might happen now...

#458 - posted by: ANONYMOUS

Someday it'll go down like this—
H: Hey, Densha Otoko, did you ever post anything on a message board?
T: Huh? "Post anything"...like what?
H: Hmm, well a friend of mine told me something and I wonder if it's true...
T: I don't get what you mean. What did your friend tell you?
H: Well, she said that a lot of stuff about you and me is written on these public forums...on one called Channel 2...

(ﾟДﾟ) KCHAK
(つ o._
と_)_) (_()、;.o:。
ﾟ*･:。

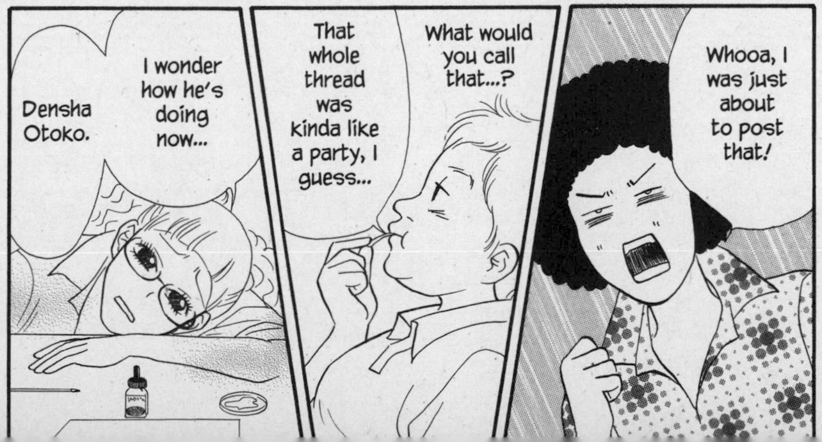
Whooa, I was just about to post that!
What would you call that...?
That whole thread was kinda like a party, I guess...
I wonder how he's doing now...
Densha Otoko.

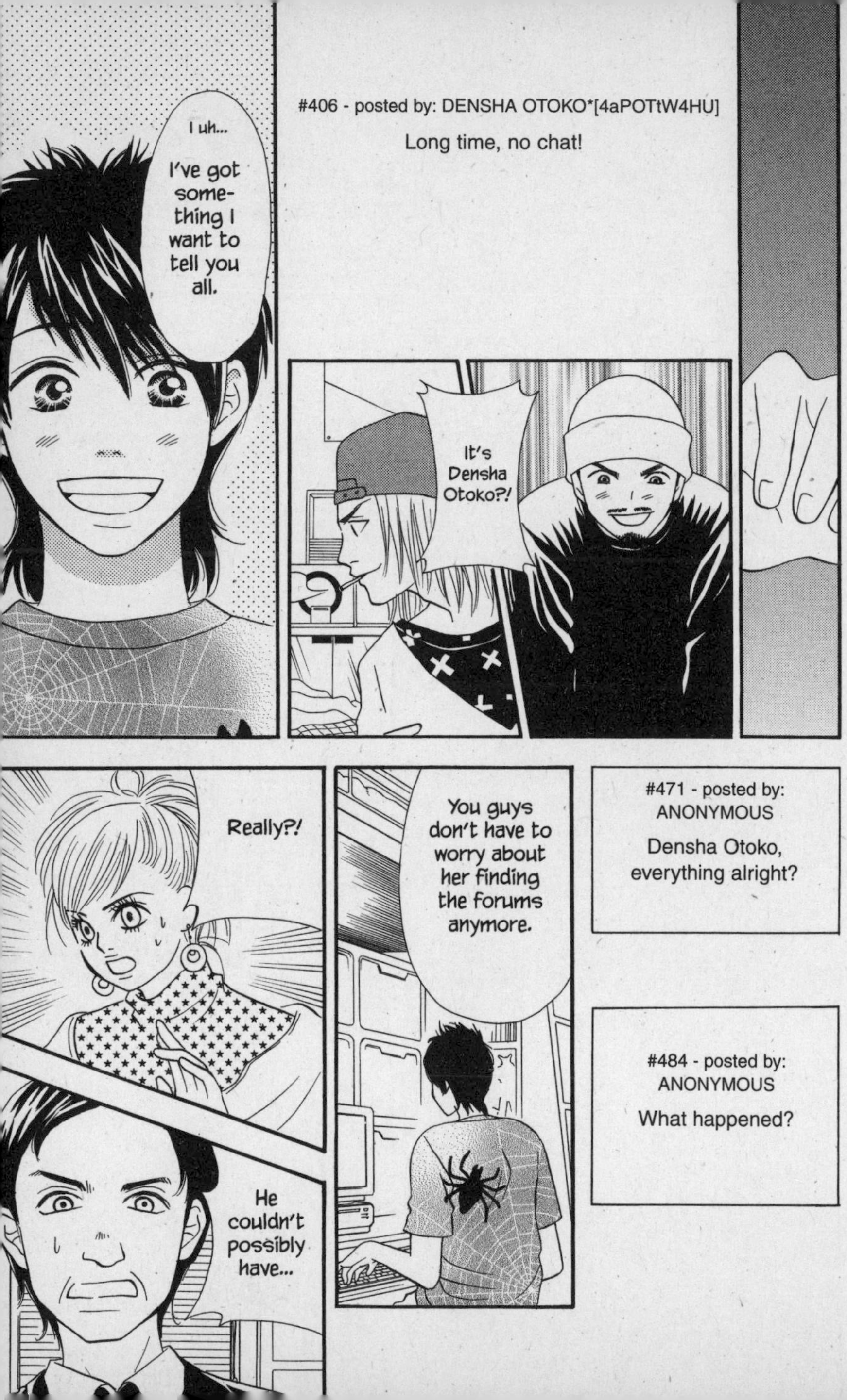
#406 - posted by: DENSHA OTOKO*[4aPOTtW4HU]
Long time, no chat!
It's Densha Otoko?!
I uh...
I've got some-thing I want to tell you all.
#471 - posted by: ANONYMOUS
Densha Otoko, everything alright?
#484 - posted by: ANONYMOUS
What happened?
You guys don't have to worry about her finding the forums anymore.
Really?!
He couldn't possibly have...

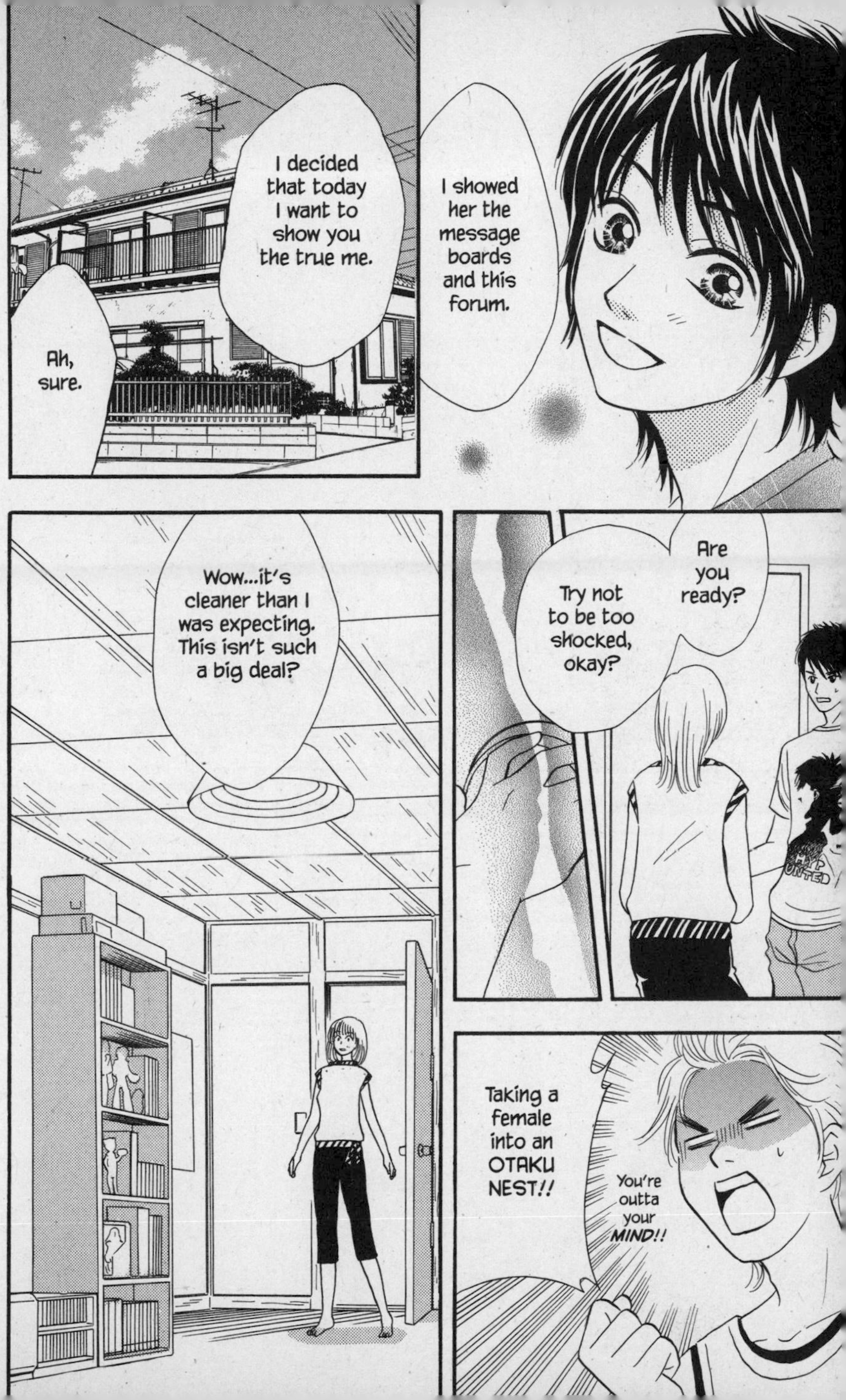
I showed her the message boards and this forum.
I decided that today I want to show you the true me.
Ah, sure.
Are you ready?
Try not to be too shocked, okay?
Taking a female into an OTAKU NEST!!
You're outta your MIND!!
Wow...it's cleaner than I was expecting. This isn't such a big deal?

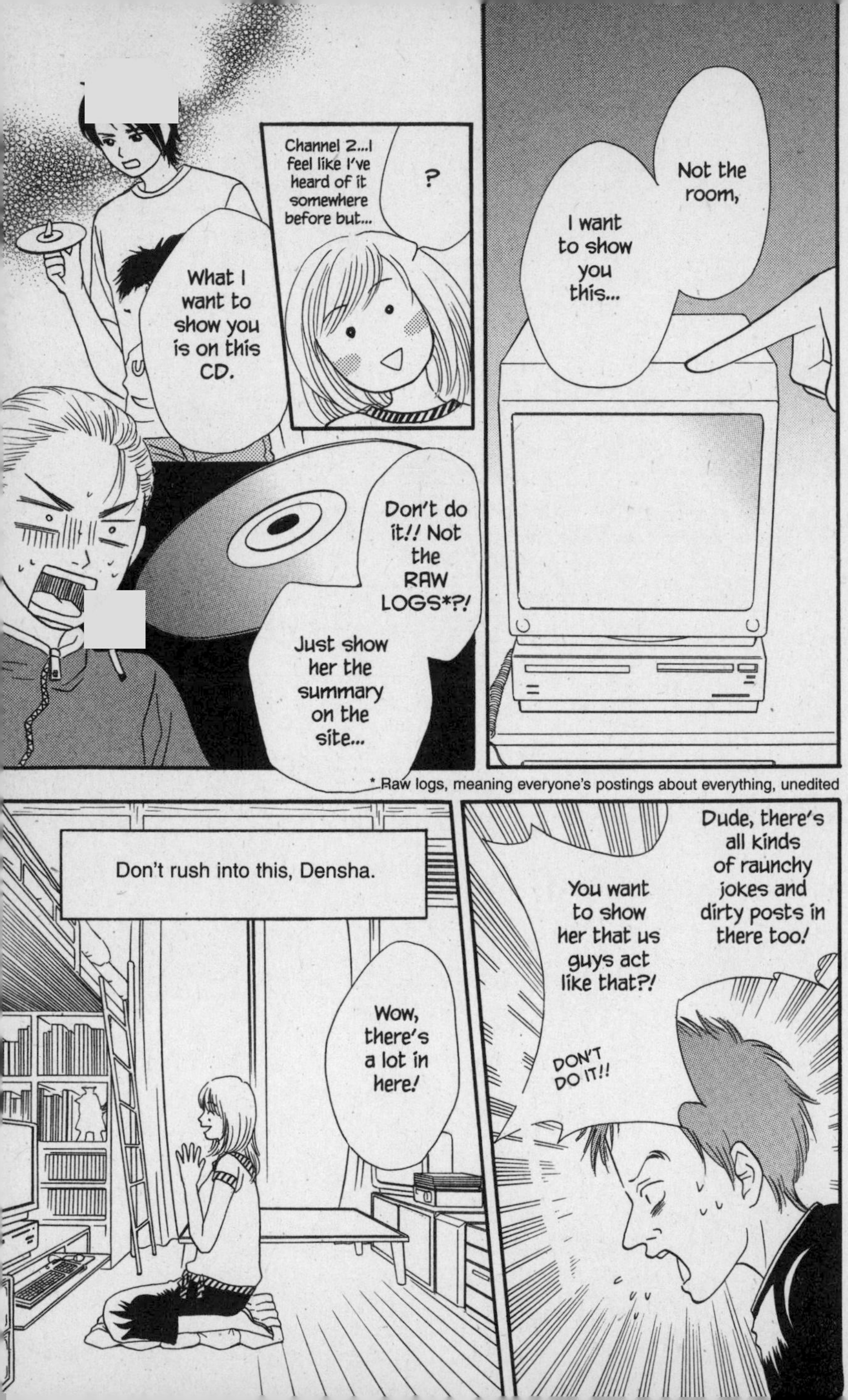
Not the room,
I want to show you this...
Channel 2...I feel like I've heard of it somewhere before but...
?
What I want to show you is on this CD.
Don't do it!! Not the RAW LOGS*?!
Just show her the summary on the site...
Dude, there's all kinds of raunchy jokes and dirty posts in there too!
You want to show her that us guys act like that?!
DON'T DO IT!!
Don't rush into this, Densha.
Wow, there's a lot in here!

* Raw logs, meaning everyone's postings about everything, unedited

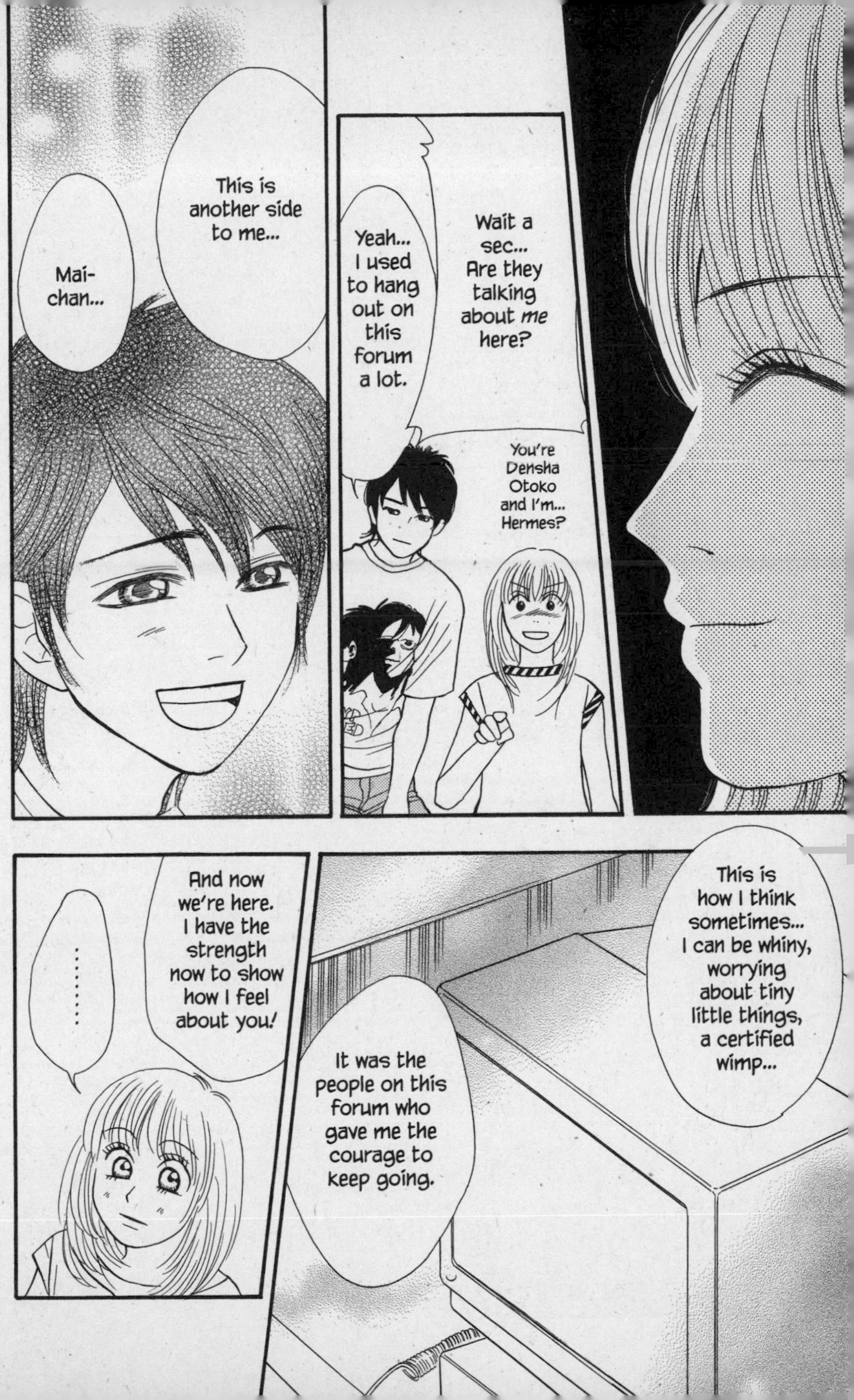
Wait a sec... Are they talking about *me* here?
Yeah... I used to hang out on this forum a lot.
You're Densha Otoko and I'm... Hermes?
This is another side to me...
Mai-chan...
This is how I think sometimes... I can be whiny, worrying about tiny little things, a certified wimp...
It was the people on this forum who gave me the courage to keep going.
And now we're here. I have the strength now to show how I feel about you!
......

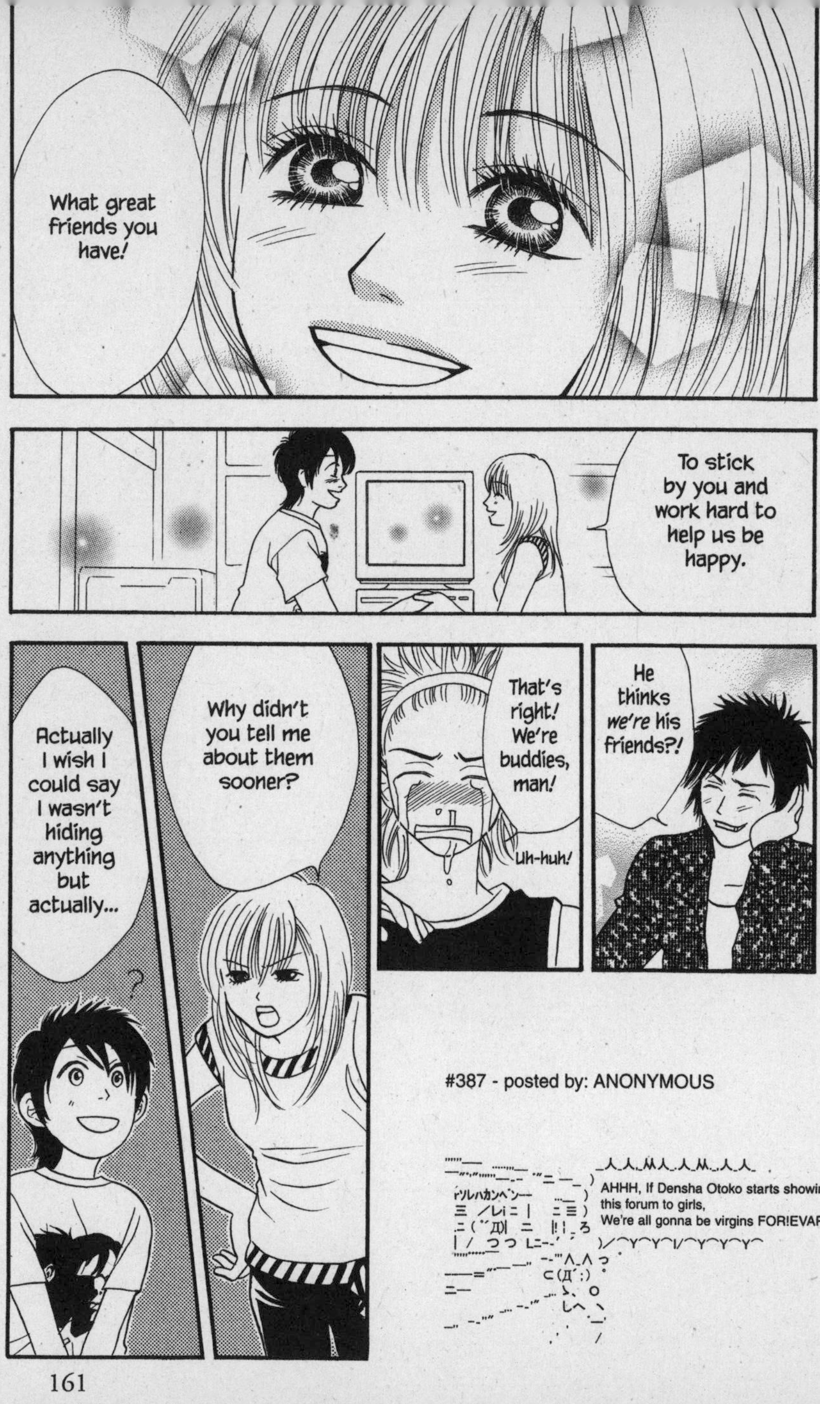
What great friends you have!
To stick by you and work hard to help us be happy.
He thinks *we're* his friends?!
That's right! We're buddies, man!
Uh-huh!
Why didn't you tell me about them sooner?
Actually I wish I could say I wasn't hiding anything but actually...
?
#387 - posted by: ANONYMOUS
AHHH, If Densha Otoko starts showing this forum to girls,
We're all gonna be virgins FOR!EVAR!!

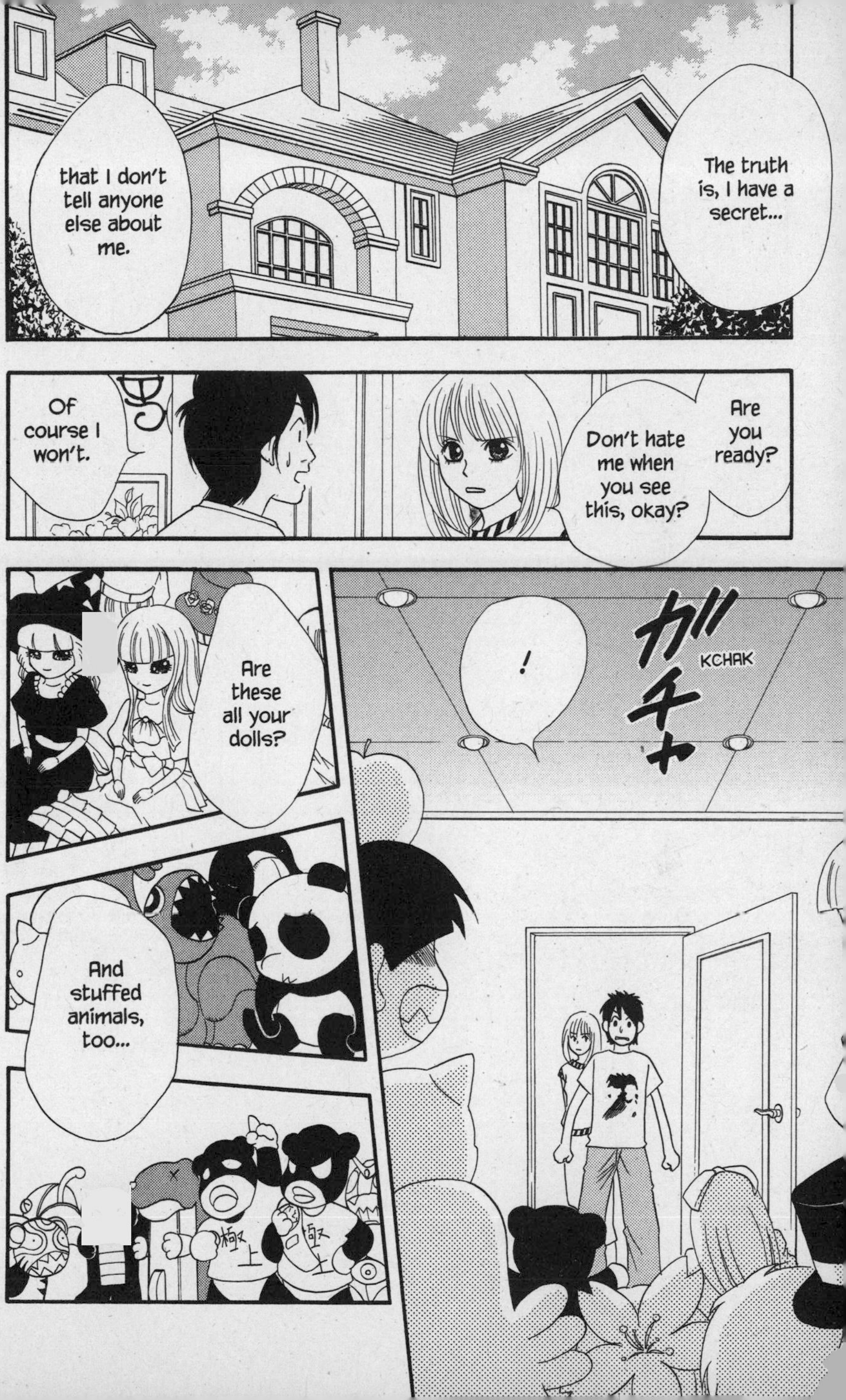
The truth is, I have a secret...
that I don't tell anyone else about me.
Are you ready?
Don't hate me when you see this, okay?
Of course I won't.
ガチャ
KCHAK
!
Are these all your dolls?
And stuffed animals, too...

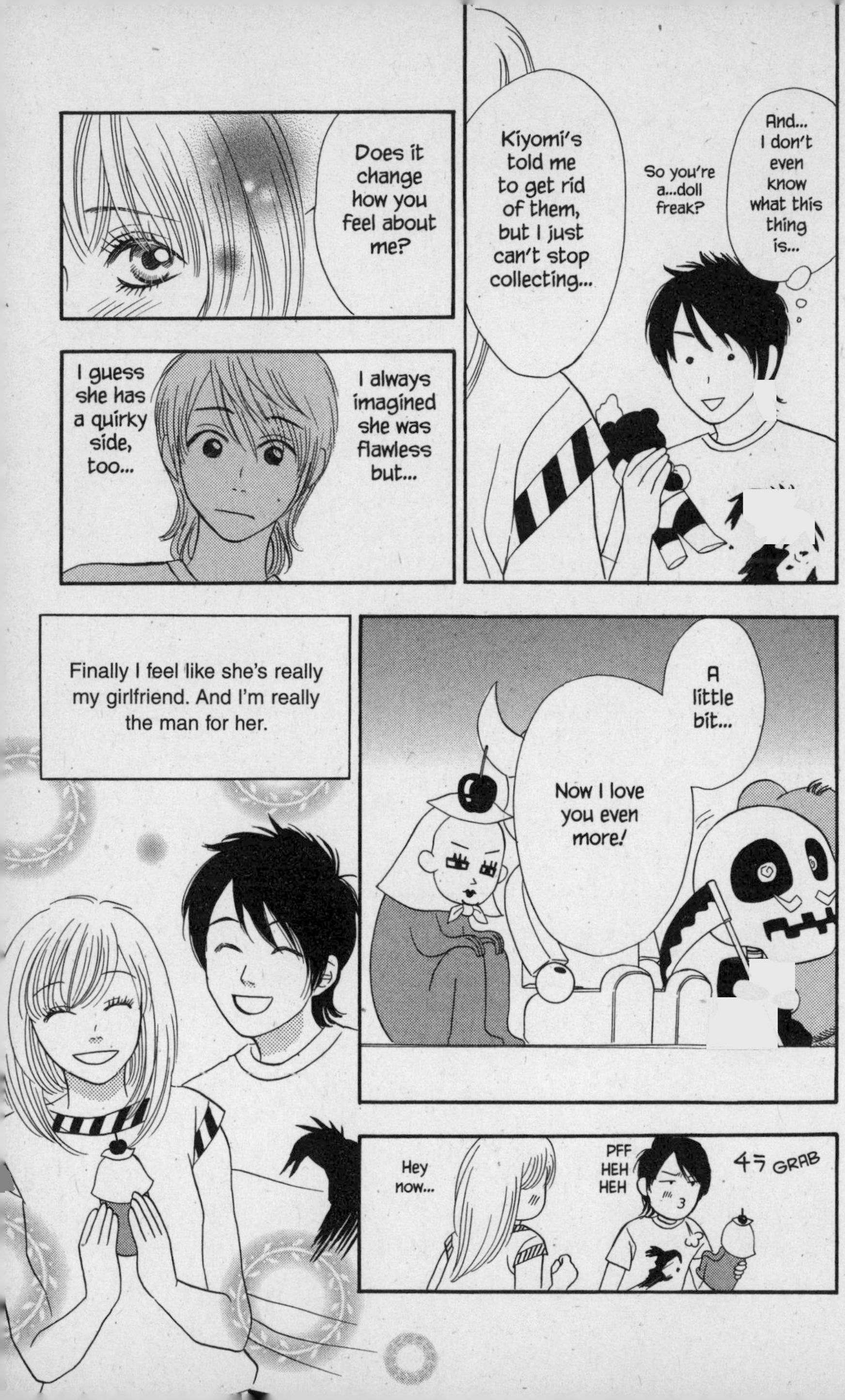
Kiyomi's told me to get rid of them, but I just can't stop collecting...
So you're a...doll freak?
And... I don't even know what this thing is...
Does it change how you feel about me?
I always imagined she was flawless but...
I guess she has a quirky side, too...
A little bit...
Now I love you even more!
GRAB
PFF HEH HEH
Hey now...
Finally I feel like she's really my girlfriend. And I'm really the man for her.

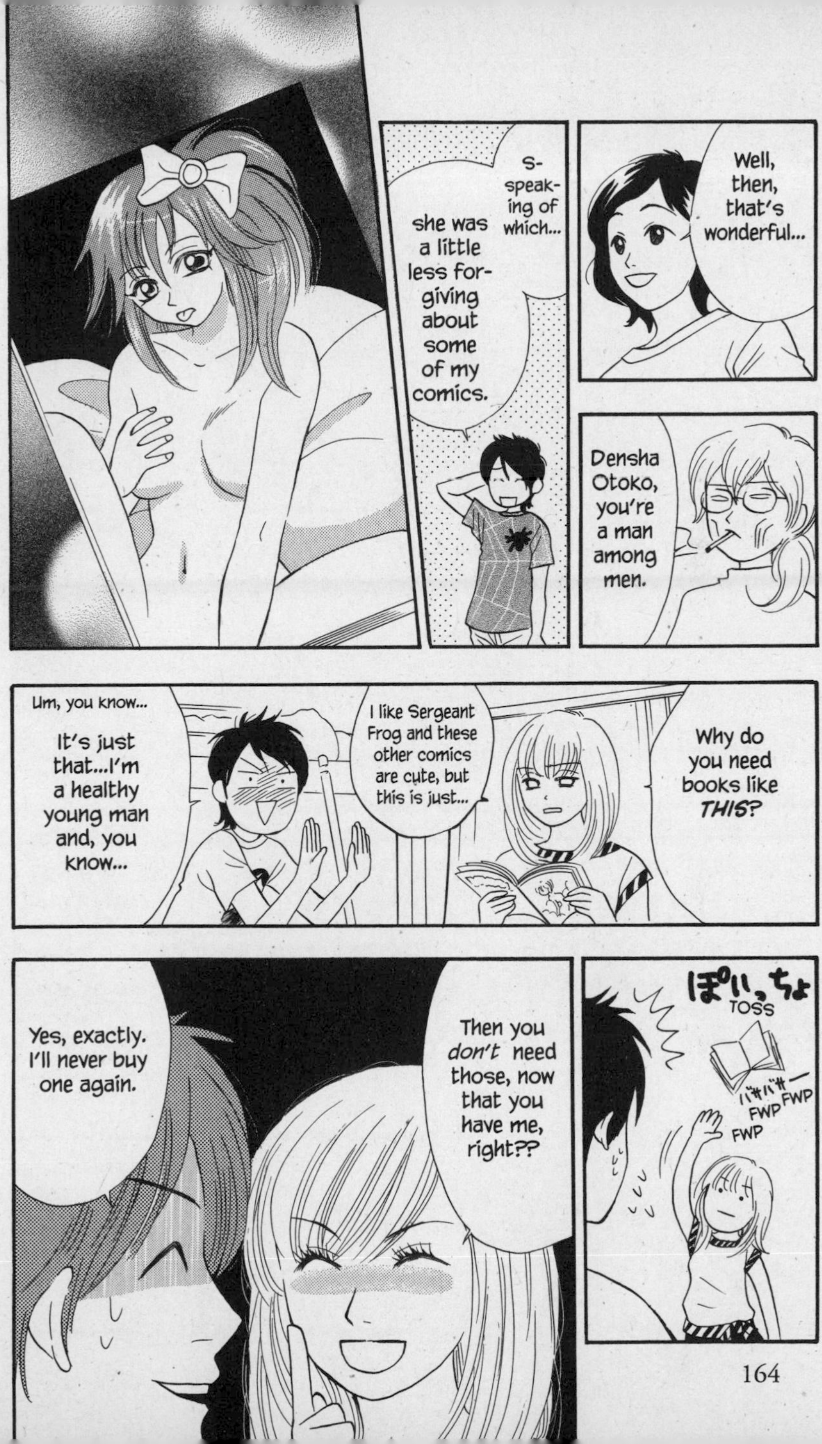
Well, then, that's wonderful...
Densha Otoko, you're a man among men.
S-speaking of which...
she was a little less forgiving about some of my comics.
Why do you need books like *THIS?*
I like Sergeant Frog and these other comics are cute, but this is just...
Um, you know...
It's just that...I'm a healthy young man and, you know...
ぽいっちょ
TOSS
バサバサー
FWP FWP
FWP
Then you *don't* need those, now that you have me, right??
Yes, exactly. I'll never buy one again.

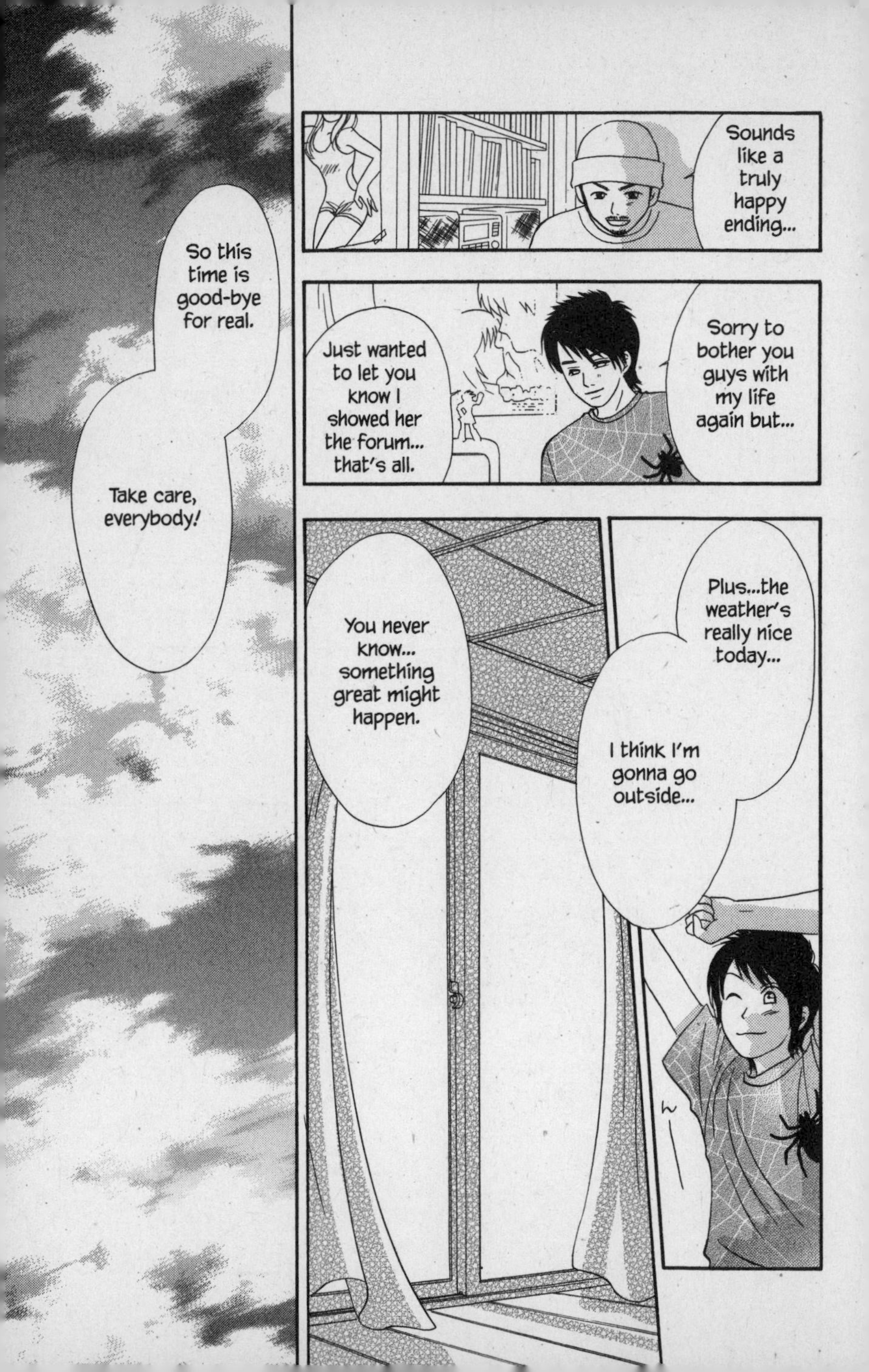
Sounds like a truly happy ending...
Sorry to bother you guys with my life again but...
Just wanted to let you know I showed her the forum... that's all.
Plus...the weather's really nice today...
I think I'm gonna go outside...
You never know... something great might happen.
So this time is good-bye for real.
Take care, everybody!

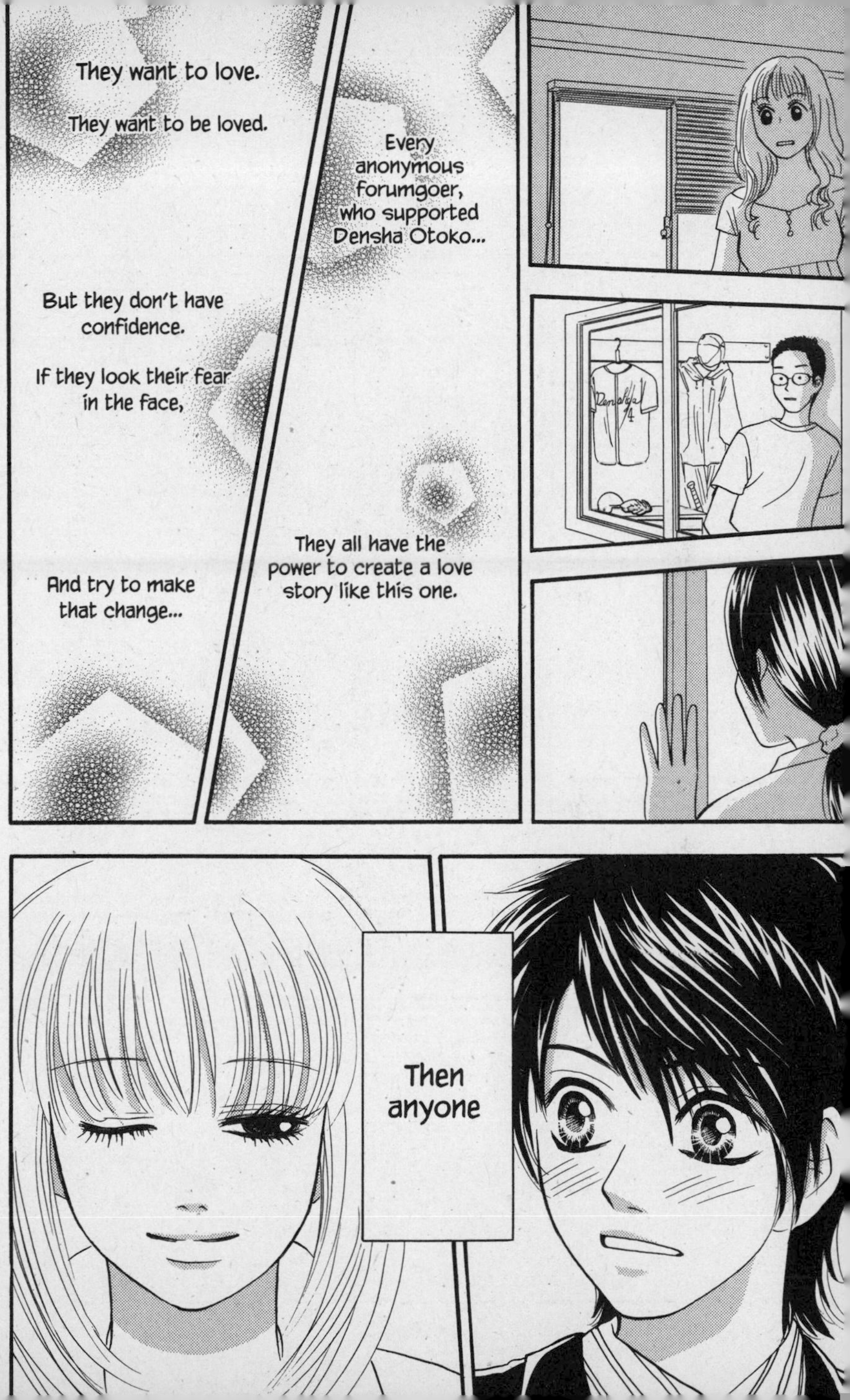
Every anonymous forumgoer, who supported Densha Otoko...
They all have the power to create a love story like this one.
They want to love.
They want to be loved.
But they don't have confidence.
If they look their fear in the face,
And try to make that change...
Then anyone

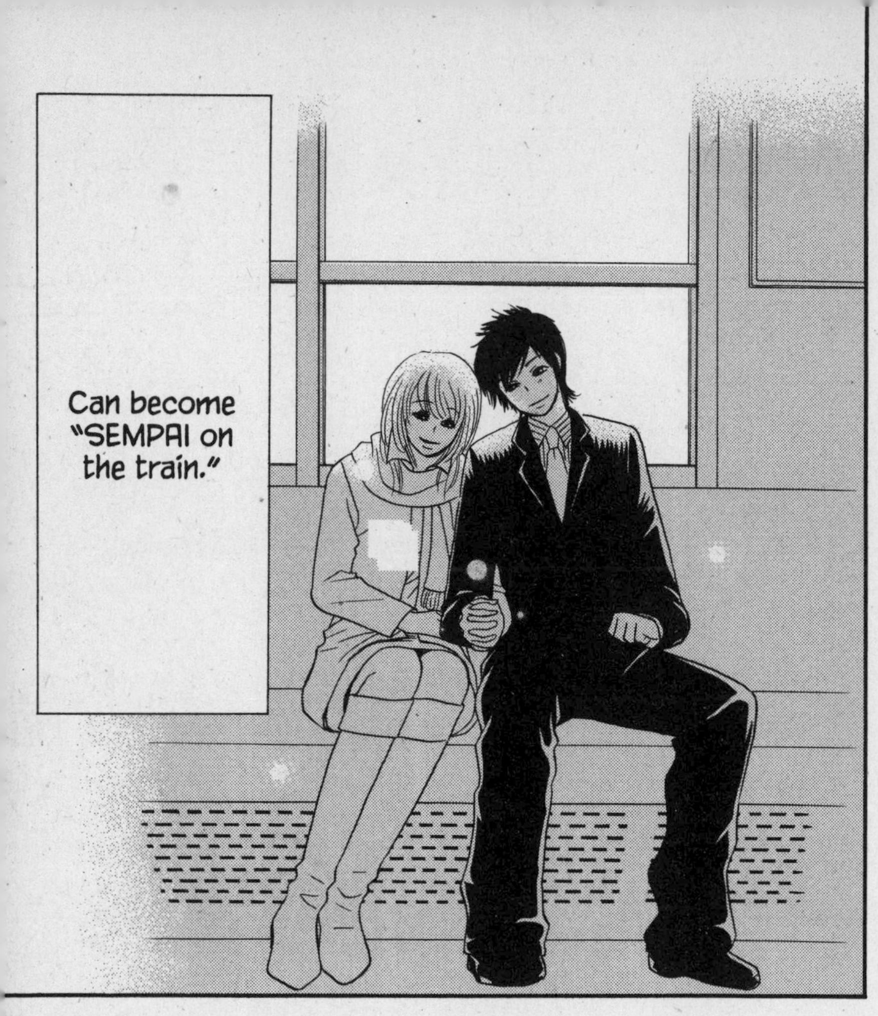
Can become "SEMPAI on the train."

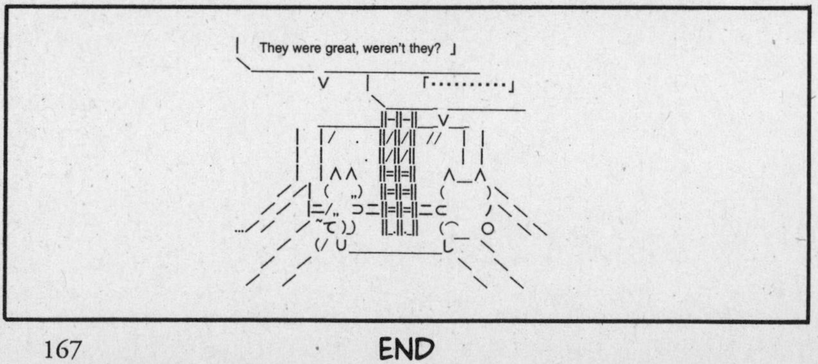
They were great, weren't they?
「..........」

END

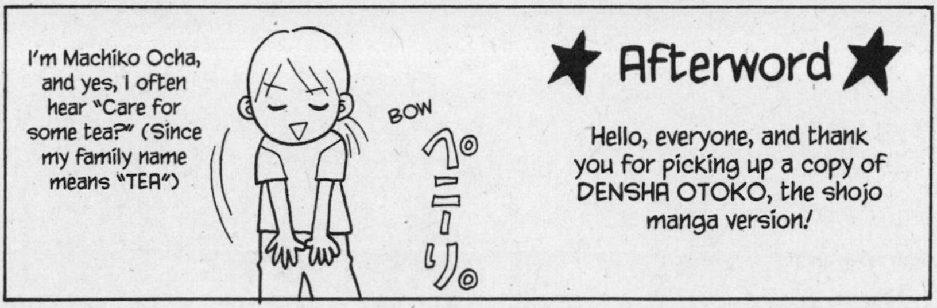
★ Afterword ★
Hello, everyone, and thank you for picking up a copy of DENSHA OTOKO, the shojo manga version!
BOW
I'm Machiko Ocha, and yes, I often hear "Care for some tea?" (Since my family name means "TEA")

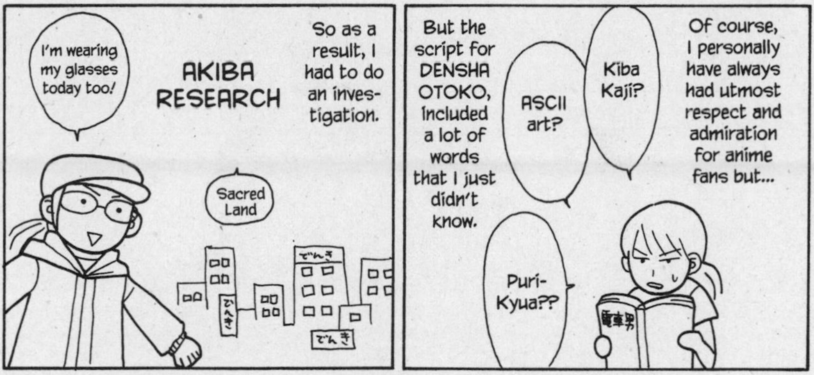
Of course, I personally have always had utmost respect and admiration for anime fans but...
Kiba Kaji?
ASCII art?
But the script for DENSHA OTOKO, included a lot of words that I just didn't know.
Puri-Kyua??
So as a result, I had to do an investigation.
AKIBA RESEARCH
I'm wearing my glasses today too!
Sacred Land

Akiba is short for Akihabara—the section of Tokyo most famous for shops that interest anime/game otaku.

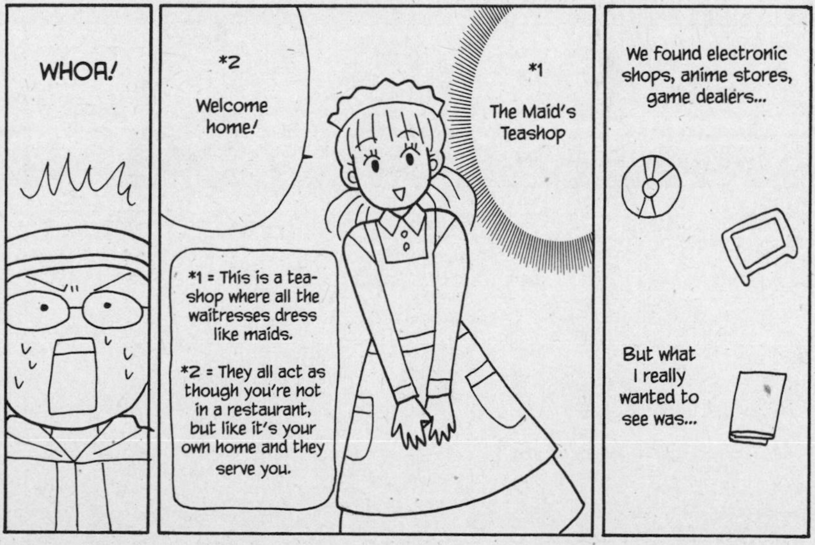
We found electronic shops, anime stores, game dealers...
But what I really wanted to see was...
*1
The Maid's Teashop
*2
Welcome home!
*1 = This is a teashop where all the waitresses dress like maids.
*2 = They all act as though you're not in a restaurant, but like it's your own home and they serve you.
WHOA!

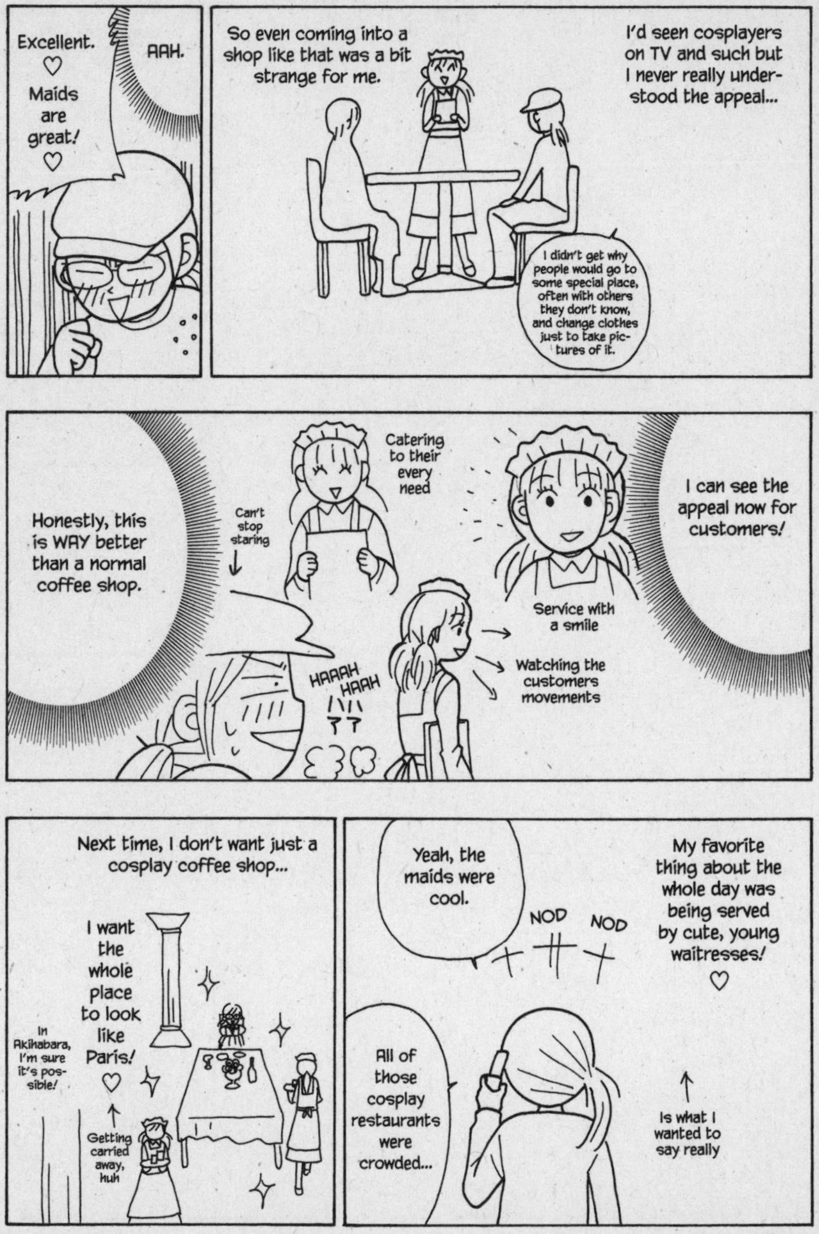
I'd seen cosplayers on TV and such but I never really understood the appeal...
So even coming into a shop like that was a bit strange for me.
I didn't get why people would go to some special place, often with others they don't know, and change clothes just to take pictures of it.
AAH.
Excellent. ♡ Maids are great! ♡
I can see the appeal now for customers!
Catering to their every need
Service with a smile
Watching the customers movements
Can't stop staring
Honestly, this is WAY better than a normal coffee shop.
HAAAH HAAH
My favorite thing about the whole day was being served by cute, young waitresses! ♡
NOD NOD
Yeah, the maids were cool.
Is what I wanted to say really
All of those cosplay restaurants were crowded...
Next time, I don't want just a cosplay coffee shop...
I want the whole place to look like Paris! ♡
In Akihabara, I'm sure it's possible!
Getting carried away, huh

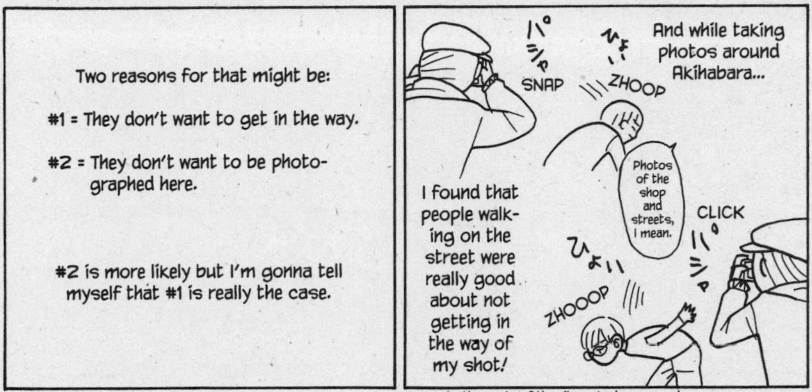
And while taking photos around Akihabara...
ひょい
ZHOOP
パシャ
SNAP
I found that people walking on the street were really good about not getting in the way of my shot!
Photos of the shop and streets, I mean.
CLICK
パシャ
ひょい
ZHOOOP
Two reasons for that might be:
#1 = They don't want to get in the way.
#2 = They don't want to be photographed here.
#2 is more likely but I'm gonna tell myself that #1 is really the case.

In most other parts of the city, nobody cares and they'll walk in front of a camera anyway.

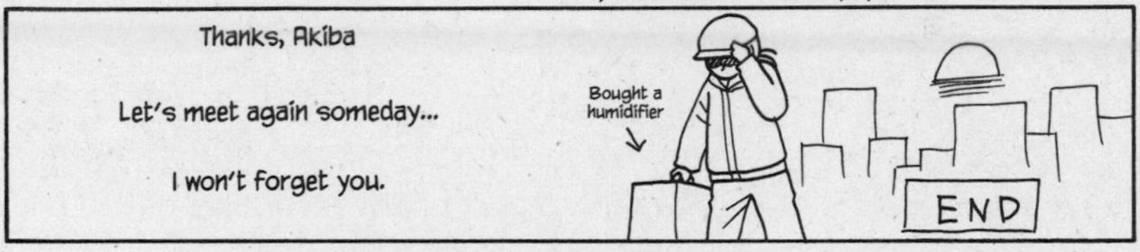
Bought a humidifier
END
Thanks, Akiba
Let's meet again someday...
I won't forget you.

I want to give an extra special thanks to everyone who helped bring this all together.

I'm truly grateful for all the people who helped and supported this project.

Ocha

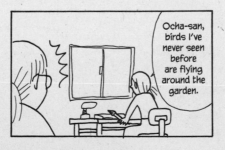

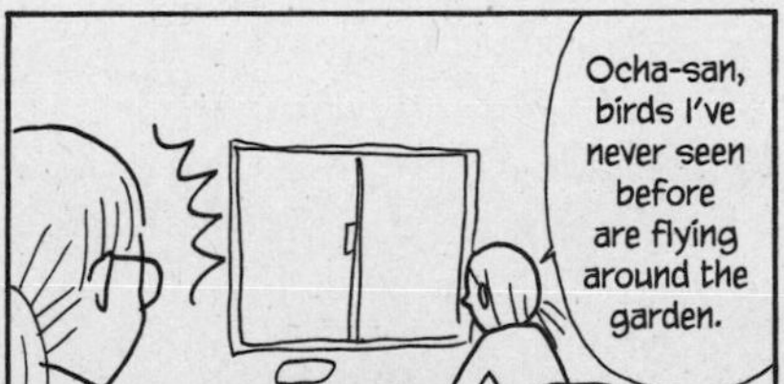
Ocha-san, birds I've never seen before are flying around the garden.

Translation Notes

Japanese is a tricky language for most Westerners, and translation is often more an art than a science. For your edification and reading pleasure, here are notes on some of the places where we could have gone in a different direction in our translation, or where a Japanese cultural reference is used.

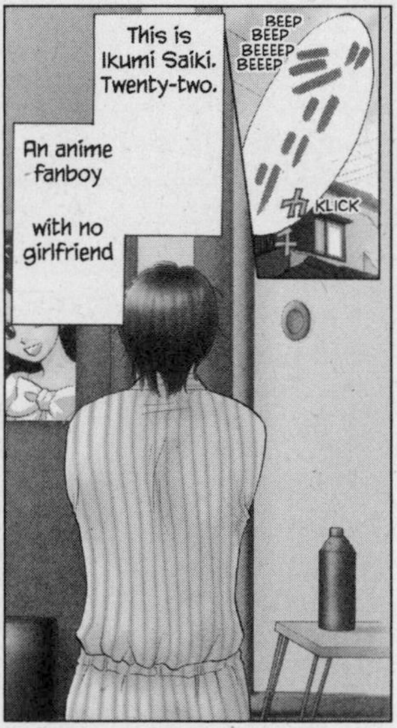
BEEP BEEP BEEEEP BEEEP
KLICK
This is Ikumi Saiki. Twenty-two.
An anime fanboy
with no girlfriend

Anime fanboy, page 3

Ikumi is part of the subculture of anime fandom in Tokyo. Most members are referred to as *Akihabara Kei*. He and the forumgoers sometimes shorten this to *Akiba*, and sometimes also call themselves *Kiba Kaji*. But all of those terms mean *otaku*, whether a particular fanboy's obsession is anime, manga, costumes, or computer gadgets.

Calbee Bento, page 6

Calbee is a brand-name prepackaged bento or lunch box. Convenience stores in Japan every so often run promotional specials on their bento. The fact that Ikumi is interested enough to notice this special shows that, rather than going to restaurants with coworkers, for example, he buys lunch at a convenience store every day.

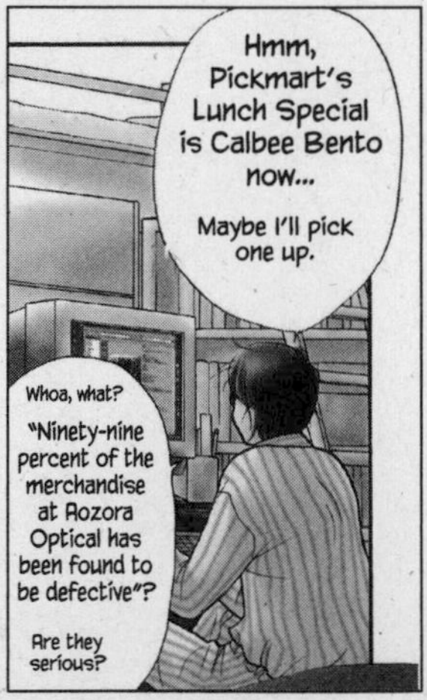
Hmm, Pickmart's Lunch Special is Calbee Bento now...
Maybe I'll pick one up.
Whoa, what?
"Ninety-nine percent of the merchandise at Aozora Optical has been found to be defective"?
Are they serious?

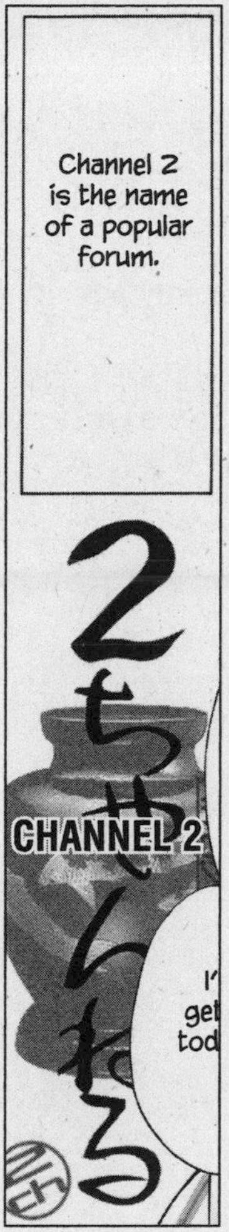
Channel 2 is the name of a popular forum.
CHANNEL 2

Channel 2 Forum, page 6

One important thing to note about this kind of forum is that it's a lot more anonymous than php/BB2 forums. On most American forums, when someone posts, a lot of identifying information is included (date joined, location: real or fictitious, number of posts, etc.), because anonymous posts are usually ignored, if they're even allowed at all.

But on the forums where Ikumi chats, almost everyone is anonymous. People get used to recognizing one another based on their speech patterns and ASCII art. Even identified posters don't show any information. There's no registration, and since anyone can view the topics and replies, even false information is too much information. Someone at the office might trace it back to a coworker and learn that he spends every night chatting on message boards.

The real 2channel message board exploded with popularity after the Train Man story became a hit. If you dig beneath the adverts, you can see the original style is still there. No icons, no sig tags, just information to throw in or take out.

asdfghjkl, page 7

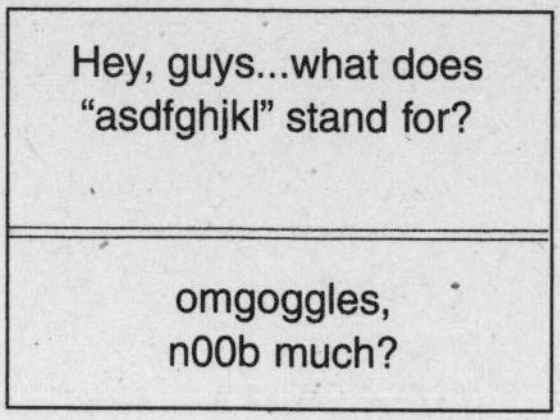
Hey, guys...what does "asdfghjkl" stand for?
omgoggles, n00b much?

Japanese message boards have as many typos and as much grammar drama as any others. But keyboards configured for Japanese input allow for a parallel world of abbreviations and netspeak that doesn't always translate directly to roman letters.

So the typos and grammatical glitches in these forums are translated for meaning, not literally. If your computer supports Japanese input, trying typing "drftgyhujiko"... See? Same meaning as "asdfghjkl"—(^_^)v.

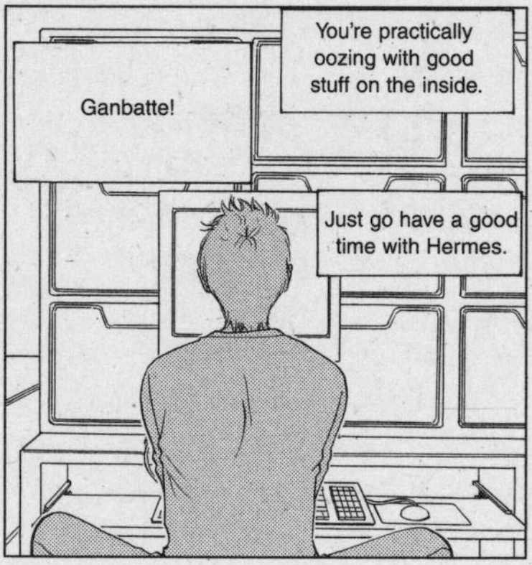
You're practically oozing with good stuff on the inside.
Ganbatte!
Just go have a good time with Hermes.

Ganbatte!, page 49

In this context, *Ganbatte!* is a nice way to wish someone good luck. An English-speaking anime fan might use the phrase here, but a Japanese-speaking fan might type something like "GUUDO RAKKU!"

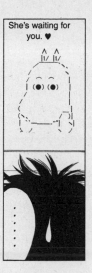

Moomin, page 60

She's waiting for you. ♥
......

This ASCII art is Moomin. Mai's friends say she looks like Moomin, so if Mai were on a forum that allowed for avatars, this would probably be the one for her.

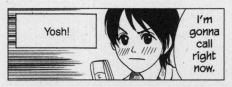

Yosh!, page 63

I'm gonna call right now.
Yosh!

Many fans have heard this word so much that they take to using it themselves—*Yosh!* substitutes nicely for "Alright!" or "Okay, here goes!"

Variations include "Yosha~!" drawn out for emphasis, as well as "Yoshi~!" as made famous by Naruto.

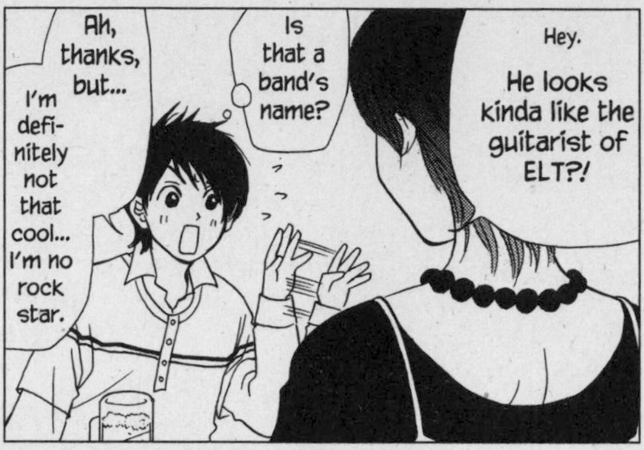
Hey.
He looks kinda like the guitarist of ELT?!
Is that a band's name?
Ah, thanks, but...
I'm definitely not that cool... I'm no rock star.

ELT (Every Little Thing), page 72

Kiyomi compares Ikumi to the guitarist of Every Little Thing, who is, unfortunately, famous for being unattractive. But Ikumi is so out of touch with mainstream pop culture that he doesn't realize it isn't a compliment.

Doujinshi, page 112

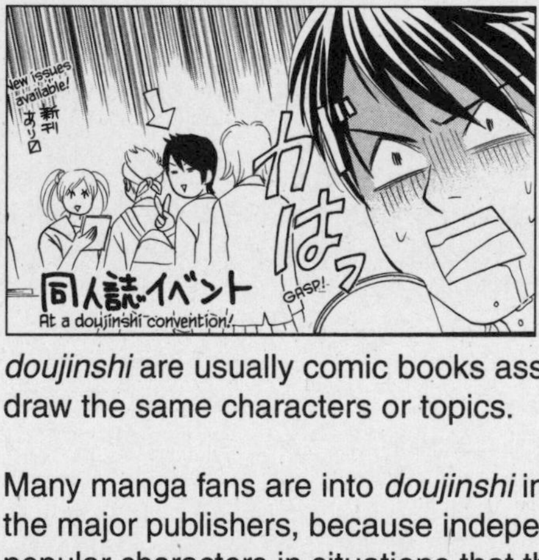
わはっ
GASP!
新刊あり〼
New issues available!
同人誌イベント
At a doujinshi convention!

Doujinshi are books or magazines published by independent artists or small groups. A *doujin* is someone who's part of a small clique or group that shares an interest, so *doujinshi* are usually comic books assembled by artists who all draw the same characters or topics.

Many manga fans are into *doujinshi* in addition to manga from the major publishers, because independent artists can draw popular characters in situations that the mainstream publishers would *never* allow in print!

Ganbare, page 122

Ganbare is a variation on *gan-batte*, another good luck wish. It's use is appropriately more familiar and intense now that Ikumi's been chatting with these same people for quite a while.

#448 - posted by: ANONYMOUS
omgogldkdkdhfshsjd!
We're waiting to hear what happens!
Do us proud!
We're cheering for you!
Ganbare Densha!

Puri-Kura

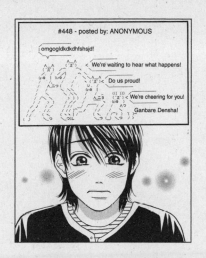

Puri-Kura, page 129

Puri-Kura is a kana abbreviation for "Print Club," a term that describes all kinds of extravagant photo booths.

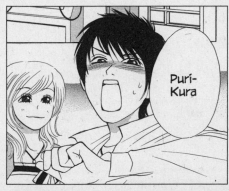

But *Puri-Kura* is distinctly different from ordinary photo booths for a few reasons: The lighting is arranged to make everyone look like a model, there's often music and/or a theme, and you can digitally alter the photos before you print them. It's kind of like do-it-yourself glamour shots. Going to *Puri-Kura* can be an all-afternoon event for a group of girls, and it's a rite of passage for many couples.

Train Man: How an *Otaku* Created a Pop Culture Phenomenon

By William Flanagan

"I might be betraying you, too," began a message board entry from an anonymous poster.

In early 2004, some of the only people in Japan who knew about the 2channel message boards were *otaku*. The *otaku* community is a large and diverse one but somewhat insular, with its own rules. This particular *otaku* posted on a section of the board that was meant for single people—mostly guys, but plenty of women posted on the board, too—and to "betray the community" was to find yourself a partner.

Only this shy young *otaku* didn't know how to go about courting the woman of his dreams, and he went to the boards for help. The rest of the story plays out in the book you hold in your hands. These events also inspired a phenomenon in Japan known as the "*otaku* boom" and created a storm of media attention that had happened only once before.

Just two years before, there was a similar pop culture phenomenon, one that began with a novel called *Sekai no Chûshin de, Ai wo Sakebu* (*Cry Out "Love" from the Center of the World*). It was translated into English with the author's original title, *Socrates in Love. Seka-chû*, as the Japanese nicknamed it, was a tragic love story that touched the hearts of many Japanese. The novel became a runaway bestseller and was the basis for an incredibly popular manga, a successful film, and the hit TV show of the season. It seemed unlikely that such an extraordinary success could ever be replicated.

However, by mid 2004, somebody had uncovered a story that was destined to be an even bigger hit. The materials for the story were out there for the finding; the drama was already playing out on the 2channel message boards. Someone collected the threads, edited out the inconsequential side conversations one

inevitably finds on message boards, and published the messages in the form of a novel called *Densha Otoko* (*Train Man*). But who did it? We don't know. The story was credited to a "Nakano Hitori," which isn't actually a person's name; instead, it's a kind of message. *"Naka no hitori"* is a Japanese phrase meaning "one of those within." Therefore, this pen name suggests that the author was one of the anonymous 2channel posters, but was it the Train Man himself—or another message board denizen with an instinct for a good story?

Initial sales of *Densha Otoko* were slow but picked up once a few celebrities started talking it up. Then the Japanese media machine, having seen in the case of *Seka-chû* what could be done with the right property and sensing huge potential in this slightly skewed Cinderella story, began pushing the story hard. Not only was the story compelling, it had a built-in audience, *otaku*, one that also happened to be the ideal consumer group as *otaku* have a strong sense of brand loyalty and plenty of money to spend. It was clear that *Densha Otoko* had the makings of a successful franchise.

Also, the story was flexible enough to stretch through several media adaptations. Since the story's events were only sketchily described in a series of message board posts, each adaptation had a lot of blank spots to fill in. Details, even down to the "true names" of the characters, were totally up to the imaginations of the adaptors, so that every version of the story has its own unique take.

For example, the first *Densha Otoko* movie, a quickie production that was rushed into theaters in June 2005, was a straight love story with some comedic elements. It featured a typical beauty, Miki Nakatani, as Hermes and a standard-issue heartthrob, Takayuki Yamada, who was dressed up in *Akiba* fashion in glasses and too-long hair but transformed into a total hunk by the end of the film. The movie was a hit, with its estimated 3.7 billion yen (more than $33 million at $1 = ¥110) in box-office receipts making it the sixth-highest-grossing movie in Japan that year.

But the TV series went in another direction entirely—into full-blown farce. The series' casting choices distinguished it as well, with noted character actors taking the lead roles: the beautiful Misaki Itoh, in her first star turn since the manga adaptation of *Taihô Shicchauzo!* (*You're Under Arrest!*), and Atsushi Itoh (no relation to Misaki). Unlike the star of the theatrical release, when Atsushi Itoh takes off his glasses, he still looks like an *otaku*! The television show outstripped the movie in popularity, with the last episode winning an almost unheard-of 25.5 rating—the highest for any TV drama that summer.

But perhaps the biggest impact *Densha Otoko* had was on main-stream attitudes toward *otaku*. In 1988 and 1989, the reputation of *otaku* everywhere was destroyed when Tsutomu Miyazaki brutally murdered four little girls. After he was arrested, thousands of anime and slasher movies were found in his apartment, and many Japanese came to believe all *otaku* were potential mass murderers. Up through the early 2000s, fear of *otaku* was widespread, and the media ran sensational stories on what they called the "*otaku* problem." But even just before *Densha Otoko*, many manufacturers and retailers had realized there could be great financial rewards in marketing products specifically to *otaku*. So the *otaku* backlash was already on the wane when *Densha Otoko* hit, but once it did, suddenly, incredibly, *otaku* were *popular*. Now in place of the "*otaku* problem," the media began capitalizing on an "*otaku* boom." *Densha Otoko* even inspired some of the "beautiful people" to seek out and date the social outcasts they once shunned!

So a shy, clueless nerd inspired a total reevaluation of *otaku* culture and changed Japan for the better. And we can hope that the real, still-anonymous man and his anonymous girlfriend are living happily ever after.

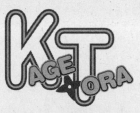

BY AKIRA SEGAMI

MISSION IMPOSSIBLE

The young ninja Kagetora has been given a great honor—to serve a renowned family of skilled martial artists. But on arrival, he's handed a challenging assignment: teach the heir to the dynasty, the charming but clumsy Yuki, the deft moves of self-defense and combat.

Yuki's inability to master the martial arts is not what makes this job so difficult for Kagetora. No, it is Yuki herself. Someday she will lead her family dojo, and for a ninja like Kagetora to fall in love with his master is a betrayal of his duty, the ultimate dishonor, and strictly forbidden. Can Kagetora help Yuki overcome her ungainly nature . . . or will he be overcome by his growing feelings?

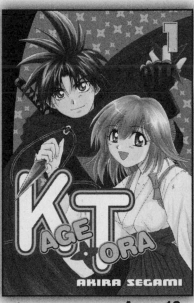

Ages: 13+

Special extras in each volume! Read them all!

VISIT WWW.DELREYMANGA.COM TO:
- Read sample pages
- View release date calendars for upcoming volumes
- Sign up for Del Rey's free manga e-newsletter
- Find out the latest about new Del Rey Manga series

Guru Guru Pon-Chan

BY SATOMI IKEZAWA

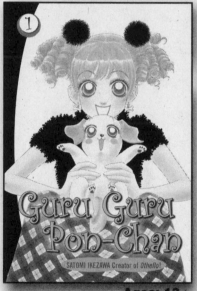

Ponta is a normal Labrador retriever puppy, the Koizumi family's pet. Full of energy, she is always up to some kind of trouble. However, when Grandpa Koizumi, a passionate amateur inventor, creates the "Guru Guru Bone," which empowers animals with human speech, Ponta turns into a human girl!

Ponta dashes out into the street and is saved by Mirai Iwaki, the most popular boy at school! Her heart pounds and her face flushes. Why does she feel this way? Can there be love between a human and a dog?

The effects of the "Guru Guru Bone" are not permanent, and Ponta turns back and forth between dog and girl.

Ages: 13 +

Special extras in each volume! Read them all!

GHOST HUNT

MANGA BY SHIHO INADA
STORY BY FUYUMI ONO

The decrepit building was condemned long ago, but every time the owners try to tear it down, "accidents" start to happen—people get hurt, sometimes even killed. Mai Taniyama and her classmates have heard the rumors that the creepy old high school is haunted. So, one rainy day they gather to tell ghost stories, hoping to attract one of the suspected spirits. No ghosts materialize, but they do meet Kazuya Shibuya, the handsome young owner of Shibuya Psychic Research, hired to investigate paranormal activity at the school. Also brought to the scene are an exorcist, a Buddhist monk, a woman who can speak with the dead, and an outspoken Shinto priestess. Surely one of them will have the talents to solve this mystery. . . .

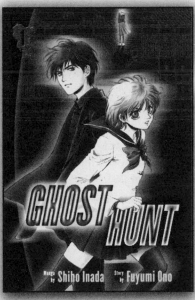

Ages: 13+

Special extras in each volume! Read them all!

School Rumble

BY JIN KOBAYASHI

SUBTLETY IS FOR WIMPS!

She . . . is a second-year high school student with a single all-consuming question: Will the boy she likes ever really notice her?

He . . . is the school's most notorious juvenile delinquent, and he's suddenly come to a shocking realization: He's got a huge crush, and now he must tell her how he feels.

Life-changing obsessions, colossal foul-ups, grand schemes, deep-seated anxieties, and raging hormones—*School Rumble* portrays high school as it really is: over-the-top comedy!

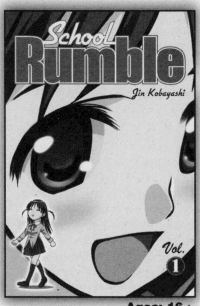

Ages: 16 +

Special extras in each volume! Read them all!

VISIT WWW.DELREYMANGA.COM TO:
- Read sample pages
- View release date calendars for upcoming volumes
- Sign up for Del Rey's free manga e-newsletter
- Find out the latest about new Del Rey Manga series

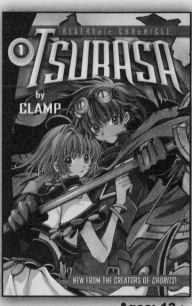

STOP!

YOU'RE GOING THE WRONG WAY!

MANGA IS A COMPLETELY DIFFERENT TYPE OF READING EXPERIENCE.

TO START AT THE BEGINNING, GO TO THE END!

THAT'S RIGHT!

AUTHENTIC MANGA IS READ THE TRADITIONAL JAPANESE WAY—FROM RIGHT TO LEFT. EXACTLY THE OPPOSITE OF HOW AMERICAN BOOKS ARE READ. IT'S EASY TO FOLLOW: JUST GO TO THE OTHER END OF THE BOOK, AND READ EACH PAGE—AND EACH PANEL—FROM RIGHT SIDE TO LEFT SIDE, STARTING AT THE TOP RIGHT. NOW YOU'RE EXPERIENCING MANGA AS IT WAS MEANT TO BE.